D-DAY GIRLS

The Spies Who Armed the Resistance, Sabotaged the Nazis, and Helped Win World War II

Sarah Rose

sphere

SPHERE

First published in United States in 2019 by Crown, an imprint of the Crown Publishing Group
First published in the Great Britain in 2019 by Sphere
This paperback edition published by Sphere in 2020

10 9 8 7 6 5 4 3 2 1

A CIP catalogue record for this book is available from the British Library.

ISBN 978-0-7515-7827-0

Printed and bound in Great Britain by
Clays Ltd, Elcograf S.p.A

Papers used by Sphere are from well-managed forests and other responsible sources.

FSC www.fsc.org MIX Paper from responsible sources FSC® C104740

Sphere
An imprint of
Little, Brown Book Group
Carmelite House
50 Victoria Embankment
London EC4Y 0DZ

An Hachette UK Company
www.hachette.co.uk

www.littlebrown.co.uk

For Gerald Rose. He fought for Title IX.

Gloucester: Is Paris lost? Is Rouen yielded up?
If Henry were recall'd to life again,
These news would cause him once more yield the ghost.

Exeter: How were they lost? What treachery was used?

Messenger: No treachery; but want of men and money.
—William Shakespeare, *Henry VI, Part 1,* act 1, scene 1

Tout simplement, mon colonel, parce que les hommes les avaient laissé tomber.
I took up arms, "quite simply, Colonel, because the men had dropped them."
—Marguerite Gonnet, at trial, 1942

Contents

Character Chart

Andrée Borrel

FIELD NAME: Denise

OPERATIONAL NAME: Whitebeam

COVER IDENTITY: Monique Urbain

Lise de Baissac

FIELD NAME: Odile

OPERATIONAL NAME: Artist

COVER IDENTITIES: Irène Brisée, Jeanette Bouville

Odette Sansom

FIELD NAME: Lise

OPERATIONAL NAME: Clothier

COVER IDENTITY: Odette Metayer

Yvonne Rudellat

FIELD NAME: Suzanne

OPERATIONAL NAME: Soaptree

COVER IDENTITIES: Jacqueline Viallet, Jacqueline Gauthier, Jacqueline Culioli

Mary Herbert

FIELD NAME: Claudine

OPERATIONAL NAME: Corvette

COVER IDENTITY: Marie Louise Vernier

Francis Suttill

FIELD NAME: Prosper
OPERATIONAL NAME: Physician
COVER IDENTITY: François Desprez

Gilbert Norman

FIELD NAME: Archambaud
OPERATIONAL NAME: Butcher
COVER IDENTITY: Gilbert Aubin

Peter Churchill

FIELD NAMES: Michel, Raoul
OPERATIONAL NAME: Spindle
COVER IDENTITIES: Pierre Marc Chauvet, Pierre Chambrun

Claude de Baissac

FIELD NAME: David
OPERATIONAL NAME: Scientist
COVER IDENTITIES: Clement Bastable, Michel Rouault, Claude Marc Boucher

France and Environs, 1940–1944
DENMARK
North Sea
ENGLAND
NETHERLANDS
London
Dunkirk
GERMANY
English Channel
BELGIUM
Utah Beach
Gold Beach
Cotentin Peninsula
Juno Beach
LUX.
Sark
Omaha Beach
Sword Beach
Paris
NORMANDY
GERMAN OCCUPATION ZONE
Blois
Orléans
Loire River
SWITZERLAND
Poitiers
FRANCE
Atlantic Ocean
Annecy (Saint-Jorioz)
ITALY
VICHY FRANCE
Bordeaux
Occupied by Germany after November 1942
Occupied by Italy after November 1942
Cannes
Marseilles
CORSICA
SPAIN
Mediterranean Sea
Utah, Omaha, Gold, Juno, and Sword Beaches invaded on June 6, 1944.
SARDINIA
© 2019 Jeffrey L. Ward

Part I

CHAPTER 1

God Help Us

London

Under the eternal gaze of Admiral Lord Nelson, high on a stone column in the center of London, Mrs. Odette Sansom raced toward her appointment at the War Office. The one-eyed, one-armed hero of Trafalgar got pelted in the rain, a bronze memorial to the glory that was *Pax Britannica,* many bloody conflicts removed from the London of July 10, 1942.

It was the 1,043rd day of the world's worst war.

Much of the city lay in ruins, a ragged collection of gaps and edifices, like a child's mouth after a lost tooth. Odette tilted her hat against the unremitting damp and sprinted past the admiral's brass lions as if spirit alone could somehow put London to rights, so that it might smile again.

Upon meeting Odette, Londoners were confronted with her Gallic élan, her essential Frenchness. She was self-consciously prettier than her English peers: big chestnut eyes, a "fresh complexion" framed by dark hair that was pulled high off her heart-shaped face and hung loose down her neck. Her light coat was cinched with a belt, the only burst of color in an otherwise bland London rain-scape; the city was full of uniforms—soldiers, sailors, airmen. The entire world had gone drab. Although she had lived in England for much of her adult life,

Odette never shed her Continental air, nor did she care to; frosty Britain seemed indifferent to sex and to women. With an inextinguishable flair for the theatrical, Odette preened and men in khaki swooned. It was said she even smiled in French.

The Victoria Hotel was a grande dame on mothballs, requisitioned for war work as the administrative home of the War Office. There were no bellhops to greet Odette; the twinkling chandeliers were packed off to safe storage; the building was dingy and practical like everything else. There were no dandies sharing cigarettes in the pink marble lobby; it was still busy, but with clerks and sergeants, men in mufti held back from the front, the old, the broken, those unsuited for battle, those too useful to be sacrificed. Someone had to run the war.

Odette arrived on account of a typed invitation—her second from the War Office:

Dear Madam,

Your name has been passed to me with the suggestion that you have qualifications and information which may be of value in a phase of the war effort.

If you are available for interview, I should be glad to see you at the above address at 1100 hrs on Friday 10th July.

Would you let me know whether you can come or not?

Yours truly,
Selwyn Jepson
Captain

For an unhappily married woman in the third year of the war, the letter on government stationery was rife with potential. At a minimum, Odette's appointment afforded a precious afternoon alone; there was a new film opening in Leicester Square, *Mrs. Miniver,* the story of how English housewives contribute to the war by coping, how matriarchs move mountains while men are at the front. There was window-shopping to do, though, as elsewhere in Europe, very little could be bought under rations on a husband's service pay. At best, the letter might rearrange Odette's life a little, for what "qualifications and information" could the army need but her native French-language skills? Perhaps the War Office sought translators. Or secretaries. She was not too old to type at speed, or she could write letters to prisoners of war in France. That would be a very worthy service.

Odette did not know what would be asked of her, and the captain's note gave away little. If the War Office had something practical in mind, she was determined to be useful.

Odette lived in the soggy countryside of Somerset. Only thirty years old, she was a single parent to three young daughters—Lily, Françoise, and Marianne—while her husband, Roy, was enlisted in the fight against Hitler. Roy was the son of the English soldier who billeted with her family during the Great War, and she had married him young—too young—at eighteen, practically an infant herself, she reckoned, so silly and adolescent; she panicked on her wedding night and refused to leave for her honeymoon. Instead, she dragged her mother and mother-in-law to the cinema.

War had marked Odette's entire young life. She was only four years old when her father was killed at the Battle of Verdun, just days before the armistice that ended World War I. He was one of 300,000 dead, a shameful, aching waste. The children of the interwar years came of age in a wounded Europe, still bleeding from the sores of Flanders and the Somme. France felt crippled by German brutality; Germany felt likewise about her neighbors' punitive reparations. Fatherless Odette was raised in her grandparents' house, her Sundays a litany of mandatory graveside visits and church offerings beside her widowed mother. As with so many daughters of the Great War, trauma altered Odette; it made her at once sweet and hard, vulnerable and ferocious.

As an adult, married but alone and mothering in England, the Blitz forced Odette to abandon the bustle of city life for the safety of green and empty farmlands. In 1940 and 1941, London's nights were pierced by bombs and lit by searchlights; the sky was a daily fireworks show of flares and flames. Had she stayed, the baby would have been fitted for a gas mask; she would have learned to distinguish between the sounds of a parachute mine and an anti-aircraft gun, even as she became bilingual in French and English. Somerset was better for the girls.

Odette's days were now an endless series of country rituals: queuing at the baker, counting out ration coupons, mending clothes when fabric was impossible to get. Propaganda posters extolled the virtue of thrift: "I'm as patriotic as can be—and ration points don't worry me!" The message was so bleak. "Go through your wardrobe. Make do and mend." Odette had been fashionable once, a dressmaker who could pin-tuck and pleat some *ooh-là-la* into any ensemble, but there was no one left to look pretty for now that she was in rural exile. "Austerity Clothes for the Fourth Year of the War," exclaimed women's weeklies; jackets without trimmings and "skirts without sin" were to be applauded. Odette longed for the thrill of London, the pleasure of companionship and attention. Rustic mothering and monasticism did not suit her. It was an unexceptional life for an energetic woman.

Captain Selwyn Jepson sat at his desk in the War Office, room 055a—previously known as Victoria Hotel, room 238—a former bedroom so small that it might have been a broom closet. Shorn of any glamour for the sake of utility, the room contained only one amenity: a sink basin. There was no furniture to speak of, save for an army-issue wood table and two plain chairs. The sparseness was deliberate, at the behest of the captain, who ordered the interview room emptied of everything that might hint of officialdom or even comfort. He was not there to chitchat or to shield himself from visitors behind a big desk. He wanted nothing to get in the way of absolute trust: no separation, status, or rank—unless, of course, he was interviewing a service member, at which point he donned his uniform out of respect.

Captain Jepson looked down his nose at the file sitting before him. Mrs. Sansom had no apparent enemy affiliation; His Majesty's Government found nothing objectionable: "Nothing Recorded Against." In other words, she possessed no criminal record. Scotland Yard and the MI5 security service had apparently decided she was an acceptable candidate for an interview. It was not piercing enough for his standards, to be sure. He would unearth objections, should they exist.

Full Christian Names: Odette Marie Celine
Nationality: British
Nationality at Birth: French

Upon her marriage, Odette became English by way of a legal concept known as coverture, meaning she was covered by her husband's legal standing; she became part of him the way a hand is part of the body.

Odette's file was opened on account of her keenness to help the war effort. In March 1942, an urgent call went out on the BBC evening news: The navy wanted photos of the French coast. On the 6:00 p.m. and 9:00 p.m. broadcasts, wedged between Proms concerts and news in Norwegian, the announcer explained that even the most boring souvenir photos would help. Trivial and mundane scrapbooks could turn the battle in Europe, and as went Europe, so followed the world. The announcement was one of many patriotic calls to service that year; the next morning Britons responded with some thirty thousand envelopes, including ten million vacation snaps.

Odette also heeded the call. She donated her family photographs to the government, a collection of snapshots of herself as a young girl on the wide beaches near her native Amiens, of picnics and parasols, sand castles and beach shacks, of her brother, her mum, her grandparents, even a father she never got to know, the plain and ordinary reminders of summers long past.

The smallest details mattered in the world's largest war. A top secret department at Oxford was at that moment pulling together a detailed map of the French shoreline. While England had ample information on France—Michelin maps, Baedekers narrating every harbor village, and nautical charts sounding every depth—the Admiralty required more specialized intelligence. To plan an invasion, the navy had to render a depiction of the country from wave height, from the prow of an incoming landing craft. The Inter Services Topographical Department (ISTD) was creating a comprehensive picture of the entire French coast and the Low Countries. The navy had to know what the harbors and beaches looked like, the gradient of each sloping dune, winding road, trickling river, any landscape feature that could yield insight into the water supply, blind spots, and approaches. No small-scale commando raid or aerial photographer could possibly produce such a map; the only way to get a broad picture was to cobble one together out of Britons' prewar holidays. A cast of researchers at the Bodleian Library pored over the scrapbook bounty, taking photographs of photographs, then returned the albums to their rightful owners, who never knew what images had been preserved or even entirely why. The ISTD built a photo mosaic, a montage of family memories, and stitched the panorama together for a colossal topographical quilt. It was the platform for a battle plan of the Allied invasion of Europe. England was at war, and the last battlefield would be France.

Odette's photographs were of no military value whatsoever. Her childhood snapshots never even found their way to the Naval War Library. Upon hearing the call on the BBC, Odette mailed her photos to the War Office, not the Admiralty; she was a non-native English speaker who misunderstood the difference. She posted her few family pictures to the wrong branch of service.

The machinery of military administration nevertheless churned. Postal clerks forwarded her note proffering assistance to a central registry, which funneled the information down appropriate, if opaque, channels to Captain Jepson.

When Odette entered the captain's office, he rose like a man practiced in gentility. The windows were framed in heavy air raid curtains, making the close room feel even tighter; the raw light between them was harsh and electric.

Captain Jepson was an elfin man, in a dark suit, forty-two years old with a squeaky pubescent voice. In peacetime, he was a working journalist and middling mystery novelist; at war, he was a cynic who held tightly to the fixtures of his own gloomy mind. With coffee bean eyes and slick, dark hair, his suspicions gave him the air of a man who was eternally constipated.

The captain, in a clipped accent sharpened and honed at St. Paul's School for heirs and aristocrats, started the interview with a rote question he put to anyone who entered his office: What did Odette think of the Germans?

She hated Hitler with a passion.

She detested what happened to France. Her mother was evacuated from her home; her brother was gravely wounded in the blitzkrieg and was recuperating in the Val-de-Grâce military hospital in occupied Paris, she said. Her country had been violated.

Oh, she figured she might find pity for the German people, but she had nothing but venom for the military occupiers.

The captain understood that French hereditary hostility to Germans was second only to Gallic enmity toward the English. At that moment in the war, it was his job, as his letter indicated, to select from the small but crucial subset of those he considered normal, common, and average British citizens, a few choice candidates who spoke flawless French, who could act French, and who were for all intents and purposes passably French.

"You would not know the way we do these things," the captain began, with Odette's file on the table before him. "We have made enquiries about you in this country and in France and we're very satisfied by what we've found."

Drama and overreaction were native to Odette, like a mother tongue. Her posture swung from demure and coquettish to highest dudgeon and outrage in less than a heartbeat.

"Well, what do you mean? Why did you have to make enquiries of me?"

In wartime England, Odette was suspect by virtue of her birth. There was resentment in Britain: The Frogs surrendered so quickly in 1940; the French army crumpled against the panzer advance; the Maginot Line was a punch line, a joke; Vichy ships in North Africa were at that moment facing off against the Allied fleet; French factories churned out weapons on behalf of a Nazi war that was killing Englishmen in Egypt.

Odette's fidelities could become a critical component of the fight for Europe. The captain was recruiting secret soldiers for a clandestine war in Nazi territory, but women like Odette were English only by marriage; foreign-born brides of Britons were considered by many to be enemy aliens.

She rejected the insinuation with enough spite to retry the Battle of Hastings. In a fit, Odette recited her patriotic bona fides: She was a good mother to English daughters, a faithful bride to a British soldier defending king and country. She lived a quiet life, did nothing treasonous or illegal. Odette was as decent an Englishwoman as any bird born in Blighty.

"What do you think I am?"

In that moment, the captain made a decision: He was willing to risk Odette's life.

WITHOUT SPECIFYING DETAILS of the job for which he was recruiting, or even the name of his employer, Captain Jepson offered Odette an opportunity to go to France for His Majesty's Government, at three hundred pounds per annum. Would she volunteer?

"Wait a minute." The captain paused. "What are your domestic circumstances?"

The minutiae of Odette's life were detailed in the file before him, but he would not send a woman to war who pined for babies in England. Her chances of returning alive were no better than even—or less.

To the captain, she appeared unconcerned about her daughters; "Oh, they won't bother," he would recall as her response.

Odette was instead trapped in her thoughts. She framed the nebulous job offer in the language of a mother. *Am I supposed to accept the sacrifice that other people are making without lifting a finger?* she wondered. What would become of her girls if both France and then England surrendered to Hitler? She might not be useful to this tiny man, Jepson; she might not be good enough to serve. But she was determined to at least try on behalf of Lily, Françoise, and Marianne.

With only the vaguest idea of what the job entailed, Odette said, "Train me."

THE CAPTAIN ROSE and escorted Odette the two short steps to the door, where they shook hands. She had a colossal personality and might not be willing to follow orders; she was too intense. Yet she met all qualifications: fluent French, British citizenship. The Allies had a need—a world-changing need—for women like Odette.

He returned to the file on his table and dashed off a quick note in the margins, his professional assessment of his newest hire:

> God help the Germans if we can ever get her near them. But maybe God help us on the way.

CHAPTER 2

Ungentlemanly Warfare

London

On Baker Street, at No. 64, a government office was hiding in plain sight of heady wartime London, operating under a false name: the Inter Services Research Bureau, or ISRB. To the employees, it was alternately known as "the Firm," "the Racket," "the Org," "the Ministry of Agriculture and Fish," and often enough "Bedlam." It was a gray and bureaucratic place, heartless and militaristic, with long hallways and functional furniture—and home to an agency dedicated to clandestine warfare in enemy-occupied territory: the Special Operations Executive, or SOE.

It was special. It was secret. It fell outside the ordinary command structure of both the Civil Service and the military, answerable only to the war's most senior planners. With Europe in the balance, this shadow organization was staffing up for the battle that would end the war.

Just ahead of Odette's meeting with Captain Jepson, a "Most Secret" document had circulated in which British and American war chiefs agreed that a second front in Europe was essential to aid Stalin's Red Army. The Soviets were single-handedly fighting the war in Europe on behalf of the Allies. But if an Anglo-American force could open a western line of battle, that would draw Hitler's attention away from Russia. He would have to fight two different wars at once, an unsustainable proposition. The strategy could finish the Nazi bloodlust forever.

The invasion would necessarily begin in France, the war planners agreed:

> Western Europe is favoured as the theatre in which to stage the first major offensive by the United States and Great Britain. By every applicable basis of comparison, it is definitely superior to any other. In point of time required to produce effective results, its selection will save many months. Through France passes our shortest route to the heart of Germany. In no other area can we attain overwhelming air superiority to a successful land attack. . . . In this area the United States can concentrate and maintain a larger force than it can in any other. A British-American attack through Western Europe provides the only feasible method for employing the bulk of the combat power of the United States, the United Kingdom and Russia in a concerted effort against a single enemy.

Possession of France was the tactical fulcrum that would tip the balance of the European theater. From the viewpoint of military geography, France was critical: It had long open coasts facing England, the Atlantic, and the Mediterranean; it was bordered by neutral countries Switzerland and Spain. Most important, though, France was in easy air and sea distance of England. It was a target the Allies could reach.

But France was in no position to fight for herself: The French government and most of its citizens were collaborating with Hitler.

"The decision to launch this offensive must be made *at once,*" the memo stated.

A date was set for the invasion of France: April 1, 1943.

SQUAT, BALD, AND very frequently drunk, Prime Minister Winston Churchill plotted the invasion of Europe while nurturing and pursuing his pet military passions: guerrilla warfare, smuggling, sabotage, propaganda, groundswells, and uprisings. From within the occupied countries, he was planning to employ the conquered peoples of Europe as a subterranean fighting force against the Nazis.

It was all the Allies had. The Nazis owned Europe. Adolf Hitler had captured the Continent with dizzying speed: In one month in 1939, he occupied all of Poland. In 1940, it took two months to conquer Norway; Belgium surrendered in eighteen days, Holland in four; Luxembourg fell in twelve hours and Denmark in under six.

In May 1940, the Nazis invaded France. During the evacuation at Dunkirk, 338,226 soldiers were ferried away from the front lines to England in a flotilla of eight hundred fishing boats, pleasure craft, and battle cruisers. What remained of the British Expeditionary Force only narrowly escaped the advancing German army. The Nazis entered Paris on June 14, 1940.

In those first fevered days of war in France, when Churchill was newly elected the head of government, Britain was stunned, alone, the only country in Europe left to fight Hitler. But with no soldiers on the Continent, how could Britannia hit back?

Memos flew about a new scheme to defeat the Reich from the inside:

> We have got to organize movements in enemy-occupied territory comparable to the Sinn Fein movement in Ireland, to the Chinese Guerillas now operating against Japan, to the Spanish Irregulars who played a notable part in Wellington's campaign or—one might as well admit it—to the organizations which the Nazis themselves have developed so remarkably in almost every country in the world. This "democratic international" must use many different methods, including industrial and military sabotage, labour agitation and strikes, continuous propaganda, terrorist acts against traitors and German leaders, boycotts and riots.

The notion of clandestine warfare was hardly new. It was, in fact, as old as war itself: The Athenians built a very fine horse in Troy. The word "guerrilla" comes from the Spanish, little warrior, and it was born of the fight against Napoleonic hegemony on the Iberian Peninsula. But until *this* war, subversion and sabotage had proven successful mostly by non-state agents for small-scale, partisan raids. War planners did not know whether it would work as a global strategy. It had not been tested on an institutional scale.

Those were days of hopelessness and fear in London. Democracies were kicked out of Europe, the Americans refused to join the war, Hitler and Stalin were still dividing the spoils of Poland. When Churchill put faith in targeted raids and resistance, they were the remaining tools in his quiver; he called them "butcher and bolt" operations. Until Britannia could fight back with machinery and military might, this secret army would continue the battle for Europe. The Allies would regroup and reequip for a triumphant return. Someday.

> What is needed is a new organization to co-ordinate, inspire, control and assist the nationals of the oppressed countries who must themselves be the direct participants. We need absolute secrecy, a certain fanatical enthusiasm, willingness to work with people of different nationalities, complete political reliability.

At a meeting of the War Cabinet at 10 Downing Street, on July 22, 1940, Churchill authorized creation of a secret agency for insurgency, a professional fifth column to attack Hitler in his new territories until the Allied Expeditionary Force was strong enough to open a second front.

The spark of resistance, Churchill believed, was waiting to ignite on the Continent. Millions suffered under the Nazi jackboot. Dissident movements would rise to challenge the Reich; sneak attacks could strain the mettle of the war machine, demoralize the ordinary ranks of German soldiers, and above all remind the European people that freedom was a birthright; justice would not be forgotten. Kindling the impulse for insurrection was a way to undermine fascism from within its ever-expanding borders.

"Brave and desperate men could cause the most acute embarrassment to the enemy," Churchill said, "and it was right that we should do all in our power to foster and stimulate so valuable an aid to Allied strategy."

Modern warfare was dependent on technology and belonged to industrial nations; never again would two countries stare at each other across a ditch, firing shots over a line that never moved. But the global war between great powers could be won by subversion as much as strength. Where regular forces provide martial muscle, the special forces are surgical and skilled, trained to be "the most potent weapons one can use": Attacking the means of production and communication—disabling factories that made the machines that fought the war, annihilating the ability to communicate troop movements over distances—was the most advanced thinking in military planning. Churchill liked to call the newly formed secret department his Ministry of Ungentlemanly Warfare.

"Ungentlemanly" was too pretty a word to put on the kind of war Churchill had in mind. It was to be the dirtiest war, beyond the rules of engagement, outside the protection of courts, contracts, or global political conventions. This was warfare by every available means: There would be murders, kidnappings, demolitions, ransoms, and torture. But when the Allies launched their major assault on Europe—with bombs, torpedoes, artillery, armor, infantry—the citizens of the Continent would be there ready to fight for themselves, armed and trained, detonating into a vast rebel army.

Long before the target date of the European offensive could ever be contemplated, it had a code name: D-Day.

Le Jour J.

"And now," Churchill exhorted in gruff understatement to his new minister in charge of the dark agency for secret warriors, "set Europe ablaze."

As WINSTON CHURCHILL was preparing to write the Special Operations Executive into existence, on July 16, 1940, Adolf Hitler signed the order to invade Great Britain. With Operation Sea Lion, the führer called for the total obliteration of the Royal Navy and the Royal Air Force. He would mine the seas of the British Isles and bombard the air, crippling trade and rending the mighty empire into abject submission. In Führer Directive No. 16, he wrote, "The aim of this operation is to eliminate the English Motherland as a base from which the war against Germany can be continued, and, if necessary, to occupy the country completely."

To PREPARE FOR a Continental invasion only a year away, to lay the groundwork for political change in Europe, SOE needed bodies on the ground in the occupied countries immediately, to fuel, fund, arm, organize, train, and command a resistance.

But with so many soldiers already at war, Britain had simply run out of men.

Captain Jepson was facing a workforce shortage, and crises are hotbeds for innovation: For covert operations in France, he unilaterally decided to recruit women.

It was a decision without much support in the Firm. Putting women in the line of fire was obscene, the brass said: War is fought by men for the sake of women and children. What use could women be in combat? Every culture on earth has a taboo against women in warfare; their bodies are purpose-built to create life, not to destroy it. Not since Boudicca led her troops against Rome had an Englishwoman taken up arms against a foreign adversary.

It was not mere chauvinism. The Edwardians who ran the war were too stiff to admit it, but they believed female recruits would deliver a new weapon into Hitler's hands: rape. As symbols and as soldiers, women are uniquely exposed; their bodies become war bounty, susceptible to other weaponized bodies. As inhabitants of an isolated island, British women had always been safe; there was a tidy division between the home front and the front lines. If women were hired for special employment in France, they would be subject to the worst of Nazi cruelties and retaliation should they be captured. And they would be: Irregular combatants had a life expectancy of less than three months behind enemy lines. Commanders said no, in defense of British maidenhood.

Captain Jepson, one sniveling man in the Victoria Hotel, set about ending a universal prohibition and prejudice as the practical solution to a staffing problem.

Captain Jepson probed international law for explicit direction. He found hiring women for combat was not against any laws of war; it was never mentioned at all.

Indeed it was acceptable and possible under the prevailing National Service Acts of 1939 and 1941, which conscripted women into the auxiliary services and brought them into the workforce in droves. The law permitted a woman to use lethal weapons if she was willing to sign a document testifying that she understood what killing and dying actually meant.

Precedent for female recruits mounted: Since those bruising days of the Blitz, some seventy-eight thousand women had begun to fire upon Germans, manning the trigger on the anti-aircraft (ack-ack) artillery. They lit up the night sky with weapons so powerful they could bring down a Messerschmitt. Winston Churchill's own daughter Mary served on a gun site in Hyde Park, about which the prime minister remarked, "A gunner is a gunner."

Women volunteered. Women were conscripted. Women got trained. Women wore uniforms in the service auxiliaries. Women killed. The women of Great Britain were already at war.

But they were not behind enemy lines.

Captain Jepson pushed his case for women further still. Women were not just useful in France but necessary. He claimed they would excel at clandestine tasks, as women were secretive, accustomed to isolation, possessed of a "cool and lonely courage." They would also make excellent couriers, he said, and have greater freedom of movement: In France, with so many POWs in Germany and every other able-bodied Frenchman pressed into obligatory service for Hitler, women outnumbered men. A man with no job, idling about, would be suspect. The captain believed German chauvinism would extend to the women of France: No Nazi could ever suspect a lady *saboteuse,* and girls on bicycles were a common enough sight. (It made no difference to Captain Jepson that Odette had no idea how to ride a bicycle. She could learn.)

In a bid to keep an exiled French general quiet, if not happy, Captain Jepson was targeting women who spoke French but who were not French citizens.

General Charles de Gaulle was a figure of defiance in London who loomed taller even than his six-foot-seven-inch frame. A general without an army, a leader without a nation, he had been feeding the furnace of French patriotism and opposition through the static of a wireless broadcast, from far across the Channel, for two years. In that mournful summer of 1940, when France surrendered to the blitzkrieg, Odette and millions like her heard the young general's first rousing appeal on BBC radio:

> Honor, common sense, and the interests of the country require that all free Frenchmen, wherever they be, should continue the fight as best they may.

The armistice was not a peace, he said, it was a cruel vengeance inflicted on a fallen nation. He was the lone voice in the darkness, raging against the Nazi occupation, conjuring resistance:

> I call upon all Frenchmen who want to remain free to listen to my voice and follow me. Long live free France in honor and independence.

De Gaulle became the leader of French exiles in London after Dunkirk. But the Firm found the Cross of Lorraine—the symbol of his Free French movement—a very heavy load. The agency was seeking native speakers of all languages in occupied Europe, but de Gaulle alone protested the battle plans. It was historically abhorrent that Frenchmen might serve in combat under British orders, he said. It predicted a future where France could become a colonial possession of the Crown. In the mind of de Gaulle, the Hundred Years' War need not be fought again once the Second World War was decided.

For the Allies, de Gaulle's tantrums threatened their invasion. The exiled heads of state for Norway, Holland, Greece, Luxembourg, Poland, Albania, and Yugoslavia had all taken up residence in London, and all consented to covert operations inside Hitler's Europe. De Gaulle was opposed. But where the monarchs hoped to return to their posts after the war, de Gaulle had no equivalent standing in France. There was already a legal and recognized head of state in the spa town of Vichy.

There were effectively two Frances in 1942, and neither was headquartered in exile in England. The armistice of 1940 had bisected the nation. In the North, there was a German Occupation Zone, encompassing the richest agricultural areas, Paris, and the Atlantic coast. It was administered by the Reich. The South was the so-called *zone libre,* the free zone, cobbled together from France's leftovers, 40 percent of the land with six million additional refugees, and only one deepwater port from which to reach France's North African colonies. Unoccupied France was governed by Marshal Philippe Pétain: the national hero of the Great War, the shame of the second. Vichy France was technically neutral, a nationalist state paying vast occupation debts to Germany; it maintained its overseas empire and an impotent "Armistice army." Unlike Hitler's other conquests, the Vichy regime offered the French a legal pretense of self-rule.

General de Gaulle was less a head of state in exile than an exile campaigning for president of France from London. He angled for a job the Allies were in no way willing to offer. If Anglo-American armies ever got a toehold in France, or in its North African colonies, it was by no means clear de Gaulle would lead the French people either during the invasion or after. The Americans preferred a wholly different French commander, one more amenable to President Roosevelt than the bilious de Gaulle. Prime Minister Churchill needed the United States' backing more than he did a vituperative and homeless Frenchman. "Every time I have to decide between you and Roosevelt, I will always choose Roosevelt," Churchill would spew to de Gaulle as the invasion loomed.

The Firm treated a diplomatic headache with a high dose of military bureaucracy. Two separate but parallel guerrilla agencies were established for operations inside France. The Free French worked with RF Section—République Française—employing French citizens; its aims were on postwar France as much as on politically uniting an "army of the shadows" during the conflict. Then there was a second organization, also commanded by the British, for non-French citizens, apolitical with an eye trained on the invasion: F Section, the French Section.

Together the two organizations commandeered every fighting-fit male Francophone in England. Between the agencies, there was a perpetual shortage of the "right type" of secret soldier. The complex knots of Anglo-French courtship only tightened demand for female recruits.

WHEN SELWYN JEPSON went "talent spotting" for women in London, he was formalizing an established fact: From the Special Operations Executive's nascent days organizing escape lines for fallen pilots inside France, women had been recruited as special agents and undercover assets. When a young Chilean actress in 1941 possessed an unexpired Vichy stamp in her passport, Giliana Balmaceda was asked to make a short reconnaissance trip across the Channel; Virginia Hall, an American journalist with a wooden leg she named Cuthbert, escaped Vichy by virtue of her U.S. passport and was enlisted in London to return to the free zone as an on-the-ground liaison for SOE. From the very start of the agency, women performed the same top secret work as men, but they weren't given commission.

Yet the brass refused to sign off on the recognition of and formal education for female agents. Facing rigid opposition, Captain Jepson appealed to a former journalist who once wrote for his magazine, a drunk old hack who penned ponderous essays about naval warfare and dreadnoughts: Winston Churchill.

If His Majesty's forces were to make a break with the proscription against women in war, a direct appeal to the nation's highest wartime authority made every bit of good sense.

In the wood-paneled meeting rooms of London, amid marble busts and oil portraits from past and prettier worlds, and behind closed doors, the upper echelon of Britain shared cigars and whispers. Everyone could know anyone. So when a mid-ranking officer sought access to the man directing the war, access was granted. They were old mates, Captain Jepson and Prime Minister Churchill.

"What are you doing?" the bulldog growled at Jepson, a man half his weight but equal in self-regard. "You're using women in this?"

"Yes," the captain said. There was a "manpower bottleneck" that could be solved with the simple application of womanpower. "Don't you think that's a sensible thing to do?"

"And good luck to you," harrumphed the prime minister in blessing.

When Captain Jepson returned to the warren of "Baker Street's Irregulars" and naysayers continued to doubt his innovative idea of commissioning women, he responded by citing his authorization.

"Would you mind talking to Mr. Churchill about it?"

CHAPTER 3

A First-Class Agent

England

Lieutenant Andrée Borrel learned to fall in the pink of an early-morning dawn. Like sixty thousand Allied paratroopers who dropped into enemy territory over the course of the war, Andrée, twenty-two, was introduced to parachuting at RAF Ringway, No. 1 Parachute Training School, near Manchester, in a course designed to explain the physical relationship between lift, weight, thrust, and drag.

Everyone strapping silk to his—or her—back was taught the physics of falling: The human body is a stone; the parachute is a feather. In theory, in a vacuum, stones and feathers will fall at the same rate. In the sky, air resistance stalls one and not the other. However compact Andrée's female frame might be, she would fall fast and hard like a rock if not for the upward force of captured air. While rigged to the canopy of the parachute, she would waft down, slow and tender, supported on a cushion of wind.

Humans must be trained to disobey instincts, to go limp when confronted with the speed of the oncoming earth. The key is to roll, to let the fleshy side parts of the body absorb the impact, while attached to a giant handkerchief.

Alongside male trainees, Andrée watched as sandbags got parachuted out of the sky. Half the chutes did not open. The sandbags with open parachutes still thumped to the ground with "a dull flat noise." The message and metaphor could not be more clear: Be prepared to land with a thud when arriving in France. Also, be prepared to die.

Andrée was buckled into a harness; then she climbed up to a riser thirty-five feet in the air where she was instructed to jump. She would be caught, she was told, by the harness clipped to pulley lines that would arrest her fall before she hit the ground. She had to get accustomed to the act of launching and plummeting, of forcing herself into the abyss.

A line of men stood on the ground looking up at Andrée. She was a bit of an "Apache-type," it was said, informal by habit, lower-class, and scrappy. The men found her accessible, playful, easy to like, easy to share a smoke and a laugh with, but innocent too, neither hardened nor hurt by the rough wear of war. Said a colleague, "She knew little of the world."

In a helmet, wearing a jumpsuit cut for a man, she stepped to the ledge and paused. The men below watched, waiting to climb the tower too, following her pluck. It was a trick of the instructors to make a woman go first. No man could stomach the idea of being shamed by a woman.

Andrée jumped. Gravity had its way with her. Instructors shouted to all students: *Feet together! Elbows in front of the chest! Head down! Bend the knees! Take the shock on your toes, not your heels.*

Paratrooping was a novel form of combat in 1942, a revelation of military strategy. Rather than breaking through a front, light infantry could fly above enemy-held territory and drop in behind the battle line. In darkness, unseen, unannounced, a whole division might arrive in secret.

The imagination of the world floated on silk canopies. The idea of a parachute army took flight long before the Wright brothers, from some of the greatest minds in history. Leonardo da Vinci sketched parachutes in his notebooks. Benjamin Franklin drew up imaginary battle plans: "Where is the prince who can afford so to cover his country with troops for its defense so that ten thousand men descending from the clouds might not, in many places, do an infinite deal of mischief before a force could be brought together to repel them?" When

Winston Churchill was first sea lord of the navy in World War I, he too envisioned dropping men into Germany from the skies. But the first wartime operation had only occurred in 1940, when Nazi paratroopers descended on Norway and Denmark. By 1942, parachutes were an entrenched weapon of war.

The British public discovered parachutes were a thrilling technology for targeted raids. The previous winter, when everything looked dire, airborne assaults gave England hope. The Allied armies could not yet count a significant victory anywhere in the world, swaths of London had been leveled in the Blitz, the Far East outposts of the empire were stripped away, but just across the Channel in France a British airborne company captured Nazi radar equipment in Bruneval. It was the kind of victory a beleaguered nation needed; headlines crowed "Parachutists in Action." "Enemy Taken by Surprise."

The Special Operations Executive wrote parachutes into clandestine strategy. "To be dropped in Occupied France was not a great adventure, nor was it an exciting pastime—it was a deadly struggle against a ruthless and savage enemy, most often with death as a reward."

Andrée was no stranger to death or to Nazis. She had been fighting both from inside France since Hitler's invasion, when she had worked as a conductor on an underground railroad, helping some sixty-five Allied prisoners of war escape to freedom over the Spanish frontier. Movement, in war, was her job. As a housemistress on a British-funded escape line, shepherding fallen pilots and patriots from secret hideaways to hidden railroad stops as they made their circuitous way to freedom, Andrée was an active defender of the Allies' most scarce and valuable resource: men.

She specialized in saving pilots. At a time when the Allies had no foot on the Continent and the war against Germany was launched from the sky, no airmen could be spared. If a flight crew managed to survive a plane wreck, they landed among French peasantry as heroes in need of an exit from enemy territory. At a time when the women of

France could not yet vote, Andrée, like hundreds of other daughters, sisters, and mothers minding the hearth fires of a fallen nation, put her life on the line to marshal the men safely home. This is how she fought for France.

War saw a shortage of every necessary thing, from wool and leather to meat and butter, but above all there was a worldwide dearth of man-power. At that moment, one in every three humans was serving in a global war that would eventually ensnare sixty-one countries. As ever in war, women by and large took up the slack when men went off to fight, flooding the labor market and infiltrating new professions. In this war, as in centuries before, women were mostly unwelcome actors on the battlefield, forbidden in the theater of combat, but Andrée was in the thick of it. She actively opposed Hitler.

Andrée had made a series of calculated counterstrikes after the Reich marched into Paris. She enrolled in a nursing course with the Red Cross, the *Association des Dames de France,* to save soldiers wounded in the blitzkrieg. Once France surrendered, Andrée and her mother joined the great exodus south, crossing the demarcation line between occupied and unoccupied zones along with more than six million of her countrymen.

Escape and evasion came naturally to Andrée, skills she perfected long before the war. As a girl in Paris, she was apprenticed to fashion boutiques for society matrons but eventually left the upwardly mobile salons for the Boulangerie Pujo. Later, she would work as a simple counter girl. Whatever hope of economic advancement Andrée—a girl who left school at fourteen—might have, she was happy to ditch it all for her Sundays off. She was an avid hiker and cyclist, a freedom lover who required at least one day outdoors.

A parachuting course in the North of England was a far cry from the manicured outskirts of Paris, but Andrée's unbounded spirit was the same. In France, she had tromped through the woods in men's trousers, never in skirts; sensible, liberating, and perhaps unwomanly, her pragmatism outstripped any idea of femininity; now she was as-signed to wear a man's jumpsuit. Andrée was action oriented, afraid of neither an awkward outfit nor a little dirt. Her family considered her a tomboy. She did not reject men, nor did they find her unappealing; indeed the men on the ground staring up at Andrée could hardly look away as she dusted off her flight suit. "She was entirely wonderful," said a colleague. "A good comrade for men, an excellent friend, but nothing more, you understand?"

At war, the men of France were in despair. The armistice was only a truce, not a legal peace treaty, and nearly two million French soldiers were imprisoned in stalag and oflag detention camps in France and Germany. (High-ranking officers would be detained for the duration of the war, for fear they might rise against the Reich.) In the Vichy zone, Andrée had ministered to returning French soldiers as they were slowly released; she shuttled from hospital to hospital, wherever a young nurse might be valuable. While working in a Vichy-operated POW camp for Allied detainees at Saint-Hippolyte-du-Fort, near Nîmes, Andrée met the officer in charge, Captain Maurice Dufour. Maurice could not resist Andrée's haunting beauty, her nerves and self-assurance. Andrée did not check her desire for Maurice, a wounded war hero and a pilot.

Together, Andrée and Maurice worked with MI9, the British secret agency financing the Allied escape route. Maurice ran his POW prison with a slackness that was entirely Mediterranean. His fellow officers were old and drunk, lax in the ways that only men on government payroll could be, pointedly un-Germanic. Maurice allowed his prisoners to roam freely in the sleepy town during the day, on their own recognizance. The Allied POWs wandered away from the fortress gates, never to return, while he adopted "an attitude of masterly inactivity until they were sure that the prisoner had a good start."

Andrée became integral to the underground escape line, a conveyor belt of some 250 partisans—nuns and priests, teachers and farmers, doctors and accountants, grandparents and teenagers—who escorted as many as six hundred Allied evaders home. She was undereducated but street-smart, meticulous about security, guiding men and moving messages between hideouts and cafés, asking no questions, greeting strangers with passwords alone in Toulouse, Nîmes, Marseilles, and Cannes. It was always dangerous; the fallen pilots were so tall and fair, those English Toms and Scottish Johns and Franks, they never quite blended in to southern France. She never knew their real names; the less information Andrée had, the safer her charges would be. She knew only addresses for her safe houses tucked into vineyards and olive groves. The links in the escape chain were independent, disconnected to stops before and after; the transfer of POWs aimed to be impenetrable. Leaks were a disease, an epidemic that would spread geometrically until they destroyed everything they touched.

This so-called Body Line stretched from the Belgian border to Spain. One daring night in Canet Plage, near Perpignan, the couple was part of an operation that liberated fifty POWs by sea to Gibraltar all at once. Said the leader, "If [the Nazis] knew how many I really helped escape, they would shoot me at least twice."

Andrée and her colleagues' success in liberating downed pilots in France changed Allied military strategy in Europe. In the maze of bomb-safe war rooms under Whitehall, Churchill reasoned that if French citizens like Andrée were willing to risk their lives to aid the Allies, they ought to have encouragement: a more steady supply of money, arms, training, communication, and orders. "France is down and we want to cheer her up."

Andrée was invigorated by resistance, besotted with Maurice and the cause. But Maurice, unfortunately, was married, though the match was not a happy one. His son, the result of an unplanned teen pregnancy, was now ten and living with his mother in the occupied zone. Andrée was a girl of few social prospects but a woman with the heart of a tiger, and she was in love. If the couple could never be married, they were very much partners in arms.

The underground became Andrée's life's work. Yet grit alone would never be enough to sustain a resistance career: Andrée got betrayed, blown, burned, *brûlée*. The escape line was violated from the inside when a high-ranking colleague, armed with names, addresses, and passwords, got caught; he handed everything to the Nazis. At least fifty-one arrests followed. Maurice was collared on the streets of Marseilles by two French gendarmes, then gave them the slip. With police whistles squealing, he sprinted seven miles to the outskirts and returned to working on the line days later; crossing into occupied France, he ferried four more evaders across the demarcation line to safety, while his identity photos were shared between secret police.

Meanwhile, Andrée's railway stop, the villa at Canet Plage, was under surveillance; a woman who worked there turned "stool pigeon" and informed the police for a mere ten-thousand-franc payout, a relative pittance. With so much exposure, the couple endangered the whole operation; they practically demanded attention from the firing squads. Their MI9 handlers ordered Andrée and Maurice out of the country.

Andrée left France by the same method she had liberated more than fifty other patriots and partisans: via the underground railroad. Where before she had been the conductor, a *passeur,* feeding, shielding, sheltering, and transporting a flood tide of evaders, now she was the cargo. With Maurice by her side, the Vichy police at her back, she crossed over the Pyrenees into Spain on Valentine's Day 1942 in the cold of winter and dark of night. The only way for Andrée to get back to the fight was to leave it.

So she went to England.

To Andrée's and Maurice's astonishment when they arrived in London, Maurice was thanked by General Charles de Gaulle for his service. They were invited to sign up with the Free French, and Maurice was offered a promotion, a raise, and a high-status posting to North Africa; his utility was obvious: He was a pilot and so could be trained to man clandestine airfields for receptions of arms and agents. He was also a skilled wireless telegraph operator, and there was a frantic need for communication from behind enemy lines. Andrée, too, had already proven her worth as an agent on the ground.

Andrée and Maurice went for interviews at 10 Duke Street, the headquarters of the French secret service.

ANDRÉE'S JOB INTERVIEW for de Gaulle's RF Section was a fiasco. She met with a French officer, the opposite number to Captain Jepson, who asked her about her work on the underground railroad. Who were her contacts? Where did the money come from? What were the addresses of her safe houses? The procedures. Helpers. Code words. Bribes. Routes. How had she gotten out of France? Charles de Gaulle's secret service demanded complete intelligence as a condition of employment.

Andrée declined to answer.

The rules of underground work were that nobody knew the details—not even her MI9 bosses. Knowledge was dangerous. The less you knew, the less a Nazi could torture out of you. Anyone caught could implicate someone else.

There was no job with the Free French, she was told, if she did not give up every detail.

Andrée stood her ground. Out of a sense of duty, security, and distrust of those who had not suffered in wartime France but instead sat out the previous two years in London, Andrée was silent. To speak would threaten future Allied evaders. Andrée's co-conspirators were not soldiers but citizens who risked their lives for a cause greater than themselves. Successful missions to retrieve fallen airmen depended on the ordinary kindnesses of the anonymous French. It was a modest, crucial heroism.

Andrée let the recruiter know where he might take his questions. She was rejected by her country's secret service.

Andrée's file was forwarded to F Section's Selwyn Jepson, who considered her "an excellent type of country girl who has intelligence and seems a keen patriot." She was engaged as a covert operative for the field, trained to be "an essential link" in the developing plan for the Allied invasion of France.

Where Andrée's meeting at Duke Street was hostile yet officious, Maurice's reception was altogether worse. He arrived for his job interview at 3:00 p.m. on May 8, 1942, and was questioned by Captain Roger Wybot, who worked for Colonel André Passy, leader of the French secret service. Both men were ferocious agents for de Gaulle, in possession of fevered cases of spymania.

Maurice's interview lasted three hours. Rather than celebrating his service, his daring defiance of Hitler, his kindness to fallen pilots, to captured POWs, and to France, Captain Wybot laid out an alternate view of Maurice's history: When he worked for the Vichy government as a prison warden, he was taking orders from Marshal Pétain. Did that not make him a Vichy agent?

The Free French were suspicious of Maurice's story: He was commissioned as a lieutenant, so, the interviewer wondered, was it not instead true that Maurice was inflating his rank? He was a lowly sergeant, fudging his status to captain to exaggerate his heroism. Over the course of the interview, Maurice claimed to have been decorated with the *Légion d'honneur,* the highest military award in France. It was a fact that could be checked.

Maurice, too, was told to surrender names, passwords, routes, secrets, hideouts, mailboxes, every last detail of the escape line. Wybot demanded answers; Maurice refused to give any. The conversation between two soldiers on opposite sides of a desk got heated, passionate, French.

At an impasse, Wybot left Maurice alone, under guard, for two hours, while the interviewer notified the British security apparatus that Maurice Dufour was a spy and ought to be jailed. The British secret police, MI5, responded that no, Maurice was a "fair cop," with a proven record of service. In the eyes of His Majesty's Government, Maurice was "most intelligent and made an excellent impression." Plenty of French patriots freelanced, but Maurice was a legitimate foot soldier who had saved at least sixty-five Allied lives; were it not for Maurice, there were mothers in England who might never have seen their sons again. They were glad to have Maurice on their side, as "can be seen from his story and connections, [he] has apparently been doing excellent work in France for the British in an accredited organisation."

Despite reassurances, the French secret service arrested Maurice. If he would not disclose information about how he aided the evasion route, he might be encouraged to speak after a night without food in the Duke Street coal cellar, a collection of dark, dank, squat cells with steel-reinforced bolted doors.

It was an open secret in Whitehall that General de Gaulle's Free French had a rough sense of justice. "Better that nine innocents are killed than one who is guilty should escape," said a report. The French secret service worked with merciless productivity; it earned the name *la Gestapo londonienne*. When Maurice revealed nothing after hours under bright lights, the stenographer was dismissed.

Two interrogators attacked him until he was bloody and insensible. In the blitzkrieg of 1940, Maurice was shot in the kidneys, then left to rot for months in a stalag with scant medical treatment. Now, in Duke Street, "they kept hitting me across my back with a steel rod bound with leather, they struck me on the place where I had been wounded and across the back of my neck," said Maurice. The beatings continued until 3:00 a.m.

Maurice was held captive for the next thirteen nights, brought out at intervals for more questioning. Each day he feared for his life: "One of the French officers knocked my head violently against the wall, breaking two of my teeth."

Maurice was "unquestionably third degreed" in the eyes of the Brits. De Gaulle's men used the same interrogation techniques Hitler was perfecting in prisons and death camps throughout Europe. Yet de Gaulle's secret service unleashed such cruelty not against an enemy combatant but toward a fellow citizen, a hero to both France and Britain. And then, in that petite Bastille in the heart of London, on French territory occupying British soil, in view of both British and American diplomats, the Gaullists issued a threat that all but unmade Captain Maurice Dufour: "We have arrested Mademoiselle Borrel and we shall make her talk using every means, even if we have to rape her one after another."

Maurice surrendered. When he was a little boy in the Great War, his sister was raped by German soldiers as he stood by, helpless. Maurice said he would agree to anything.

Induction papers were presented, a blank employment document. Maurice became a French soldier again, under the command and jurisdiction of General de Gaulle. The European governments in exile had vast sovereign privileges, operating as states within the British state: They had autonomy over political decisions and internal legal affairs;

they could maintain small armies and secret police and oversee military matters such as discipline and punishment. With Maurice's signature, the Free French acquired the lawful authority to court-martial him for refusing to divulge sensitive military intelligence. With the stroke of a pen, he made his own torture legal under the Crown.

Maurice was imprisoned in the stockade at the Free French camp outside London, at Camberley. Meanwhile, Andrée, at the behest of Captain Jepson, went to the countryside for secret agent training. She received glowing reports from her instructors:

> Of sound intelligence, if lacking somewhat in imagination. She has little organising ability and will do her best to work under definite instructions. She is thoroughly tough and self reliant with no nerves. Has plenty of common sense and is well able to look after herself in any circumstances and she is absolutely reliable. Has lost her attitude of overconfidence and has benefitted enormously from the course and developed a thoroughly level-headed approach towards problems. A very pleasant personality and she should eventually develop into a first class agent.

WHILE COMMANDERS LAUDED Andrée's sangfroid, it was tested immediately upon her return to London.

The second Friday in July was full of surprises. Bastille Day had been celebrated around the world with demonstrations in support of France. In London, General de Gaulle led a military parade from Buckingham Palace Road to the statue of Marshal Foch, the general who won the Great War. In France, the holiday was illegal, and celebration of *Quatorze Juillet* was forbidden.

Andrée was billeted at a Kensington mansion, Moncorvo House, which was the assistance home for French refugee women, a dormitory for the *Volontaires françaises*. She was a guest of the Allies, lectured on decorum. "You are not free," the house matron scolded in plush drawing rooms. "You have been chosen to be bound by duty and honor to show the world what the real France is like and what French women can be, and, indeed, are—a great factor in the world struggle against tyranny."

For Andrée, the days following *Quatorze Juillet* were a reunion: Maurice had escaped from prison. She had not seen him for months, but now he had found her and they were together again, in a women's dorm. She looked different now, her thick dark hair was rolled back off her forehead like clouds over an angry sea, but it was necessarily collar length, as required by the uniform she wore. With blue eyes the color of a Riviera beach, Andrée searched Maurice's face and saw a suffering man.

De Gaulle's goons had underestimated him. The torturers did not view Maurice as Andrée did: a partisan who openly challenged the Gestapo, cashed a military paycheck while defying Vichy, and escaped arrest and death many times over to save the lives of Allied servicemen. The idea that Maurice would just submit to an illegal imprisonment on the pretense of a coerced signature was laughable. He had been a prison warden; he knew the daily patterns and cycles of a jailhouse, the weak spots and willingness of guards. Against orders, after three months, Maurice bolted like Napoleon at Elba.

However passionate and filled with longing their reconciliation was, there was a gulf between them. The love of Andrée's young life was broken, tortured, hysterical, and traumatized—on her behalf, at least in part, whether she knew it or not. And Andrée was now a British agent, the only female parachutist SOE had—the first, and, at that moment, the only woman combat paratrooper in the world.

In stolen moments, on that chilly English midsummer night, Andrée could tell Maurice nothing about what she knew, where she was going, what her training entailed. To his everlasting credit, he did not ask it of her. They shared a lover's trust and a guerrilla's fear.

They had one night together. Baker Street was provoked when Maurice went missing, as it threatened Andrée's imminent mission to help lay the groundwork for the invasion. "She is expected by an agent of ours who is already in occupied territory and her presence there fits our prearranged plan, which it would be impossible to change now."

An officer from the MI5 security section discovered Maurice with Andrée and "stowed him away" to a safe house in Guilford, under twenty-four-hour watch. The Firm was in the tricky position of now siding with Maurice over the Gaullists; it broadcast the discomfiting "position that the FF [Fighting French] are court-martialing DUFOUR because of animosity arising out of his previous service to the British."

A diplomatic crisis stewed to boiling. The Firm walked a line with de Gaulle's secret service: They fought for the same cause, in broadest strokes, but not for the same country or the same leader. One secret service could not oppose the other while working jointly to defeat Hitler. Dufour's case strained the tenuous legal and diplomatic relationship between the two: The so-called French government in exile was in violation of the British Constitution.

It riled the British sense of fair play. There are rules, even in war and especially in this war. Maurice, though not a citizen, was entitled to due process, to habeas corpus, to a jury trial; he was protected against arbitrary and inhumane punishment. Everything hinged on his signature, which, as the British said dryly, he was "jollied into." Once Maurice became an unwilling member of the Fighting French forces, he fell out of England's legal purview, subject to military justice. In time, a man would die under the same "jolly" treatment Maurice got in the Duke Street dungeons, presumably tortured to death.

Andrée Borrel's love saved Maurice. If the Firm handed him over to de Gaulle, it would undermine her trust in her handlers; it would risk every agent she might contact in the field and by extension jeopardize the invasion. As long as Andrée was key to the Allied operations in Europe, Maurice's safety was guaranteed. The Firm invoked a masterful dodge: "The proper course would be for MI5 to say to the Fighting French that DUFOUR was of great interest to MI5 at the moment and that they would appreciate the opportunity of holding and observing him for a few weeks."

In the summer of 1942, Andrée Borrel was a weapon. She was expensive. While the Royal Air Force spent billions to develop sophisticated aircraft for bombing campaigns on the Continent, Andrée was the human equivalent. Bombers are messy, imprecise; they have a hard time pinpointing targets at night—with the unfortunate side effect of civilian casualties. The most sophisticated precision bomber in the world is a secret agent behind enemy lines. Andrée was needed for D-Day.

Maurice would stay under watch of the British security services in case he tried to contact Andrée. He was not authorized to see her again before she deployed. Upon successful completion of her assignment in France, they could reunite.

After one surprise of a night together, Andrée returned to Moncorvo House, her cloistered ward for demure French exiles.

Maurice was brutalized, but so too was France. Between Andrée's love of country and her love for Maurice—as if it were any choice at all—Andrée chose France.

CHAPTER 4

The Queen of the Organization

The New Forest

It was high summer in the New Forest, the hottest August in memory. The sky was clear, but there was a haze over the full moon, a dull pall of a halo. In the copses of old trees, in the deepest hours of night, an entire class of women failed secret agent training.

Visitors approaching Special Training School 31 saw what in peacetime was a private estate, a Tudor pile where the teenage lord, then at Eton, had inherited a rumored twenty-seven bathrooms while still in diapers. Known as Beaulieu, it had been in the Montagu family since Henry VIII's dissolution of the monasteries, but now the Crown claimed it—as it did so much—for war work. Great houses were appropriated all over Britain, their Van Dycks and Gainsboroughs yanked off the walls, the ghosted outlines of picture frames now overlooking lecture halls, map rooms, conference tables, and examinations. SOE got the nickname Stately 'Omes of England, for its posh digs and upper-class officers, a play on a popular Noël Coward radio ditty:

The stately homes of England
How beautiful they stand
To prove the upper classes
Have still the upper hand.

In one of the smaller houses on the property, the principals of French Section gathered for a meeting.

Major Maurice Buckmaster and Squadron Officer Vera Atkins argued past midnight with the chief instructor and commandant of the Beaulieu area.

The French Section was at the time still a young operation. Buckmaster was the overworked leader, a balding blue-eyed blue blood with the same head-boy background that seemed to attach to everyone at 64 Baker Street (Eton College, Continental ties, family bankruptcy). He was informally known as Buck, and in the secret service officers were frequently addressed by their coded titles: As the head of F Section, he was "F."

F was backed up by his number two, his assistant go-to girl Friday, Vera, the intelligence officer, "F-INT." Brilliant, iron-willed, square-jawed, Vera was a high-caste immigrant who hid her Romanian-born Jewish heritage behind an RP—"received pronunciation"—accent that would have daunted the queen.

They were a team, Buck and Vera.

The Special Training Schools were manufacturing secret soldiers under the banner of a modern military for the very first time. In August 1942, five women received top secret commando training and intelligence on the future battle plans for Europe; of those five, only one got even a notionally passing mark.

The room was clouded with cigarette smoke and discord. Around the table, Buck and Vera were opposed by the man known as "MT," the chief of training for SOE, Lieutenant Colonel Stanley Woolrych, who was outraged that only one student of the entire STS 31 Party No. 27.OB School No. 36 was minimally fit for deployment.

A stalwart security officer, Lieutenant Colonel Woolrych was more successful in combat than as a civilian. He was a veteran of the Great War, fluent in French and German, decorated, and dangerous; he was known to cross enemy lines during Christmas Day cease-fires and speak to the *Boches* in their own language. Gruff, thick-necked, bald like a potato, he was a gamekeeper turned poacher, a failed lingerie importer, and an accomplished classical pianist.

Woolrych said the single candidate in the class who was acceptable—by standards set for a man—was the model recruit, Lieutenant Lise de Baissac, thirty-seven years old.

And even she should not go to France.

A FEW NIGHTS EARLIER, not far from the house where the commanders were arguing, Lise de Baissac was snatched out of a deep sleep. She was marched in her nightclothes across a dewy field, hands above her head, away from the women's dorms to an empty garage where men in gray uniforms, their collars marked with braids in two twin lightning bolts, SS, shouted, "*Achtung! Raus!*" With a bright light shining in her eyes, she was grilled on her cover story as the psychological games of Nazi officers were practiced on her. Men barked, *You have been caught. What is your name?* She could recognize the voices of the supposed German examiners; they were the groundsmen and batmen, servants of Beaulieu. Every agent candidate was subject to the mock arrest and interrogation.

Lise's time among the ancient oaks had been otherwise pleasant, and she was part of a lively group of women. They woke early for daily physical training (PT), splashing through swampy bogs and groping their way over border fences. Each morning a man with calves like cricket bats ran alongside, shouting, "*Allez! Allez! Bougez!*" Lise was a natural athlete, raised in a house full of brothers. "I was really more, well, at ease with jumping, running than playing with dolls," she said. What most candidates would remember about commando training was the exhaustion, the particularly English masochism of running through the woods long before breakfast on nothing but a stomach full of coffee, but not Lise. She was powerful and fierce; she took pleasure in the schedule of daily runs, pack marches, and obstacle training courses. Every morning she got a little faster; then every day the runs were longer and the pack weights heavier. To many of the students at Beaulieu, the logic of field training defied explanation: Lise was supposed to look like an "ordinary everyday" Frenchwoman—war bedraggled, worried, weakened by rationing—but her job was to get as fit as a track star.

Lise was an ordinary enough Frenchwoman already. From what she understood, that was the critical requirement for the job. She had grown up in Mauritius, the French-speaking British colony off the east coast of Africa, a coaling stop on the sea route to Asia that was captured during the Napoleonic Wars, so she held a British passport. As an island girl, Lise played outside all year and lived with the perquisites that attend a colonial aristocracy, servants and property, but at the age of fourteen she left for schooling in France and lived there until the occupation. Hers was a Paris of privilege. She ran with a fast set, intellectual and arty, who weekended in châteaus and took spins in private airplanes. Lise was a fully habituated Parisian.

But France was no longer itself and no place for a British subject. With the fall to Hitler, Lise became an enemy alien, an instant threat to the Reich. Thousands of Britons were rounded up and imprisoned in detention camps inside France—retribution, it was said, for the jailing of German citizens on the Isle of Man. In June 1940, Lise abandoned her apartment in Paris and fled with nearly six million French citizens by foot, bicycle, horse, and car, away from the Nazis and south of the newly drawn demarcation line; it was a mass exodus, *un exode*.

France was shamed by the armistice, Lise thought. "Pétain was awful, opening his arms to the enemy." In Cannes, she approached the American consulate—neutral at the time—which arranged her passage to England on behalf of Greater Britain.

In London, Lise's brothers were enlisted in the war effort; her brother Claude was also commissioned by SOE. He had worked for the French underground after the blitzkrieg until he was imprisoned in Spain; then he, too, fled to England by virtue of his colonial citizenship. It was through her brother that Lise came to spy craft. Once Claude was recruited for special employment, Lise's personnel file found its way to Selwyn Jepson's desk. (The Firm was frequently a family affair; native bilingualism runs in siblings.) Jepson saw that Lise was self-confident, worldly, and astute, that she had a driven and analytic mind, like her brother. Training to become an agent was an uncomplicated choice for Lise. "I went to England to help with the war effort and I thought that

I was more useful doing that sort of thing, and [it was] more interesting also, than working in an office in London."

The Special Training School coursework was at once an indoctrination into soldiering, freedom fighting, and national service. But where male recruits got extensive instruction in demolitions and night raids, the women, the so-called Amazons, were treated to a much more cursory education. The first groups of women skipped most military training and were sent directly to the top-level security classes, the "finishing school."

For three weeks, Lise and four others attended courses in subjects previously thought inappropriate for soldiers, let alone women: Lise sat through lectures on invisible writing; she learned to pick locks and crack safes, and the king's gamekeeper from Sandringham taught her how to catch, snare, and skin a rabbit to feed herself in a dark wood. When burgling a house, agents were told to mask their scent from a dog by running into a barn and taking a "crap in the corner" like the livestock. In service of sabotage, and rebel recruitment, Lise was taught how to blend in like a civilian, build up a network, lose a follower; she learned to be an arsonist, a train wrecker, key maker, forger, blackmailer, stalker, and assassin. An instructor by the name of Harold "Kim" Philby designed courses on the black arts of foreign propaganda. Lise was schooled as a thug and expected to behave like a socialite. In all, it was not, Lise thought, terribly useful stuff. She was going to France to be French and to aid the French Resistance, not engage in cloak-and-dagger minutiae.

Lise was nevertheless given an education in violence as a necessity and an art form, something to master, process, and hone. After her morning runs, she was pitted against a grown man and told to bring him down with a single throw. Officers from the infamous Shanghai police taught a style of "all in" alley fighting that looked nothing like the sport of boxing or wrestling: Lise learned how to deliver a smashing blow with an open palm and the side of her hand. It was not how hard the hit landed, she was told, but where it was delivered; she was told to follow every attack with a "knee kick to the testicles." In her unarmed combat classes, Lise learned "at least 100 ways to kill people without shooting them."

Lise came from a family of gentlemen hunters, but Beaulieu was not interested in hobby shoots. Lise was introduced instead to the so-called sweets and toys of the .45 Liberator and .32 Colt pistols. Pistols are guns not of defense, the instructors said, but of assault. Lise took to weapons training as befitting her station in the world: regally, as if the laws of gravity only tangentially applied to her. Daily, she practiced shooting with natural movements, premised on speed of attack and accuracy under fire. She shot outdoors and in firing ranges; she fired while stalking. She learned to take aim from a distance, at night, and on the run. Targets bobbed and moved toward her, on pulley strings, and she neutralized the paper Nazis that came her way. It was noted that the women in the course were all crack shots. "They took up, funnily enough, pistol shooting with great ability," said Captain Jepson. He watched female recruits absorb recoil from a .45, fall on their backs, "get up and fire again and fall on their backs. It was that sort of determination."

That steamy August, Lise learned to use the Bren and the Sten guns, which looked much like a tommy gun from some Hollywood gangster film. The Sten submachine gun was the preferred weapon of the Resistance—easy to assemble, quick to clean, simple to use, lightweight. It fired five hundred rounds a minute. Thousands of Stens were to be dropped from the sky into France in steel containers each month. They were to be issued widely to partisans for the day when the Allies arrived; Lise had to know not only how to build, break down, clean, and fire it but how to teach those skills to others—young men hiding in the woods from Nazi conscription and old farmers too ancient and bent to be useful in a German war factory. These were the Frenchmen, she was told, who would be the foot soldiers of the rebellion.

In important ways, however, Lise and her class fell behind their male counterparts. Where most recruits who came through Beaulieu had at least passing knowledge of war and warfare—what little boy had not positioned tin soldiers on a carpet on a cold winter night or played chess with a doddering uncle?—women had to be taught basics of troop movements, supply systems, and battle strategy from the ground up. The logistics for the D-Day assault were near impossible to fathom; it would be the single largest amphibious invasion in the history of mankind. At Beaulieu, Lise and others learned exactly what that meant. It was elementary war school.

The women were trained as couriers, messengers, mercurial go-betweens for more prominent men in command. The courier was the point of lateral contact: Members of different networks were not supposed to meet; there was to be no cross-pollination between groups. Lise thought the messenger job was too small a thing: "I didn't want to be a courier. I didn't want to work with anybody else." Lise would not be parachuting into France as some lackey, to follow other men's orders. It was beneath her, she thought, and she told her superiors so: "I want to be alone." Buck and Vera listened. Throughout Lise's brief military education, she maintained the clear sense that her subservience to men was no part of any winning Allied strategy.

The most interesting lessons, to Lise's mind, were the schoolroom lectures on how France had changed under Hitler's dominion. With the clownish exception of her faux interrogation, Lise had never seen a German soldier in person; in classrooms, she learned to distinguish details on the uniforms of the security police, the *Schutzstaffel* (SS) and the Vichy *Gendarmerie*. She had not had to buy food under Pétain's rationing scheme; there were now bread tickets and meat tickets and ornate rules about what day of the week each was available.

France was a whole new country, and so Lise, too, would arrive as a different person. At Beaulieu, she wrote herself a new life history, invented a secret identity: that of Irène Brisée, a widow from Paris. She learned addresses for places where she had never lived, memorized the faces of siblings who didn't exist, and concocted a love story of war and loss for a husband she never had. (Romance in real life was not a priority. There had been one moment, when she was seventeen years old, when an artist proposed, but her mother rejected the match as she was not yet twenty-one. Other men had asked for her hand in the years since, but Lise never said yes. "I didn't want to get married. I don't know why. I'm very happy not to have done so," she said. "I would have been just . . . a wife and mother during the war.") As another female agent would say of the classroom texts and lessons, "In a sense, you see, your life had been taken apart and rebuilt."

> Cover is the guise you assume to make it possible for you to do subversive work.
>
> (a) Spend a good deal of time choosing what profession you are going to adopt.
> (b) Your story.
> (c) Your name.
>
> Know every detail backwards. Remember that within five minutes of landing at your destination you may be questioned by a hostile official. On your ability to tell your story slickly, your liberty and still more the success of your mission, may depend.

Lise was prematurely gray and preternaturally wise. Forging a convincing French identity did not worry her. With pale eyes and white hair, she was sufficiently French, Dutch, Russian, or English, whatever; she blended into the whole of northern Europe. "I can be anything." Nevertheless, her "outlook" was always Gallic. "Nobody asked me 'are you French?'"

Lise was issued a false name for training purposes so she could get used to living as a new character. The Beaulieu trainees and teachers were not supposed to know each other's real identities, for safety's sake. Lise still had family in France, and her mother remained in Paris; the pseudonyms would insulate them too, if Lise was arrested. Beaulieu's lessons were designed to help Lise not merely fool the Germans—who were easily deceived, as France was full of foreigners after the rise of Hitler—but fool the besieged and distrusting French. She had to pass as convincingly and innocently local.

Lise's childhood, spent living under one flag while fluent in the language and customs of another, was excellent preparation for navigating two competing life histories. To be a secret agent is to inhabit two worlds at once, in the field under a cover story and as a soldier answering to headquarters, carrying out the aims and goals of a foreign adversary. Many bilingual speakers say they "feel like a different person" when they speak different languages; the mission in France required Lise to simultaneously *be* two people: She moved with ease between them.

Lise grew fond of her classmates, despite the anonymity of secret scholarship where she was expected to keep her distance. There was a lithe Irish intellectual, Mary Herbert, nearly forty, a deep thinker who spoke six languages and had worked for the British embassy in Warsaw. There was also a gutsy Jewish arrival, Hélène Aron—as Parisian as any Jew could be in 1942. A third student, much younger, was movie-star gorgeous but uncertain of herself in the otherwise all-male, buttoned-up atmosphere, Jacqueline Nearne. But of the small group of women on the course, Lise never warmed to the temperamental mother, Odette Sansom, who had to be the center of every room she occupied and kept comparing herself to Joan of Arc. "Not my type of girl," Lise said.

After three intensive weeks, Lise alone was judged to be very much Beaulieu's type of girl. Her commanders wrote in their summary,

> Intelligent, extremely conscientious, reliable and sound in every way. Is quite imperturbable and would remain cool and collected in any situation. In both practical exercises and theoretical problems she has shown a capacity to sum up a situation, make a decision and stick to it without becoming flustered. A considerable experience of the world has built up for her a very high degree of self-confidence. A pleasant and quiet personality. She was very much ahead of her fellow students and, had she been with others as mentally mature as herself, she would have shown herself even more capable. We would certainly recommend her for employment in the field.

A FULL MOON shone through the forest canopy, casting lattice shadows against the windows in the conference room. A cloud of smoke hung low, just above table height. Vera drew on her cigarette with abandon; before one was extinguished, another got lit. Everyone was exhausted. Arguments circled for hours, then ricocheted back.

Woolrych fumed about the mere existence of the female students. Women should not land behind the lines, he declared, and now five inexperienced and scarcely competent women knew enough classified intelligence to endanger Allied operations in Europe.

The D-Day landing preparation was the world's largest secret. Not just the time and date of the offensive but the mechanics of each element were kept compartmentalized from all but the most senior military officials. In the coming year, officers of the secret army would train thousands of Frenchmen to attack the Nazis all at once, on the same day, at the very moment of the Allied assault. France would have to shut down in a single night: all the phones, all trains, all major roads and bridges. Years of preparation would come down to one narrow window, and the earliest days would be decisive. If the partisans could keep Hitler's reinforcements away from the Channel coast while Anglo-American troops captured a beachhead in France, there would be little to stop a cross-continental march to Berlin.

Democracy and peace were high stakes. Putting women in the field who might imperil the invasion by virtue of ineptitude, or physical inferiority, was too great a gamble, said Woolrych.

The arguments for and against sending these five women into a war zone were rehearsed until cock's crow. Representing Baker Street, Buck and Vera put up a fervent defense of their *Corps féminins*. Bodies were needed immediately for operations inside France; with the invasion imminent, networks had to be launched and nurtured. It was Beaulieu's job to teach qualified candidates to meet the growing demands of battle—even women.

Woolrych insisted there were objective standards that the women had not met. Female soldiers just lowered the bar too far. Buck was not dissuaded, and F Section was his organization. "I should have been failing in my duty to the war effort if I had refused to employ them," he later said. "I should have been unfair to their abilities if I had considered them unequal to the duties which were imposed upon them."

It is not that Buck had any formal qualifications that would recommend him to head a secret military agency; when his family ran out of money, he went to France as a journalist between the wars and rose to an executive position in public relations for the Ford Motor Company. He was qualified for command of the Firm's French operations only in that he spoke fluent French; as he would say, "It was no use trying to do things by the book, there was no book."

From both Buck's and Vera's point of view, the most charitable read on the commandant's dismissal of an entire class of women was that he and his instructors "were deterred by old-fashioned chivalry from agreeing to girls taking risks of this nature." It would not do in war.

Like it or not, women were on their way to France, said Buck and Vera, so they had better be prepared. The prime minister was on board. Best to get the women over there immediately, for there was work to do: A thriving underground would raise national spirits and possibly encourage France's colonies to lean the Allies' way, today, when the entire war felt hopeless.

The world was unspooling, and the Allies could hardly claim a victory anywhere on earth. It had been only a year since the end of the Blitz; thousands of Londoners had died in the Battle of Britain. It was only nine months since that day at Pearl Harbor when 2,335 military personnel were killed. Stalin and Hitler were in a stranglehold, fighting street to street in Stalingrad. Greater Britain had shed its Far East empire—Singapore and Hong Kong—in a blink, and India was agitating to leave. When Tobruk, in Libya, fell to Rommel, it seemed all Britannia did was retreat.

In a despondent moment, there was no time to wait for fictional future perfect soldiers, said Buck and Vera.

Just before dawn, in a deep and forsaken wood, Woolrych relented. Party No. 27.OB was begrudgingly graduated from STS 31.

Lise de Baissac alone passed with unanimity. She would be sent straightaway for parachute training. "I understand you are the Queen of that organisation," she would be told. It made her "very proud."

The Firm put a pin in the question of the other women, at least for the night: F Section admitted the intellectual one, Mary, and the pretty one, Jacqueline, back into the organization in the morning; they would be quartered in London pending orders. One female candidate would be investigated: Hélène Aron. And Major Buckmaster would take the theatrical Odette aside for a chat.

The Firm was in a hurry. The war was fought on the moon's twenty-eight-day rotation of light and dark, sight and shadow. Agents parachuted in on a full moon, when pilots could see. There were only three more weeks until the next moon to France.

CHAPTER 5

Merde alors!

Tempsford, England

The autumn night was unusually clear on September 23, 1942, from Bedfordshire all the way to the Channel. The moon was full.

Andrée Borrel and Lise de Baissac stood in coveralls in a hut at the RAF base Tempsford to say their final good-byes. To Vera. To Buck. To England. It was time to go home, to France. It was time for Operation Whitebeam/Artist/Monkeypuzzle.

Andrée had been ready. She was ready in July, when Maurice showed up at her door, but she did not go on that full moon. In August, the second half of the first class of women was trained at Beaulieu—Lise's class—and so that moon too was missed.

It was annoying, waiting for the September full moon—Charlotte, the moon was called in the agency's code, a woman's name. Andrée waited for Charlotte to grow pregnant in autumn to light the way to France in the darkness.

On the night Andrée was to leave, she met Lise, her jumping partner, for the first time.

"Now the time has come," Vera told them.

Floodlights bounced against curved steel walls of the temporary Nissen hut, casting a spooky glow on the tense ritual of takeoff. Andrée and Lise were selected to jump together, each the best of her group. Andrée, in the first set of Amazons through Beaulieu, was a practical student who dreamed up new ways to murder Germans. (A sharpened pencil jammed through the ear of a sleeping Nazi would not be too cruel a fate, she said.) Lise, in the next group, was the "queen" who preferred to rule alone. Both women were quiet and prepared, steeled against their doubts. As Lise put it, "If you're frightened, you can't do anything."

Lise and Andrée took to each other at once. Andrée was unsophisticated but quick, a "very charming, very simple little girl," thought Lise. Their past lives bridged opposite economic ends of Paris: Lise bought her daily baguette on the ritzy Avenue Kléber, where Andrée had been a counter girl before the fall. They would have met a hundred times. War made them equals.

They were to land in a field in the middle of the French countryside, but Andrée was jumping into the heart of the fight: She was assigned to Paris. The jewel of European civilization, the communication and commercial hub of Nazi-occupied France, Paris was also Andrée's hometown. She would set up a base there, working and living in constant sight of the Gestapo, Hitler's mechanistic counterintelligence and anti-espionage services. Building British-backed networks north of the capital would be critical to the Allied offensive across the Channel. Fanning out into the occupied zone, Andrée would be a courier and go-between, her bosses said, "to expand our various organizations to the maximum possible without pyramiding them and to deliver at least 1500 lbs of stores immediately."

When D-Day arrived the following spring—maybe only six months hence—coordination and command for the underground would come from Paris.

Attending the send-off was Captain Francis Suttill, a tall, poised, clean-cut thirty-two-year-old barrister who would be Andrée's commanding officer in Paris, her organizer. Andrée and Francis spent the summer getting briefed together. She would land before him, to smooth his way in France. For days prior to her departure, the two agents did nothing but sit in meetings: recounting, remembering, reciting, rehearsing, planning their strategy. They had been "talked at and talked at" until Francis could scarcely think at all.

Francis was a born winner: quick-minded, politically deft, physically capable, and solution oriented. He had the skills to bring together Communists, Gaullists, students, professors, Jews, and teenage patriots as a cohesive subterranean fighting force. But it would take a woman like Andrée to connect those diverse parties, one to the other, for it was not just Andrée's guts that would bolster their mission: Francis was dependent on her local knowledge and her native Parisian French. Francis's language skills were imperfect: His mother was French, but he was raised in England, so he spoke with a nursery lilt, almost like a child. Or a Belgian. He could understand everything, but when he spoke he sounded incorrect, suspicious. By way of explanation, he could say that he was educated abroad, in Canada. By his side, Andrée would normalize Francis, give him necessary cover, Frenchify him.

Francis was anxious to see Andrée go, but for reasons of his own. He was unnerved by the choice of a woman courier (at least this woman) and discreetly let the bosses know that he would have preferred someone else. To a man with two young sons and an overwhelmed wife, a beguiling work partner was a temptation. Andrée was just too beautiful, too appealing. He was a happily married man and wanted to stay that way.

Buck was unyielding: Andrée would work with Francis. She was the best and only agent for the job. Privately, Buck assured himself the pair could travel as brother and sister—though their accents did not match—and it was a story that explained away any possible sexual tension, at least in Buck's head.

For the sake of his colleagues, Francis appeared collected; he was "showing off" with a smile and a brave face. Watching a woman set off on such a dangerous task was tough to swallow; it would be simpler, he thought, when it was his turn. When times were difficult, Francis, like a good English schoolboy, calmed himself with poetry. He was drained, yet he would sit down and take pains to copy out Rupert Brooke's words for his wife as he recounted Andrée's departure:

Now, God be thanked who has matched us with his hour,
And caught our youth, and wakened us from sleeping!
With hand made sure, clear eye, and sharpened power,
To turn, as swimmers into cleanness leaping,
Glad from a world grown old and cold and weary.

The airplane hangar was empty; planes were out on the tarmac lit by blue moonlight. The farewell was formal, altogether different from Andrée's impassioned parting from Maurice.

Andrée was assured her lover would be safe. She had not seen him since July. It was a security risk to spend time together after his jailbreak, but MI5 promised he would not be left to the whims of Free French heavies. She put the drama behind her. There was work to do.

Buck regarded his two agents, Andrée and Lise, certain he was dropping his two most competent, most capable. Each was a girl who kept her head when all about were losing theirs, as Kipling might have said.

Though two female agents were already in the field in France—Yvonne Rudellat and Virginia Hall—Andrée and Lise were the first women to land by parachute. The RAF Special Duties Squadrons ordinarily called their clandestine passengers "Joes." These were "Janes."

Buck pulled a small package from his pocket and presented it to Lise. The male agents got gold cuff links, gold cigarette lighters, watches, pens. But the women got daintier parting gifts: gold compacts, a necklace, a gold pencil. Lise was given a gold cigarette case. Buck delivered each with the same sentiment of dark hope and realism: It was something to "remind them that, back in London, there was always a link ready to try to help them in their difficulties." It was also something that could be pawned on the black market, he said, if she got in a pinch. Presentation of the agency's golden gift was a ritual

Buck would perform at least thirty-nine times with women over the course of the war. They would not all make it home. At every send-off, his stoic British reserve was unmade a little.

Vera, composed and erect, went over her departure routine, emptying Andrée's and Lise's pockets, rummaging through their small suitcases, looking for loose change, a movie ticket, a matchbox, a clothing tag in English—a snapshot of Maurice Dufour—anything that might give them away.

If there was a power behind F Section's paterfamilias, it was Vera, whose informal remit expanded as the war went on. "She was the soul of SOE, more than Buckmaster," said Lise. Vera's daily duties as the intelligence officer included gathering news headlines and on-the-ground reports from inside France and pasting them together under the heading "Comic Cuts" and "Tid Bits." Her nightly responsibilities included sending agents off and welcoming them home at the airfields. Vera declared her title, F-INT, actually stood for F-Interference. Where there was a human need in the organization, Vera was ready to fill it; advancing paychecks to agents awaiting assignment, witnessing last wills and testaments, forwarding reassuring notes to worried mothers, befriending pregnant wives of deployed agents, and sending secret messages via the BBC to France once the baby was born. (*Joséphine ressemble à sa grand-mère,* for a girl; Joseph looks like his grandfather, for a boy.) Vera was the "Fairy Godmother" of F Section, Buck said, handling the "social side" of saboteurs. All the while, she lived a double life of her own. Few at the Firm knew she was an immigrant; no one knew she was Jewish.

After a thorough look at Andrée's and Lise's most personal items, Vera could find no stray bits of England to mar their cover. The contents of their kits were functional down to the details. Agents were provided with medicine, four very specific remedies: There was a sleeping pill, which, mixed into coffee or cognac, would render anyone insensible for at least six hours. There was Benzedrine, an amphetamine, should they need to stay alert for days on end. Another pill would induce cramping and diarrhea, good for a cover story. There was also an optional medicine, the very last pill anyone would ever take—and because it was lethal, it was nicknamed the L-pill—coated in rubber, sewn into the lining of a sleeve, it was filled with cyanide. If swallowed, it was harmless. If bitten, it was fatal.

The ground crew helped Andrée and Lise into their harnesses, straps over each shoulder, buckling at the chest. Under her flight suit, Lise was in a fashionable dress, nipped at the waist with some volume in the skirt, a slight extra bit of fabric that was an extravagance when wool was tightly rationed. The buttons and finish were precise; expert tailors reconstructed the design from clothing off the backs of French refugees, down to the labels. It inspired confidence that the Firm spared no expense and paid such close attention to detail. Once Lise shed the jumpsuit, she would arrive *à la mode.*

The particulars of the exit were rigorously attended to, complete with redundancies, fail-safes, and contingencies. Agents jumped with a revolver, in case the reception was unwelcoming. They might not keep the weapon upon landing, many preferred not to; it was a damning thing to be found in a police search when every firearm in France was confiscated. In their sleeve pockets, there was a folding switchblade, if they had to cut loose from their rigging. The leg pockets had room for a flashlight and provisions for surviving a night in the forest. They were prepared.

Andrée had fled France without her passport, and now she carried a *carte d'identité* for Monique Urbain. To the crew at Baker Street, she was known by her code name: Whitebeam. (Winston Churchill thought it intolerable to give silly code names to agents, imagining the poor mother who might learn of the death of her child Ballyhoo or Bunnyhug. On this point he was often disobeyed.)

To London, Lise was known as Artist. She was on her way to tiny Poitiers, a city on a hill in central France with "an ecclesiastical air," where she would be a network of one, running a safe house, greeting agents who dropped solo. Her orders downplayed the significance of the role, saying that for any other purposes she was considered not "otherwise operational." But in fact she would be the person greeting many of Baker Street's agents. Not "otherwise operational" meant liv-

09:35:52 13/06/2024

Receipt for Borrow

Patron details:

Name ------------------C************
******d

ID ------------------2***********
*7

Outstanding fees -------------- £0.00

Battle of Britain : the pilots and planes that made history

Item ID: 30129085904077

Due back: 04/07/2024

A history of treason : the bloody history of Britain through the stories of its most notorious traitors

Item ID: 30129090537060

Due back: 04/07/2024

Elizabethans : how modern Britain was forged

Item ID: 30129084725564

Due back: 04/07/2024

The greatest invention : a history of the world in nine mysterious scripts

Item ID: 30129088946414

Due back: 04/07/2024

Item count: 4

Successfully borrowed: 4

Norfolk Library and Information Service

Please keep your receipt

ing in a hostile country under a false identity while giving aid and comfort to men whom Nazis called "terrorists."

Andrée's and Lise's papers were minted in Roydon, where the Firm ran a forgery shop; the factory faked any document an agent might need: ration coupons, travel papers, marriage certificates, demobilization papers, health certificates. Totalitarians used these to control their populations; it was critical to have one's papers in order. Propaganda posters throughout France demanded: Are you in order? *"Êtes-vous en règle?"*

Packed into a cushion that rested between their backs and the parachutes, they carried heaps of cash. Andrée had some 250,000 francs in crisp notes, almost five years' salary, worth about £1,400 then, or about $250,000 today. It was an unholy amount for a woman of modest background, but more than enough to get by until her rendezvous with contacts in Paris. If all went as planned, the money would fund her circuit. If the reception went awry, it would get her to safety.

In the realm of what could be controlled, Andrée and Lise had everything locked down: They knew their mission instructions, backup plans, postboxes. Their ciphers were memorized. Nothing was in writing. They were fit and ambitious, certain of themselves, of their assignments, and of France. *It's all so very exciting,* Lise thought. *What's going to happen?*

The "dispersal" meeting drew to its natural conclusion. There were handshakes, kisses on each cheek. Good-bye. Good luck. *Merde alors!*

It was the unofficial motto of the agency: "Well, shit!"

THE DAY WAS AS LONG AS THE NIGHT, hovering around the equinox. At sunset September 23, 1943, Ensign Yvonne Rudellat sat in a safe house in France, listening to the French-language broadcast of the BBC. It was illegal to listen to foreign radio, yet nearly everyone in France did—as much as half the nation. At 7:15 p.m., the whole country, in both the occupied zone and the free zone, leaned toward polished-wood radio cabinets to hear the familiar clarion call of the world news in French.

The broadcast began with timpani pounding out Morse code for the letter *V*, for "victory."

Dot. Dot. Dot. Dash.

It was also the opening bars of Beethoven's Fifth Symphony—*Dot. Dot. Dot. Dash*—a small ritual of anti-Nazi propaganda, a triumphal reminder of a gentler and more civilized time, one that would return to Europe someday. Listening to the radio was an act of rebellion, and it could get a citizen killed.

Yvonne heard the announcer's daily script, recorded at Bush House in London:

Ici Londres! Les Français parlent aux Français.

This is London calling! The French speak to the French.

The BBC French broadcast was forty-five minutes; it began nightly with five minutes of world news, followed by five minutes devoted to Charles de Gaulle. The next thirty minutes were a buoyant variety of poems, songs, slogans, comic plays, political essays, commentary on the war, and calls to resist the demands of the Vichy government, to slow factories and undermine production. Early in the war, the French service broadcast twice daily, but it was such a hit—the nightly call from a land of democracy—that the BBC increased programming at every turn, up to five hours daily as the invasion approached.

The news program was inevitably on the progress of the war. When it came to reporting world events, there was no puffery, just facts: The Vichy government was instituting labor requirements for men between the ages of eighteen and fifty, exchanging French workers for captured POWs. The Russian front was holding in Stalingrad, where Hitler's forces were pitted against bomb and bayonet.

The final five minutes of the nightly show were the most crucial to the burgeoning French Resistance. At the end of the program, there was a running list of static-filled personal messages, which were a mélange of gibberish, riddles, rhymes, fairy tales, and couplets. The *messages personnels* were codes:

Jean a des cors aux pieds.
Jean has horned feet.

L'arc en ciel fait naitre l'espoir.
The rainbow gives birth to hope.

Some sentences were just noise, distractions, to divert, clutter, and confuse the majority of listeners—especially the Germans. Within the jumble of nonsense, however, were a few phrases intended as coded messages to operatives in the field. Via encrypted telegram, Baker Street would arrange details for airdrops and battle plans. In Morse dispatches, the signaling sentences for BBC broadcasts were set and confirmed. Some radio messages were for Frenchmen on the ground: A nursery rhyme might assure a banker that the money he lent a Resistance circuit would be backed by an IOU from the War Office; an aphorism could tell a factory owner that volunteering to scuttle his own machinery would guarantee the RAF would not later bomb the entire works from above. Other *messages personnels* were for agents, confirming airdrop reception and flight information.

In those last five minutes at the end of the program, Yvonne listened for her sentence announcing that Andrée and Lise were on their way. *Les Français parlent aux Français* played twice, at 7:15 and at 9:15; the first announcement would indicate that Andrée and Lise's flight was preparing for takeoff.

Around 8:00 p.m., Yvonne heard:

Les singes ne posent pas de questions.
Monkeys do not ask questions.

Operation Whitebeam/Artist/Monkeypuzzle was going forward. Yvonne knew Lise and Andrée were in their harnesses and chutes.

All was contingent on the second broadcast: If the same message was repeated, takeoff was confirmed.

On the night of September 23, 1942, the sentence beamed out a second time from London to the empty fields of the Loir-et-Cher.

Monkeys do not ask questions.

The rebels would always remember "the joy of hearing the message through the static, this tangible proof that contact existed," that the Allies were working to liberate France.

CHARLOTTE HAD ARCED more than halfway across the heavens when the pilot spotted the French coastline. The moon was a clock tracking in the sky.

Between low and broken clouds, the pilot spotted Pointe de la Percée; his landmark was halfway between beaches that would someday be known as Omaha and Utah. He took a fix on his position, aimed toward the city of Orléans, then at the last minute dropped below the cloud base, becoming as visible to the enemy as the moon-dappled waters of the river Loire were to the navigator.

Like so much confetti, a cloud of pamphlets fluttered into quiet, curfewed streets of a tiny French town. The leaflets contained slogans, drawings, and patriotic reminders: One fight for one country. *Vive la France*. Charles de Gaulle. The notes served two Allied purposes: as propaganda to tell France that the nation historically considered "perfidious Albion" had not forgotten her, and to give cover to the aircraft so that in the morning the Germans might assume that the enemy flew in on a public relations or reconnaissance mission, not to infiltrate agents or drop supplies. The RAF pilots called the payload "*Mein Pampf.*"

Sighting Orléans, the Whitley descended to five hundred feet. Between steeple and treetop, the aircraft approached a dark and empty field outside Blois.

The pilot dropped his flaps and made a low pass, just over stalling speed, a moment of high vulnerability, ripe for shooting and visible to enemy searchlights. He had little room to maneuver, so low and slow, focused on his targets.

"Action stations," shouted the dispatcher over the engine noise.

Andrée was curled around her knees, tucked in the tight fuselage of the Whitley. She got up, moved to the hole in the floor of the bomber, checking her harness and the pin that clipped her static line to the aircraft. She kept her eyes fixed on a red light ahead of her, her feet in the wind, waiting for the green to go.

It was good to be first. Lise would have preferred it. She assumed it would be easier, choosing her own exit time, rather than depending on another, but they drew lots and the honor went to Andrée. The jumps would be quick, one right behind the other, or they would land miles apart.

Passing over the drop zone, the navigator looked for the flare path, three red lights in a triangle with one light downwind, flashing white. The pilot made sweeps over the target, seeking the beams, searching for a confirmation signal in Morse: the letter *F*.

Nothing happened.

"We can't drop you because the lights are not right," the dispatch officer shouted.

The signal was wrong. No one seemed to be waiting for Andrée and Lise.

ON THE LOIRE RIVER, there is a spot where five hundred years ago a girl named Jehanne Romée, daughter of a peasant named Jacques d'Arc, marshaled an army that would give birth to the nation of France.

Not far from there, in a dark pasture, Yvonne Rudellat took a seat and waited for the plane. The ground was damp and cool. Days were still warm, but the night had a chill. The harvest was nearing an end, grapes were picked, potatoes and apples were set in cellars for the winter;

there would be frost any morning now. It had been two years since the Nazis first forbade hunting in the Sologne region; now the night felt alive with critters.

Yvonne sat still, listening for airplane engines. Her culottes were bunched up around her waist, displaying the tops of her stockings and her bare thighs. She neither noticed nor cared; she was not a woman to "worry about no-essentials."

Yvonne was with an all-male reception committee; it sounded so English, like something attended by men in waistcoats and white boutonnieres, but they operated at night in a climate of ruthless intimidation. Three men stood in the field, arranged a hundred yards apart, the evening dew soaking their trouser cuffs, berets pulled low. If they were caught, they looked like common poachers. With so much produce diverted to Germany, France was malnourished, and 1942 was the first open hunting season of the war. The punishment for a rabbit-gauge rifle was no longer a stiff prison sentence. It was not a revolver. Grouse were not the Gestapo.

Yvonne looked up and tilted her head toward the roar of approaching engines. Out from the noise, she expected two women to flit down like autumn leaves, their canopies blocking the moonlight as they fell.

The Whitley made runs over the empty farmland. For fifteen minutes, the low plane circled before the two men threw their lights into the sky. One man did not. Maybe his bulb was out. Maybe a switch got stuck, or a wire was loose. Perhaps his lights were set too close to the tree line, obscured from the sight of the navigator. One man was deaf in one ear, so perhaps he did not hear the aircraft.

When Andrée's and Lise's airplane arrived, there were only white lights, no red.

Andrée and Lise did not jump.

Against a harvest moon, the silhouetted bomber nosed up and banked away. From a great thundering crescendo, the engines died back to faint hums.

Then the night was silent. So quiet that Yvonne could hear a wristwatch tick.

The next day, all was calm in the small village of Avaray, near the Loire. Life in the hamlet continued as it always had, unhurried, as if nothing were wrong, as if the demarcation line did not exist.

The flare paths were in place again at 1:00 a.m. The committee waited, in a long uncertain silence, and from a distance, hardly discernible, came the throb of approaching engines.

A large shadow appeared over the moonlit field as the plane, for the second night in a row, made its low pass toward the drop zone. The correct Morse signal blinked toward the stars.

Dot. Dot. Dash. Dot: F.

The Whitley dropped Andrée, then Lise, on pinpoint.

Un, deux, trois, quatre . . . the committee counted parachutes opening like flowers. Andrée, Lise, their suitcases, and twelve Colts with ammunition, ten kilos of plastic, eight hundred primers, detonators, and other devices landed in France under a wide orange moon, one right after the other, not fifty yards apart.

Into the flight log, the pilot recorded,

Everything ok.

Shrugging off their parachutes, unclipping from their harnesses, Andrée and Lise were greeted by the committee who ran up to collect the silk and suitcases.

Barely speaking, the women were walked to a shed in the forest to wait until morning, when curfew lifted.

Well, now I am living on the soil of France, thought Lise.

At first light, a horse and cart brought the agents to the small home of an elderly and patriotic refugee couple, the Bossards, fish merchants who had fled the bombing on the coast for the Loire valley. Yvonne was there to greet her colleagues. She was a friend of Andrée's from their days together in the summer's first training class of women at Beaulieu.

It was not easy to find Frenchmen sympathetic to a British-backed resistance in 1942. Anglophobia was never far from French consciousness, and the nation still resented the *débâcle* at Dunkirk, which it continued to see as Britain's abdication of the war. Even after two years of occupation, Frenchmen spat at the name Churchill. After all, the very first thing he did after the fall was to threaten France: Send all French battleships to a neutral port, the prime minister had ordered, or scuttle your own navy, lest the fleet be surrendered to the Germans. When the Vichy admiral refused, Britain bombed the harbor at Oran, Algeria, on July 3, 1940; some 1,297 sailors died. It was an agitprop coup for Hitler and Pétain.

Older French people were likely to be forgiving of the British, to remember the friendships forged at the Somme. The Bossards lived close to the demarcation line, where the countryside was heavily guarded and daily routines were upended; said Lise, "It wasn't quite free."

Yvonne arranged for a radio message back to London: Monique and Odile arrived safe.

Andrée and Lise rested a few nights in the small village, talking with the couple, acclimating, "to make us feel happier about it before we were sent out." The first female soldiers to parachute behind enemy lines began their missions with omelets and wine.

Lise bought a ticket to Poitiers.

Andrée went home to Paris.

CHAPTER 6

To the Very Last Man

Sark, Channel Islands

In the English Channel, an island shaped like a flattened bug was quiet and still, a waiting link in Hitler's great Atlantic Wall, the vast chain of steel and concrete mined defenses stretching two thousand miles, from above the Arctic Circle in Norway all the way down France to the Iberian Peninsula.

The island of Sark was recently British. Now it belonged to the Reich. Hugging the coast of France, only two square miles, it was tucked between Guernsey and Jersey, just off the Cotentin Peninsula, a place lost in time: Islanders still traveled by foot and by donkey; they read books by gaslight. But after the fall of Dunkirk, the war came to the Gulf of Saint-Malo and to Sark's beaches. The Channel Islands were indefensible, Churchill declared, so close to Normandy, and strategically unimportant to the safety of England. Britain demilitarized and pulled out.

The Nazis seized the islands. Those pleasant pastures were lost without a fight. Now Hitler made the Channel Islands an integral part of his strategy against the coming Allied invasion.

Breaking the silence of the autumn night on October 3, 1942, a motorboat nicknamed "Little Pisser" drew up to the sea cliffs of Sark. Twelve men debarked and scaled the sheer rock wall up onto the island's spine. Faces blackened, guns loaded, knives at the ready, the team ran toward a Nazi encampment. The mission was Operation Basalt.

Six commandos reached the German barracks. Lining up in a long hallway in front of six bedroom doors, at the signal, the raiders entered the soldiers' quarters, where Nazis snored in iron beds. The occupiers woke to the faces of their enemies.

The raid went quickly and as rehearsed: British commandos tied the hands of their German prisoners with bedsheets, hustled them into the hallway, then collected books, newspapers, every printed thing.

With prisoners in tow, the raiders regrouped for the long run back to their escape vessel. Abruptly, as the Nazi soldiers realized what lay ahead, all the raiders' preparation and forward planning fell apart. The Germans were captives; they began screaming, complaining about their treatment, demanding to wear uniforms rather than bedclothes, rousing nearby villagers. The commandos retaliated: "Helped by some blows they became quieter—or at least we thought so."

In the ruckus, one German broke free and ran for open ground. He was captured immediately, but undeterred, he raced out again, shouting and fighting. He was shot in the back. Seeing the melee, three other Nazi prisoners made for escape. Two were fired upon immediately, point-blank. The third, still in restraints, screamed, in hopes of a rescue.

A young British soldier moved to silence the German with the butt of his revolver, his finger still on the trigger. He blew the prisoner's head clean off, "accidentally." In the scuffle, two Nazis got away: one injured, the other naked. They sounded the alarm.

One remaining German prisoner surrendered, deferring to the British commandos' brute strength. Better to live another day as a captive of the British than to die a hero of the Reich.

The town and garrison were alerted to the raid. Under reports of gunfire, the raiders and their hostage escaped to Little Pisser, motoring away from Sark into a black sea.

All the British commandos returned alive. They brought with

them a Nazi prisoner, who was an engineer on the Atlantic Wall. He had information about construction of the concrete antitank barriers, double-wire fencing, minefields, pillboxes, and heavy artillery all along the Channel. They had collected a handful of other intelligence: notes, orders, plans, and ledgers. Operation Basalt was A-1-0, a rollicking success.

TO THE NAZIS, it was an execution: German soldiers were shot at close range while restrained and in their nightshirts.

In response, Hitler issued a commando order, *Kommandobefehl,* October 18, 1942, with instructions for the highest officers of the Reich. It was marked "Secret." Only twelve copies were made.

"This order is for commanders only and is in no circumstances to fall into enemy hands," the missive warned:

> From now on all sabotage troops will be annihilated without exception to the last man. Whether they are soldiers in uniform, saboteurs, with or without arms; whether they are fighting or seeking to escape; it does not matter if they come into action from ships or aircraft or if they land by parachute. Even if they give themselves up as prisoners, they will not be excused. No pardon will be given. . . . That means that their chances of escaping with their lives is nil. Under no circumstances . . . can they be expected to be treated according to the rules of the Geneva Conventions.

The implementation of Hitler's illegal order took a poetic, if dark, turn: The Nazis loved documentation and kept detailed records, so when they were ordered to commit crimes against humanity, but were loath to leave evidence of the fact, prisoners got designated with the code N+N. It stood for *Nacht und Nebel,* a reference to Hitler's beloved Wagner, a lyric from *Das Rheingold:*

Nacht und Nebel—niemand gleich!
Night and fog—as if no one was there!

The N+N designation was a way to identify the unidentifiable, to signify those who would be erased. German jailers were instructed to punish N+N prisoners with pain, terror, and suffering, tempered neither by compassion nor an eye toward international covenants. In secret, Hitler gave preemptive pardons to his commanders for any past, current, or future war crimes.

If captured, Lise, Andrée, and Odette were fated for the most violent treatment of the Reich. Isolation. Torture. Slavery. Summary execution. Total eradication from all living memory. Night and fog.

Part II

CHAPTER 7

A Thousand Dangers

Paris

Avenue Foch is the wealthiest street in Europe, Paris's most exclusive address. It stretches from the Arc de Triomphe to the Bois de Boulogne, with wide gardens flanking either side of the boulevard; it is planted with ancient Indian elms and expansive chestnuts that predate Napoleon Bonaparte. During the occupation, Avenue Foch remained a promenade of elegance and grandeur, with bridle paths and wandering walks that curved between copses of flowering bushes and stone monuments. (The brass sculptures of Paris, however, were carted off and melted for bullets.)

In war, Hitler's administrators made Avenue Foch their bureaucratic home.

On the north side of the avenue, toward the Porte Dauphine, there was a six-story home at No. 84 with stripes of iron fretwork banding tall front windows. The mansion was set to be headquarters for the security force that in Paris was colloquially known as the Gestapo: Together the *Sicherheitspolizei* and *Sicherheitsdienst* (Sipo-SD) made up the secret service of the Nazi Party, staffed by stalwart followers of the führer, whose job was to root out, capture, and execute all enemies of the Reich.

In the afternoons, Paris sunlight slanted into a Beaux Arts office as grand and imposing as the man who commanded it. The room was centered on a large Louis XV desk that spoke to leadership, order, opulence, and strength; it belonged to *SS-Sturmbannführer* Karl Bömelburg, who was moving in as 1942 rounded to 1943. The top counterintelligence officer in Paris was a barrel-chested party loyalist and veteran of World War I nearing retirement. He was tall, with graying hair, an Aryan mien, and the posture of a practiced equestrian; Bömelburg was often seen riding through the Bois de Boulogne to a villa where he kept chickens, his lifelong dream. He decorated his personal apartments and his home with lavish gifts from collaborators in the Paris mob, stolen silver, and young male prostitutes.

Major Bömelburg followed Adolf Hitler with conviction and cruelty from his earliest days in Berlin. In the 1930s, before the war, he set up the Gestapo headquarters in Paris, but for provoking the extreme-right wing of France, he was exiled to Czechoslovakia in 1939, as police counselor to the Gestapo. There he made a healthy profit swapping Jewish children for cash, sparing 669 innocents in the remunerative process.

Now in a conquered Paris, in the waning days of his military career, Bömelburg hunted the French Resistance and French Jews with equal fervor. At Avenue Foch, they were often considered the same thing.

Avenue Foch was quiet, as if from an earlier century. There were few cars in Paris; there was no gas. Instead, there were the bells of bicycles and pedicabs, the syncopated clip-clop of horse-drawn carts. Once a day, the goose steps of soldiers on parade echoed down from the Arc de Triomphe, accompanied by the trumpet bombast of the "Horst Wessel Lied": "Millions are looking upon the swastika full of hope. The day of freedom and bread dawns."

Like all of Paris in the war, the facade of No. 84 was coal stained, dark gray. From inside, Bömelburg commanded a professional and punishing police force.

Beyond the gates of No. 84, a narrow driveway stretched into a courtyard where chauffeurs polished to a high sheen a fleet of luxury cars requisitioned from escaping Parisians and former Jewish residents. There was a shed in the courtyard too where reluctant citizens were encouraged to reveal private information in ways that made grown men piss blood.

At the heart of the mansion, a central stairwell swept upward to posh apartments populated by an assortment of Nazi secret police: ranking commandants, clerks, enlisted men, drivers, and goons. The second floor was headquarters for counterespionage investigations, for arrests and interrogations inside occupied France; it was packed with desks, file cabinets, photostat copy machines, and plump blond secretaries in uniform. A tasteful bathroom in the corner of the house boasted a deep iron tub, useful for interrogations.

On the top floor, in what used to be the servants' quarters, were prison cells for enemy spies. In the cellar, there was a cave with fine vintage wine.

Major Bömelburg took a particular interest in the third floor, which would see a new team of expert spy hunters moving in during the third winter of the war in France, a group of radio and language specialists. Telegraph traffic and signals were in the air; the radio was wide open to anyone who could listen in with a receiver. Transmitters were illegal, but nevertheless remained weapons of resistance. They were easy to build and conceal; radio signals were the fastest means to communicate. The Gestapo was always listening in.

On the third floor, any suspicious encoded message was typed out onto carbon copies and filed away. Most secret messages were a seemingly random collection of Morse letters, meaningless without the keys to the code. Radio specialists nevertheless examined each new missive closely. Bömelburg's team could not yet read messages the underground was sending to London, but it was only a matter of time. Code breakers looked for patterns and applied statistical analysis. For example, *e* is the most frequently occurring letter in the English language, used about 10 percent of the time. The letters *j, k, q, x,* and *z* occur least often; there are only two words that are one letter long, "a" and "I." So with simple counting and a little deduction, any message can be cryptanalyzed. Bömelburg's team learned to tune in to suspect radio frequencies and recognize the "fists" of the Morse radio operators, the *pianistes,* they were called; Nazis knew radiomen by their unique typing fingerprints. The Allies themselves unwillingly aided Avenue Foch in their quest: Over the course of the war, the Gestapo arrested rebel agents and then used psychological coercion and physical torture to persuade them to give up their codes.

In radio espionage, Hitler gained the upper hand early. For well over a year in Holland, captured British radio sets and codes had been deceiving Baker Street's Dutch section. The captured sets would pretend to be operated by British agents, and the Allies unwittingly dropped agents and arms into the hands of the Reich. The German propensity for inventing new nouns was deployed, and such deception was nicknamed *Das Funkspiel,* the radio game. Or more often and more accurately, *Das Englandspiel,* the England game.

For Bömelburg, it was a waiting game. While Hitler worried that "a large city like Paris can hide a thousand dangers," no amateur spy network could hide forever. The day would come when a rebel in Paris would be captured, when the keys to his coded messages would be found on him—or her—and would unlock Bömelburg's orderly files full of back traffic. A wireless set tuned to London's bandwidth might even fall into his hands. On that day, it would be possible to understand previous messages and control signals to the Allies going forward. The Gestapo might be able to send disinformation about landing zones and conditions to the enemy. Bömelburg believed he would hear advance warnings about the coming invasion of France.

From his opulent apartments, as a coda to Herr Bömelburg's vaunted career, the *SS-Sturmbannführer* worked on a scheme to also capture the written text communiqués between the burgeoning French Resistance and Allied command.

Some rebel messages went by radio; others traveled by hand, by courier. Partisans crossed into Switzerland or Spain, where there were British diplomatic missions, carrying dispatches that arrived later in England via diplomatic pouch. Alternately, when a VIP French leader or British rebel had to be picked up in France via airplane, at those moments a mailbag could be included on the flight out, often carrying letters in plain text, *en clair,* or notes using simple word-replacement codes that contained veiled references to operations behind enemy lines.

Bömelburg knew about the mail and developed a plan to get it: He was in contact with a Frenchman, a stunt pilot who had escaped over the Pyrenees to Britain and got trained by the Special Operations Executive. The French pilot would command his own landing zones and oversee the airplane pickups and landings in the vicinity of Paris. He was young, slick, greedy, and corrigible.

His price tag was four million francs.

Avenue Foch itself reflected the recent history of Franco-German enmity. It was known originally as Avenue Bois—the road to the forest—but after World War I was rechristened for the heroic French general Ferdinand Foch. It was in General Foch's private railway car that the kaiser's forces surrendered, for the cessation of hostilities that was scheduled to begin at 11:00 a.m., on November 11, 1918. General Foch disparaged the Treaty of Versailles for its lenience toward the conquered Krauts. "This is not a peace. It is an armistice of twenty years," he blustered when it was ratified, on June 28, 1919. Hitler's war in Europe started almost exactly twenty years later, on September 1, 1939. Foch was off by a mere sixty-five days.

When the belle epoque mansions along the avenue were requisitioned for the Reich, there was great pleasure in retribution for Nazi command. What had once been a boulevard populated by nobility, Renaults, Rothschilds, and the Aga Khan, in war became the concentrated seat of an occupying power. The avenue earned its whispered nickname among Parisians, Avenue Boche—the contemptuous slang for Germans.

Major Bömelburg tracked all rumors and rebel movements. For the first years of the occupation, he kept to a broad strategy of monitoring rather than intercepting "terrorists." His counterintelligence officers were seasoned spy hunters, whereas most saboteurs were novices and outmatched. The Gestapo did not mount campaigns against rebel attacks with any vigor, because it served Bömelburg to wait. Coups de main on German soldiers or targets were rare and made good pap for propaganda; posters and exhibitions went up decrying the violent "Jewish Bolsheviks" who were invading and debasing France. Beyond race-baiting, however, the partisans were themselves useful sources of military intelligence; they could be followed, detailed, and described. They drew out their friends. Bömelburg made a cold calculation: Each time partisans completed a successful sabotage, the underground became visible, and the links between rebel groups grew more obvious. With each new assault, the Resistance stopped being a collection of trees and grew into a forest.

When opposition was small, fractured, and incompetent, there was little downside to Bömelburg's strategy of watch and wait. Paris was a mousetrap: When and if the underground got guns from the Allies, it would be easy to round up the mice once the time came. Until then, partisans were leaving a trail of useful data: hideouts, helpers, compassionate cafés, and covert mail drops. If the underground grew and got organized, if rebels got Allied matériel on a consistent and reliable basis, that would signal an imminent turn toward the seaborne assault on France. The Gestapo would monitor—but seldom interfere with—the growing opposition.

A race was on: Bömelburg had to know the date of the landing before the Resistance grew too powerful. Axis and Allied officers alike believed a landing in France could happen as soon as the seas in the Channel calmed down in the spring of 1943. Rumors abounded: The invasion would take place "as from the 21st of March," rebels heard through the grapevine. The dates could be Nazi-manufactured gossip, disinformation, it was impossible to tell, but throughout Paris news of a 1943 landing spread "firelikewise."

The prize of the Gestapo was to predict the day and hour of the Allied return to western Europe.

CHAPTER 8

The Dark Years

France

Tucked into the tight little Rue de Caumartin was a small Parisian café Andrée Borrel knew from happier times and easier days. She sat at a small round table waiting for the noon hour, not far from her sister's apartment. It was the third year of what was to be a thousand-year occupation of Europe. The hard work of organized rebellion began with a coffee.

The women of the secret army operated in the fog of war. With all the planning at Baker Street and the education at Beaulieu, clandestine life was improvisational. Agents lived the war on the ground, day by day, and built circuits around the vicissitudes of occupation. For Andrée, her first assignment was to activate an Allied-backed Parisian network. Every other move would be decided later.

In the café, voices were at a soft mumble, broken occasionally by the footfall of a wooden-soled shoe against worn tile flooring. Mirrors, aged and cloudy, offered sight lines around the room. It was perfumed by coal smoke, stale cigarettes, and the bitter smell of counterfeit coffee made from ground acorns and chicory; it approximated the taste, if not the stimulation, of caffeine. Like *diktat* and *blitz, ersatz* was new to French vocabulary, an ugly word adopted from the brutish invaders.

Andrée had been in the field for two weeks. Landing in France, she began behind enemy lines with a single lead: a woman named Germaine Tambour. The Tambour family flat on Paris's Avenue de Suffren was a central point of contact for newly landed agents, a "live letter box," or post office, for the personal exchange of messages. Germaine was a centerpiece of the British-supported Resistance, if not a soldier: "She was antimilitarist and paled at the sight of a weapon." She was a rebel administrator, a storehouse for covert knowledge dating back to the very first days of the armistice. Andrée announced to the Tambours that she was a friend of Charlie's—that was her password, she came "*de la part de Charlot*." From there, she was welcomed into the fold, given contacts, addresses, and assurances.

Andrée listened nightly to the BBC French service as the October moon waned to darkness. Long conversational radio essays counseled the nation in a time of grief. To the women of France, the announcer, Jacques Duchesne, exhorted, "We count on you, our mothers, our women, our sisters, to stand firm and continue to give men the strength to hold fast." Andrée waited until the end of the program for her specific BBC personal alerts that Francis was on his way.

Each day of autumn grew a little shorter, tilting toward winter, and beginning on October 1, Andrée returned to the café. The mornings began late, and her days ended in curfew. One of Hitler's first acts after the fall was to put France on Berlin time, making it a suburb of the Reich. Darkness lasted deep into mornings, casting a pall over each war-deprived day, and so the years of occupation came to be known as "the dark years," *les années noires*. Andrée spent a narrow bit of daylight nursing a drink in the Rue de Caumartin. Waiting. She listened for a bell to chime.

At the bar, men with rolled sleeves wiped glasses from the inside. The barman was potentially Andrée's greatest ally. Or enemy. Bartenders knew secrets and held power over their customers. The only good meal to be had in Paris in 1942 was on the black market. Very few Parisians could afford it; those who could were in on some scheme to eat beyond their meager rations as winter drew near. But in the cocoon of the Rue de Caumartin, the great tradition of café privacy was resilient in the face of Nazi subjugation. Andrée relied upon it.

As noon approached, time grew leaden. The clock's second hand labored upward from six, then began its final climb. Her instructions were clear: Wait five minutes. It was the shortest possible window for contact. She had a limited exposure for the rendezvous before she was ordered to leave. The meeting must be precise, or it would not happen at all. If her rendezvous failed today, she was to do the same thing tomorrow.

The door swung open, and a slice of daylight sashayed across the floor. Francis Suttill limped into the bar. He was always on time. With a brave smile strung between two big ears, his blue eyes scanned the room in a glance toward his partner. He looked French enough, his hair neatly parted, high-waisted trousers and a suit jacket no more scruffy or fine than any Parisian's three years into the war. But his aching leg commanded attention he did not want. Plenty of men walked with war wounds in France; for most, the injuries were mature, sustained in battles prior to the armistice. Francis winced with a fresh pain.

He took the seat opposite Andrée.

"Where might one find gasoline?" she asked in earnest.

For Paris in 1942, it was an anodyne request; gas was commandeered for the occupying forces. Most cars had been converted to work on charcoal combustion gasogene engines. Where could one get petrol on the black market?

"Fuel, you mean?" Francis responded.

Confirmed by code, the Parisian network was now operational. Agent Prosper had arrived only days before, albeit not safely. Or with his luggage. Francis dropped blind, that is, with no committee to receive him. Jumping in a fog, he landed hard, popping his knee from the socket, ripping the cartilage. It was not a promising start. He was in agony, but that was something he was accustomed to; he had muscled his way out of a childhood weakness from polio with a self-imposed gymnastics program; he could do so again. After the hard landing, availing himself of any relief zipped into the medical kit in his flight suit, he hid the giant bundle of silk that had not put him down softly in France, as intended, but instead with a bump and a yelp. He stumbled away from the field carrying what he believed was his valise. It was not.

Instead, he shouldered a leather suitcase that hid a wireless radio transceiver. He had no idea for what agent it was intended. Nor did Andrée. She would get a message to Baker Street inquiring after the set.

The Paris leadership got to work. Francis composed a note, a shopping list of needs—including his missing suitcase—paired with the coordinates for an empty field near the Loire River. Andrée moved the letter physically and by stealth to a radio operator who coded and transmitted the missive to London, along with requests from other organizers. Soon a message from London came back: Congratulations, Prosper. Also, keep the radio. London said the Paris circuit might need it.

In the reply from Baker Street, parameters were set for an operation code-named Monkeypuzzle III. London assigned a BBC message to confirm the drop—"The crayfish walk sideways"—and acknowledged the landing zone address.

As for Francis's lost luggage, he was given the assurance of airline passengers the world over: There was a mix-up.

The suitcase—rather like the Allied landing in Europe—was on the way.

All across France, there were small acts of rebellion. Schoolchildren refused to meet the eyes of Nazi soldiers. Students marched in silent protests. Spontaneous coughing fits broke out in darkened cinemas for German newsreels. The occasional *V* for "victory" or *K* for *Kollaboration* got chalked on walls and painted on doorways as acts of petty defiance and denouncement. Factory workers made deliberate miscalculations on the size of ball bearings. Secret newspapers were slipped under doors. Vichy propaganda was stripped from the walls of the metro. Occasionally, clergy offered care for Jewish detainees. It was an atomized opposition. The Allies had to harness such fractured and furtive activity.

In the fall of 1942, commanders and war planners in London were a bit hapless. There was no obvious way to coordinate partisan action across the Frances, occupied and unoccupied. There was no one rebel leader, no candidate to command the diverse and opaque anti-German factions. Just as Vichy failed as a single effective governing body between the two Frances, so too the partisans lacked a body issuing directives, assigning rank, planning assaults. It could not come from General de Gaulle, a distant voice on the radio, who had been in exile for years with very little idea of what was happening at home. He had no control inside France.

Someone had to organize secret soldiers on the ground, the British thought, but who and how? Andrée's remit was to put organization and weapons into the hands of partisans in the North, where citizens came face-to-face with German soldiers daily, where subversive activity was riskier, necessarily small, and secretive. Baker Street authorized "Bangs" in the occupied zone—targeted acts of small-scale sabotage. Other female agents, such as Odette Sansom, would end up in the Vichy zone, south of the demarcation line, where there was a policy of "No Bangs." Instead, agents were to concentrate on recruitment, propaganda, reconnaissance, the laying in of arms and personnel, and the escape of politically useful allies and fallen pilots.

Agent by agent, drop by drop, leaders for the rebel networks arrived in France in the autumn of 1942. The guns piled in too. They fell from the sky with every full moon. It was the advance drumbeat of the invasion. Andrée's mandate was to receive arms and train secret soldiers, and each month as moonlight grew brighter, action would increase. Once the moon reached its most fulsome, Andrée's days would be spent on trains out to the country, her nights sleepless in cold fields rolling metal canisters of guns, gelignite, and tea toward the haylofts of sympathetic and eager peasants. But there were few established networks or reliable contacts, and no master plan for mobilizing disparate elements of the underground with a view toward the Allied landing in the spring.

In the first years after the blitzkrieg, there were not yet enough Frenchmen willing to die for the dream of a free France and no belief that things would change. After nearly three years of occupation, however, the loose and growing collection of angry antagonists reached a critical mass: factory workers, intellectuals, former soldiers, railway men, trade unionists, Jews, Freemasons, farmers, socialists, Communists, noblemen, and the bourgeoisie. Together and separately this became *la Résistance.* Now the British gave them guns.

For the Paris underground, years of occupied frustration coalesced around hope. Andrée's and Francis's presence heartened local dissenters who had an ache to rise up but no clear sense of how to do it or no faith that the Allies would come to their aid. "With PROSPER's arrival, we felt we could at last be of some use and this was so exciting," recalled a Parisian, long after the war. "We were not just working for the Resistance, we now worked for a purpose, for a date, for a reason—for a military goal. *The invasion.*"

By All Saints' Day, the full moon was waning. The October lunar period was Andrée's first in action. Soon there would be too little light to drop containers or agents. On the eve of a frigid and dark November, there was stubble in the countryside, winter wheat was laid in, and the air smelled like manure.

In fields throughout France, gifts had already come from the sky: Weapons. Explosives. Bicycle tires. Radios. Wireless operators. Lost luggage.

Two large networks were forming in the occupied zone: the circuit in Paris, Francis's PHYSICIAN network, and in Bordeaux, Lise de Baissac's brother Claude's SCIENTIST. (By policy, code names for circuits in France honored professions—BRICKLAYER, RATCATCHER, PUGILIST.)

Each circuit and every agent was directed to move independently, in isolation, so that there was no lateral communication or cross contamination. But with limited resources, the task of welcoming new agents required cooperation between networks.

In the deepest hours before sunrise on October 31, 1942, a cheerful group of British agents gathered in the Loire valley, in Avaray, to greet agents and celebrate their accomplishments over bottles of local wine.

"We were all young together and on an adventure with a spice of danger," recalled a newly landed radio operator.

Attending the party were three of the first women the Firm deployed to France: Andrée, Lise, and the agent who received them, Yvonne Rudellat, the first member of the *Corps féminins* to be seconded to combat. Barely one month after their own moonlight jumps, Andrée and Lise were accomplished operatives welcoming novice agents to their posts. "Experience as an agent was picked up very quickly" in clandestine work, recalled a network lieutenant.

Two agents had only just dropped, and Andrée was drawn to one in particular: Gilbert Norman, a dashing wonder of a radioman. Handsome, gray-eyed and swarthy, mustachioed and capable, Gilbert was the living example of the ideal Firm recruit; at twenty-seven years old, he was, said his trainers, "perfect in all ways, has great qualities of leadership and physical endurance." Not tall, but a natural athlete—hockey, tennis, soccer—"extremely fit, extremely active." He was the type of chap France needed as the Allied landings approached, a man "popular with all." Women could not get enough of him, and he seemed to know it; Andrée took note of his upper-caste upbringing and savoir faire—summers in Biarritz. He grew up outside Paris, where his father was vice president of the British Chamber of Commerce before the war. He could realistically pull off the cover story that said he was too rich to work and physically incapable of French army service; he had medical papers testifying he'd had syphilis since 1936 but that it was in remission and his trust fund was enough to support a princely convalescence. With the self-assurance of a rich child who has never known want, Gilbert wore success as his birthright. It was a blunt but enthralling contrast to the shrewd and "common" Andrée.

The group would be together for only a few days. Lise was to shepherd the second radio operator to Bordeaux, to Claude's network. Gilbert would say adieu to Andrée and cross the demarcation line, traveling south to Corsica as a radio operator for the Riviera networks in the unoccupied zone. He would be very far from Paris.

The warm and encouraging Madame and Monsieur Bossard, the couple who had met Andrée and Lise upon their landing, again greeted the agents, generous with the food and comforts of an agricultural region. Throughout France, such couples played great hosts to incoming rebels. "They felt this was the way they could best contribute," an agent remembered. "All were so pleased to be able to do something."

It was a party of big personalities enjoying a rousing night in a nation under siege. It took no time at all to become close within the anonymity of rebellion. Women's relationships cemented with speed, and they forged fast friendships. The *Corps féminins* were never just on the job; they retained an identity as mothers, sisters, girlfriends, wives—or ex-wives—even behind enemy lines.

The Firm had recognized such "feminine" traits as assets in clandestine tradecraft by 1942: If empathy does not come immediately to mind for special operatives trained to kill, the very first agents in the field reported warmth toward the partisans they enlisted, and agents were listening to rebels' needs in exchange for cooperation. It was a large part of the assignment. Rebels were recruited from a disaffected population on the fringes of France. Caretaking would become a substantial core of resistance work.

"Everybody was very friendly and I suppose had a strong sense of comradeship," recalled Roger Landes, the second radio operator who arrived that evening. It was collegial, but the room was too cozy, too free with information, too insecure. It made him uncomfortable.

THE FARMHOUSE WAS SNUG, the conversation lively, the wine ample, and at the center of the scene was Yvonne Rudellat, who ran that evening's reception committee. Yvonne's rebel cell in the country operated as a satellite circuit to Francis's PHYSICIAN network in Paris. It was her first *parachutage* as leader; not only was she the first of her class deployed to France, but she was the first woman to command a covert air reception.

Older, giddier, and more petite than her peers, Yvonne was fully reborn in the rural neighborhood; her position of authority mapped to her growing skills as an agent. Said Francis, "She cycles about at night with her plastics [explosives] and is extremely handy when it comes to blowing [up] things."

"Here's to the King of England," Yvonne would say with a giggle on nights with the partisans, raising her glass of wine in toast. "He pays for all of this."

The relationship between agents inside France was impossible to anticipate from London. The type of frisson between Andrée and Gilbert was a concern to Baker Street. ("We had to be very careful to select our groups in such a way that they would get on well together," said Buck, "but not too well, [so] that the organizer wouldn't want to go to bed with the courier all the time.") So the brass breathed a sigh of relief that Yvonne, at twice Andrée's age, was beyond the reach of adolescent attraction.

Yvonne had an "old maidish look"; her forty-four years and hard life "brought lines in her forehead and a rather weary stoop to her shoulders." But she was natively French, and the need for French speakers overwhelmed instinctual objections against age and sex. Yvonne's commission made her spritely again, her trainers at Beaulieu had said:

> The first impression of fluffiness is entirely misleading. Her air of innocence and anxiety to please should prove a most valuable "cover." She is extremely thorough and sincere in anything she does, and together with her preserving and tenacious qualities, she will see any job through to its conclusion.

Women become invisible as they grow old, but for Yvonne it was a professional advantage. With a shock of white hair and deep-set eyes cresting above high cheekbones, she had never been pretty. With a pencil-sharp jaw and a nose that was handsome at best, her face settled into a bland obscurity in middle age. Yvonne's most notable quality was her ordinariness: the more she cultivated it, the better she was at her job. The manual for her training course emphasized the average and the familiar: "The secret to being secret is to be natural. Behave naturally."

If Yvonne was no longer considered fecund, she still used womanhood as her cover. She worked with a locally recruited partisan named Pierre Culioli and took on the role of his "wife." Marriage was a terrific clandestine pretext. "She lives *en ménage* with Culioli in a small chalet—very much liked by the whole neighborhood who know them as a refugee couple from a bombed area," wrote Francis.

Yvonne and Pierre were both puckish and inclined to silliness; the pairing was a physical, psychological, and practical fit. Pierre would later name the splinter group ADOLPHE, a poke at the führer himself. (He grew a toothbrush mustache to complete the caricature.) "It was much easier traveling about with a lady," said Pierre. "As a couple and living like husband and wife, nobody paid any attention to us."

Yvonne was in the same Beaulieu class as Andrée, but she was ready in July, when Andrée was delayed by the unexpected prison break of Maurice Dufour. Yvonne, deemed too old for parachute training, arrived in France via ship from Gibraltar.

As the first woman of the *Corps féminins* to deploy, Yvonne's departure presented a new administrative dilemma to Baker Street: Few of Captain Jepson's colleagues were comfortable with the heavy burden and irrevocable step of writing orders to send a lady behind enemy lines. In the grand tradition of governments everywhere, men shied at the responsibility of doing anything new. Training women was a big step, and no one actually wanted to be the one to send Yvonne to the field. The decision was handed up the line to officials more senior and consequential.

In the summer of 1942, the first sea lord, the chief of the Imperial General Staff, and the chief of the Air Staff all weighed in on the question: Would they send Yvonne to France or not? Around a dark wood table in Whitehall, the war chiefs and the Foreign Office met regularly to chew on cigars, secrets, and strategies. The most senior commanders of the British armed forces ran a global war between great powers, and there was much to discuss: Hitler was in Stalingrad, Gandhi was arrested in India, the Nazis had deported some 300,000 Jews from Warsaw; Generals Erwin Rommel and Claude Auchinleck fought a stalemate in the desert.

For a brief time, these men of import stopped to consider the practical problem of moving ahead with Captain Jepson's radical idea. "It would be the first time that we had sent a woman out, but anyway what was against it—except her age and possibly her physique?" offered Buck.

It was not that Yvonne was female; Prime Minister Churchill had already signed off on women recruits. What the service chiefs were most worried about was that Yvonne was old enough to be a grandmother. Would she be taken seriously when explaining the finer points of *plastique* explosives and machine guns to teenage boys? "We wondered how tough resistance fighters would react to having her as a tutor," said the political liaison for SOE. Yvonne in middle age did not project strength. She might be laughed out of France. Would the French take her assignment "as some kind of joke and say 'The British must be in a bad way to send us a frail old lady!'"

Yvonne was the test case for all female agent trainees. "If everything worked out alright, as we hoped, then the others could go afterwards."

Two months later, Andrée and Lise jumped from the sky.

FULL MOONS WERE for parachute receptions. New moons—when the whole sky went dark but for the stars—belonged to sabotage.

As autumn turned to winter, Yvonne and a small party traveled to the little village of Montrichard, on the river Cher. Petite, barely five feet two on her toes, she was a student of yoga, a vegetarian whose weight hovered at only eighty pounds. She was the only person who could do the job the Allies needed done that night.

Yvonne hung suspended in a parachute harness, her rigging lines quadrupled for strength, dangling over railroad tracks while searching for the ground. Her flashlight beam sliced through a cloud of breath. Beyond her light there was nothing, an ink-black railway tunnel in France at night. No hints of light bled in from the openings on either end of the underpass; there were no noises either, but for a steady drip of water, somewhere.

Her hands were cold and sticky and smelled like almonds from the chemical residue of plastic explosives. Her clothing was tattered: culottes, and a pair of underwear she washed and wrung out every night. She looked bedraggled, gaunt, but also somehow much younger than the year before. In the best possible sense, war took years off Yvonne's life, said Francis. "She looks fifteen years younger and has definitely found her niche."

Her torchlight flooded the tracks below, revealing a shadowy zipper running across the seams of France.

There was a straight drop down. No obstacle would impede a package of explosives if it was lowered from the air shaft above. The path to the tracks was one of empty and elongated space.

Montrichard was a sleepy place: a cathedral, a ruined castle, a town hall, bakers and butchers facing each other across narrow, cobbled streets. Villagers knew each other well but saw each other infrequently, gathering now and again for a dance, a christening, a funeral, but mostly their intimate lives were separated by vineyards, forests, and orchards. It was a place where farmers drove livestock with phlegmatic resignation—eternal France.

Swaying back and forth, a human pendulum marking time on a moonless night, Yvonne was swinging under a hill that ran just above the small village. The railroad tunnel lay in the middle of a triangle of larger cities—Blois, Vierzon, and Tours—on the north bank of the Cher, an arbitrary physical boundary that formed the dividing line by which Hitler separated the zones of occupation. Winter was here; Yvonne dangled by a thread in the center of a European storm.

In war, the river town closed completely at night under curfew. For almost three years, it had been a silent crossroads for human violence and international catastrophe: Nazi troops, guns, freight, and food moved through; the tiny village was a node in the rail network linking Berlin to its vast subjugated continent and the Battle of the Atlantic. It was the direct supply line between Germany and its *Kriegsmarine* warships and submarine wolf packs hunting Allied shipping convoys.

Railroads were the veins by which the Reich bled France. When Hitler invaded in 1940, he acquired a vassal economy nearly as large as

Germany's and demanded more than half of France's fiscal output for occupation debts. The rich produce of France crossed the length of Europe to feed German soldiers on the eastern front, who were locked in a frozen death match against Stalin's Red Army. Indemnities claimed 50 percent of France's iron ore, 99 percent of its cement, 92 percent of the trucks it produced, and 76 percent of the trains. In total, some 55 percent of the national revenue was paid in tribute to the occupiers. Hermann Göring, vice chancellor of Germany, told his colleagues, "Let them deliver whatever they can until they can't deliver any more." France did.

The trains ran on schedule in wartime France, though there were fewer of them. Patriotic railway men would take note of military runs to send news up and down the line. Yvonne could fumble in the dark on her swing knowing that no locomotive would steam through. It was all clear.

Yvonne signaled to her man on belay that she had what she needed: a view of the center of the tunnel, the depth and grade of the tracks under the sloping hill. She was hoisted aloft with swift precision: By virtue of her delicate stature and flexibility, she was the only person who could wriggle up through the ventilation shaft of the railway passage. She was also the only one who could perform the reconnaissance by education and authority, who might lead the mission of French partisans to blow up the railway tunnel. "After all," she said, "I am the only one who has been specially trained."

The sabotage party was far from the underground explosion when it began. There was a small flash of light, like a bolt of lightning. The sparks blossomed into a blaze, and black smoke filled the tunnel. The blast pulsed and breathed, like an animal, alternating between the bright white light of a star and the warm yellow of a bonfire. The flames grew until they consumed the oxygen in the passageway. Shock waves ricocheted against the arches and shattered the walls. Boulders, bricks, and debris tumbled down, littering the tracks.

Yvonne did not need to be near the village to follow the choreography of the Montrichard explosion: The blazes, the concussions, the familiar symphony of elemental chaos roared like a thousand tin cans crushed at once and lingered long after in hisses and pops.

She knew it all too well. She had been home on the night of April 16, 1941, in London, when Hermann Göring had one of his best nights of the Blitz. By the spring of 1941, his targets had progressed from strategic military points, such as ports and factories, to a campaign against British morale—terror attacks, *Terrorangriffe*. In the Blitz, London would be hit with 50,000 tons of high-explosive bombs and 110,000 tons of incendiary bombs, designed only to set fire to cities.

In that one night of precision bombing, the Luftwaffe damaged St. Paul's Cathedral, the Houses of Parliament, the Admiralty, the Law Courts, and the National Gallery. Nazi command called it a Baedeker bombing, declaring, "We shall go out and bomb every building in Britain marked with three stars in the Baedeker guide." They also destroyed Yvonne Rudellat's home in working-class Pimlico.

Near Victoria Station, on Warwick Way, two parachute mines and three high-explosive bombs went off at once, and the blast took out an entire terrace of houses. The top floor of Yvonne's home was leveled. It was the house where she had raised a daughter to adulthood and watched a marriage crumble; where she had studied Confucian philosophy and practiced meditation; where she had played boardinghouse mum to a haphazard collection of bohemians, eccentrics, and kooks; and it was substantially gone. Ceilings collapsed onto floors, chimneys stood alone, severed from their surroundings, gas mains exploded, sewage flooded up from pipes, the fires burned through the morning. At daybreak, the neighborhood smelled of charred wood, masonry dust, and decay. Her large Edwardian house was declared uninhabitable.

Everyone survived except the family cat, Bones.

"It was this," said Yvonne of her cat's untimely demise, "more than anything else, which made me determined somehow to fight back."

CHAPTER 9

Alone in the World

Poitiers

Poitiers was a city on a hill, with Romanesque churches, medieval universities, and, as 1942 became 1943, bitter cold and creeping paranoia. The town of climbing streets, cobblestoned squares, aqueducts, and buttresses reached backward in time to Charlemagne, the Crusades, and the Holy Roman Empire; its ramparts had weathered the wars of Visigoths and Caesars.

Joining a trickle of refugees from the coast to central France, Lise de Baissac thought Poitiers would be an easy place to blend in, to avoid a hotel, as so many night managers sent registers to the local Nazi command. In the ancient academic town, it was typical for students to let private rooms and apartments. To the public, she was the widow Madame Irène Brisée, there to learn about Eleanor of Aquitaine and Richard the Lionheart. For the Firm, she was a "liaison agent," assigned to meet incoming agents dropping to empty fields, procure contacts and safe houses, and arrange for guides across the militarized border that separated France.

Lise needed a flat of her own from which to operate. She began with only one name, an auctioneer, a friend of the Bossards', and he knew of the perfect place: a ground-floor apartment belonging to a woman who was going to North Africa to escape the war. The stone building was on a busy, slanting street on the way to the station, with no nosy concierge; spacious and homey, luxurious even, it was good for entertaining. Lise at last settled in, "as if I was going to live all the rest of my life [in Poitiers]."

Lise's home was only one door down from the Gestapo headquarters. Her address was an excellent cover: No British agent would be so reckless as to live next door to Nazis, and no one would ever suspect the neighborhood widow. "I was just an ordinary person; they couldn't care less about my being there or not." In proximity to the enemy, Lise was vigilant but aloof. "You'd say good morning if he says good morning, I said good morning and that's all." She studied the behavior of the men who were out to kill her. "The German troops [have] been given strict orders to be polite to the population and on the whole they [behave] with great deference. They are never seen drunk on the streets. If they do behave badly it is in town, [and] they are sometimes shot the next morning." (Lise warned Baker Street that when British troops arrived for the invasion, they too ought to mind their manners, like the upright, goose-stepping Nazis, or the French "people would be ready to throw themselves" at the English.)

Locals were xenophobic and Anglophobic, as potentially threatening to Lise as any neighbor in the SS. They celebrated Philippe Pétain's revanchist fantasies and Catholic pastoral of a pure former France. But no one approved of the original circumstances that put Vichy in power: France's devastating loss to Hitler. The Nazis stationed in Poitiers were "afraid of being killed in the streets. They never [went] about alone."

The region grew callous as the war dragged on, even cutthroat. French peasants could not be relied on to side with Lise or any coastal exile. They were wary of strangers, often reporting them to the Gestapo for reward, sometimes out of pique. Locals were obsessed with getting enough to eat, choosing no side other than that of their empty bellies. Denunciation was rampant; *délation,* it was called. Collaborationist newspapers ran step-by-step instructions on how to make a proper accusation and to which authorities, fingering anyone suspected of being anti-Vichy, or worse, Jewish. Such reports were by and large anonymous, inevitably signed "A loyal Frenchman" or "Long live Pétain." Times were lean, and trading names to the authorities for money was a painless quid pro quo. Germans and French alike were paying inflated prices for basic goods on the black market. "The chief concern of the people is their own well-being," said Lise, "and they will support anything if it will result in their personal gain."

There was charity in the small hilltop city still, but it was silent by decree. The large network of churches and convents meant there was an attendant collection of priests and nuns. While supporting Vichy's Catholicism, many French clerics viewed the occupation through the narrow aperture of compassion. (The Vatican itself remained neutral during the war and did not intervene on behalf of the persecuted.) But in the region around Poitiers, some members of the church operated in determined and intrepid silence: Prelates were roaming the countryside, seeking Jewish orphans, hiding them in abbeys, enrolling them in schools, finding foster families, providing food and funds. Others penned fake baptismal certificates giving Jews new identities. One Jesuit priest went daily to a local detention camp near Poitiers—carrying in news, liberating children on his way out. Working with a rabbi, he entered the camp at least two hundred times. When the rabbi was arrested, the priest became lead adviser to the Jewish community, saving at least one hundred Jews and providing aid to some thousand more.

This, too, happened under the Nazis' noses.

THE RIFTS CLEAVING France on the problem of *les Juifs* predated Hitler, but the fall of the Third Republic was a rich opportunity for anti-Semites. Among Pétain's first acts in power was the "spontaneous and autonomous" decision to pen laws parroting Nazi racial edicts against the Jews. Vichy called for the total eradication of Jewish culture, the expulsion of foreign Jews, the denaturalization of foreign-born Jews, and the isolation and exclusion of French-born Jews while directing "half-bred" Jews to assimilate. In both occupied and unoccupied France, Pétain implemented the Final Solution with enthusiasm. In the North, he volunteered to target Jews as a way of asserting French sovereignty in the Reich-administered regions. In the South, Vichy partnered with the Gestapo to make the so-called free zone *judenfrei,* promising ten thousand Jews to Hitler.

The eradication of French Jewry was abrupt. In October 1940, the "First Statute on Jews" stripped Jews of citizenship rights using criteria more strict than even the Reich's Nuremberg laws. Several statutes followed. Jews were kicked out of the army and public office and forbidden to sell businesses or practice law or medicine. Radios, telephones, bicycles, and cars were confiscated; students were forbidden to attend school. There were curfews, detention, and deportation. If France's homegrown anti-Semitism was not virulent enough, the Nazis stoked it: In October 1941, six Parisian synagogues were bombed; a seventh device failed to go off, and while the attack looked like an act of terrorism, it was orchestrated by a German commander seeking a Paris encore to *Kristallnacht*. By New Year's Day 1942, the first roundup of Jews had begun in Paris: Doctors, lawyers, bankers, scholars, merchants, and scientists were sent to an internment camp at Drancy. Deportations from France to Germany started in March of that year. By May, the Eighth Statute was declared: All Jews were ordered to wear the yellow star. Shortly after Bastille Day in July 1942, some thirteen thousand Jews were rounded up in Paris and held in a sports stadium for days, including at least four thousand children. The tragedy at the Vélodrome d'Hiver was condemned around the world; gruesome details were broadcast into France on the BBC. Babies younger than two years old were held captive without food or water, then shipped to Auschwitz in cattle cars without their parents.

THE WINDOW-BLACKED Baker Street headquarters of F Section was experiencing its own Jewish problem, in the form of Hélène Aron, the petite Parisian with the law degree who attended STS 31 Party No. 27.OB School No. 36.

Women made up some two thousand of the approximately thirteen thousand employees of the Special Operations Executive. As London in war toggled between mania and depression, pageantry and resignation, tradition and pragmatism, these women arbitraged the contrasts, advancing in a man's world. They were translators, radio operators, secretaries, drivers, and honeypots. Only eight were deployed as special agents in autumn 1942, when SOE's first class of female trainees was seconded to France, among them Andrée, who was in Paris with Francis Suttill. Lise was in Poitiers, and the "little old lady," Yvonne Rudellat, was in the Loire valley. Sailing toward the French Riviera were Odette Sansom, the mother of three, and Mary Herbert, the scholarly language expert. Hélène Aron was still waiting for her orders.

To an adolescent secret spy agency experimenting with women for the very first time, Hélène posed a challenge. She had completed the training course at Beaulieu over the summer. She could now code messages in secret ink, set explosives under a train carriage, and bring down a fully grown man with a throw, then kill him silently. She shared the same lessons, had the same expectations—and received some equally dismal final reports—as her peers. And she was briefed on plans to detonate the clandestine army behind enemy lines during the coming Allied invasion. She possessed operational information at the level named Most Secret. Like many in her course, she "wanted to kill as many Germans as possible by any means possible." But in contrast to her peers, the F Section leadership and Beaulieu trainers believed Hélène might be an enemy spy. By virtue of her race and religion, she was suspect.

In a national act of psychological projection, Britain was in the grip of a spy panic. The island nation had always had a greater sense of inviolability than other European countries, which saw territorial wars with every generation. But when Rudolf Hess, Hitler's best friend and co-author of *Mein Kampf,* parachuted into Scotland in 1941 to single-handedly negotiate peace, Britain got spooked. It set off a torrent of spy rumors: Hundreds more German parachutists were ready to land, disguised as clergy, with collapsible bicycles concealed beneath their cassocks. Six cows stampeded on the minuscule island of Eilean Mor in the Scottish Hebrides, and it was attributed to clandestine enemy maneuvers. Fleet Street splashed stories of infiltrating Axis agents: "Vice Consul a Nazi Spy," "German Spy Shot at the Tower," and "My Husband Was Never a Spy."

Jews were ready targets for spy anxiety and teatime fifth column neuroses. It was said Jewish merchants in London were profiteering black marketeers who minted millions off the misfortunes of the Blitz. Jews were called draft dodgers when they were not deployed to the Continent to fight the Nazis who were interning the Jews.

The Firm was no more anti-Semitic than the rest of Britain. Hélène received the same treatment that most Jewish refugees and many Jewish Britons got in an anti-Semitic era: skepticism bordering on overt racism. F Section had a general sense of discomfort about Hélène. Agents frequently complained about so-called Israelites in their midst. "In my opinion it is unwise to send out so many Jews as they are not liked by the French people," said one agent. Female trainees too commented on the recruitment of "girls who were very obviously Jewish and I couldn't understand [why] the organization [did] that." Jewish heritage was not always a black mark against a candidate: Baker Street did employ a few Jewish agents, and an all-Jewish network was building in Paris. Some Jewish recruits were given plastic surgery to correct for perceived racial imperfections such as large noses, so they might arrive behind the lines less noticeably Semitic.

For secret operations in enemy territory, the government had to be vigilant. The F Section head, Maurice Buckmaster, ordered a full MI5 review of Hélène's bona fides. "Without going so far as to suggest that she is a Vichy spy, the view is held that the circumstances of her arrival were peculiar."

Hélène's circumstances were like any other émigré's from the occupied countries of Europe. On landing, she had been vetted at the Royal Victoria Patriotic School. She earned the label of NT upon entry, "No Trace" of allegiance to an enemy government. But that screening was too cursory, Buck said. It was not enough. She was as legally British as his other Beaulieu trainees—by way of a British father and French mother—but her allegiance made him uneasy. To her potential employers, Hélène's escape to England was itself questionable.

France had not been so bad for Hélène, investigators reported. She was insulated from France's anti-Semitism as the daughter of a wealthy man; her British father was a luxury goods wholesaler. But however upper bourgeois and assimilated Hélène might have been, under the Pétain regime she could not "pass"; her surname, Aron, was always a tell, as it meant that her patriarchal line descended from Moses's brother Aaron, that her father's origins could be traced to an ancient elite Levitical priesthood. She was marked. Nevertheless, the Firm dismissed any threats to Hélène. "She was not molested by the Nazis but only had to register as a Jewess" in the Paris census. In October 1940, Hélène claimed the British passport that was hers by right of her father but that she had not seriously considered using until necessitated by war. "It is at least probable that being a practical Frenchwoman, she was beginning to see on which side her bread was buttered." (She was cunning, as Jews stereotypically are, investigators implied.) In Paris, it took a year to process Hélène's paperwork. She was scheduled to leave for England in 1942, but days before her departure in April, while visiting a girlfriend in the countryside near the demarcation line, the women were accosted by a Nazi soldier, who took them back to his guardroom for the night. In the morning, he "fined" Hélène for her own release. Inquiring what became of the levy, the investigator noted, "The money evidently went into his own pocket." Records are silent on the matter but suggest Hélène might have been charged for her own violation. She crossed the demarcation line, obtained her emergency exit papers at Lyon, kissed her mother good-bye in Marseilles, then escaped to England via Portugal.

Judaism tainted Hélène's evaluations at the Firm. Captain Jepson believed she was an excellent candidate but noted "the only thing he could find against her was that she was a Jewess." To the trainers at Beaulieu, she at first "appeared intelligent with a well-organized mind," with degrees in languages and political science, but during the course instructors concluded she was "slow and stupid." When she first got to the New Forest she had been "a slip of a thing," and after weeks of generous meals intended to strengthen secret soldiers in PT, she filled out, compensating for the depravations of wartime Paris. "She tells me she is now enjoying her three square meals a day!" investigators observed.

Buck could not shake his unease about Hélène: "I appreciate that it is rather unreasonable of me to act purely on instinct in this matter, but my own instinct is backed by other people and I shall not be happy until I am satisfied that she got a clean bill." F Section mother hen Vera Atkins, who took pains to hide her own Jewish heritage, offered no appreciable defense for Hélène.

Hélène's Judaism, womanhood, and innate incapacities as an agent were, taken together, disqualifying. The Firm decided she would not go to France. "She is unlikely to be of the slightest use to this country's war effort." More, the officers declared Hélène unfit not only for deployment but even for England. "In my view, Miss Aron should never have been allowed to come here and should be repatriated to France where she belongs," investigators said. "I only hope that someone will have the strength of mind and energy to make an issue of this case."

Baker Street was faced with a question: Now that Hélène was trained, if she didn't go to the field, what would happen to her? The Firm maintained a home for the recruits who failed the so-called finishing school courses at Beaulieu. While not every student passed special training, by the time they had made it to the New Forest, they were considered at least minimally fit for the field. Beaulieu was the final test: Agents who were flawed, indiscreet, profligate, libidinous, unstable, drunk, and in any other way useless, and who went through the course, would necessarily be sent away to Scotland, to Number 6 Special Workshop School, otherwise known as the Cooler, or "the Forgetting School."

Inverlair Lodge, in the cold and remote Scottish Highlands, was the holding pen for incompetents. Failed trainees were warehoused at a hunting estate far away from the war until their knowledge of secrets grew dusty, until they were not considered a security risk. The mansion for useless agents was a quarantine for the resentful, a ghetto of the bored.

The Cooler was standard procedure for failures. Yet policies were often rewritten for the women of F Section. Did Hélène's case merit a second look? Was it appropriate to send her to the Cooler when she would be the only lady there? The camp was not designed for women; there were no provisions by way of facilities, rooms, jobs, or activities for her. Some at Baker Street questioned the morality of His Majesty's Government banishing a lady to the hinterlands of Scotland for the misfortune of being born Jewish.

Bureaucracy kicked into inaction. Hélène might not be much of a security risk, they reasoned; she was only a woman, after all. The first class of women was not trained with the same rigor as male recruits, who studied in-depth military subjects at several other secret schools. Less was expected from women.

Beaulieu said no. "The fact that it was the only school she attended does not make the knowledge she gained there any less dangerous," said the training chief.

The government had a duty to find some suitable placement for Hélène, if the Cooler was not an option. So Baker Street became Hélène Aron's new employment agency; it would be the only way to keep an eye on her movements. Had she been an enemy alien, the government was within rights to keep tabs on Hélène, but she was British—her citizenship was only questioned, never revoked—and under the logic of a free and civil society, a government does not spy on its own people. It was suggested de Gaulle's Free French might find a use for Hélène, because she had received special training. Let the Gaullists struggle with her Judaism.

Hélène, like Andrée before her, interviewed with de Gaulle's secret service and was grilled for information about her schooling at Beaulieu.

> She did not answer. It would be illegal to speak of what she learned; she had signed the Official Secrets Act: I declare that I will never disclose to anyone any information which I have acquired or at any future time acquire as a result of my connections with this Department unless such disclosure is necessary for my work for the Department.

If Hélène revealed anything at all to the Fighting French, it was punishable with up to a two-year prison sentence, "with or without hard labor."

"She refused to divulge what she was doing," approved the investigator. "She would not play."

Charles de Gaulle declined to extend a position to Hélène.

The failed job interview buoyed Hélène's British minders. She could be trusted, even as a Jew. A new solution was presented: She should resign her FANY commission (First Aid Nursing Yeomanry) for a post in the WAAF, the Women's Auxiliary Air Force. The WAAFs provided administrative support to the Royal Air Force, clerking, catering, and driving. There were some thrilling air force–related jobs too; the Air Transport Auxiliary trained female pilots to deliver fighter planes to airfields.

Hélène preferred the FANYs to the WAAFs. The FANYs were a volunteer corps of upper-crust ladies who provided the bulk of SOE's support staff. (Every women's auxiliary had a diminutive pet name; if FANY wasn't suggestive enough, they were also nicknamed the "First ANYwheres" with all intended innuendo.) After Captain Jepson decided to hire women as agents, he met with the FANY commandant to procure commissions for his elite *Corps féminins*. The "Amazons" got uniforms—khaki, belted, straight skirted, and practical to the point of ugly—but more than an ensemble, the commission gave SOE's female agents cover: Their loved ones need never know about courses in safecracking and map reading; they could assume the girls were learning to drive, take dictation, and type. Other women's auxiliaries—the ATS (Auxiliary Territorial Service), the WRNS (Women's Royal Naval Service)—were attached to the military, and so a combat role would be in more obvious violation of international conventions. The FANYs, as an independent and volunteer civilian corps—and not formally aligned with the services—squeaked a legalistic end run past the fuzzy international prohibitions on female combatants in a war zone.

Hélène, a liberated thinker, was unhappy about the regimentation of the WAAFs. For FANYs in the Firm, salutes were not mandatory.

The suggested transfer from one auxiliary to the other offended her "*amour-propre,*" her self-regard.

"I have been played a dirty trick," Hélène said.

In that case, replied His Majesty's Government, she might be happier in civilian life.

Paperwork was drawn up for her dismissal. Said one security officer with a sigh, "I suspect that she thinks her rejection was solely on account of her Jewish extraction and not because her Jewish extraction might have endangered her in the field."

Had Hélène been top of her class, she was unlikely to get to France in late 1942. By then, the fate of Europe's Jews was known worldwide. In Berlin, Göring had declared, "This war is not the Second World War, it is the war of the races." And Hitler shouted in a celebrated speech, "It will not be the Aryan peoples, but rather Jewry, that will be exterminated." The future led to ghettos, work camps, medical experimentation, and mass extermination. While the Firm contemplated Hélène's position, a member of the Polish Resistance snuck into the Warsaw Ghetto and took to London details of what happened behind the walls and at transit camps. "The German Record in Poland: Torture and Murder," read *The Times* of London. More than 2.5 million people had disappeared since Hitler's 1939 invasion, most of them Jews, with at least 550,000 already murdered—staggering numbers, almost incomprehensible to Britain, with a mere 45 million citizens of its own.

At the highest levels of Allied command, the state-ordered slaughter of Jews had been known since 1941. In an operation code-named Ultra, women at Bletchley Park had decrypted secret communications detailing the monstrosity of Hitler's Europe: the public executions and systematic killing of the so-called subhumans, *die Untermenschen,* the Jews.

In the case of Hélène Aron, the Jewish genocide in Europe gave the Firm a moral cover it did not entirely deserve. It created a rationale for kicking her out of the agency when her Judaism rubbed bureaucrats the wrong way. It was for her own good. She was returned to "civvy street," taking a job with Peter Robinson's department store in Oxford Circus. The position of shopgirl was beneath her, a legal scholar doing the work of an illiterate teenager, but she was alive, in a democratic and free country, while storms thundered down on the Jews of Europe.

Once Hitler's Final Solution was publicly acknowledged, the Allied nations drafted language to censure Germany. On December 17, 1942, a proclamation was read aloud in Washington, D.C., Moscow, and London:

> From all the occupied countries Jews are being transported, in conditions of appalling horror and brutality, to Eastern Europe. In Poland, which has been made the principal Nazi slaughterhouse, the ghettoes established by the German invaders are being systematically emptied of all Jews except a few highly skilled workers required for war industries. None of those taken away are ever heard of again. The able-bodied are slowly worked to death in labour camps. The infirm are left to die of exposure and starvation or are deliberately massacred in mass executions. The number of victims of these bloody cruelties is reckoned in many hundreds of thousands of entirely innocent men, women and children.

The House of Commons stood for one minute of silence, a symbolic, if inert, moment. The only way to stop the murder of the Jews was to win the war.

By the end of the year 1942, Hélène had a new job: General de Gaulle's Fighting French at last agreed to take her on as an employee, in spite of her unsavory heritage. The nature of Hélène's new assignment was not recorded in SOE's notes. The Firm simply closed Hélène's file. The Jewish Amazon was de Gaulle's problem now.

F Section had to focus on its female agents behind enemy lines.

LISE DE BAISSAC was deployed to central France to help the army of the shadows, not to build an army of her own. Poitiers was not a hub of resistance. Early in the war, there had been some opposition to Hitler and Pétain there, but the partisans were "blown" months before Lise arrived; "some of the members were shot and the rest were in jail."

The quiet bothered Lise. Days and then weeks passed between communications from London. To be good at her assignment meant not getting caught, not raising awareness, instead performing daily, mundane tasks for an adversarial state, transporting matériel, messages, and men while the Gestapo hunted her and everyone to whom she spoke. Or so Lise had expected. Instead, she grew bored.

She could watch the Nazis next door all day long, but it was not enough to keep Lise busy. She took Spanish lessons and typing classes; she would need a job after the war and was thinking ahead. University courses and the daily schedule of a war widow at leisure were hardly stimulating. She hoped to make as many friends as possible, holding frequent dinner parties. The "object was to have a lot of people coming and going so that agents who visited her would not be noticed by neighbors and passers-by," reported London. (Also, she couldn't find good restaurants in Poitiers.) Over time, Lise grew close to her Spanish professor, who never knew she was anything other than an enthusiastic midlife student. "I had to take some interest in something," she remarked. "Time is very long, you know."

Above all, the work of a secret agent was lonely. "You have false papers; you never have a telephone call; you never get a letter," Lise lamented. "I arrived [in Poitiers] and didn't know a single soul!" With no radio of her own, she had to travel to Paris to see Andrée when she needed to send or collect information. Other times she went to the coast, to Bordeaux, to meet her brother Claude (known as the agent David). Those visits reached back to a time when things were warm and safe, to when she had companionship. "And well, it was nice to know that I had somebody somewhere. Because if not, you are alone in the world."

Claude was drawing up a rebel army of fifteen thousand partisans, despite popular resentment against the English. Mary Herbert, the language expert who was Lise's classmate, was assigned to Claude as his courier. He said he enjoyed working with women. "Contrary to his expectation, women were better than men when used as couriers and for taking W/T [wireless telegraph] sets and material from one place to another. They were very enthusiastic, did not talk as much as men and got through controls more easily," read a report. Mary arranged Claude's meetings as he only spoke face-to-face with his circuit, there were never written messages, and he did not use letter boxes—dead or live—or send reports in veiled word-replacement codes, or even use the telephone or telegram in a pinch. He obeyed the tightest security protocols, far more stringent than the safety dicta from Beaulieu. He moved homes so often that Lise never knew where to find him except at the Café Bertrand, at the same time of day, where she just had to wait. Sometimes he didn't come. When she saw him again, it was always a reunion. "Two friends meeting, and that's all. Just ordinary life!"

The Firm considered Claude "extremely French and volatile," but he quickly became one of the finest organizers in the field. Like his sister's, Claude's heart was tropical, hot-tempered. "He was a vital, very sensual man," recalled his family. War was good for opinionated people, like the de Baissac siblings; the wishy-washy ones take orders, have a safe time in the ranks. Lise and Claude were brilliant, funny, and determined; they had an inner compass pointing to a North that only they could see. Said his trainers of Claude, "He is conscientious and hard working but is inclined to worry about difficulties that exist only in his own imagination." Such cautions, real and imagined, could keep Lise and Claude alive.

"I think in the family we are like that. We are glad to do what we feel like doing," said Lise. "That's the way we've been brought up."

Lise had more knowledge of wartime France than her handlers in London. In a time of capitulation and terror, she believed the occupied French could be better partners in their own fight for freedom. Unilaterally, she expanded her original mission orders. "I thought it wasn't enough to receive agents from the sky and put them on their way," she said. "So I started to [take] a little more action."

Lise began exploring the countryside, looking like any woman on a bicycle, but she was instead scouting landing grounds. She sought flat fields in the middle of nowhere, mostly hidden by trees, far from main roads, with a sympathetic farmer or absent landlord. She sent the coordinates to London, but waiting to hear news on her agricultural and cartographic choices, expecting approval to come by radio through her long, slow channels, was still not enough: "They agreed or they didn't agree."

In that dull mid-war Poitiers winter, Lise grew ambitious, inviting more danger and increased scrutiny. She began to build her own rebel network, recruiting a mortician, a doctor, and a young family with a teenage daughter who would become Lise's travel companion. She sounded out the individuals who, for private reasons, chose risk and civil disobedience, opposing both the state and the bulk of French society. They procured ration cards, train tickets, and clothing and provided safe harbor to incoming agents or those crossing the demarcation line, in full awareness that even simple errands could be fatal.

"They *knew* what they were doing," Lise said. "They knew what they were undertaking." They were assets. She called them her "helpers."

Always in the Nazis' direct line of sight, Lise did not consider her mounting aspirations brave, merely sensible. "Everything will turn 'round all right," she would say. "I'm not a pessimist."

CHAPTER 10

Robert est arrivé

Unoccupied France

On a crisp November day, a train from Marseilles bound for Paris rocked past thin poplars and sun-cooked vineyards. Rolling stripes of grapevines ticked by in long strips, picked over and pruned back for winter.

On the overcrowded train, a beanpole of a man was on an errand. The courier was traveling from the free zone to the occupied zone on behalf of one of the largest partisan networks in France. The emissary could not use the mail (it was censored), or the telephone (the police were listening in), or send a telegram (copies of all wires went straight to the Gestapo). Instead, he carried with him an address book, a list of trusted associates, their home addresses, passwords, safe houses, and postboxes, contacts for the whole of France. It was the prize of the rebellion, a catalog of two hundred officers, not encoded, a roll call of the Resistance.

The courier was lucky to get a seat at all in a second-class compartment. With a briefcase at his feet, he took a rare and necessary rest. He was nervous by nature and terrified by practice, a dedicated dissident. He had neither money nor a livelihood, so he worked for the underground, attending group meetings in darkness, mixing into crowds during the day to avoid identity checks by French police. Once

Pétain's armistice paired France's future to Hitler's tanks, the courier crisscrossed his country in hopes of one day liberating it. Trains were as much his home as his bed.

THE MOONLESS AUTUMN NIGHT of November 3, 1942, saw a forty-foot fishing boat rounding the point at Cap Câble, maneuvering into the mouth of a thin bay slashed deep into the Mediterranean coast between Marseilles and Cassis. A low thump from the motor was the only noise breaking the still darkness. *Seadog* cut her engines, let out chain, and dropped the hook. The felucca looked as if she were back from a trip out netting sardines, had there been shoals nearby. There were not. Like a typical fishing boat, she was a double-ender, narrow bottomed, with a short mast and lateen sail, guided by a tiller, but *Seadog* had been fitted with a new engine for outrunning Nazi gunboats. Like the cargo she carried, *Seadog* worked undercover: She sported French colors on her bow—red, white, and blue—painted in the last two days after she passed Ibiza and Mallorca, where she had displayed the hailing banner of Franco's Spain, the yellow and red.

Odette Sansom arrived in France on a swell of discontent; no part of her training prepared her for the indignity of homecoming. With five other agents, she stepped off *Seadog* into a dinghy, smelling of sardines and seawater. They had been traveling for a month and had not slept in four nights, had eaten nothing but tinned food for days; there was no bathroom aboard. *Seadog*'s foulmouthed Polish captain kept something soft and squishy stapled to the bulkhead, which he told passengers was a "dozen German foreskins."

Onshore, an Englishman in French clothing steadied the disembarking agents, Odette and her classmate Mary Herbert. Just behind, a matronly woman and three men stepped ashore. When the last agent gripped the man's wrist, taking the hoist, he stared into the eyes of his own brother: One was homeward bound to London, his first mission now complete; the other's first assignment was about to begin. It was a shock. The brothers did not linger, though they might not see each other alive again. They could not know what would happen in the days and years ahead. By the end of the war, one would be named a torturer; the other, a traitor.

Odette was dressed for function, with no mind to fashion, in a canvas bin bag with armholes. (The standard kit for poison gas attacks was also fairly waterproof.) It was not how Odette hoped to return to France: After putting her little girls in a convent school, to be looked after by an aunt, she was scheduled to fly on the September moon, around the same time as Andrée and Lise. But Odette thumped her head in parachute training and got concussed. She was then set to come by aircraft, climbing down the ladder of a Westland Lysander directly into the occupied zone, yet each night her flight was scheduled, something went wrong: Bad weather. Engine failure. A crash. Finally, Odette and Mary Herbert were sent to Gibraltar by destroyer, picking their way through a sea of U-boats. At last, they got to the Riviera, ghosting in on a rising tide so their footsteps would be washed away as the seas ebbed.

In the South of France, the Firm was searching for leadership. General de Gaulle was still disliked by Churchill and distrusted by Roosevelt, so Baker Street believed alternate rebel commanders were a political necessity. Ideally, the leader would be a man who had the advantage of actually being inside France, someone less churlish than de Gaulle.

In the Riviera networks, an appealing candidate had risen up in the Resistance, a dynamic artist who anointed himself chief, André Girard. Some men are born to lead; Girard got people riled up, engaged. Graced with charisma and abundant imagination, he accumulated a purported 300,000 followers behind his dreams. He was a visionary, as dramatic and moody as his notebooks; speaking in quick strokes, he elaborated ideas with outrageous colors, explosive contrasts, and dreamlike swirls of confusion. "All around the mighty German army, there is an invisible and patient hatred in every house; in the soil, it is waiting," Girard declared, "for the terrible awakening that is possible someday."

The French art scene went dark during the occupation; it was collaborationist to show at a gallery while French châteaus were scavenged for old masters and Nazi officers pilfered fin de siècle treasures from Jewish dealers. Prior to the war, an artist could make a living off political cartoons, but such work was now forbidden under Hitler and Pétain. In the gloom of fascism, France was no home for art. Had war not intervened, Girard would have been the aesthetic heir to Expressionism; he was a student of Georges Rouault and Pierre Bonnard. Instead, he channeled his creativity into animus, into plans for a new propaganda radio station, Radio Patrie, aimed to rival the French-language broadcasts of the BBC and America's NBC, but as a product of the people themselves, the organic voice of those actually living and suffering under Hitler. He aimed to compete directly with Nazi puff blasted out on German-controlled Radio Paris.

Churchill's military intelligence was seduced by Girard and gave support to Radio Patrie. Girard promised Baker Street that he was linked to voices of opposition in France and North Africa. He said he had contacts with high-ranking members of Vichy's Armistice Army who might be amenable to working with the Allies to undermine Hitler.

Girard "is engaged in the organisation of every strata of society without regard to variations in opinion. [His network] is well informed and strong," read an internal Baker Street memo. He recruited from the breadth of France: He was a magnet for retired French military men and guerrilla exiles from the Spanish Civil War; they formed the core of his covert troops. But Girard's friends—artists, poets, jazz musicians, and intellectuals—were sophisticated and cosmopolitan. They understood how the spirit is crushed by totalitarianism. Communists opposed the German occupation once Hitler turned on Stalin; peasants, too, joined after able-bodied young men were conscripted for slave labor in Germany. Jews signed on from the beginning, as their days were numbered. The courier sleeping on the train was only one man in a large army of patriots ready to follow Girard. The sheer scope of his stealth membership seemed to be a ready-made extension of SOE's plans, reaching deep into the heart of France.

Odette and Mary landed in the Riviera two years into France's war, at the apex of André Girard's career as rebel leader. Where most underground networks were starved for guns and ammunition, receiving only the most meager rations from London, Girard's circuits got boatloads of matériel and millions of francs to supply his invisible army. He was at "the pinnacle of his power; power that he wielded as though born to it. And, unlike Hitler, he was a man of considerable charm and his powers of persuasion were not those of a raving maniac, but those of a man who talked people intelligently around to his way of thinking," said a British organizer, an early admirer of Girard's prowess.

"She will never die!" Girard would say of his beloved France. He paid his men in meals and incentivized resistance with cash. Food is the eternal obsession of the French, and among the casualties of war were cheese, eggs, butter, meat, oil, and potatoes. In the Riviera, where the sun shone all day, the soil was poor, and there was a monoculture of citrus, olives, and wine. It was not enough to sustain a population in wartime, let alone a region flooded with refugees and deeply in debt to Germany. To Girard's rebels, Britain air-dropped tinned rations with English labels, to remind the French who was backing them from afar while the Nazis starved them; every little detail was an opportunity for pro-Anglo propaganda in a nation disinclined to trust England. ("I now feel the old power of the Empire arm," wrote a British leader to HQ in gratitude for tea and biscuits.) For partisans who risked their necks to disperse the contraband, there were special treats, such as chocolate, chewing gum, and cigarettes. "This is progress, Thunder of God, and makes one feel very proud of the department."

London's leadership coveted Girard's secret army, but his partisans were not competent. Upon receiving Britain's backing, Girard's movement descended into a comedy of bumbling and catastrophic errors. In the fall of 1942, for instance, in a dark harbor off the coast of France, a crew of five young rebels loaded a dinghy with "one thousand pounds of danger"—explosives—and a radio transmitter and rowed to sea where the cache would be sunk off a buoy for storage; it was enough firepower to blockade a port, mine a harbor, or sink a battleship. Overweight and unbalanced, the rebel boat turtled into the ocean, capsizing. It was a total loss. The teenage *résistants* whooped and yowled, waking an entire harbor village, "like a Bank Holiday crowd on Derby Day." After the accident, the *Chantiers de la jeunesse française*—Pétain's version of the *Jungsturm,* now known as the *Hitlerjugend,* Hitler Youth—dredged the channel for the explosives and marked the spot. (This was the tragedy of France: Schoolboy was set against schoolboy in a game where the guns were entirely real.)

Once Vichy police retrieved the sunken ammunition, houses all along the coast were searched, and a precious landing beach where the underground could come and go in darkness was unveiled to the enemy. The harbormaster watched, complaining, "I close my peepers to what the Albions do right under my very nose, but in the name of the Holy Virgin why do they not help me and themselves?"

An incompetent network of amateurs would not survive a war against career Nazi spy hunters. Girard's code name was Carte; as rebel groups often adopted the name of their leaders, his vast circuit was also named CARTE. The word *carte* might translate to a business card, map, chart, or menu. And Girard had an unfortunate, childish affection for making lists of names and filling out *cartes.*

After their sodden arrival, Odette and Mary overnighted in a safe house in Cassis, then traveled by train to Cannes, where they were greeted at once with cookies, wine, and the local British organizer, Captain Peter Churchill.

"You must be terribly hungry and tired," Peter said with a smile, welcoming the agents to a hidden flat by palm gardens. "And probably longing for a bath."

Odette looked up. Through long eyelashes and sea-weary eyes, she saw the handsome, bespectacled face of a man so tall, slender, and agile he looked like "a question mark with a mustache." He appeared to be laughing at his own joke, though he had yet to make one.

Peter was the English model of a modern secret agent. A former Cambridge ice hockey star with an aquiline nose, he was a born raconteur, as flamboyant, sloppy, and entitled as any upper-class athlete in his prime. He was the kind of man who kept wineglasses full. Men like Peter were having a "good war." Before his commission, his sense of entitlement made him a failure. He bounced from job to job—"publicity, metallurgy, silver fox farming, and the British consular service"—neither amounting to much, nor trying very hard, but having a jolly time. He maintained a glib sense of well-being in a frightening world with an existential love affair with the literature of Damon Runyon and Raymond Chandler that would become an asset for the absurdities of war. He wrote his messages in Runyonesque code. Peter possessed the crucial skill set for the Firm: fluency in French and English, with studied competence in Spanish, Italian, and German. The war had a way of focusing men like Peter; urgency transformed peripatetic rakes into leaders. For once, Peter could concentrate in every language. His smart-aleck posture looked like professionalism within the oddball ad hoc structure of the Firm, and if Peter's arrogance grated on the French—it did—he believed he was a magnificent first sight for at least two of the three women just off a sardine sampan: the younger ones, Mary and Odette.

Among Peter's many duties in the South of France—communicating with London, coordinating with CARTE, receiving airdrops, and helping POWs out of the country—he was tasked with greeting arriving agents and settling them into the toughest job of their lives: to ensure that they cost no one else theirs. The first days in the field could have "a quality of strangeness and uncertainty, everyone working in a fog."

Lunch was in a café populated by strangers, French police, Jews who fled south after the invasion, unlucky former citizens of the Reich endowed with enough money to buy black market horse meat but not in possession of enough luck to purchase exit papers out of France. The Riviera was the hungriest place in a starving nation. ("We sell tourism, the rest we import" was the local motto.) There was a tight quota on consumption of food, but Peter had a bottomless supply of ration coupons, "hot from the rolls."

Without breaking his grin, the veteran organizer took stock of the women in his charge: They were green, nervous, and new. For months, Peter had been working with the Firm's one-legged American agent, Virginia Hall, who was competent, warm, and assertive. By contrast, these women all seemed delicate and needy.

Mary Herbert was clever, articulate, and looked younger than her forty years. She was a brigadier general's daughter, studious about her surroundings, reserved. Peter doubted she would amount to much as an agent, though he had been surprised before by "hidden depths."

Odette captivated him. With her mop of brown hair and eyes that glowed like polished wood, he found he could not stop looking at her. Odette was accustomed to the attention of men; she cultivated it, recognized its utilitarian value. Peter watched as she raised her glass and took a sip, her first taste of French *terroir* after nearly three years of blockades. A whole lifetime had passed since Odette's last French lunch, with bread on the table, wine in a jug, and sunlight streaming through plate-glass windows. The lack of hurry, the excess, was foreign to her now and inconvenient. The Côte d'Azur was a world away from London fog and English food, from gray puddings and ration famine.

Peter bequeathed Odette a personality she had not yet earned: He decided she was fearless, discerning, a challenge. Over the course of the meal, he became obsessed. He fell for her hands. "I observed a telltale expanse between thumb and forefinger, denoting extravagance, generosity, impetuosity," he said, fixating as if he were a palmist at the fair. Or a lover. Peter found no less eroticism in Odette's knuckle than Victorians found in an upturned ankle. "The ambition in the index fingers; the unusually wide gap between them and the second fingers, showing independence of thought only matched by the independence of action that almost cried out from the gaping valleys that lay between the fourth and little fingers." He searched for her wedding ring, or the ghostly reminder thereof. He had an agent's eye for detail: Odette's wedding ring was sawed off in London, replaced with one whose engraving mapped to her new backstory: As a fatherless teen, her cover story went, she was married off to an elderly Frenchman who died suddenly of bronchitis. The loveless marriage produced no children.

"This reception is all very nice and in keeping with what I expected," Odette said to Peter, with annoyance. "But I'm anxious to get on with the job."

Her job was similar to Lise de Baissac's: establish safe houses in which to receive traveling agents. Odette was to be on her own, not a courier to a circuit; she was to live in France, to be French, until otherwise notified, at which point she would be invoked as a British housekeeper and quartermaster. She was to be based in Auxerre, in the center of the country. But Peter had disappointing news: Auxerre, in Burgundy, was cut off from Cannes by the demarcation line, the almighty frontier between the two Frances. Travel between the zones was potentially deadly, and he would not be able to get her across. Through no fault of her own, she had arrived in the wrong France.

Odette needed help, he said, a smuggler, someone who knew his way around the militarized checkpoints dividing France. She would also need a forged travel pass, an *Ausweis,* to explain why she was moving so far from home. Every detail could be arranged through the CARTE network, but André Girard, the French leader, and Peter Churchill, the British commander, were currently vying for control of the Riviera rebels.

Peter had a headache on his hands, and catering to this new woman—however delicious her digits—took a backseat to managing the tempestuous artist. The Firm's partnership with CARTE was fast falling to pieces. Barely two years old, they counted few successes: André Girard never got around to making the introductions between British agents and ranking Vichy leadership. Radio Patrie was a dream. London urged progress and demanded measurable results, but this wounded Girard's ego; he became autocratic and abusive.

By the day of Odette's arrival, Girard and Peter were sworn enemies. Instead of battling the Germans, they lobbed attacks at each other. "Security just doesn't exist here," Peter raged in frustration upon cock-ups like capsized weapons. Peter called Girard "lord of the manor" and decried his incompetent underlings, "flashy characters full of ballyhoo." CARTE's rendezvous were too much like salons, "happy-go-lucky meetings on park benches with . . . up to half a dozen of the local top Resistance men sitting around and scribbling their orders and instructions under the public gaze." In a report to London, Peter finally recommended that the connection between the Firm and CARTE be severed, despite the high hopes and heavy investment. As far as positive results from the CARTE partnership, Peter wrote, "I challenge you all even under the influence of benzedrine to scrape up one gnat's navel full of gravy."

London soon radioed orders recalling Girard to London to account for himself.

Odette's mission was a lost cause. She asked Girard for help, for a guide to get her to Auxerre; he refused. He took orders from London, he said, not from British agents in France; unless and until a message came through the radio from Baker Street, he was on strike when it came to aiding the friends of Peter Churchill. "He was rather rude to me," she reported in frustration.

"I suggest you start off by having a good rest," Peter offered instead.

"I don't need any rest, thank you."

Odette could not get across the line. Mary had a contact in Tarbes who would arrange for her passage into the occupied zone. She would soon leave to join Claude de Baissac and his SCIENTIST network in Bordeaux. But Odette had to remain with Peter. She was not happy being idle. She demanded to be put to work, so Peter gave her a bicycle and sent her out into Cannes with a message.

Within minutes, he heard a scream, a crash of metal against cobblestones, followed by the shrill curses of a woman lamenting bloodied knees and torn stockings.

She had tried to learn to ride on the fly, balancing as she pedaled.

Why hadn't she told him she couldn't ride a bicycle? Peter wondered.

"Because you seemed to take it for granted that everybody is as . . . competent as you are yourself. It is most irritating. Why should I give you the satisfaction of admitting ignorance?" Odette said.

Peter decided Odette was "dynamite."

On November 8, 1942, the BBC nightly broadcast to France began as it ever did with Beethoven's Fifth.

Da. Da. Da. Dum.

In the safe house, Odette and Peter listened to the radio for the evening news in French: In Egypt, the Axis forces were on the run, the El Alamein offensive was a "complete and absolute victory." In America, President Roosevelt's Democrats maintained a narrow majority in the midterm congressional elections. The U.S.S.R. was to celebrate its twenty-fifth birthday as Soviet soldiers pinned down the Wehrmacht in the streets of Stalingrad. In England, some forty million poppies were ready for sale on Remembrance Day.

At the end of the program, as the personal messages began, there was a persistent and repeated announcement:

Attention, Robert est arrivé! Attention, Robert est arrivé!

The simple sentence sounded the length of France, down through the Mediterranean to Gibraltar, and deep into the desert oases of Morocco and the dunes of Algeria. The whole of Francophone Europe and North Africa heard the call.

The Allied forces recognized it as an action alert. That night,

Anglo-American armies invaded North Africa. On the heels of the British victory in Egypt, France's colonies were in play. It was the first major offensive by the Allies and the first landing of American troops abroad. Only one year after the Japanese attack on Pearl Harbor, America was now in a world war, and its troops were fighting Nazis in the desert: Operation Torch.

The fight for North Africa was a war for the Mediterranean. Control of the placid waters would ratchet back Hitler's dominance in southern Europe. And just as critically, it was a proxy battle for the hearts and minds of the French.

The fight to reclaim Europe began on November 8, 1942, only five days after Odette and Mary landed on the southern coast of France. Some thirty-three thousand troops were preparing to go ashore in Casablanca, another thirty-nine thousand were heading toward Algiers, and thirty-five thousand men were set for Oran. They crossed the Atlantic on 350 warships and 500 transport carriers. The American forces were untested. The German generals were hard and calculating. The French military leadership was in turmoil. But it would be a battle that might turn the war: If the Allies could cleave the North African colonies from the government in Vichy, it would send a signal to the French people that the marriage to the Reich was not destined to last a thousand years. (As a French journalist put it, "The Valkyries will go back into their hole and die like something out of one of Wagner's operas.")

"Now this is not the end," Prime Minister Churchill cautioned in a speech. "It is not even the beginning of the end. But it is, perhaps, the end of the beginning."

Robert est arrivé!

ROBERT ARRIVED, and Hitler retaliated.

On November 11, 1942, Remembrance Day, when Europe and America honored the war dead from World War I, Adolf Hitler invaded France. Again. The Wehrmacht breached the demarcation line, pouring into the free zone, occupying the southern cities of Lyon, Limoges, Agen, Marseilles, and Vichy itself. The Reich swallowed what remained of free France, putting paid to the farce of the vassal Pétain government. The armistice agreement was vitiated and the Armistice Army was demobilized.

Two Frances became one. France was now a fully occupied territory of the Reich, though the demarcation line remained in place as a way of controlling the movement of the population. Hitler told Marshal Pétain the takeover was for his own benefit; it was to defend France against attack from the south, from the Allies now fighting in North Africa.

On German-controlled Radio Paris, the führer spoke to the French people, to let them know he "took the action out of friendship." No harm would come, he said; orders were given to "disturb as little as possible."

The Allies jammed the airwaves with taunting rhymes:

Radio Paris ment, Radio Paris est allemande.
Radio Paris lies, Radio Paris is German.

Depuis Strasbourg jusqu'à Biarritz
La radio est aux mains des Fritz.
From Strasbourg to Biarritz
Radio is in the hands of the Fritz.

THE SECOND NAZI invasion of France roiled the world; the chess pieces of Europe were again rearranged. France's disgraceful peace was in tatters. When Hitler's tanks rolled beyond the demarcation line, he raised France's occupation payments from a crippling 300 million francs per day to 500 million, in yet another act of legalized looting to which Pétain numbly agreed. As the costs of German plunder grew, the French desire for freedom kept pace.

Winston Churchill saw an opportunity for SOE. The embers of rebellion, so far dormant in France's free zone, should be fanned to flames at once. "It seems most important to intensify operations in the newly occupied regions of France in order to make the relations between the torpid French and the German invaders as unpleasant as possible."

There would be Bangs.

On the day of Hitler's advance, British agents in the Riviera looked out their windows and saw clouds of dust kicked up by military trucks as Mussolini's troops pressed in from Italy, taking possession of the twinkling beachfront necklace. Cannes was annexed by Il Duce, Italian territory now.

London's policy in what had been the unoccupied zone changed daily. With no Armistice Army, Girard's alleged high-level contacts became as worthless as his other promises. Odette was an agent in the field for a little over a week, and she could not get to her assigned destination. Attached to Peter Churchill's network by default, she became his courier.

Peter stayed in a garden flat, just off the sunbaked beach promenade, the croisette. ("A lovely house, beds and the whole shooting match," Peter said.) Odette joined him there.

Only a few days on the ground, in her new bed, in her old country, Odette fell asleep watching wispy curtains wave in front of an open window. She contemplated her new self, her new identity: The last time she lived in France, she was Mademoiselle Odette Brailly, ingenue. In England, she had been Mrs. Odette Sansom, dissatisfied wife, burdened mother of three. Now in the war, as an agent, she lived under the name Madame Odette Metayer: widowed, childless, enticing.

Odette could not know it, but Peter watched her while she slept, as intensely as he studied her hands. "She smiled," he said, "with a look of childlike peace upon her face."

By the eleventh hour of the eleventh day of the eleventh month of the year 1942, when Europe and America stopped in silence to honor the dead of the Great War, Hitler had subsumed all that was left of France, and at that moment Odette and Peter were already living together as "husband and wife."

THE CARTE NETWORK'S MESSENGER, André Marsac, was slumped in his seat while the coal-fired locomotive climbed up through France in a cloud of smoke. Train carriages rocked back and forth like babies' baskets. He was tired. He was accustomed to moving nonstop, a tangle of energy, a live wire of a man who was still growing into his job as a secret soldier.

The train was hypnotic to Marsac. He had worked himself thin, all bones, knees, and elbows. Eyes heavy, chin to chest, breathing slow and even, syncopated with the drive wheel of the engine, Marsac fell asleep.

When he awoke, his briefcase of CARTE names was gone.

CHAPTER 11

The Paris of the Sahara

Morocco

Winston Churchill was an enthusiastic amateur painter; at least he was before Britain locked horns with Hitler and he was named head of government. Oil painting helped beat back what he would call his "black dog," his depression. After the war ended, Sir Winston would have time to sit at his easel again, but during his tenure as prime minister and minister of defense he completed only one canvas: in January 1943 in Marrakesh, Morocco. "Simply the nicest place on earth to spend an afternoon."

Morocco was cool in January, newly liberated, and a very good place for what Churchill decided to call his "summit," a meeting of the Anglo-American military chiefs. It had been a little more than a year since Pearl Harbor; it was time to plan the war for the year 1943.

Churchill had a deep love for Morocco, with its "fortune-tellers, snake-charmers, masses of food and drink, and on the whole the largest and most elaborately organised brothels in the African continent."

Brothels can claim the most extraordinary offspring: For ten days at an Art Deco hotel in Casablanca, generals and diplomats sat around conference tables and maps, with gold braid weighting their cuffs and collars, puffing on pipes while they hashed out the future of the conflict and by extension the planet. Two nations would settle on a global military strategy together, as partners. In Morocco, Britain and America wrote the plans for D-Day.

"I MUST BE with you when you see the sunset on the Atlas Mountains," the prime minister pleaded to the American president. He also had to render the moment on canvas.

It is an optimistic painting: Bright pink minarets of the Koutoubia mosque are set against the dusky purple mountains and robin's egg sky. Shadows hang in long triangles upon worshippers in caftans entering for evening prayers. Churchill painted as the sun grew orange, while the muezzin called out to barreling sparrows, snowy peaks, and devotees. If his wartime moods were marked by gloom and mania, his days in the French colony were sweet, saturated in color, bright with uninterrupted vistas of calm.

"You cannot come all the way to North Africa without seeing Marrakesh," Churchill said to Roosevelt. He called it "the Paris of the Sahara." The Yanks had, indeed, come a very long way: It was only a year after the Japanese bombed the U.S. Navy's Pacific Fleet. American soldiers were young; killing was still a fresh idea, something that happened on far shores to other countries. The American war machine was only just coming online, pumping out B-17s and battleships with a vigor and dedication that would ultimately turn the nation into the greatest war power the world had ever seen.

At the oasis, after his Allied summit, Churchill painted the Atlas peaks. He stood on a mountaintop and carried the fate of the world on his shoulders.

ON WALL-SIZE MAPS, when generals moved their armies and fleets with pins, they began moving in the Allies' direction. The landing in

North Africa, Operation Torch, was a success. The Allies controlled the mouth of the Mediterranean; Britain and America, Churchill and Roosevelt, counted a solid win against Germany—the very first.

The year 1943 would see a second line of battle in western Europe, all were adamant. The Desert Campaign was an important triumph, strategically and morally. American forces got their necessary combat experience. With the Middle East harbors under control, there could be a southern shipping route to supply the Red Army. Secure access to the Suez Canal would provide a shortcut to the war in Asia, where Japan was threatening British India. If the Allies could control the Mediterranean, they would forestall a global pincer movement that saw Hitler and Tojo shaking hands together in the Middle East. Should the Axis powers capture the oil wells of the Arabian Peninsula, the war might go on for years.

Torch was a win for France too, also its first in three years. The North African colonies were returned to the French people as a counterargument to the capitulation of the Vichy regime. "French Africa is the only place in the world where our flag flies freely, where the army carries its arms, where the navy flies its flag and where our air force can use its wings," announced a French admiral after the Allied landings in the Mediterranean.

Allied troops now committed to Africa would soon be free to launch a major offensive. The question around the table was where to take the fight: The Pacific? Southern Europe? France? War planners took a considered breath in January. They were in a solid position from which to make an inventory of men, guns, and ships, to study maps, moon phases, and tides, and to concoct a strategy for the end of the Reich.

But another massacre of a winter lay ahead, with Stalin screaming for help from his Allied partners; he demanded a second front in Europe. Now.

Among the Allied commanders assembled in Casablanca, disagreements threatened all sense of accomplishment. For Britain, the war was moving into its fourth year. She had escaped Dunkirk, survived the Blitz, but had lost Singapore, Hong Kong, and Burma, then secured the win in Egypt and North Africa. Britain's forces were battle forged and fatigued; her soldiers were on a different footing from the fresh-faced American troops; her generals were senior, seasoned, and conservative.

The American brass agitated to take on Hitler directly in the coming year. General Dwight D. Eisenhower called for the immediate return to Europe via France, followed by a push to the Rhine. His plan, Operation Roundup, required a major decisive strike on the Continent as soon as possible, as soon as weather permitted. If the Allies did not invade France soon, the führer would get one more year of slave labor to fortify his Atlantic Wall defenses. An overpowering invasion would draw the Reich's attention away from the Soviets and, if all went as hoped, secure democracy's place in Europe again.

The particulars of the cross-Channel offensive loomed over the summit. It would require a massive troop buildup in England; the Allies had to strike down the U-boat wolf packs in the Atlantic, to free up shipping from America; an air campaign would be launched against Germany, to cripple its war-making capacity and demoralize its citizens. This would all culminate in an assault on the beaches of Europe, which Churchill would call "much the greatest thing we have ever attempted."

Americans debated where to hit France first: The Pas-de-Calais? The Cotentin Peninsula? Along the Atlantic coast, below Brest in the Bay of Biscay? Or up from the south, from the Mediterranean?

The British chiefs were unenthusiastic about the invasion of France in 1943, and they insisted it was not a good year for a total Continental war. The alliance was not yet where it needed to be in terms of leadership and planning, training, manpower, and equipment. The coordination of supply and doctrine were challenges no modern military had been asked to confront. Rommel was still digging in, claiming resources for the desert that would be needed in a cross-Channel push. For the novice Americans and overstretched Brits, Churchill's planners insisted on exploring some kind of half measure, a lighter lift than the complete invasion of Europe.

The prime minister was worried. He did not want to lose Roosevelt's attention in Europe. If the Americans were not engaged against

Hitler in 1943, it would be all too natural for them to turn to the Pacific theater. President Roosevelt might abandon the "Germany First" strategy and look instead toward the global war.

Roosevelt, for his part, was anxious that an exhausted Britain might pull out of the war once Hitler was defeated, leaving America alone to claw back the Pacific. The American chiefs considered any invasion short of a complete assault on northwest Europe a "sideshow."

In the meantime, Stalin might just finish off Germany first, for everyone. Russian troops were indefatigable by order and training; wounded Soviet soldiers were told to "pull yourself back together, get ready to fight, and even if you're half dead, if you've only got one good arm, use it to shoot the enemy." They had been holding the Wehrmacht steady on the eastern front for almost two years.

"Is it really to be supposed that the Russians will be content with our lying down like this during the whole of 1943 while Hitler has a third crack at them?" Churchill shot at his advisers. The year 1943 could not go by without a major landing in Europe, he said. The prime minister had even named his ideal target date for D-Day, a midsummer moon, waxing full: July 12, 1943.

The top brass performed an audit. The balance of power was on Britannia's side: America had 150,000 active troops in the Mediterranean against 450,000 of Britain's forces. For an invasion in 1943, the Allies could count on four French divisions, nine American divisions, and a whopping twenty-seven British divisions. Unless Hitler collapsed under the weight of his own hatred and overreach, losing Europe of his own accord, the year 1943 was to be a British show—tempered and measured.

"We came, we listened and we were conquered," said an American general, of the plans made in Casablanca.

THE SUN SHONE in Churchill's painting, but it was soon to set on the British Empire. The prime minister was stunned when President Roosevelt uttered an impromptu idea at a press conference that fixed the endgame strategy for the war, even though it had not been previously agreed. The war, Roosevelt said, would not end without "unconditional surrender." Any kind of negotiated cease-fire—such as the one Eisenhower set with Vichy's admiral of the navy only weeks before—was now off the table. From Casablanca forward, there could be no amenable terms with Hitler, no armistice with Germany, only complete and total submission.

Two words. "Unconditional surrender." The phrase betrayed a larger truth of the Casablanca meeting: As American military strength grew, Great Britain's would be eclipsed. For the first years of the war, Britain fought alone on behalf of Europe, a story that served the national ego; it was the last great flowering of a colonial superpower. Then one infamous day in Honolulu, America joined the war, and the balance of the world tipped westward.

Casablanca would mark the very last time Britons would sit around a table and dictate the future of entire continents. In the long history of the British Empire, it marked an end to England's global hegemonic dominance. The British would be junior partners going forward. Geopolitical strategy was to be an American show.

But the year 1943 still belonged to Great Britain. And for a few days in Morocco, everything was beautiful.

CHAPTER 12

Our Possibilities

Paris

Andrée Borrel lived in a city she did not recognize. Wartime Paris was petty, beaten down. The winter of 1943 was colder; coal was scarce. Women were thinner; food was rationed. People grew stupid: They pulped their own books for firewood, and newspapers were full of collaborationist swill. Paris had not known want before. Now it was a city of plunder.

Streetlamps, cabaret signs, and cinema marquees were shut off well before curfew. It was so dark that Andrée could scarcely see as she angled around anti-aircraft installations in the squares. Streets echoed with emptiness, her wooden "armistice shoes" sounding off the cobbles.

In the bleakest days of winter, Andrée handed off a message to a radio operator. The note was from Francis, the agent Prosper, written jointly with the agent David, Lise de Baissac's brother Claude, in Bordeaux.

February 1, 1943

FROM DAVID AND PROSPER. UNITED OPINION OF THE ONLY TWO ACTIVE RECRUITS OF YOUR SECTION THAT QUOTE NOS POSSIBILITES PRATIQUEMENT ILLIMITEES SONT EN FONCTION DE L'AIDE QUE VOUS NOUS APPORTEZ UNQUOTE

With your help, our capabilities are virtually limitless.

The letter was scrambled by code and converted into electrical dots and dashes that pulsed through the atmosphere to England, where they were received by a giant aerial antenna on the grounds of a manor house. Formerly known as Grendon Hall, Station 53, in Buckinghamshire, it was the heart of communications between occupied Europe and London.

In a room that smelled of "talcum powder and dry rot," some twenty FANYs in khaki drill skirts, with no-nonsense haircuts, sat hunched over a row of wireless transceivers "listening" for messages from Europe. On the wall, there were blackboards with the names of agents such as Broccoli, Cloak, and Butcher. In chalk next to the names was a schedule of times that transmissions were expected, as well as the wavelength on which they were to be broadcast. Messages arrived as a cluster of seemingly random letters, an encrypted text. A nearby room of FANYs had the job of unwinding the transmission: The cipher was ornate, with two separate codes layered on top of each other, a process called double transposition. When letters were forced twice through the algorithm, sense and syntax emerged.

The FANYs of Station 53 were the critical link between the resistance movements of Europe and the spymasters of Baker Street. Every day, they received hundreds of coded messages from agents in the field—from Norway, Holland, Poland, Yugoslavia, Italy, and France. The women got it all first. Most never met the foreign correspondents with whom they were in daily contact. The girls in bobby pins and flats would not know until after the war that, for instance, Butcher was the handsome, twenty-seven-year-old Gilbert Norman, now hiding out in Paris.

Gilbert had never arrived at his original assignment in Corsica. His mission parameters vanished before he got there. Immediately after he jumped into France, Hitler invaded the unoccupied zone, Mussolini claimed the Riviera and Corsica for Italy, and the CARTE network reorganized, a victim of its own flamboyance. The erstwhile CARTE head, André Girard, got recalled to London, and his thousands of imaginary patriots went back to their little lives. Gilbert ultimately went instead to Paris to become a radio operator, joining Andrée and Francis.

The FANY operators felt tenderly toward Gilbert, as they did toward all their distant secret pen pals. They understood him, down to the pauses between dashes and the cadences of his dots. Every radio operator had a unique sending style, a "fist" as individual as a fingerprint. The women seated around tables with headsets could recognize an agent by the rhythm of his traffic alone. It was intimacy in Morse.

Radio was the deadliest assignment. As Paris was the hub of the northern Resistance, it became a bottleneck for underground communication. Gilbert was one of the few radios in the region; he transmitted for his group, for other sub-circuits, for de Gaulle's RF Section networks, and for escape lines. There were times when it seemed as if he was on air throughout the day, long enough for direction-finding vans to triangulate his signals. "Each W/T transmission is a blood transfusion," said the signals officers to the FANYs. The life expectancy of a radio operator was less than six weeks behind enemy lines. Gilbert kept sets hidden in eleven different places and moved between them, switching frequencies daily, changing his schedules to keep the Huns guessing. He was up to the task, Baker Street thought, "one of those rare agents who encoded even better in the field than they did in practice."

Amid the chattering of Teletype machines, wireless receivers, and scrambler telephones, the mood at Station 53 was young and giddy. The FANYs were reminded to "at all times conduct themselves like ladies" but were as likely to call themselves "girls." They were generally in their twenties and single, and in 1943 they were mostly new recruits, civilian volunteers who could leave their jobs at any time. They were not hired for their looks or their sophistication; the most competent ones specialized in puzzles, music, and foreign languages. Their conversations bordered on silly, if not downright dirty, but their work was dead serious. They were keeping agents alive.

It would surprise the FANYs to find out that some agents working behind enemy lines were also women. The first graduates of Party No. 27.OB were in the field by the winter of 1943—Andrée, Lise, Odette, Yvonne, and Mary among them. Female agents behind the lines had a more exciting war than those pounding telegraph keys at Station 53, but were not more important to the outcome. While some women worked at Bletchley Park to crack the German Enigma intercepts, the FANYs of SOE were both decoding agents' messages and creating foundations for new codes to fool the Nazis. As codes grew more sophisticated, the FANYs were asked to write original poems as an underlying base for agents' ciphers; the lyrics became the puzzle platforms for encrypting messages.

One such ditty composed by the FANYs went,

Is de Gaulle's prick
Twelve inches thick
Can it rise
To the size
Of a proud flag-pole
And does the sun shine
From his arse-hole?

Signals traffic between London and France increased exponentially in the winter of 1943. With the crop of new agents in France finding their footing, Baker Street hoped the moon periods of February and March would be the most active to date, scheduling more agents for deployment and tons of guns, explosives, munitions, and rations for dispatch.

The Allies were ramping up the war of terror against Hitler. F Section was in a sprint to recruit, arm, and train the French. But the Paris PHYSICIAN network made slow progress in the winter of 1943. Often known as the PROSPER network—after Francis's code name—it was not prospering as it might. The airdrops were not coming off as planned, headquarters could not deploy enough radio operators, and sub-circuits were too hamstrung by a lack of weapons to be much trouble to the Nazis. It was a growing source of frustration for agents on the ground: Each month in the darkness, Andrée recruited and trained young rebels in sabotage and receptions; then, as the moon grew full, they splayed out into the provinces, stood in frozen fields, stared at the sky, waited for the growl of engines and the inflation of silk parachutes, only to go home dejected when the moonlight did not bear fruit. Only two airdrop operations would come off successfully at the start of 1943, out of fifteen attempts. Two drops amounted to all of seven containers, each the size of a coffin. It was not enough weaponry to supply a secret army.

February 21, 1943

THIS BEING A NEW AND VERY KEEN GROUP A DELIVERY THIS MOON IF POSSIBLE WOULD BE A BIG HELP.

Nineteen forty-three would become the watershed year for the French Resistance. At Avenue Foch, Major Bömelburg and his colleagues noted a sudden and surprising white-hot "hitherto unknown Germanophobia in France."

Between collaboration and resistance, there was accommodation: It was the category into which most French citizens fell. Few thought violent resistance was sensible; there was a broad nationwide fear of young men living in the woods, with neither jobs nor families, clamoring for guns and revenge. What reasonable person would support lawless adolescents with bombs?

Whereas the first three years of Paris's occupation saw mostly small-scale and uncoordinated acts of opposition, so-called terrorist attacks in 1943 spiked against the Reich. Though Andrée and Francis felt they could not get enough guns, those they had were put to immediate use. "Germans are killed daily in the streets of Paris," said a top secret report from France to London that spring, "and 90 percent of these attacks are made with arms provided by us, e.g. to the Communists."

After the fall of France, assaults on the Nazis were inchoate and inexpert; the targets of anger and sabotage were likely to be soldiers rather than strategic coastal installations or munitions factories. The slaying of soldiers set off chain reactions that would stoke hellfires of both retribution and rebellion: When one Wehrmacht soldier was killed on the streets of Paris in 1941, the Germans retaliated by executing three French hostages. From Berlin, Hitler reproached his French commanders, insisting that the body count must be higher; a three-to-one ratio of reprisal did not go far enough: One German life was worth far more than three French terrorists'. As a matter of policy, Hitler insisted on the "most drastic measures"; at least fifty more French hostages had to be executed and an additional three hundred Frenchmen were to be rounded up and imprisoned for every German death. Reciprocation must expand geometrically. The next attack against any soldier would result in one hundred further executions, Hitler said, and so on, until the French understood the full force of the führer's rage. In a play for sovereignty, Vichy insisted on drawing up the lists of hostages. The victims were mostly innocent.

The reports of firing squads ricocheted through France.

In Paris, yellow Nazi propaganda posters with thick black borders listed names of terrorists recently shot. In public parks and in the metro, billboards and placards declared,

Anyone committing acts of violence against the German army will be shot.
All close male relatives over 18 years old will be shot.
All female relatives will be condemned to forced labor.
All children, up to 17 years old, male and female, will become wards of the state.

There was collective guilt for every dead German soldier; French mothers, wives, and children were to answer for the perpetrators.

Resistance took root in France by way of these assassinations. As the Reich's reprisal rules fueled opposition, they led to more angry attacks, then more German reciprocation, then more resistance, then more Nazi rage, ad-bloody-infinitum. It was a spiral of death that some of the most unsentimental Nazi Party members had no wish to oversee. One military commander in France, Otto von Stülpnagel, resigned after presiding over the execution of ninety-five French hostages.

Exponential murder was a nuisance for Hitler's commanders in France. Berlin's passion for revenge kept Bömelburg's spy hunters busy while simultaneously undermining the Reich's governance. The retaliation policy strained relations with Vichy, upending the "functional collaboration" and détente between the two regimes, making it near impossible to deliver willing workers to German war factories.

National sentiment, never warm toward occupation, grew chilly for the disproportionate bloodshed. The reprisal orders served as an excellent recruiting tool for Andrée's underground army, as Winston Churchill pointed out to his advisers: "The blood of the martyrs is the seed of the Church."

At last, Vichy and the Reich found a political answer to the führer's obsessive bloodlust: the systematic execution of "Jewish Bolsheviks." Many Jews were no longer even French citizens by 1943; Vichy had stripped them of their passports. As these Jews were set to be rounded up and deported anyway, the innovative answer to Hitler's insane counterterrorism policy became an integral part of France's Final Solution.

Long winters at war, too, eroded national faith in the Vichy regime. The longer the occupation lasted, the more it discomforted France's workers, the little people, *les petites gens*. The pressures of occupation were intolerable; inflation had risen 50 percent since the Germans rolled in. Women rioted against food shortages, queuing for hours for basics. Paris had the lowest rations in all of Europe. Vegetable patches sprouted in the Tuileries gardens; Parisians got 3.2 ounces of oil a month, 2 ounces of margarine, and so little meat it was said the portions could be wrapped in a metro ticket—unless, of course, it had been punched, for then dinner might slip through the hole. Starvation diminished France; one-third of the children born during the war had stunted growth, three-pound newborns were common, and only one in five was born at normal weight. Women grew gaunt, and their periods were infrequent or stopped altogether; if menses came, women joked it was as if the English had finally arrived—the "redcoats" have landed.

Hitler broke France not all at once but over the course of years. In 1942, Vichy had instituted "voluntary" labor conscription to Germany—"the relief," it was called, *la relève*—an unfulfilled promise to repatriate one wounded French POW in exchange for three strapping young workers. The *relève* was followed by mandatory conscription, *Service du Travail Obligatoire* (STO), which cemented the foundations for a nationwide opposition, whisking away 650,000 men of France to German factories. When any mother's son was vulnerable to expatriation and slave labor, rebel activity was poised to expand from a small intellectual and urban exercise into a mass movement. The STO brought the war to every parish and into each family's living room. If officials hoped conscription would empty the ranks of potential terrorists by sending idle boys to Germany, they were fatally mistaken; it simply created more.

International events also incited the French. After Germany invaded the Soviet Union in 1941, French Communists were ordered by Stalin to avenge Russia and turn against the Nazis with a vehemence that betrayed their revolutionary ideology. By 1943, with the Allies in French North Africa, Pétain's armistice was violated and his army disbanded. There was no more pretext of French national sovereignty. The marshal looked ever more like an inert lackey emptying France's pockets for Hitler. Then, in February 1943, news came from Russia that Hitler's forces were routed in Stalingrad.

Three years into the occupation, the pendulum of war swung toward the Allies. In Paris, an expectation of victory took root.

If only the guns would arrive.

March 2, 1943

PEOPLE DISAPPOINTED THEY SPENT TIME AND RISK AND PETROL FOR NOTHNG WHY RPT WHY DID YOU NOT TRY EARLIER THIS IS BAD PROPAGANDA AND DIPLOMACY.

From the point of view of London, the Paris network (Denise, Prosper, and Archambaud—Andrée, Francis, and Gilbert) made a good team. The trinity enjoyed one another—"inseparable friends"—rare for a business and military pairing. "As a general rule, the three of them [were] always together," recalled a Paris agent. "Suttill was like a father to Gilbert who admired him as a leader and was ready to obey any order," said a colleague. "In our dangerous and trying situations strong friendships and admiration developed for each other's work."

Lacking firepower for sabotage, the circuit spent moonless nights at the Hot Club, a secret jazz society known for gypsy rhythms—home to the great Django Reinhardt. When Andrée and Francis walked into the club for recruitment meetings, they "were veritable gods to the people, gods in person." Accompanied by the clarinet and the saxophone, London's agents taught Parisians how to assemble machine guns and load a pistol, which they then stashed in the hollowed-out base of a bookcase. Someday, when Allied matériel arrived as regularly as the moon, those lessons would be put to patriotic use. The Vichy regime rightly considered jazz a threat to law and order; Andrée's club companions, *les petits swings,* planned big trouble for the Reich.

Francis said Andrée "had a perfect understanding [of] security and an imperturbable calmness." She pulled her hat low over her eyes, knotted her scarf, drew her fur collar close, and disappeared into Paris. In traditional theaters of war, an opponent is identifiable: He is in uniform, he is the enemy, there is a dynamic of "us" and "them." But in an occupied city, the nation lies down with the conqueror; citizens befriend, support, work beside, and sometimes even become those whom they despise. For any woman engaged in covert operations, the enemy might as well be everyone. "You couldn't sort of openly trust the first person you saw," said one female agent.

In the winter of 1943, Andrée was powerful and, in a new way, beautiful. Undercover and in disguise, her hair was blonder than it had ever been, higher; she rolled it up behind her ears and piled it over her brow as if gravity and bobby pins could defy the dour Nazi stare. The couture houses of Chanel and Dior profited on Fräuleins and collaborators, but Andrée, like so many *Parisiennes,* played the part of a gamine *zazou*. Paris fashion had witnessed a wartime youth movement take flight, the *zazous,* who modeled defiance on jazz. Clothing was in short supply, the Allies blockaded the coasts, fabric manufactured in France went for Wehrmacht parachutes and uniforms; domestic wool was spun with 30 percent wood fiber, and it was said termites flew out of hand-knit sweaters every time it rained. Yet it remained a point of pride for Parisian women to stay chic through the privations of war. They still made sartorial statements: Deep-necked seductive dresses ran counter to Pétain's Catholicism, mocking his national calls for modesty, and tighter blouses helped solve a fabric shortage. In the coldest winters Europe had ever known, women wore outsize rabbit fur coats made from the skins of the domesticated bunnies that became meat. (Guinea pigs too were a source of both food and fur.) For ease in bicycling, they donned their boyfriends' trousers and hiked hemlines ever higher. Men too, so smart and turned out before the war, took up the *zazou* banner, sporting sloppy, square-shouldered suits, and kept their hair too long and slicked back—all in a physical manifestation of social rebellion and conscientious objection.

Andrée avoided Germans for the obvious reasons, but also because she hated the sight of them: Bundled in black leather trench coats, high boots, peaked caps, gray-green wool, and insignia hanging off in chains, those blond, hollow-eyed men looked so warm and well fed. The Nazis spoke an awful guttural French, when they even tried, like a dog's bark. Most soldiers were from rural Germany, hayseeds who had never left the family farm; Paris glittered with sophistication and beauty. The city was their war bounty, a playground of prizes and delights—opera, restaurants, prostitutes. The Germans binged, mindful that at any moment orders might come, sending them to join their Aryan brothers dying on the Russian front. Some soldiers were dispatched to Paris to convalesce, a reward for surviving Stalin's winters. The city was cheap for the *Boches:* They were paid in reichsmarks; they spent in francs, which were officially debased. There was hardly a Nazi soldier who did not return home from Paris without a suitcase full of luxuries: chocolate, perfume, Armagnac. War was a mechanism of export. It all disgusted Andrée, recalled a colleague. "For the enemy, she had complete contempt."

Other women found comfort with the Germans. Paris cherishes its culture, its love of music and literature, which maps to a Teutonic ideal of Europe as the center of learning; there were similarities between occupier and subject, points of intersection and pride. When Wehrmacht officers had unfettered access to real coffee and warm clothing—and French citizens did not—cozying up to soldiers seemed a reasonable decision. There were so few Frenchmen of marriageable age left in Paris, at any rate. Such coupling was labeled "horizontal collaboration." By 1943, some eighty thousand French mothers had babies fathered by German soldiers. When women collaborated, it was sexual; when men collaborated, it was called political. The standards were double; the enemy was the same.

If occupation means, literally, a place taken over, it was achingly true of Paris in the winter of 1943: Street signage was in German; swastika bunting flapped in bitter breezes; emptied apartments were filled by German troops. The French had a new word for their own sense of dislocation—*dépaysement*—not feeling at home. They were de-countrified.

Andrée wanted France back. She did not give in; her spirit did not falter. Said Francis, "She is the best of us all."

ANDRÉE ARRIVED HOME late on March 8, 1943. When she entered her building at 51 Rue des Petites-Écuries, the concierge delivered bad news. In a skeptical city, it was standard practice to pay off building minders in advance, compensating them long before they were needed, to give warning of future suspicious interactions or official inquiries. A secret agent would not have neglected this task.

Andrée climbed the stairs to her flat in possession of breathless new information: Police had been snooping around her room that afternoon, while she was out, at around 5:00.

The neighborhood in the 10th arrondissement was an otherwise easy place to avoid, a difficult place to be tracked down, a grubby area known for landlords who would not demand documentation, favored by men avoiding forced labor. The locals were idle; the women were for sale. It attracted the dregs of society, but Andrée could hold her own in any dark alley long before she was trained to kill.

On the ground floor of her building, there was a café, small and cubby-like, tucked into a street that was built snugly for horse carriages and now saw only bicycles. Below her bedroom, café patrons swallowed good wine and smoked genuine tobacco into the night.

The so-called Carlingue, the notorious Bonny-Lafont gang, sought out the café. They were a corrupt bunch of former policemen who collaborated with the Nazis and were known as the *Gestapo française*. The semi-deputized mob recruited heavily from the criminal underworld, scouring Fresnes Prison for killers and smugglers. The group was headquartered on Rue Lauriston, in the tony 16th arrondissement, where members staged home raids, kidnapped families, then tortured everyone until they surrendered their jewelry, paintings, antiques, cash. The gang plied their trade in the 10th for the same reason Andrée lived there: It was an easy place to vanish. The area was known for off-market trades in stolen goods and gold. They would organize illicit purchases, arrive at the rendezvous, reveal themselves as police, then seize the bounty and hand the culprits over to the Nazis for a sizable commission. It was a lucrative grift.

When Andrée arrived home between nights at the Hot Club and anticipated air receptions in the countryside, her flat was within a bullet's distance of men sipping brandy who would have congratulated themselves for either capturing or killing her—both were on the menu.

Andrée entered her room: Her possessions remained, her clothing undisturbed. Her flat was a nucleus for other female agents: Mary Herbert had a key; Lise contacted her to collect and send messages; and Yvonne was often in town. Andrée looked around the small flat for any cues that would give away information about the rebellion to an industrious police inspector. Were there used train tickets? Michelin maps, false ration cards, the flotsam and jetsam of a subterranean life? It was too close.

Andrée was cool in the face of danger. She reported the police visit to Francis and told him she was prepared to "bluff" the inspectors when they returned, should they give her any grief. The near miss only redoubled Andrée's determination to rid Paris of the Nazis. "Nothing would deflect her from what she felt her duty."

To Andrée's relief, the police did not return that night. But the mob continued to frequent the café below and run rampant in Paris, murdering innocents, raiding homes, manipulating the black market, shaking down the remaining Jews, working hand in leather glove with Hitler's barbaric security state.

By Baker Street protocol, the surprise visit should have signaled a time for Andrée to go dark, to let her trail grow cold. She was too hot; she could resurface later. But there was no lying low for Andrée; there was no time: London pressed the Paris agents to prepare for the invasion, to grow networks quickly—even before the guns arrived.

Going forward, Andrée felt ever more encouraged to sleep somewhere other than her own apartment. She had an alluring alternative in Gilbert, the radio operator. In the winter of 1943, Andrée spent her days couriering messages, guns, and money. She spent her nights with Gilbert.

March 9, 1943

Letter from PROSPER, *en clair,* via courier.

Am attacking Chaingy 10 Mars and Chevilly four or five days later. I will send you a report on the affair by my men.

. . . I want to repeat again Archambaud [Gilbert] and Monique [Andrée] do a really remarkable job. Hurry up your landings because all three of us need a small holiday.

March 12, 1943

GERMANS IN FRANTIC HURRY TO CLEAR ALL FRANCE BEFORE INVASION. HURRY UP ALL YOUR OPS THIS MOON.

March 19, 1943

FOR GOD'S SAKE HURRY UP ALL OPS WHY SUCH A DELAY.

March 21, 1943

ON SATURDAY NIGHT STILL NO MESSAGES NO OPS WHAT IS THE GAME WEATHER GOOD ALL OF US MOST IMPATIENT RISKS ARE GREAT DO NOT LOSE TIME LA FORTUNE EST AUX AUDACIOUS.

Fortune favors the brave.

Despite the dearth of weapons, the rebellion grew in might and size. With mandatory forced labor and a surfeit of teenagers itching to join the partisans, central coordination was urgent. To organize individual factions into a single cause, General Charles de Gaulle sent to France a personal emissary through RF Section, the parallel agency within SOE. (Andrée and Francis were in Paris to launch and arm a resistance, regardless of politics, but RF Section worked to create a rebel force under de Gaulle's leadership.)

Jean Moulin's mission was to unite insurgency groups—the students, manual laborers, socialists, Communists, ex-military, police, Jews, subterranean newspapers, and escape lines—under one single Gaullist banner.

Moulin was uniquely qualified for the job. He had been a politician under Vichy, prefect of a *département,* when he was captured and tortured by Nazis. Despairing in his jail cell, afraid he would crack under pressure, he recited Hamlet's soliloquy—*Être, ou ne pas être?*—and attempted suicide by slashing his own throat. A guard stopped him just in time. The fanatical move secured Moulin's release. He was known thereafter for his raspy voice and for always wearing a scarf, branded for life for his anti-Hitler credentials.

When Moulin flew to France on behalf of de Gaulle in 1943, he united the Resistance, and competing rebel leaders mostly stepped aside. By that winter, some eighty thousand paramilitary members were coordinating, mobilizing, and organizing sabotage, helping Allied pilots travel back to England, escorting Jews across the Spanish border, forging false documents, distributing partisan newspapers, liberating POWs from detention camps, hiding weapons caches, and training teenagers to shoot a Nazi or blow up an oncoming train.

Between both F and RF Sections, command, coordination, and strategy in France would come together that winter. The partisans were enthusiastic for action, and organizers kept agitating for more than simple recruitment; they needed arms. Yet there was no regularity to the shipment of chocolate and grenades; RAF planes could not land enough agents or containers to satisfy an emerging secret army.

The rebellion had only just started to grow, and now it grew discouraged. When partisans joined up but there was no fight, the task of liberation felt futile, and the war seemed hopeless, as if the Reich's occupation of France would last ten times longer than a millennium.

The Resistance needed something to do.

March 22, 1943

AM BECOMING INCREASINGLY UNPOPULAR DUE TO BRITISH APPARENT INACTION AND INABILITY TO HELP THEM OVER LA RELEVE. I FIND MORALE LOW THE MEN RELUCTANT DO SERIOUS SABOTAGE. CAN START GUERILLA WARFARE WITH MEN UNWILLING TO LEAVE FOR A RELEVE IF YOU SUPPLY ARMS FOOD AND MONEY CONTINUOUSLY. PLEASE ADVISE.

March 23, 1943

AS FOR OPS THIS MOON WE ARE NOT IMPATIENT WE ARE DISGUSTED.

March 24, 1943

WE LACK GUNS AND BANGS DUE TO OPS NOT PERFORMED WEATHER REASON GIVEN OUR PEOPLE BUT I DO NOT DARE TO GUESS THE REAL REASON.

March 28, 1943

RUSH ALL ORDERS NEED MATERIAL URGENTLY. PROSPER.

March 28, 1943

OWING NO RECEPTIONS FEB MARCH SECURITY AND MORALE TEAMS FAILING RAPIDLY. NORMANDY GROUNDS MAY BE UNUSABLE APRIL OWING GERMAN HEADQUARTERS. FURTHER OPS DEPEND ON MARCH RECEPTIONS. CANNOT AGAIN RELY ON STALLING GERMAN. RELY ON YOUR CO-OPERATION AT ONCE. DISAPPOINTED. PROSPER.

CHAPTER 13

The Demolition Must Never Fail

Chaingy

Andrée Borrel bicycled in the countryside on an early-spring day in 1943. The air smelled of fresh dirt and wood fires. The fields were raw; last season's stubble was plowed under in neat, combed seed rows. Just below the soil, life was sprouting, awaiting the long days of summer.

The hills were not steep, and the country was inviting. On a new moon, when there was no luminary in the sky at night, no air missions could fly: It was a time for combat. Andrée thrilled to a day of physical activity, like any holiday excursion outside Paris before the war.

Chaingy was a strategic target. In a series of bombing raids, the RAF had attempted to blow up electricity exchanges in the area to cripple railways. From the air, the Allied bombers managed to cut a few power lines but "lost three or four planes" in the attack. Then, in the type of mob justice little seen in France since the Revolution, the Nazis found the fallen airmen and "left the bodies of the aviators [in the square] for four days which caused intense anger in the neighborhood."

Gilbert Norman coordinated a precise and rehearsed response. If Chaingy's power transformers came down, the knock-on effects would be titanic. Whereas coal-driven engines were still used on the national north-to-south railway, the routes bisecting the country from the

Atlantic coast to the Alps were electrified, and therefore vulnerable. The two thousand miles of high-voltage track were a perfect target for the Firm's sabotage operations. The plan was to cut off power at the source, at the stations, with a series of explosions.

Cutting power lines was an impermanent act of vandalism—electricity seldom went down for more than a day before it could be restored—but it interrupted the choreographed east-west movement of manpower and heavy equipment between Paris and the Atlantic coast to Hitler's Europe. The Nazis' war depended on supplies from France's industrial North: airplanes, engines, and trucks. The ancient soot-spewing coal-fired locomotives would still supply food to a starving country north to south; it was important not to turn citizens against an incipient resistance movement. Gilbert mapped out entrances and exits and calculated blast ratios. He "took up the hunt and made a reduced scale model on which practice charges were laid." Finally, when the first spring moon was dark, it was time to put Gilbert's plan into action.

Andrée pedaled past small farms with grace and ease. Her backpack was overstuffed, filled with bricks of explosives. "She hoisted it on her back as if it was a feather," her sister said. Three bricks of *plastique* were enough to blow up a truck; Andrée's rucksack could take out three trucks or at least a few electricity pylons. "She thought nothing of carrying it out of Paris, neither for its weight, nor for the danger it entailed. She enjoyed her work . . . she had found her métier."

Andrée cycled down tree-lined roads in the daylight. She was "a perfect lieutenant," Francis said, "an excellent organizer, who shares all the dangers."

Beside Andrée rode a colleague, a short and chatty man with whom she pretended to be "sweethearts" for the sake of a cover story. Gilbert was her boyfriend now, replacing Maurice Dufour, but in a conservative Catholic country it was helpful to have plausible reasons to be alone with a man, so she took on yet another lover, at least in show. As Andrée was told in training, "In our business, improvisation must be resorted to."

Andrée's bicycling companion was Jean Worms, who had worked with CARTE's southern network before the Firm recruited him and trained him in Britain. Worms was infiltrated back into France with a brand-new identity after a death sentence was set upon him for being "100 percent Jew." Jean only looked Jewish now—small, dark, and bespectacled—his forged identity card revealed nothing. He led an all-Jewish network in Paris that operated in parallel to Francis's PROSPER circuit. The Firm's policy on training Jews remained inconsistent: Jews could be game recruits for the fight against Hitler, but they were also a field liability—as noted in the case of Hélène Aron. Jean was judged worth the investment. He seemed to know everyone and had deep connections in banking and currency markets. Like an alley cat, he had survived many narrow escapes. Together, Andrée and Jean were to test yet another run of luck.

In an open field, far from town, Andrée dropped her bicycle into the long grass. The Jewish agent was not a naturally physical man, neither an athlete nor commanding, not like Francis and Gilbert, but Andrée and Jean nevertheless had much in common, a venomous hatred for the *Boches*. Jean's trainers noted, "He seems to have one aim in life: revenge." They walked like lovers, without hurry, without apparent care, toward three electric pylons in a field. The massive metal latticeworks carried high-voltage current.

Andrée shrugged off her rucksack at the base of a metal tower, removing slabs of explosives marked with the warning "Do not handle for long with bare hands or you will get a bad headache." Together with Jean's, there were "20-odd" charges all told. The standard charge was a one-and-a-half-pound block of pliable rubberlike explosive, with a tube of booster charge contained inside. The volatile blocks were wrapped in rubberized fabric and then strung along a length of Cordtex, a blistering bead on a giant necklace of destruction. Andrée taped charges to the base of the pylons at each of the legs, covering the breadth of the steel support so it would shear the metal. The breeze was perfumed with the strong chemical stench of almonds and axle grease.

For acts of sabotage, agents were repeatedly admonished, in textbooks and in classrooms,

THE DEMOLITION MUST NEVER FAIL.

All around the region, seven other teams, including Francis and Gilbert, were at that moment performing the same action on twenty-four other pylons carrying 300,000 volts each. Partisans were also laying charges along railroad tracks nearby.

Once Andrée set the charges under the towers, she removed a set of pliers from her bag and used it to crush a thin and hollow metal tube no bigger than a pencil fixed to the charges. The steps were drilled into Andrée in training: Squeeze the copper cylinder; shake it. Then repeat with a second cylinder. These were time-delayed detonators—known as time pencils—that would start the explosive reaction. When the end of the tube was crushed, a small glass vial of acid broke open inside; the corrosive liquid would, in time, erode a spring-loaded lead wire that connected to a striking pin. Once Andrée pulled out the safety tab that held back the strikers, the clock started ticking. If the first device didn't work, the second would.

The timer was set.

As the acid worked its way through the wire, eating away at the tension, the "loving pair" picked up their bicycles and returned to the road.

Andrée was barely two miles away and could still see the towers when the time pencil wires snapped. The striker dropped, hit the percussion caps, and then the Bangs began.

The field roared. White sparks flew toward the sky, like fingers of lightning stretching upward from the towers. It happened faster than the eye could process; explosions can grow at some twenty thousand feet per second. Nitrogen-containing molecules flew apart, separating from the rest, leaving water vapor behind, which expanded in a cloud of steam. Carbon dioxide and carbon monoxide inflated seemingly out of all proportion; excess oxygen molecules were set free. What had recently been sticky bricks of unharnessed energy was now a fire fifteen thousand times bigger than Andrée's rucksack. Black smoke enveloped the base of the pylons, glowing from the inside like the flame in a backed-up chimney. Then the gaseous expansion retreated on itself, curling toward the middle of the blast. A second set of explosions went off.

Andrée cycled away, listening for the concussions, checking over her shoulder, as calm as a girl on a picnic. The first pylon toppled and fell, bringing down wires with it. The second tower descended right after, ripping the high-voltage cables free and yanking them to the ground in a "sparking and spitting blue flame" that sent up flares until the power was cut.

But where was the third explosion? Andrée and Jean had set charges for three towers, and yet there were only two explosions, two gas balls, two clouds of black smoke. They were warned, "Incomplete detonation means incomplete destruction."

The demolition must never fail.

The last explosion did not go off. Something had gone wrong. But you could not circle back to double-check on terrorism.

Andrée kept pedaling, her backpack now light and empty. From across the field, she saw a Citroën speeding down the road toward the scene of her so-called crime.

She cycled onward toward safety and her alibi, always toward the kind of small and typical French village where "there were priests on bikes and little kids in black overalls, and the smell of bread."

IT WAS REPORTED that the third explosion went off some time later, when Andrée was already in hiding.

Three SS men exited the Citroën to inspect the crumpled base of the pylons. As they stood at the hot wreckage, the delayed bomb exploded. The chief officer got blown "to smithereens." Two other Germans were injured.

Death tolls were often exaggerated to bolster popular sentiment for the anti-German Resistance. The story of Andrée's demolition was repeated and retold, embellished by lieutenants who wished they had been there. But there was a core truth: a clear and growing pattern of coordinated and strategic assaults in France in the spring of 1943.

For the French, the period of waiting—*attentisme*—was nearing an end. For the first time, Andrée and Francis were beginning to feel that Europe was inching its way to freedom, as long as partisans could get a steady supply of weapons and explosives. Arms dumps were exhausted almost as soon as the canisters dropped into a dark field. "The record of achievement and of possibilities is so great but the record of assistance from this side [London]—particularly in the matter of supply—is so small. It is obvious that the [stakes are] big and it is to be hoped that the effort in the next few months will be sufficient to make up the leeway before it is too late," read an internal memo. The only limiting factor now was the availability of Bangs.

Baker Street ordered organizers to set aside at least some weapons in reserve for the upcoming summer invasion.

On Avenue Foch, *SS-Sturmbannführer* Bömelburg took notice.

The Nazi strategy of monitoring rather than intercepting "terrorists" was always a tense calculus. Early in the war, there was little downside to the Gestapo strategy of watch and wait. When resistance was small, fractured, and incompetent, the harm was localized and contained, but 1943 was the year the scale of damage multiplied throughout France, north and south. And by that spring, there were some four hundred rebels linked to the PROSPER networks, with as many as twenty thousand militia members ready to rise.

Between December 1942 and January 1943, some 282 German officers were killed by partisan activity, 14 trains were wrecked, 94 locomotives and 436 coaches were destroyed, 4 bridges went down, 26 trucks were destroyed, there were 12 major strategic fires, and 1,000 tons of food stores and fuel were destroyed.

The Resistance finally put up major wins on the board. "A train taking foodstuffs (wheat, hay, etc.) to Germany was set on fire and destroyed on leaving Paris," organizers reported. Ten "informers" of French nationality were "neutralized."

News even made it to the international papers. *The Times* of London reported that a troop train running eastward at top speed through Châlons was "blasted off the rails" at Chaingy—in the region of Andrée's demolition—killing over 250 German soldiers. The Allies broadcast to the world that there was successful opposition to Hitler within France and it was coalescing around de Gaulle.

Once spring arrived, Andrée, the RAF, and Baker Street hit their collective stride. Bombers took off on night raids, hammering French factories working for the Nazis with thousands of tons of high explosives: in Rennes, Rouen, Boulogne-Billancourt. The RAF Special Duties Squadrons unloaded agents and canisters into France with a newfound efficiency; there were guns to distribute and a secret army uniting behind de Gaulle that was at last armed by the Allies. "It was decided to call for sabotage immediately and on as large a scale as possible."

By April, the Paris-linked networks would commit sixty-three acts of sabotage. In Blois, where Yvonne Rudellat and Pierre Culioli worked, demolition teams derailed three troop trains, with 43 Germans killed and 110 wounded. According to a Baker Street report, "The rate of 'density' of sabotage has increased tremendously and we are now receiving almost daily reports from one sector or another."

At last, Andrée and her colleagues were succeeding in the fight for France.

The western front might open in a matter of weeks.

As coordinated attacks grew increasingly costly, Major Bömelburg began paying closer attention to Andrée and the PROSPER network.

CHAPTER 14

An Obstinate Woman

Paris

André Marsac was a lanky man; his days in Fresnes Prison were organized around the sound of squeaky metal-wheeled carts: One cart came in the morning to deliver coffee and bread through a so-called Judas slot in the door; the second cart rolled around at night bringing a thin broth that no Frenchman would consider soup. It was sufficient to keep a man alive, but barely.

Behind the yellow brick walls of the prison, in the network of narrow cell blocks stacked one atop the other, Marsac was one of two thousand political prisoners in the spring of 1943—captive members of the Resistance.

History's clock stopped for the denizens of the dark turrets and barred passageways. They were held in squalor, waiting to be summoned for questioning or transported to Germany for the long and indefinite duration of the war.

The courier who lost a suitcase while sleeping on a train, Marsac, lieutenant to CARTE, had been betrayed in a café while trying to restore lines of communication between Marseilles and Paris, cobbling a rebellion out of the Riviera network's rubble.

Now at Fresnes, guards escorted him down stairs, through tunnels, to an interrogation room where he was seated opposite his arresting officer, Sergeant Hugo Bleicher, an agent of the Abwehr, the intelligence service of the German army.

Sergeant Bleicher lived to extinguish the Resistance. He was a dandy. Balding and slight, he adored Parisian fashion, wore bespoke suits, hand-hewn shoes, and round, horn-rimmed glasses. He spoke fluent French, and in the interrogation room he recited his list of questions: What was Marsac's role in the British organization known as CARTE? What were his duties? Who were his colleagues? Their code names? Where was the Riviera underground headquartered?

For three days after his arrest, Marsac refused to answer.

By Bleicher's third visit, however, the young and "imprudent" Marsac began to speak, just a slight back-and-forth, repeating a personal history he assumed the Abwehr had already gleaned: He had fought in the army for France against the blitzkrieg.

Bleicher caught the tidbit—Marsac said he was a former soldier—and launched a natural follow-up: How might the humiliation of France inspire his commitment to the underground?

Marsac "shut up like a trap." He held other agents' fates in his hands, and he wanted to give nothing away that might compromise his colleagues. The network had just moved from the coast to the mountains near Annecy; Marsac had worked with Odette and Peter.

From his offices at the Hôtel Lutetia, Bleicher returned to Fresnes daily, plying his prisoner with gifts, wooing with excellent French grammar, good tobacco, and generous, fatty, fulsome, black market Parisian food. As part of the dance, Bleicher described his own war experiences. He had been a prisoner of the British during the Great War, captured crossing enemy lines while wearing a British uniform. Jailed as a POW "not only with handcuffs on his wrists, but manacles on his ankles"; it was an insult. After the war, Bleicher clerked at a chemical firm in the wealthy port city of Hamburg, until the crash and the war in Spain ruined the business. He signed on to become a civil servant, a censor, and claimed he was shocked to discover that he had in fact enlisted in the Wehrmacht. When Hitler launched the invasion of Poland in the summer of 1939, Bleicher was called up, not as a government reader, but as a counterintelligence agent in the Abwehr.

Bleicher was hired as an insignificant bureaucrat, tallying denunciations, corralling working-age boys who hid in the homes of their grandmothers, generating paperwork to satisfy a Teutonic need for documentation. But to everyone's surprise except his own he rose to stardom, capturing more than sixty British-affiliated partisans and rewarding himself with a "requisitioned" flat in the posh 16th arrondissement.

Bleicher worked by flattery. He used his affability to win his prisoners' confidence and performed the same speech to all his victims: He opposed Hitler, who was a megalomaniac; the recent loss in Stalingrad proved it was time for Germany to sue for peace. He was a patriot, but that did not mean he supported Adolf's war.

Marsac blinked to attention. He had visited Germany once, he said, and went drinking with a bunch of small-time local Nazi Party bosses; they were boorish and loud. "I cannot believe that the Germans are happy under such a debased regime."

Out of the slightest agreement between prisoner and captor, rebel movements can fall. Bleicher pried a little from his prisoner every day. Marsac was a good catch—he knew where the rebel shoals were—but there were bigger fish, leaders trained in spy craft in England, who answered to Allied commanders, who knew details of the incipient invasion of France.

As Marsac grew comfortable with his German jailer, he believed he might be able to seduce Bleicher. "Can't we arrange this between ourselves?" Marsac pleaded. He had access to the network's funds and understood the power of wealth to change a man's mind. Could Bleicher be bought for one million francs? There was a hotel in the Latin Quarter; the German should tell the concierge that he was there to collect Marsac's belongings from room 13, and there he would find a suitcase with one million francs in addition to four radio crystals tuned to frequencies in London. Bleicher could take the cash, lob the crystals in the Seine, and let Marsac go free.

Bleicher bargained: One million francs is very nice, but liberating a prisoner from the catacombs of Fresnes was all but impossible under a regime that fetishized paperwork. It would be the end of Bleicher's splendid career to spring Marsac for money alone.

So Marsac sweetened the deal. The raw value of names was not new to him: The previous autumn, asleep on a train, he had lost the entire CARTE roster. He knew more details now, real names as well as noms de guerre, addresses for arms dumps, coordinates for landing grounds, the locations of bridges to be blown, and the BBC signals to launch the attacks.

More than British cash and rebel addresses, the jewel for Bleicher was Marsac's connection to England.

"I would be in a position to get you to London at any time," Marsac offered.

Bleicher's ego dictated his terms. He demanded a flight to London. He wanted an air pickup as an agent for peace, fantasizing he might gain an audience with Prime Minister Churchill. The deputy führer, Rudolf Hess, proposed something similar when he parachuted into Scotland in 1941. But where Hess was high ranking and putatively sought a cease-fire ahead of the Soviet invasion, Bleicher was an enlisted man; his scheme was to use Marsac's offer to double-cross the Allies, return priceless intelligence to his Wehrmacht commanders, and become a German national hero.

"But I must proceed carefully," said Bleicher. "Who guarantees that nothing happens to me in London?"

Marsac promised he would not be harmed.

The negotiation was comic: Marsac was all bluff. He could deliver no such thing without Baker Street's approval, and in jail he was not in a position to get it.

"Do you really believe, Marsac, that your people can keep out of our clutches for long? If we have succeeded in getting you, it will be easy to catch the smaller fry, one by one," Bleicher threatened. "We have now occupied the whole of France. Most of your comrades are under observation already . . . and it is probably no secret to you that many are working both sides."

In a dark interrogation room in a prison from which there was no escape, an agreement was fixed: One million francs. Safe passage to England. A radio and a set of Allied codes. And a list of arms caches, landing grounds, and British officers.

"But I can give my word they will not be treated as spies," Bleicher assured him. "They will be regarded as prisoners of war."

André Marsac wrote two letters: one to his wife, and one to the British networks. He introduced Sergeant Bleicher, whom he called Colonel Henri, his old friend. The sergeant savored the thought of a possible trip to London: "My success surprised me."

For the second time in six months, Marsac surrendered his secrets to Hitler—among them, the location of a new rebel hideout in the Alps where Odette was now living with Peter.

Spring was just arriving on the shores of Lake Annecy. The Rhône Alps were kaleidoscopes of magnolia, azalea, and pear blossoms. Annecy was a resort town of winding canals and red-roofed medieval buildings, an Alpine Venice. In peacetime, the region was both a park and a playground, a stylish retreat for skiers in winter, a beach resort in summer. But bourgeois holidaymakers were scarce in the spring of 1943.

Chalets dotted the foothills. The Alps rose from a mirror of glacial waters, snowcapped and looming like an occupying force, magnificent in the spring sunlight.

Like guerrillas the world over, Odette hid in the mountains. In the aftermath of CARTE, her remit was to impose structure and safety on the loosely banded southern networks. She left Cannes for the hills almost a month after she arrived and had been working as a courier for Peter the whole time. Together they accomplished little—there were few airdrops and no sabotage of note—yet they were alive, and that was no small feat. Peter got recalled to London to rehash his arguments with CARTE's former leader, André Girard—summoned by Baker Street in an effort to negotiate a truce between secret soldiers.

Odette lived on the road to Annecy, at the Hôtel de la Poste, one of the countless stucco-and-wood lodges littering the mountain roads. The four-corner village of Saint-Jorioz was only a ten-minute bicycle ride to the lake; she could hide there in plain sight. She was near train tracks—crucial for trips to and from the coast—close to the hills and to the beach, with plenty of opportunities to blend in or to get away, if need be. The hotel was closed for the season, but the proprietors, a sweet couple, allowed her to stay, in full knowledge of what Odette was doing and what danger it brought.

The Hôtel de la Poste was the calm center of a circuit that had descended into chaos. The Riviera networks splintered after the CARTE leadership went to war with itself. Where regular troops must follow a chain of command, dissidents and partisans are no tidy force. Add to the mix the French tendency to resist authority in general and the English in particular, and it was a powder keg. When arguments broke out, Odette was given orders to tie everything up connected to the network and await a new assignment.

She was staying until the April moon, when Peter was scheduled to return to France. He had been gone a month. As Peter briefed Baker Street, Odette counted the days until their impassioned reunion.

Odette lived in seclusion, far from the stone-faced German invaders of Marseilles, but as she pedaled her bicycle through the mountains—now like an expert—evidence of a three-year war was everywhere: With husbands, brothers, and sons away, farms were managed by mothers, children, and old men. What cows were left marched alone from hay barns to the high Alpine meadows. Under rationing, the many thousands of francs she carried were often worthless compared with barter items such as tobacco and sugar—which fell from the sky in containers, with any luck.

The BBC signals from London still got through to the mountains each night with news of hope, triumph, and tragedy: The Nazi general Rommel made a quixotic stand against the Allied generals Patton and Montgomery in the desert; in Warsaw, an extermination began in the ghetto. In the days surrounding the equinox, there was a tender balance between forces, the dark and the light.

One morning in early April after an appointment in Annecy, as Odette returned to Saint-Jorioz on the bus, she saw "a very strange looking man." He was drawn, with "prominent veins," a "puffy red face," and thinning black hair, and dressed like a parvenu.

The foreigner likewise took note of Odette: He considered her eyes "dark and sparkling." He already knew who she was; he had learned everything from his prisoner André Marsac in Fresnes.

Odette got off the bus, and the strange man alit at her stop. He walked to a villa down the road where several members of CARTE then lived as one big happy—and all too obvious—family, "ten or fifteen young people who did not look at all like country folk." Locals believed they were Jewish refugees, which was marginally better than a group of rebels arming the neighborhood, albeit not by much.

The Alps were an ideal home for partisans. The steep slopes and dark caves were good places to hide. Young men fled there to avoid forced labor. Annecy city clerks sometimes gave rebels and Jews new travel documents and identity cards. With hiking trails to Switzerland, furtive travelers could climb the high passes toward freedom, if the Swiss did not turn them away, as they did so many Jews.

The rebels now called themselves the maquis—the Corsican word for a stubborn and dry evergreen scrub, native to the Mediterranean coast of France. The partisans could be just as thorny, hardy, and dangerous. A recruiting leaflet read,

> Men who come to fight live badly, in precarious fashion, with food hard to find. They will be absolutely cut off from their families for the duration; the enemy does not apply the rules of war to them; they cannot be assured any pay; all correspondence is forbidden.

The maquis toughed it out in the limestone peaks, eager for each pending drop of Allied guns, impatient for the advent of the flotilla so they could fight for France.

Odette observed the dapper stranger from the Hôtel de la Poste's terraced gardens, where bulbs planted before the invasion—daffodils and tulips—were poking up in optimistic bloom. Though the hotel was technically closed, the restaurant fed locals with staunch mountain food. The man ordered a sweet omelet with sugar and jam; he enjoyed it so much he asked for a second while chatting up Odette's rebel colleagues.

The peculiar German seemed to have made fast friends with Odette's maquis. One British agent joined the group, "talking in a very silly way and in a rather loud voice about their work." It was an appalling breach of security.

Odette had taken charge of the network when Peter left for England. When she saw the conversation between the agent and the strange man, she dressed down the Briton, who responded with an eye roll and shrug. Circuit members did not support Odette; they thought she was just some honeypot courier, sleeping her way to the top of the organization. The little German sat silent and still; he looked at Odette "very hard and smiled."

He was "quite all right," the British agent told Odette. He was Gestapo, but a friend, not some Nazi maniac. He produced the letter from André Marsac, in prison in Paris, which introduced Colonel Henri.

"I would bless the day of my arrest if my ambitions are realized," Marsac wrote. If Odette would kindly radio Baker Street for an aircraft pickup, Colonel Henri would arrange for Marsac's manumission. The colonel would tell the War Cabinet about secret details of Hitler's Atlantic Wall ahead of the approaching landings. He would establish a German government in exile—much like de Gaulle's—and negotiate a lasting peace with Winston Churchill, provided, that is, he was not jailed as a war criminal like Rudolf Hess. Could Odette please communicate this deal to the War Office? the maquis asked. Colonel Henri would single-handedly bring peace to Europe.

Odette's undercover world was full of double-crossing amateurs, fantasists, eccentrics, and misfits, each with a plausible enough story, so why not a defecting German colonel too? He might be as good as his word, but any letter from prison was written under duress and was itself coercive; from her training at Beaulieu, she knew Marsac had likely flipped in jail.

Odette said she was in no position to make such a request. The plan was stupid, traitorous, perhaps both. The circuit wanted to free Marsac, but she insisted they drop the scheme. Colonel Henri was not the one Nazi in all of Europe who could be trusted; there was no such thing. What kind of idiot volunteers to work alongside an officer of the Abwehr?

The rebels, loyal to Marsac over Odette, threatened to leave for Paris on the next train. It was mutiny.

CYCLING INTO THE mountains overlooking Lake Annecy, Odette could see her breath in thick plumes of steam. She biked toward a secret safe house where her radio operator, Adolphe Rabinovitch, was staying. A surly Russian-Egyptian Jew, Rabinovitch swore like a sailor when Odette explained her chance meeting with Marsac's so-called friend, Colonel Henri. She had a detailed report for London, which Adolphe coded in disgust for the security breaches it contained. He took pains to transpose details of the colonel, of Marsac's arrest, his letter, the proposed air pickup, the negotiations with the prime minister, the peace plan. Rabinovitch sent news that, by Colonel Henri's own account, once the British bomber was summoned to the Alps to collect him, the war was practically won.

The Russian radio operator had a temper more expansive than his vocabulary for genitalia. When Rabinovitch heard the deputies were off to Paris to see Marsac in jail, he grabbed a pistol and said he would kill the men in Annecy if they boarded a train to Paris.

Odette pedaled back to Saint-Jorioz alone, hoping to calm the sedition. She let the insubordinate maquis know that Colonel Henri's request was transmitted to Baker Street and the German could expect a flight on the April full moon, around the eighteenth, only a matter of days.

It was a lie. The Firm's response included no such pickup offers:

```
HENRI HIGHLY DANGEROUS STOP YOU ARE TO HIDE
ACROSS LAKE AND CUT CONTACTS WITH ALL SAVE
ARNAUD [Rabinovitch] WHO MUST QUIT FAVERGES
AND LIVE BESIDE HIS MOUNTAIN SET STOP.
```

London said it was a trap. Go to ground. Disappear. She was blown. With Colonel Henri on the scene, Baker Street demanded Odette end her relationship with the Saint-Jorioz operation, except for the radio operator. Wrap everything up, find an isolated hideout, and await future instructions.

But Odette refused to leave the area until Peter was infiltrated back to France. Of her own obstinate choice, she remained at the Hôtel de la Poste, defying direct orders from London.

On April 14, 1943, the BBC French-language evening broadcast ended as it always did, in a stream of silliness and buried cryptograms:

The gold bug must do his spring cleaning.

It was the prearranged sentence Rabinovitch had set with Baker Street, an oblique reference to an Edgar Allan Poe story about secret codes and the signal for an incoming reception: Peter was on his way.

Peter was instructed to avoid Odette at all costs on his return. Baker Street briefed him: Marsac was under arrest. Colonel Henri was on her trail. Any contact risked Peter's life as well as what was left of the Riviera networks. Odette was contaminated. Peter had no idea she would ignore Baker Street's explicit instructions.

On a moonlit plateau above Lake Annecy, six thousand feet high, at 12:10 a.m., an RAF bomber buzzed the Semnoz peak. The bay doors opened, and Peter's parachute swelled into a black balloon against the silver sky.

Odette was waiting for him. She stood in a snowy field, her face turned toward the stars. As Peter wafted into the pine-scented clearing, his touchdown was slowed by a gust of wind. Hovering just above the ground, he spoke to Odette for the first time in a month: "If you take a step back, I shan't land on your head."

Odette threw up her arms, as if to catch him.

THE FOLLOWING DAY was a frenzy of action: Saint-Jorioz was a target. Odette and Peter had to flee. Hiking down from the mountain by 8:00 a.m., they scouted a new hideout across the lake. Together they cycled into the hills to collect messages from Rabinovitch, sending him packing as well. It would be Peter and Odette's last night in the Hôtel de la Poste; they would be out by first light.

At 11:00 p.m., drained from the parachute operation and a day on the move by foot, boat, and bicycle, Odette undressed in the bedroom she shared with Peter.

There was a knock at the door; it was the hotel proprietor and his wife. "There is a strange man downstairs, who says that Henri is talking in Paris."

Peter thought it was a terrible idea to investigate, but Odette disagreed. The proprietor was a friend to the maquis. "My reflex action at this moment was absolutely nil," Peter recalled.

He put his head on the pillow and was out.

As Odette reached the bottom of the stairs, she saw Colonel Henri. He stepped forward, flanked by Italian soldiers and counterintelligence officers in street clothes. One German was tall, thin, and blond, very jumpy, the other short, dark, and slow, with a Belgian accent and a slouchy hat pulled over his eyes and scarf up around his face. There was no escape, Henri said, offering a hand to Odette, which she did not take.

He acted wounded by the rebuff. "I think a lot of you," he said.

Odette did not care what he thought.

In the lobby of the hotel, the colonel was solicitous. "You have done a very good job . . . and you almost won the game," he said, but Marsac's friends talked too much. "It is not your fault you lost."

Odette paused: What options did she have? Where were the doors? What would happen if she screamed?

The tall officer stepped forward and shoved a pistol in her back. There were no moves. Had she raised an alarm, Peter would have jumped out the window to a cordon of Italian soldiers surrounding the property.

She marched up the stairs.

"There is the Gestapo," she said.

Colonel Henri and his companions threw on the lights.

Peter awoke to the barrel of a revolver. Asked his name, he instinctively used his cover: Chambrun.

"Your other names are Raoul and Captain Churchill and you are nothing more than a saboteur," Colonel Henri said. "And anyway, I can hear your English accent."

Odette cursed at the colonel as if she were raised in a dockyard—as if she worked side by side with Adolphe Rabinovitch. Peter ordered her to stop speaking.

They were both told to get dressed.

As the tall man searched the room, Odette lifted Peter's winter coat off the bed and laid down his suit jacket in its place. His coat was long and boxy, with a fur collar and a breast-side inner pocket in which he kept his wallet. Hugging it close to her body, folded over her arms, she slipped Peter's billfold out and into the sleeve of her own coat. The wallet held his forged identity card, seventy thousand francs, and five incriminating messages decoded by Rabinovitch. The texts were orders for the maquis in the mountains. Peter saw the sly substitution and donned his suit jacket instead.

Do you want to go with the Germans or the Italians? Colonel Henri asked.

Peter said he would sooner be arrested by Italians.

Odette moved around the room collecting things a man might need in prison—shirts, socks, soap, the overcoat. Peter would later remember that she "went about it as though she had rehearsed the scene her entire life."

The soldiers, meanwhile, found Peter's diary, complete with names and numbers of other network members, including the agent Virginia Hall's. Peter used aliases, noms de guerre, their "war names," but he had been taught not to write anything down at all. Yet he had trouble memorizing the long telephone codes for France; he was still the shirker, even at war. It could have been worse: Upon landing, Peter also left his suitcase with the hotel proprietor for safekeeping; it contained his revolver, another one million francs, his parachuting gear, and the decoded text of more than thirty messages exchanged between his network and London while he was away. The diary was enough for Colonel Henri; it contained long threads tying together rebel cells across the whole of France.

As Odette ducked into the backseat of a green car, she caught her stocking on the car door. It was deliberate. Reaching back around to unhook her hose, she slipped Peter's wallet out from her sleeve and tucked it between the cushions of the car seat.

"Take good care of these two," the colonel said to the Italian soldiers. "We can't afford to lose them."

CHAPTER 15

An Endless Calvary

France

Odette and Peter were moved together, from cell to cell, jurisdiction to jurisdiction, through the Alps to ever larger and more secure prisons—Grenoble, Turin, Vichy, Nice—on their way to Paris and Fresnes. They were prisoners, living and sleeping alone in fusty cells on straw mattresses but seeing each other at moments of transition and travel. Each point of transfer was an opportunity; any stray moment could be an escape, a play for freedom, the difference between life and death. Had Peter been captured alone, he figured he might have made a break for it; he was the more experienced agent, and other men had escaped the Nazi net in such moments. But he was less sure of Odette's chances. Instead, the couple remained together, stealing sighs and cherishing small glances. Now and again the guards allowed them to pass notes. Peter sent messages "as a man would to a woman he loved"; romance appealed to the Italian jailers. These brief encounters were enough to sustain them through long days of captive worry.

After three weeks, on May 7, 1943, on a train from Marseilles to Paris the two were seated together, with time to speak privately, "as much as we liked," Peter recalled. His face was cut and bruised from scrapping with the Italian police; one foolish night, despite his chivalrous intentions toward Odette, he tried to punch his way to freedom as he was offered a cigarette. When the *Alpini* attacked in response, they had not called him by his code name, Raoul, nor used the names on his papers, Pierre, but shouted his true Christian name while delivering the blows: Peter Churchill. In a drunken rage, they beat him beyond bloody recognition with the butts of their rifles, landing blows they said were intended for the man they believed to be his uncle, Prime Minister Winston Churchill. They broke his nose, his ribs, and two fingers; his face was cut and his eyes were swollen shut. They did not question him.

Peter was cuffed at the wrists and ankles. After his attempted escape, he was considered a threat. His glasses and shoes were taken away. He told Odette he would rather be dead than in jail; he wished he had been killed when he was caught.

Odette was outraged. "As long as there is life, there is hope," she said.

In dejection, Peter said it was ridiculous to have any hope at all; this was the end of the line. She filled his pockets with the butts of half-smoked cigarettes hoarded from prison guards; she placed boiled eggs into his bag like a mother packing a lunch.

"It was I who told them your real name," she whispered to Peter immediately after his fight. Odette gave up his identity on the night they were arrested. Her instinct for high drama and self-aggrandizement was an asset for a cornered agent. She had concocted a story that she hoped the Nazis would believe: that Peter was Winston Churchill's nephew and that she was Peter's wife, Odette Churchill. The gambit seemed to be working if the Italians had indeed landed blows on the prime minister's behalf. It gave Odette courage; perhaps the lie would hold once they were transferred to the Gestapo's command, for, as she said of Nazi convictions about the master race, "the Germans are the most frightful snobs."

"I always thought it rather a dangerous name to travel under these days," Peter replied. In fact, his relationship to Winston Churchill, he believed, was "sixty-second cousin."

"Wrong psychology altogether," Odette said. She reasoned it was better to be a high-value diplomatic prisoner who might possibly command the attention of world leaders and international press than an irregular soldier with no protections under the laws of war. She bet their lives on it.

Once the Winston Churchill fib was told, it had to be believable. They had not been thoroughly interrogated while the transfer of ownership moved from the Italian police to the French to the Germans. They had to nail down a story: They decided to say they were married on December 24, 1941, Christmas Eve, in a registrar's office on Baker Street. The marriage was witnessed by Odette's aunt and Peter's younger brother, Oliver, in uniform, also on his way to war. In their brief time together before guards separated them, they traded names and addresses of each other's relatives, questioned and rehearsed each other's backstories, exchanged the prosaic details of a married life. They took an oath, its own sort of marriage vow, to maintain their fictive partnership until the bitter end, whatever form that might take.

"If I ever get the chance, I shall ask you if you'd care to make it a lifetime measure," Peter told her. Odette was already married to Roy Sansom, the father of her three girls. But she was in love with Peter.

She promised that every night at 6:00 she would remember Peter; it would be a kind of prayer.

On May 8, 1943, Odette and Peter arrived in Paris, at Fresnes Prison, the home for political enemies of the Reich and other undesirables. They were in Colonel Henri's—or, rather, Sergeant Bleicher's—jurisdiction now.

In Fresnes, Odette and Peter were starved, lonely, afraid, and Odette swiftly grew ill. Days stretched ahead in agonizing terror, said Peter, "an endless Calvary."

There were no clocks in Fresnes. No church bells rang through the prison yard. Through a single window in their cells, they watched the arc of shadows play against the walls, and at what seemed like 6:00 every night, each stopped to think of the other.

———

At 84 Avenue Foch, Sergeant Hugo Bleicher ascended a swirling staircase in smart civilian clothes, au courant in a city where no one but Nazis or collaborators owned anything new. He gave an obligatory "*Sieg Heil*" upon entering the office of the head of the Gestapo in Paris, *SS-Sturmbannführer* Karl Bömelburg.

Major Bömelburg raised his right hand and locked his elbow for the *Hitlergruss;* a black diamond on his sleeve boasted an embroidered wire emblem that read *SD,* for *Sicherheitsdienst.*

The two men could not have been more dissimilar. Bleicher was a middling but self-professed intellectual serving as an enlisted man in his second war, a diligent functionary who had yet to rise above sergeant. Bömelburg was known to all as a lion of the Reich, a career soldier, and a devout Nazi whose professional fortunes rose with the grandeur of the führer. Wearing the death's-head skull and crossbones—*der Totenkopf*—on his peaked cap, he was stiff and handsome in belted tunic, riding pants, and high leather boots. When the colonel met the younger officer in street dress, it was with an air of agitation.

That there was an audience at all between the two testified to the seriousness of Bömelburg's concerns about the tinderbox that was Paris in 1943. The sergeant's star was on the rise; despite his modest rank, he had a string of successes to his credit, including the newest feather in his beret, the capture of the CARTE lieutenant André Marsac, who "flipped" at Fresnes Prison. The dragnet that followed had resulted in the arrest of a valued prisoner—a bargaining chip, who would claim the attention of Allied political leaders: the nephew of the prime minister and his pretty young wife. In Berlin, it was suggested the couple might be worth a swap for the prize inmate of the British Isles, Rudolf Hess, Hitler's dearest friend. Bleicher's success had an unexpected consequence: He came to the attention of the German leadership in Paris.

The senior officer took the measure of the junior and gave a direct order: Stop your work with the British underground. Give up the double cross entirely. Hold off on every arrest. Now.

The meeting between Major Bömelburg and Sergeant Bleicher was, in fact, a showdown between party and country, between Hitler loyalists and German patriots. Ending resistance in France was the shared goal of the two men, but they did not answer to the same organization. While both served in intelligence and sought to snuff out rebellion in all its forms, the elder officer was chief of the Paris Gestapo and belonged to the Nazi Party's independent economic and military state within a state known as the SS, the *Schutzstaffel*.

Sergeant Bleicher, by contrast, worked for the German army. He was an underling in the Abwehr, in military counterespionage. The Abwehr was a Wehrmacht holdover from the days of the kaiser. It sustained a nineteenth-century soldierly conceit while in service to a psychopath. Bleicher was loyal to the army, to Germany, and not necessarily to Adolf Hitler.

The Gestapo and the Abwehr were bitter rivals. Where the Abwehr was cold and militaristic, the Gestapo was inhumane. Paris saw an administrative tangle of government-sanctioned atrocities, and with so many professional spy hunters rooting out espionage and sabotage, the varied intelligence services got in each other's way. "The exact nature of the [Nazi] party organization that was fighting SOE was complicated enough to baffle a theologian," said the official French Section historian.

Bömelburg expected obedience. He might concede that the recent arrest of Marsac was well played, the follow-on capture of the Churchill nephew a glorious accident, but Bleicher had to stop recruiting for his double cross. His scheme for the army took manpower and resources away from the SS and Bömelburg's most ambitious plans: to determine the date of the invasion.

Bleicher thought small and was small, whereas Bömelburg was a master strategist with an agent of his own, named BOE48, the forty-eighth secret agent of the Paris Gestapo. The information gathered by BOE48 was vital to the war effort, kept under lock and key in a safe in Avenue Foch. Through this single source, it would be possible to discern critical intelligence about the Allied assault on France many weeks—if not months—ahead of a landing. According to various reports, Bömelburg was offering four million francs to learn the location and time of the Allied attack. He hunted the most critical piece of military intelligence in the war. Bleicher's trivial spy games and incidental arrests kept bumping up against the movements of BOE48, embedded deep in the Paris Resistance. Nothing must interfere with the goals of the thousand-year Reich.

The order was clear and it was also a threat. It would not have gone unnoticed that Sergeant Bleicher misrepresented himself to the rebels as a higher-ranked colonel; he told them that he opposed Hitler, whom he called a tyrant, and said that he thought Germany should win the war without the Nazi Party, that there should be an amenable peace between powers rather than a persistent war premised on the ravings of a cult leader.

Such statements were treason. Bleicher could say it was all a con, an act, a way of lulling the enemy into a false sense of trust. But he couldn't escape the fact that the Abwehr represented a legitimate threat to the Nazi Party. (Bleicher's rant mirrored an institutional position: The Abwehr's commander, Admiral Wilhelm Canaris, was at that moment making secret peace feelers to the Allies, and in little over a year's time Abwehr officers would try to assassinate Adolf Hitler, using weapons collected from British parachute operations.)

Any soldier would be a fool to move against a senior Nazi official with the party record and corporate authority of *SS-Sturmbannführer* Karl Bömelburg, chief of the Paris Gestapo. Yet the elder officer was nearing sixty, about to age out of the position. He would be replaced. His power was on the wane.

It could only have given Hugo Bleicher a tremendous sense of gratification to disobey.

After two weeks in Fresnes Prison, Odette was brought to 84 Avenue Foch, the palace intended for gentlemen and diplomats, full of fine wine and Nazis.

She was marched upstairs to the top floor, to a small office. The officer in charge looked German, solid, and northern; he did not speak to Odette. He was there to oversee but not (apparently) to understand, as he spoke no French.

A second man entered the office. He wore civilian clothes and took his seat at a desk. He would be her interrogator.

In educated French, accented with hard *k*'s, like a Lorrainer, the interrogator began his practiced script of questions and set pieces. Each time he spoke, typewriter keys responded at speed to take down the information in carbon "quintuplicate."

The Nazi summation of Odette's story was read aloud: She was married to Peter Churchill, and her husband was a nephew to the prime minister. Her radio operator was Adolphe Rabinovitch, they said, so where was he hiding? The Germans had knowledge of her organization, stacks of single-spaced pages detailing the operation, letters from Peter Churchill to his network. The name CARTE kept popping up, as well as the name Marsac. The source of betrayal was soon obvious to Odette.

Odette was called to account for each moment of her mission. What day did she arrive in France? What became of the other passengers on her felucca, and where was the agent Mary Herbert?

The interrogator preyed on Odette's fears, those of a woman who had gotten her lover arrested and now might never see him again. They did not know she was also a mother, who might never see her babies again. Odette was prepared for the confrontation. She role-played her own capture during training at Beaulieu and many more times in her mind. She knew that the Nazis were not her friends, that their courtesies were not reliable. She had been taught to answer promptly and simply, if she was forced to speak at all, to provide information as close to the truth as she could without giving up essentials; elaborate lies unravel under hours of questioning. She knew not to bargain, beg, or concede any detail that could betray another agent, for though she and Peter were captured, Rabinovitch was free and transmitting to London, a precious and essential lifeline to the maquis with the Allied landing on the way. His continued safety, not her own, was the only outcome Odette could effect.

In the midst of her interrogation, Odette grew meditative, withdrawing into her thoughts. Her lifetime of displacement and make-believe, of wishing herself into adventure, became a weapon in a war of minds: She knew she could endure, like Joan of Arc. *If they kill me, they will kill me physically but that's all, that will not mean anything. What's the point? They will have a dead body, useless to them, but they will not have me because I will not let them have me,* she thought. In that moment, Odette believed she was granted "grace."

The interviewer treated her with disdain: She was a woman, a terrorist, a conquered Frenchwoman, and an enemy Briton. He walked Odette to the window overlooking the verdant Parisian boulevard below. "Have a look at those happy people outside!"

It was spring. Paris was a daily mix of wet and dry, chill and warm. Over aluminum rooftops, bright sun broke between gray clouds, sometimes by the hour. The women in the gardens of Avenue Foch looked gay in their coats and dresses, ambling to the Bois. The gap between their freedom and Odette's captivity was intended to wound. The German seemed to be making an offer, a bargain.

"Are you doing this for money?" he asked.

It was for love of country, said Odette.

A pity, the commander replied. The investigator seemed bored, dismissive.

There are ways and means of making a woman speak, the man said, summoning an underling, a younger man who was French, with "very beautiful eyes," who had an educated Parisian accent and smelled, Odette would remember, like soap and eau de cologne.

Little more than a teenager, the young man reached in front of Odette to unbutton her blouse. She shoved his hand aside and undressed on his behalf. A second soldier kneeled near Odette and held her hands together behind the chair.

She was unable to move. The young Parisian with the pretty eyes took something hot—a poker from the fire, a cigarette, she had no idea—and pressed it to her back, right between her shoulder blades.

The stench of burning flesh rose to her nostrils, mingling with the soapy scent of the boy torturer.

———

On the door of Odette Sansom's cell at Fresnes, there was a sign: "*Grand Criminel Pas de Privilège*"; she was to be held in secrecy, without privileges. "You would have thought I was the most dangerous woman ever," she recalled.

The alleged Mrs. Churchill arranged rituals to make her prison days pass: Each morning she shifted her skirt by one inch around her waist, to make it feel new, as if she were putting on a clean outfit. When her stockings fell to shreds and tatters, she used the scraps to curl up her hair at night. Odette's body, however, betrayed her rituals and fictions of hygiene: She was sick and growing delusional; the burn on her back was a weeping sore; she had a painful swelling on her neck that kept her awake and sapped her spirit; tuberculosis was spreading throughout her lungs. But she said, "If I am going to die I want my hair to look nice."

In interviews with Odette, Sergeant Bleicher tried to cajole her into friendship; he dangled meetings with Peter as rewards for complicity, proffered concerts, baths, and packages of food. She never gave up the location of her radio operator, Adolphe Rabinovitch. When she disobeyed Baker Street's orders and greeted Peter after his return from London, she had endangered his life with that heedless affection; now she could save other agents with her silence.

Bleicher told Odette that he was arranging a swap—Peter Churchill for Rudolf Hess—and that Odette was no part of the deal. Peter was ready to let her rot, he said, playing his prisoner against the man he believed was her husband. Odette did not flinch; she did not respond at all.

"Of course you don't love [Peter], it cannot be?" Bleicher asked, then made a proposition: Odette would be better off working with him, her Nazi jailer, as his girlfriend.

Odette declined.

Peter was a lucky man, Bleicher said. She didn't belong in prison, and he would do "any little thing" that might please her. It was an odd seduction: The German was confessional about his hatred for the Nazi regime. At the same time, he was probing and personal, like "visiting a psychiatrist."

Odette accepted only his cigarettes.

"You are not the sort of person who would wear dirty clothes like that," he said of the outfit in which Odette was arrested, her thin blouse and dingy skirt. "Do let me have one of your blouses and I will get it washed for you."

She was better off under his protection, he cautioned, under the jurisdiction of the Abwehr. The Gestapo, by contrast, were sadists. If she fell under the Nazi Party's dominion, he could no longer protect her. But Bleicher's protection did not amount to much. She was being tortured regardless, and her confinement was destroying her. Officials at Fresnes requested permission for Odette to see a doctor, but the Nazi commanders said no: Medical care was rationed, reserved for prisoners "in danger of death." As she grew frail, she was moved to a communal cell, where other prisoners took pity on her desperation. "Her weakness was extreme: she could no longer even eat the small amount of filthy and repugnant food," said one roommate. The act of eating was the organizing principle for the prisoners of Fresnes, the fact of food itself, "one tin finger full of beans," made the calendar move, but the squeaky wheels of the bread carts were not enough to get Odette out of bed. She was seldom strong enough to stand.

In time, Bleicher gave up on Odette. Ever feebler, she attended interrogation upon interrogation at Avenue Foch and in Rue de Saussaies, another Nazi stronghold in Paris, fourteen interrogations in all.

Within the Gestapo, English prisoners were considered more useful alive than dead. At war crimes trials, the denizens of Avenue Foch listed three reasons: Captured agents could identify new prisoners and inflict peer pressure during interrogations; British prisoners had English accents, and a new radio technology allowed agents on the ground to speak to pilots flying overhead during airdrops, so voices were needed for deceit and decoy operations. Last and most important, live agents had utilitarian value as hostages, where corpses had none. Once the invasion came, prison swaps might be necessary.

The officials at Avenue Foch considered themselves civilized men, even as they behaved like war criminals. They shared fond reminiscences about "how fine it was in the good old days when they used to knock about and ill-treat Jews." In the mansion's courtyard, there was a glass greenhouse providing cover for pitiless questioning. "I have heard screams from the shed," one English prisoner recalled. As the victims were returned to the top-floor interrogation rooms, the shed's purpose was clear; agents were "in such bad condition from the ill-treatment they had suffered that they could barely walk up the stairs." Some officers kept handy riding crops and hazel switches to make their points upon a prisoner's body; some got carried away with wet towels, truncheons, and clenched fists; others used the method of questioning known as "the bathtub," *la baignoire,* "the cold water cure," now commonly known as waterboarding.

Always, the question from the German interlocutor was, when were the Allies arriving, where would the flotilla land? Said one British prisoner of the interviews, "Really all they wanted to know was when the invasion was coming, on and on and on."

Odette was instructed to remove her shoes. She slipped her feet out, unrolled what was left of her stockings, laddered and tattered from months in prison and daily hair rituals.

A young soldier kneeled down and took a pair of pliers to her toenail and yanked at it. Blood filled the space in the nail bed; the pain was blinding. She did not cry. The soldier then proceeded to the next toe.

At any moment, it was within Odette's power to stop the exercise, to spare her next toe, to give up what intelligence she possessed that might be useful to Hitler.

The torturer worked his way down one foot and onto the next.

The secretaries kept typing.

The young soldier glanced up at his commander with a questioning look as if asking to continue to her fingers.

"Do you like what you are doing?" Odette asked her torturer. "You are not doing it for any other reason."

It was a game, she realized. She always lived in her head, trusting her romanticism to carry her through the pain. The Nazis relied on their own dogma too; Hitler's canon, his alleged struggle, his *Kampf,* excused his henchmen from any shame. This was not, she thought, a "clean game."

Odette looked like death itself, "a wreck, unkempt, hair all over the place," said a captured pilot under interrogation. To an agent contemplating his own fate, seeing Odette was its own kind of intimidation. The Nazis took note of her impact on other prisoners. "My mouth must have hung open," he recalled, as he watched Odette hobble from the interrogation room. "I was absolutely petrified."

Odette was presented with a stack of papers listing her sins. In both French and German, it said that Mrs. Churchill was condemned to death on two counts: first as a British spy, second as a Frenchwoman working against the Reich.

She was ordered to sign her own judgment.

For which country would Odette die? Hitler would just have to take his pick, she thought. "In every tragedy there is an element of comedy if you can see it."

A woman can only die once.

CHAPTER 16

The Swap

Paris

An echo of bouncing balls rattled off the facades of buildings at the Square de Clignancourt, while mothers coaxed children inside for an afternoon nap. Grandmothers stood in the breeze for a moment and noticed the blessing of a normal May day, a regular childhood moment, girls and boys running under the belvedere, playing tag, like in real life, the life of a neighborhood at peace. Petulant little ones, reluctant to come indoors, were told that the warm weather would be waiting when they woke up, that it would be there all summer long.

The park, not far from Montmartre, was just up the street from the local police station. It had an air of suburban calm in the middle of a city. A fourth-floor apartment at No. 10 was a safe house used by the PROSPER network. It was not currently hiding agents; there were no secret meetings taking place. In the living room, little hinted at wartime terror, nighttime drops, or invasion plans. With the summer assault on its way, Francis had been recalled to England for a debrief. So while the *chef* was away, Andrée and Gilbert played a game of poker.

The day was marked by laughter, as if the war would not find them. It was a time to unwind, to live like people: A game of cards at the Square Clignancourt spoke of leisure and not of invasions or offensives, guerrillas or guns. The luncheon was warmed by friendship; Andrée and Gilbert had made it through the winter together. They were now inseparable and in love. In a time of mild weather and broad smiles, they were a handsome pair.

Andrée and Gilbert were joined by two other couples in the underground: their hosts, the Bussozes, whose son was old enough to be inducted into Vichy's forced labor scheme, and a pair of married British agents—a radio operator, Jack Agazarian, and his wife, Francine.

Gilbert and Jack, as the main radios in Paris, were overwhelmed with work as D-Day loomed. Every agent who passed through the city needed help communicating with London. Gilbert and Jack spent nights after curfew coding and days traveling between radio sets, faithfully meeting schedules with the FANYs back at Station 53. London spymasters knew—as a result of the Ultra decrypts of the Enigma code—that the Gestapo was getting better at hunting illegal radio transmitters. "There is good ground for believing that it is very unlikely any transmitter can hope to exist for any length . . . in German occupied territory without being detected, identified, and located." Gilbert, in the field for six months, was coding on borrowed time.

The war was long, and agents would remember the moments of downtime more than the sabotage: "These were the important things—the personal associations one had with people during the period, associations born of a tension of which one was really not as aware as one might have been." The coziness and cohesion might not last as the agents started receiving new assignments for the invasion: Francis was in London getting updated orders. Time with Gilbert now was precious.

No one could be blamed for relaxing while Francis was gone. The Agazarians, in particular, were frustrated by Francis's tense leadership; Jack, likewise, was an irritant to his network chief. "He is not being very useful," Francis complained in a report to London. "He is imminently [*sic*] unfit for our work in the field." Jack was known to drink too much, to flirt with strange women; he begged for a promotion, to become an organizer of his own network. He adored his own success.

Francis denied him: "He has not the slightest organizing ability." Jack's wife, Francine, seemed to think she was beyond the reach of the network command structure, that Francis's authority did not touch her, which made her useless in his eyes. "She has not been able to fit into the picture."

While the afternoon was lazy, the war came knocking: The buzzer at No. 10 rang, and a stranger arrived, asking to speak to Hélène Bussoz. In one of the many small, daily ways women aided the Resistance, they were the first point of contact in a rebel home. They opened front doors and answered phones so that partisans with weapons and a target on their backs might escape. Hélène answered, the correct passwords were exchanged—"I am a friend of Roger Dumont. I have not seen him for over a month"—and the visitor asked for Gilbert, who went down to the park.

There were two men to greet Gilbert on the street, one a guide from an escape line, the other an agent from the Dutch section of SOE. The smuggler introduced himself in accented French, like a Belgian. His name was Arnaud. He was stout, strong, blue-eyed, fair-haired, with rosy cheeks and meaty hands. The second man, the Dutch agent, had a broad, fat face and the high-strung, nervous gestures of a man who "looks and behaves like a waiter." He called himself Adrian and spoke no French whatsoever.

The men told their story: Baker Street had wired The Hague to recall Adrian to headquarters to report on subversive action in Holland. He was ordered to cross into France and secure a seat on an upcoming flight to London. In Paris, he was told to speak to a man called Gilbert.

When every agent had four or more names—operational, Christian, alias, documentary, and otherwise—mistaken identities were common. Gilbert said he was not the man they were looking for; to London, he was Archambaud. There was a different British agent who handled the airplanes, an agent known by the code name Gilbert—Flying Officer Henri Déricourt.

Jack was the radio operator who transmitted all information for flights to Déricourt's landing grounds, and he told the Dutchmen he would make the arrangements. But because the May full moon was nearing its close, it was not possible to fix anything right away. All seats on outgoing flights were booked.

It would be better, Jack said, if the Low Country agents returned the following month; so the strangers went away with the promise of a June flight to London.

The day remained fine. There were cigarettes to smoke, cards to play, lovers' hands to hold. There would be plenty of work to do once Francis returned to Paris.

The decisive moment of the war—the summer offensive in Europe—lay ahead.

IN STARK CONTRAST to the ruined glamour of France at war, London remained a gentlemanly city, a place for bankers, stockbrokers, accountants, and politicians—smart, calculating, and expert. In the aftermath of the Luftwaffe's Blitz, the city stayed powerful.

Dry, sunny, and warm, London was as optimistic as possible under the circumstances—for being at war and for being English—even if Francis was not. Battleships were moored in the snaking Thames. The streets were sluices of soldiers: Brits, French, Poles, Canadians, Americans, readying for the invasion of Europe. In daytime, Piccadilly lights were on, as they had ever been. *Bovril. Guinness Is Good for You.*

The fight seemed to lean the Allies' way. The prime minister was not at 10 Downing but instead in America meeting with President Roosevelt and the U.S. Congress, plying the case for a war strategy that would be launched in Europe and extended to the Pacific. "The defeat of Japan would not mean the defeat of Germany, the defeat of Germany would infallibly mean the ruin of Japan," the prime minister insisted, still worried the Americans might turn their attention to Hirohito and away from Hitler. To bolster his argument, Churchill emphasized positive news from Europe: Widespread bombing raids were crippling the Reich's factories, enervating Germans, and inspiring the conquered nations. The Battle of the Atlantic, too, had turned for the Allies; the Admiralty rarely announced public details about German submarine wolf packs, but in May 1943 it issued a statement that ten U-boats were sunk in one week. The assist the Allies got from Ultra decrypts of the Enigma code would not be known to the world for a generation, but the effects were immediate: Hitler was losing the fight for the seas. Munitions, ships, and aircraft could now reach Europe in enough mass to open the much-heralded second front.

Every full moon had the potential to change the world, as each one could signal the landing in Europe. No one would tell the Firm when the offensive would start, or where; the only thing that was certain was there would be a second front on the Continent in 1943. To catch Hitler off guard, it was all hush-hush; details were not shared even with the French Section. Only the highest levels of Allied command knew the specifics. All services were told to stand by for D-Day.

The wait might not be too long, generals warned. In a flash, Hitler's regime could collapse, bankrupted by its own grandiosity; if that happened, the fall of the Reich would be swift, and a cascade of occupied nations would join the effort to free Europe. The French networks were told to prepare, to kick into action "in June, July, August, as quickly as possible in view of the events which can take place at any moment."

Francis stayed in a hotel on the south side of Hyde Park. It was a welcome change from his digs in Paris, where he lived among rabble and moved constantly. France was his mother's home, but it lacked any sense of comfort; instead, Paris reeked of sweat and fear. Agents noted the dissonance between life in occupied France and in London on a secret government budget.

Francis had been recalled to London for a week, and it was not a good week. The visit with HQ was fraught. He explained that the Gestapo was cracking down: Bömelburg was now paying collaborators one million francs for the capture of British officers in the underground. Betrayal was incentivized; "denunciations have become more frequent," it was reported, now that the Gestapo penalized people who failed "to 'do their duty' in this regard." A growing list of mistakes and accidents put Francis and his fellow agents in danger. His safe houses were inexplicably blown. The organization's "secretary" in Paris was just arrested, a woman who came from the CARTE network, Germaine Tambour. Now the Nazis were using injectable drugs during interrogations, "which rendered the victim quite irresponsible and talkative," Francis said. He was most "perturbed" by the rumor and what effects such drugs might have, were he or his team arrested. What had it done to Germaine? The Tambours' apartment was the very first place Andrée went once she had cast off her parachute and made her way to Paris. Every agent descended on Germaine eventually; hers was the warm and maternal face of the Paris Resistance.

Meanwhile, the British intelligence services understood, Avenue Foch seemed to be planning a sweep ahead of the anticipated invasion. As a result of deciphering the Enigma code, it was known that the Nazi counterespionage police were now drilling down on the PROSPER circuit. A direct order was sent to Bömelburg's men on Avenue Foch that the partisan "organization in Paris must be rooted out as an overriding priority task."

Baker Street acknowledged Francis's frustration. Buck—now promoted to lieutenant colonel—and Francis ate together every day during the visit. The topics to cover were vast: from cauterizing the CARTE bleed to the logistics of the invasion.

There was a growing disconnect between agents on the ground and supervisors barking orders from London. Francis, too, wanted a promotion—to major—and Gilbert deserved one as well. Francis argued the Firm was not doing enough for the women in his command: Andrée and Yvonne were working themselves thin and had not gotten enough congratulatory messages or words of encouragement from HQ. They deserved every bit as much praise as the men, and the silence was insulting.

The arrest of the CARTE lieutenant André Marsac had far-reaching effects on the circuits in France, beyond Odette's and Peter's capture. Other members of the underground had been identified, tailed, picked up, and presumably turned. Francis was trying to cordon off the PROSPER circuits from anyone affiliated with Marsac. He canceled addresses, demanded new letter drops; every operative detail was compromised, tainted, he said to his commanders. "Please, please,

please avoid all contact. . . . I have reliable reports which induce me to distrust [a CARTE member] or at least his methods. I can, if necessary, give you chapter and verse for this." Andrée had told Francis she thought there might be yet another traitor in the extended network—with no relation to CARTE. She suspected parachute receptions and airplane pickups were being monitored by the Gestapo.

Francis hammered on about field security. In order to do what was asked, he was growing his sub-networks fast, launching satellite circuits all over the North to lighten the load on his overburdened shoulders. With every full moon, he welcomed new agents arriving from London. "Life for him was continually tense and active," recalled one of his French lieutenants. He was "terribly headstrong and firm, almost hard in character. He had such an elevated sense of his own responsibilities." He commanded an army of as many as twenty thousand.

The Firm recognized the dangerous communication bottleneck in Paris: Seven networks in northern France were funneling messages through the capital. It was functionally impossible to keep circuits watertight and independent when so much traffic was distilled into so few radios. Many more operators had to be landed to relieve the pressure. From D-Day on, they would need a permanent and continuous twenty-four-hour link between the French guerrillas and the Supreme Headquarters Allied Expeditionary Force, or SHAEF, located in England. French Section was staffing up radios in anticipation: In one year, the number of radios in France had increased tenfold, from three to thirty, and was set to grow to eighty operators in the field, but as long as there were more rebel cells than radiomen, there would hardly be enough capacity to handle the traffic for a forward assault on the western front. Buck wanted Francis to know that new operators were preparing to join his extended network immediately. One would go to the Jewish circuit in Paris; the other—an Indian woman, the first woman to be deployed as a signals operator in combat—would go to Trie-Château to join one of Francis's sub-circuits.

Really, under such conditions, the entire PROSPER team needed a rest, so the sooner D-Day arrived, the better, according to Francis. The exhaustion was hard on him: He watched Andrée and Gilbert falling for each other and saw that codependence made their lives better, work easier. "I cannot praise them too highly and wish to state that any success we may obtain will be very largely due to their efforts."

Francis, in the end, got what a man longs for most on leave: He saw his wife, Margaret. At Baker Street, he negotiated hard to be allowed to travel with photos of his children. Security rules forbade it, but Francis was a man on edge; permission to look at his sons from time to time was granted with reluctance. He could write to his wife. She was allowed to write back.

D-Day was the massive, dense object around which all conversations orbited. When "matters are at a head"—that is, immediately after the invasion—Francis's assignment was to go to Gisors to lead the northern circuits from there. Gilbert would go to Orléans and take command of his own circuit in the central Loire.

ACTION FOR "D" DAY

It has been agreed that the provision of a universal password, or even a universal recognition sign, is quite useless, since the communication of this password or sign to large numbers of troops would have obvious dangers.

The following procedure should, therefore, be adopted:

You should send back to us a list of 3 or 4 safe houses for use only on "D" Day, and you will make arrangements for . . . yourself and—at most 2 or 3 of your chief Lieutenants to go to ground in those houses at the moment when the battle begins to pass over your area. You will remain in these houses until picked up by one of our Officers attached to the invading troops.

Your organisation will, obviously, have a most important harrying function right up to the time when the battle reaches your area.

THE BRITISH ISLES were becoming the world's largest weapons stockpile and muster zone. The plan would call for the deployment of 326,000 Allied troops, as many as 5,000 ships and landing craft, 11,000 aircraft dropping 13,000 paratroopers, and 54,000 vehicles sailing across the Channel, hauling 100,000 tons of supplies for the march to Berlin. The massing of men and heavy equipment in southern England was so immense it was said the island might well keel over and capsize into the sea.

In all this, Francis and his lieutenants were synchronizing plans for the coordinated effort to hobble France's infrastructure during the assault. The combat zone was necessarily the point of focus. The elite panzer tank divisions had blitzed through northern France in 1940. Those same tanks had to be kept far from the beaches as the Allies came ashore; if Hitler's armor were to reach the invasion zone, his panzers were powerful enough to blow the Anglo-American offensive back into the water. Once the attack came, the maquis would be tasked with preventing a sequel to the blitzkrieg.

No one could know where the armada would land. Only that it would come to an area under the PROSPER umbrella.

AFTER SIX DAYS IN ENGLAND, Francis parachuted back into enemy territory on the full moon of May 20, 1943, carrying an "alert" message for his entire network: Stand by for the invasion.

In a clearing, the trees above Francis were black filigrees against the sky. He and his jumping partner rolled up their parachutes, shed their flight suits, balled it all up, and buried it.

"Darling Child," Francis would later write to his wife, Margaret, of his soft landing. "My journey was very comfortable and my leg gave me no trouble at all—I may have done it good."

His homesickness was mollified, for a time. "I keep thinking of all the things I should have said to you," he penned onto ruled graph paper. "I hope my next visit won't be the same rush."

They had only recently parted; emotions were fresh; the softness of her cheek when he kissed her still a new memory. He had not gotten to see his sons in London and it stung: "Anyway, I have the photographs now and they make me feel much better."

Goodbye darling

All my love

F

FRANCIS WOULD HAND his letter to a courier, who would meet someone in a café to pass it off again, and then the missive would wing its way back to England, to Margaret, his darling.

In the next full moon, two Westland Lysander aircraft descended into the valley where the Loire meets the Sarthe for a textbook landing. It was always thus: The French-born pilot who organized airfields never made mistakes. Flying Officer Henri Déricourt would meet some sixty-seven agents and rebel leaders in the field by war's end, including a young François Mitterrand.

Déricourt worked his airfields with deft authority. As arriving passengers disembarked, he waved forward the agents going home for the return trip. Luggage was handed down from the open cockpit; a mailbag was passed up into the plane. Francis's letter to his bright-eyed and freckle-faced wife would be included in that courier bag.

But in the days and hours before the airplane touchdown, Déricourt had taken all the England-bound mail to the men of 84 Avenue Foch.

In the Firm, Henri Déricourt's code name was Gilbert.

To *SS-Sturmbannführer* Bömelburg, he was known as agent BOE48.

UPON HIS RETURN from London, Francis had a clandestine meeting near a corner café at noon, on the east side of Paris. He sat "sipping a tasteless wartime aperitif"; blossom petals collected in white lines along the curbs. Across the leafy expanse of the city park, he studied the Château de Vincennes, a fourteenth-century fortress that had housed military installations for several Louises, three Napoleons, and one Adolf. Francis was alert, in expectation of a prison release, an exchange of bodies for money.

Francis was awaiting the arrival of a Citroën containing two middle-age women, the beloved Germaine Tambour and her sister, Madeleine, both betrayed by Marsac. Germaine was originally the CARTE leader André Girard's secretary, his right hand—until she broke off contact when the artist's ego grew poisonous. From the Riviera, she returned to her native Paris, to the bebop beats of the jazz scene, to help build circuits on the Channel coast ahead of an invasion. She worked from 38 Avenue de Suffren, her family home, and it was this address that Marsac gave to Sergeant Hugo Bleicher.

Throughout the spring on Avenue de Suffren, Bleicher's Abwehr had monitored the apartment. Inspectors sat in a little restaurant below, sipping coffee in the shadow of the Eiffel Tower, photographing all who entered the building, noting when they left—inevitably members of the Resistance. When Bleicher pounced, it became a crisis for the PROSPER network: If Germaine were tortured, she "knew too much and we could not risk her standing up to any sort of interrogation." Germaine's arrest had been a blow to the spymasters at Baker Street, Buckmaster wrote in his diary: "Awful PM. Staggering news. Sold down the river!"

So Francis put the Firm's money where his heart was. There was little in Paris that could not be bought for the right price; it was the largest barter market in Europe. With the plan in place, he wired London for money and put 125,000 francs down as prepayment on the sisters' freedom. ("You are not the Salvation Army!" Baker Street had shot back at the notion of purchasing prisoners.)

Funding the enemy directly was a high-stakes scheme that put Francis in perilous range of war criminals. It financed men running protection rackets who murdered Jews and tortured children. Irregular soldiers always tread a line of moral indeterminacy. ("It isn't cricket, you know, blowing people up, which is what we did," said a FANY of the Firm's top secret actions behind enemy lines.) Now Francis inched closer to the sorts of people whom he loathed, collaborators and Nazis. But Germaine was worth it.

The handover was set to look as if the sisters were being transferred between prisons—from the lockup at Fresnes to the cells of Vincennes. Officials on both sides would claim the car had been hijacked along the route.

From his perch at the café, Francis watched as a black Citroën approached the rendezvous, slowing to a stop. The doors opened, and two French inspectors stepped to the street escorting two female prisoners.

After life in Fresnes, the women were haggard, ill-fed, and unbathed; they looked as if jail had taken years off their lives. They did not resemble the elegant Tambours.

Germaine and Madeleine, brunettes, were nowhere to be seen. The inspectors produced instead "rather tired looking blondes."

Francis, it soon became clear, had paid a fortune for the release of "young ladies of doubtful virtue from Montmartre." The German official attending the rendezvous was furious at the French officers for the botched job. The French inspectors apologized for the mistake but demanded payment for the wrong merchandise. There was no returning the women to the prison whence they came; it would rouse suspicions even more. The officers must be paid for their time and risk, not for results.

Germaine and Madeleine remained locked up in Fresnes. The 125,000-franc deposit was surrendered. Some Nazi somewhere along the chain had a hearty laugh. The Resistance had just bought the most expensive prostitutes in Paris.

But Francis could not give up on the Tambours. He plotted a follow-up scheme, this time with better fail-safes but the same bad idea: buying a jailbreak.

The second rendezvous would be far across town at a café near the Porte Maillot. As insurance against the kind of cruel comedy that produced women of the night instead of soldiers of the underground, the notes for one million francs were cut in half: one-half delivered in advance. The remaining half would be handed over at the time of the confirmed exchange. To annoy the Nazis, the rebels mixed up the notes, scrambling them, "like a storm of confetti."

At this rendezvous, there would be secure identity checks. A third party, a cutout, would be accompanied by someone who knew Germaine, who could vouch for the sisters' authenticity. When the right prisoners were produced, she would signal the middleman, who would then hand over the suitcase of half notes.

Francis and Gilbert would monitor the swaps.

For the second attempt, Francis chose a popular café, Café Sport, a happy place: canvas awning, bent wicker seats, brass trim, bad coffee. Close to a metro, the neighborhood was busy, flanked by alleys, sharp corners, and a nearby park: lots of ways to foot it out if the plan went to hell.

On the day of the handoff, a snub-nosed Citroën bus rolled down the Place Maillot—the fearsome Black Maria transport van of the Gestapo. When it stopped around a corner, some twenty police filed out, all moving in the direction of the café, ready to claim the second half of the million francs and the heads of a few terrorists.

Someone had tipped off Avenue Foch.

The barkeepers of Café Sport remained casual, but the room was vigilant. A PROSPER lieutenant arrived in time to sound the alarm. No one was arrested. But Gestapo plants were in the room.

Francis's second calamitous ransom attempt accelerated the chain reaction catalyzed by the CARTE collapse and Marsac's double cross. Bleicher was gaining. Bömelburg too. The sisters were lost, and the Parisian networks were now firmly in the scopes of two arms of the German secret police: the Wehrmacht's Abwehr and the Nazi Party

SS's *Sicherheitsdienst.* From that day forward, there could be no question that members of *réseau* PROSPER were known by sight to Avenue Foch.

To the partisans' surprise, the suitcase of halved banknotes was returned. It took three days to paste together one million francs.

PARIS GOT HOT, but the underground continued to believe a crowded café was a safe café. In full view of the French and the Germans, rendezvous were arranged, passwords confirmed, messages swapped. In summer, the Resistance conducted its business on the *terrasses*—Café de Flore, Le Colisée, the Montholon—where men with briefcases and women in wispy scarves and sunglasses smoked, gossiped, argued, and drank. Waiters met patrons with a nod—collaborators and patriots alike. Café society was a French ritual that withstood the deprivations of war. It predated Hitler; it would outlive him.

Only Andrée Borrel took notice when Jack Agazarian hurried into Café Napolitain on June 9, 1943, looking as if he had stared death in the face. Jack detailed a recent and narrow escape: The terror happened only minutes before, Jack said, at the Café Capucines. He went from one café right to the next, certain he had not been followed.

But Jack swore he was a marked man. He had rendezvoused with the Dutch agents—the men who came to the Square de Clignancourt on the day of the lazy poker game. One man needed a flight to London, and the other was his guide; in the days since the poker game, Jack had organized it all with Henri Déricourt. Precautions were used; no one else even knew of their meeting. Then it all went wrong. Out of nowhere, the Dutch agent got arrested in the café.

Jack had spoken to the guide through a shorthand vocabulary used by those on the run, all in ellipses, vague words like *sévite,* crackdown . . . *plaque tournante,* hub. They were deeply engaged *en français,* while the other agent sat detached, as he spoke no French.

At once the café had seemed to grow busy; the room went from empty to bustling in minutes. Two Nazi soldiers arrived, announcing a roundup. All patrons in the room were ordered to take out their papers.

At that moment, the uncomprehending Dutch agent stood, shoved his hands into his pockets, and hurried to the door. The demand for identification—so commonplace in Paris—was a death sentence to a man with no French language and forged documents.

The German officers looked up and watched the Dutchman leave, continuing their investigation.

They did not run after him. *But why?* Jack wondered. He realized it was because they didn't have to; there was a plant: The agent was apprehended at the door by a man in a mackintosh who sat on the *terrasse* with no coffee or cognac. It had to be a setup.

The Dutch smuggler watched as his charge got escorted across the road by the stranger in civilian clothes. "They have arrested Adrian," he said out loud, only to be stared down by Jack; it was imperative to act as if there were nothing to hide. In whispers, they forged a new cover story, something simple that might explain why the third man ran.

The Nazis made the rounds of the café and got to Jack. He produced his documents—all in order, as were the smuggler's. For whatever reason—fate, or the skill of a good forger—both men were spared. The Dutch agent was not.

Once cleared, Jack vanished. The Germans in uniform would return to the café every five minutes for the rest of the afternoon, checking papers, harassing Parisians, making life uncomfortable and cafés uninviting.

A storm came over Andrée's face as she heard the story: The Dutch agent from Baker Street was arrested and was now at Avenue Foch. He was being interrogated that very moment, likely tortured. Or had he flipped already and was now a pawn to draw in other players? He had an assignment for the flight to England. He could identify everyone at the poker game: Jack, his wife, the hosts, Gilbert, and Andrée.

How many members of the PROSPER circuit were now infected?

Jack would have to go back to London. Gilbert's workload would only increase.

Catastrophe. Débâcle. Désastre.

As was typical of the Resistance, Andrée and Jack knew the captured agent only by his code name: Adrian.

The agent's real name was Karl Boden. His companion was Richard Christmann. They were not, in fact, employees of the Firm.

They were the enemy. Both men were Abwehr agents from Holland, where an intercepted British radio set was at that moment in the middle of a years-long *Funkspiel,* a radio game, duping the FANYs of Station 53. British radios, with SOE codes, were under control of the Nazis in The Hague. When the Dutch radio sent dummy messages to home station, the FANYs believed they were receiving vital information from genuine Allied agents. The Abwehr had been deceiving Baker Street for well over a year. It was double cross by radio.

Now Hitler's *Englandspiel*—his England game—was playing in Paris.

CHAPTER 17

The Dog Sneezed on the Curtains

Loire Valley

It was the first quarter moon, June 10, 1943. There was optimism, as there ever is when summer is young, and the BBC fueled the hopes of the French. In a prophetic speech heard around the world, the British prime minister spoke of "amphibious operations of peculiar complexity."

Bombing raids out of England were at their fastest pace yet, crippling military industrial installations—munitions and aircraft factories, oil refineries, submarine pens—and racking up civilian deaths. The BBC tried to warn the French ahead of bomber runs to stay away from targeted sites, to no avail; the death toll rose to about sixty thousand by 1943. The Germans exploited the casualties. *Paris-Soir* published pictures of babies' corpses. The surprise strike must be near, France thought. The intensification of the air campaign was a sure sign of a looming attack.

Winston Churchill's speech reported on France, hinting at imminent change: General de Gaulle had just formed a Free French cabinet in Algiers with a new French constitution. Across the dissident spectrum, rapprochement was achieved under de Gaulle. He was "the sole authority over all Frenchmen seeking to free France from the German yoke," said Churchill. The extreme Left and the extreme Right together cast their eyes upon the "light of victory."

After the prime minister's speech, as the moon waxed to full in the next two weeks, France had every reason to ask, would this be the day the Allies returned? The night skies were brightening, weather was warm, winds were mellow and sweet. It was an excellent time for an armada.

The farmland along the Loire was ripe; each sunny day felt like a gift. Rebels in the countryside saw parachute operations nearly every night of the full moon: Three hundred drops were scheduled for June, and so many were on the mark; twenty-seven missions would unload some 205 containers.

Yvonne Rudellat's landing grounds were long established and often used; her reception teams were practiced, her sub-leaders trained and competent. Remarked an SS colonel, "The resistance terrorists in this area were the most arrogant and difficult in the whole of France."

On June 10, 1943, a personal message came for Yvonne:

The dog sneezed on the curtains.

She heard the phrase, repeated like a mantra, and set off with Pierre Culioli on her bicycle toward an empty landing field, an asparagus crate attached to her handlebars.

Under the freshening June sky, Yvonne expected ten containers, an enormous payload, but well within her team's capacity. The night's committee was a collection of motley local patriots: two crippled ex-POWs, a veterinarian surgeon for large farm animals, a father-and-son electrician team, and nobility from a nearby château.

It was a typically fine June evening. "We find ourselves with happy work to do, rapidly, methodically, in silence, with straining muscles and full arms," recalled a network member of those evenings in the fields, "to unfasten and fold the parachutes, to unscrew the metal braces holding the containers together, five by five; to group them and transport them to the hiding place. Two, three hours, sometimes more, of tiring work but exciting in the extreme. The certainty—arms with which to fight, a promise of victory. Rare moments, where for a little while, we no longer felt so alone. Time to breathe." When the guns dropped from the sky, each barrel and stock foreshadowed the day when the weapon might at last be used against the Germans.

The signal lights were in position, the ground was firm, the wind was light, visibility high. It was the Thursday before the feast of Pentecost. From the horizon, the sounds of Halifax engines overpowered the night hum of crickets.

When the pilot spotted the landing lights, ten canisters launched from the bay door: one after another, parachutes blooming in sequence.

Then there was an explosion.

"A blinding glare came up from the ground as if a phosphorous bomb had been substituted for a container," partisans would recall. The sky lit up like day, and the countryside was all fireworks: dazzling, brilliant, devastating. Where the moon had been a spotlight only an instant before, now the field shone like morning, each detail coming into sharp focus, from the pocket on a man's jacket to the dirty hem of Yvonne's culottes. Flames engulfed parachutes.

Booms filled the night, as if the whole firmament were splintering. The moon retreated into a penumbra of thick smoke. Geysers of ash flew heavenward, roiling what only minutes before had been a perfect summer night for rebellion. Men were thrown by the shock.

The blast could be heard ten kilometers away.

This was it, the group thought, the Nazis were making their assault on the local maquis. They were under attack.

"We are betrayed," one man cried out.

Men fell to the mud. Others hid in a ditch. A countess ran into a swamp, hip-deep in bog. Newer members of the group "lost their petals."

"Look at them," barked the countess in outrage. "They are behaving as they did in 1940. Running away like rabbits."

From the point of view of the RAF Special Duties crew, nothing seemed amiss. The rear gunner saw a brief flash of light, but by then the bomber was too far away to wonder at it.

Yvonne's team was in anguish. Were more explosions coming? Were German fighters giving chase to the British bomber?

Yvonne alone stood her ground and did not recoil. Lit by blazes, everyone in her committee watched her. The explosions felt tectonic, but they were not new to Yvonne. She had survived the Blitz, had seen her home blow up, created a whole new life from the cinders. She was a student of Eastern meditation. The sky was on fire, but her role was clear: In the face of attack, she showed her crew that flinching was a choice, defiance a moral posture.

Hands over their heads, facedown in the dirt, the men of the committee peered up to see Yvonne standing firm, surrounded by flames. "I thought she was marvelous: a splendid little woman. I was struck by her calmness."

After the sound of engines died away, the partisans understood what happened: The blasts were not German anti-aircraft maneuvers but arms canisters catching fire in sequence. They became their very own gargantuan pipe bombs, containing hundreds of mortars, grenades, guns, and gelignite. When the canisters crashed to earth, dry grass and leaves caught fire. Once the incendiary explosives in the canisters detonated, they would burn for a solid hour. *Le chien éternue*—the dog had sneezed.

The air was bitter with the smell of smoke and the partisans were rattled. The police were surely now onto them. The explosions were signals launched into the sky telling Hitler: Find us. We are here.

Go back as you came, shouted the reception leader, in twos and threes, in various directions, heed the shortcuts, stay out of sight, steer far from the main roads.

Yvonne and Pierre collected their bicycles and pedaled home to their cottage in the woods. The little house was booby-trapped all around with British ordnance, mined with enough firepower to blow up the entire city of Blois.

Soon Yvonne was asleep under silk sheets made from parachutes, on a pillow stuffed with grenades, with *plastique* explosives stored under her bed.

On the morning of the longest day of the year, June 21, 1943, in what had already been a long war for Yvonne's rebels, the hot weather had overnight turned cold and moist, casting a gray chill over the Loire valley. There was a shift in the air; no one had yet put their finger on it. It was not just the wind and rain but the temper of the countryside.

The Germans were back in force.

After the explosions in the woods the week before, the Wehrmacht was visible again in the farmland near the demarcation line. An entire battalion, or so it seemed, moved to the area to root out the terrorists from the underbrush.

Barricades went up at each road crossing, checkpoints on every bridge. The Luftwaffe flew over the woods, at treetop level, circling open fields, to locate the telltale marks of impromptu landing strips and drop zones. Covered trucks were parked in town squares, troops mustered in pavilions, and farmers noted the glint of sunlight reflecting off soldiers' helmets as they marched through open fields. The villagers assumed the increased presence was a training maneuver. Members of Yvonne's circuit understood they were being hunted.

Nazis chased the partisans as London was racing the moon. The police pressure did not stop Baker Street or the Special Duties Squadrons from squeezing every advantage out of June's waning lunar period. As long as the night's beacon could still light the way for a mission, they dropped more containers and "bods."

In the early hours of that June morning, four separate airdrops flew from England to Yvonne's landing grounds in the Loire. The containers fell on pinpoint; the planes returned to their air base counting the night's missions a success.

As one of the reception teams moved a ten-container haul toward Yvonne and Pierre's woodland cottage, they were intercepted at a German checkpoint.

All five partisans were arrested. No one sent notice to the other members of Yvonne's circuit; there was no one left to get out the news.

By daybreak, Yvonne and Pierre had left home. They were on their way to a safe house to collect two newly arrived F Section agents from

Canada: Lieutenant Frank Pickersgill and Lieutenant John Macalister, Pick and Mack. They were going to Paris.

Yvonne and Pierre had a new car, a Citroën abandoned by refugees fleeing south of the demarcation line.

The couple arrived as scheduled at 7:00 a.m. to collect the Canadians. Yvonne was gleeful in a new set of clothes, borrowed finery. The women of her circuit were tired of looking at her single tatty British-made suit, which she had been wearing constantly for almost a year. The network included women of taste and refinement; Yvonne's thoughtless sartorial sense would not do. From Blois, she would take a train to Paris and must look the part, so they gifted her a summer-weight wool suit, in a Glengarry-check weave, the fabric favored by the exiled Duke of Windsor. (The abdicated sovereign was sympathetic to Hitler and so dispatched to the Bahamas for the duration of the war, at Winston Churchill's insistence.)

Snaking through a network of wooded roads, having picked up the Canadian agents, the full Citroën passed so many German soldiers, military lorries, horses, and motorcycles it seemed as if some general or Nazi noteworthy were on parade with an honor guard.

It was unusual, Pierre thought. It occurred to him that he and Yvonne ought to have checked on the previous night's airdrops, made contact with the teams, before setting out to retrieve the Canadians for the trip to Paris. Had Yvonne been less exhausted, she might have insisted on it. She had been on the ground for nearly a year, working without pause. The clandestine life that had once energized her was now draining. In confidence, she admitted that she wanted out of espionage. "Whatever happens, I must get back to England," she said. She had a feeling it was time to go home, before the Allies arrived. "I'm too tired to think properly but I am sure a disaster is about to happen."

Tucked between Yvonne and Pierre on the wide front seat of the car was a brown paper package, tied in twine, marked *Croix Rouge Française,* labeled and stamped for a fictional prisoner of war. Three years after the invasion of France, relatives and church societies still pooled resources to feed Hitler's French captives. The tight little package contained no links of dried sausages, packets of cigarettes, or letters from loved ones. Instead, it held un-encrypted messages from London—one for Francis Suttill, two for Gilbert Norman, one for Mary Herbert—and six quartz radio crystals tuned to Station 53's frequencies.

At a crossing near the small village of Dhuizon, Nazi soldiers raised their hands and brought the Citroën to a stop, demanding papers, travel passes, license. Yvonne and Pierre produced their documents: husband and wife—Monsieur and Madame Culioli. Everything was in order. Pick's and Mack's papers were minted in England; their French accents were forged in the schoolrooms of Canada. It was a tense moment, but the car passed inspection.

"Do not be afraid, we are not here for you," the German sentry said, waving the car onward. "But we are looking for someone."

Rolling forward through tight streets, between stucco-and-brick buildings, a butcher shop, a bakery, a church, with soldiers manning the roads throughout, the cars in the neighborhood were stopped every ten meters or so. The town had become a garrison.

At the next check, the Citroën was called to a halt again, and the inspection was repeated: identity cards, passes, questions.

Pick and Mack were ordered out of the vehicle. A young German soldier with a machine gun took their place. What was in the package? the soldier wanted to know. "Charcuterie," he was told.

The Canadians were marched toward the town hall, and Pierre was instructed to drive there too, for a more thorough interrogation.

The *mairie* was stuffy, feverish with suspicion and queuing country folk. Locals surrendered to a gauntlet of German critique: Where had they been, where were they going, what had they done the night before, the week before? Pick was so tall and blond he was easy to spot; both he and Mack had hundreds of thousands of francs tucked in their money belts.

In the pandemonium, Pierre clung to his briefcase, hoping to mix into the flock of unhappy citizens. Like all too many in the underground, he kept circuit reports and lists, in violation of all good safety measures. He carried his briefcase on him, everywhere, as if he were personally inviolable; he was egotistic enough to believe that he was.

Standing beside his "wife," mindful of the incriminating evidence in his grip, Pierre slipped the leather case behind a chair when no one was looking.

An inspector asked for Yvonne's papers, then Pierre's, and yet again that morning they recited their family history: He was a civil servant posted to the region; they had been displaced by British bombing on the coast, that's how he got stationed so far from home.

The German looked over at the mayor of Dhuizon. Did he recognize Pierre? Was he indeed a government official?

"I have often seen him around," said the mayor, noting Pierre didn't come to the region much.

They had never met.

The Nazi wrote out an official travel pass, an *Ausweis*. Yvonne and Pierre were free to go.

Pick and Mack were not.

YVONNE AND PIERRE hurried down the steps, across the lawn, back to their Citroën parked on a nearby corner. Should they drive away, they wondered, take advantage of the pass and abandon Pick and Mack? The Canadians could fend for themselves, feign their way out of the scrape, just as Yvonne and Pierre had. But if the boys were left behind, it would be suspicious. If they were all innocent, why wouldn't their friends wait for them? And that tall blond Canadian spoke such truly awful French. Yvonne and Pierre could not, they reckoned, trade two men's lives to save their own. But it was insane to stay at a Nazi control. They were in the enemy's line of sight, with an incriminating package; that put four officers at risk rather than two.

There was no obvious answer: Yvonne and Pierre agreed to split the decision, to both stay and go. Pierre turned the key in the ignition, the Citroën sputtered and drummed to life, but he did not drive away. They sat idling at the corner, in view of soldiers, military trucks, and the whole installation. Their eyes stayed on the doorway of the brick-and-stucco town hall.

They would wait as long as seemed reasonable. The town clock above the entrance sat in a curved pediment, as if teasing the question: How long was too long to wait?

A few uneasy minutes later, German soldiers ran out of the municipal building.

Come back! They shouted. *Revenez!*

Pierre's briefcase had been found.

He let out the clutch, stepped hard on the accelerator, and drove back through the town, while soldiers lifted their guns and took aim.

Three military cars gave chase out of Dhuizon. The Citroën raced past troops massed on either side of the road, trying to outrun the pursuit, blowing beyond the checkpoints. The tight village streets gave way to farms, mostly downhill toward a river.

Time bent and stretched, like the road. It felt suspended for an instant as the car took its head start to roar ahead of the Nazi vehicles. Along winding roads, as they clocked past fields bordered in poplars, the morning sun blinked through dark evergreens. Yvonne and Pierre took screeching turns, trailed by cars of Germans with machine guns poised.

Each mile under the chassis, the soldiers gained. The engine on Yvonne's car had sat abandoned in a field near the demarcation line, a victim of weather and neglect, only to be coaxed back to life by an old mechanic doing his small part for the liberation. Survival was a matter of horsepower: The Wehrmacht's Fords had petrol unadulterated by black marketeers.

Nearing the next town, Bracieux, the Nazis leaned out of their windows with Yvonne and Pierre in their sights and sprayed the car with bullets.

The windshield shattered, splintering into sharp webs, obliterating the contours of the road ahead. Yvonne slumped over onto Pierre's shoulder. Blood pooled out from her collar, staining her brand-new Glengarry-check suit.

Unable to see, Pierre banked a turn just outside the town and lost control, turning off the road into the side of a small inn. The Citroën groaned to a stop.

The soldiers approached the wreck, guns drawn. They threw open the door and dragged Pierre from the driver's seat. He punched at his captors, who beat him to the ground. To go down fighting was the only way to go, Pierre thought.

Standing back from the scrum, a soldier took aim and shot Pierre in the leg. He was now a prisoner of the Gestapo, to be transferred to Paris and to Avenue Foch.

In the crumpled sedan, Yvonne was still. The bullet was lodged in her head but had not penetrated her skull. She was not dead.

CHAPTER 18

Hunted

Paris

André and Gilbert sat together late into the night of June 23, 1943, as they often did, before a pile of paperwork. In a smart corner house with windows over the wooded *bois,* they were comfortable and at ease, the air rich with the after-dark perfumes of climbing roses from a garden below. Paris was blacked out, there was not much of a moon to beam in through an open window. In the dark sky of a new moon, landings and *parachutages* stopped. It was time in which the lovers could pay attention to administrative matters and to each other.

Andrée was still dressed from dinner with her network. In defiance of the war, gaiety was in vogue in Paris that summer; floral-print dresses clung to women's hips and swayed in the breeze. Andrée never had money before the Resistance, and now she was in a swank home, with a suave boyfriend.

Andrée and Gilbert spoke softly; he called her Denise. Cigarettes spooled wisps of smoke into the lamplight. Strewn before them were blank cards on heavy paper stock and a series of postage-stamp-size black-and-white photographs, their colleagues' head shots, in profile.

The room was comfortable; the night was unhurried. They were working in the office of Gilbert's childhood playmate Nicolas Laurent, whose house looked onto the Bois de Boulogne. The friendship between Nicolas and the radio operator was deep and trusting; Gilbert knew the wealthy Laurent family from Saint-Cloud, long ago, and while Nicolas and his wife had an easy enough bourgeois life that would allow them to wait out the war, they offered up space to Gilbert. It was the most important work in the world.

But rebellion was taxing to Andrée and Gilbert's hosts. These nights frustrated Nicolas's British-born wife, Maude, who considered it an abuse of hospitality when they treated her home as if it were a hotel. Houses in the 16th are generous, elegant, and private, with inlaid-wood floors, high ceilings, arched doorways, mirrors, crystal, art, and other class comforts. The PROSPER network "came and went as they wished" from the Laurent home; Francis, so often the third wheel to Andrée and Gilbert, was a frequent guest, so too were Yvonne and Pierre, who would visit to discuss business, arrange details of *parachutages* and arms storage, and ponder the action items assigned for D-Day. The network members made no secret of their activities and plans but seldom included the Laurents in details—for everyone's safety—and so Nicolas paid little attention. (Gilbert never transmitted messages from the Laurent family home; it would put his friends too directly in the Gestapo line of fire.)

Andrée's assignment for the night was atypical but not altogether unusual in clandestine Paris: She and Gilbert were forging new identity cards for the entire network. Throughout the war, authorities changed the long list of documents required for law enforcement—work cards, identity cards, census data, demobilization papers, ration tickets, health certificates, travel passes—and each required stamps and signatures, a visit to the local *mairie*. For the Germans, it was a bureaucratic way to keep a population in line, under constant police scrutiny. For the underground, it was a nuisance. "It is impossible to imagine in just how many back rooms or parlours of France amateur forgers were at work," recalled a circuit leader.

The trade in fake IDs grew as more Parisians slipped through the Nazi net: deserters from forced labor and the Jews. In the summer of 1943, the revised minutiae of *cartes d'identité* dictated that head shots could no longer be face on to the camera, but in profile, and pictures could not be stapled to the heavy cardboard but instead had to be attached with metal rivets. Repeat visits to police stations were not risks that any agent could safely take, so Andrée manufactured new cards.

There were three levels of false documents: "the fake fake papers" supplied in London; the "true fakes," acquired in France and illegally forged; and "the fake true papers," issued by prefectures in the name of some Frenchman who actually existed. The Parisian networks had money to spend on the true fakes, *les vrais faux*. They sought out jewelers, experts in engraving, who carved metal plates to match the block lettering on the official blanks or sent copies home to London to be reproduced. Paris police were demanding negatives every day from professional photographers; it cost extra now to have portrait takers burn originals. (The Paris underground was aided in forgeries by an Irish exile and playwright, Samuel Beckett, who received "arms and money but not . . . orders" from the PROSPER network. As a printer and publisher, Beckett manufactured a "quantity of false papers, visas, circulation cards, etc.," for Andrée's group before he fled from Paris.) No ration tickets could be procured without identification. It was an awful lot of trifling administrative work to create identities for several hundred network members. Rebel lives depended on it.

Andrée had energy for the task; she could stay alert all night as if it were morning. "She never tired." It was nearing midnight, past curfew. Andrée and Gilbert sat with pens, photos, and scissors, entering agents' cover identities: last name, first name, occupation, nationality, birthplace, address, working down a list of network names. Strewn across the desk were the official seals of every German headquarters post in every department, the *Kommandantur*.

Nicolas and Maude Laurent returned from their stroll and a coffee with friends to find Andrée and Gilbert in the office. Occasionally, Maude would help with forgeries, but on that night she was too tired. The couples exchanged pleasant good-nights, and Nicolas and Maude retreated to their bedroom.

As Maude got ready for bed—removing jewelry, running a comb through her thick and tightly curled hair, washing off makeup, performing a woman's evening ablutions—the bell rang at the front door below. Maude fetched her husband, who was already fast asleep.

Annoyed by the late hour, Nicolas went down the back stairs, through the garden, to speak to the visitor from the opposite side of a gate. The young man was neatly dressed, about twenty-five, with polished and learned French. He asked to speak to Gilbert.

The request took Nicolas aback. They were not expecting anyone, and Paris was under lockdown. To be roused so late was uncommon, though not past possible for a house given generously over to the underground. He went back upstairs to fetch the leader, his dear friend.

Andrée was deep in concentration before the lists of names, stamps, photos, rivets, pliers, and detritus of forging when Gilbert stepped away. He left her among the civil luxuries of polished furniture and rich carpets to a pile of unfinished paperwork. It was a brief and casual parting.

In the city darkness, Gilbert and Nicolas spoke to the young man. He said he had the radio crystals that Gilbert was expecting, the ones that Pierre Culioli was set to carry to Paris. Gilbert opened the gate to receive them, and the stranger slipped behind him into the garden.

Gilbert spun around to see the young man holding up a pistol.

At once, some twenty men in civilian clothes came out of the shadows and filed through the gate shouting, "Gestapo!"

Nicolas shouted up the stairs, "Maude, get dressed!" A husband would not want his wife to be arrested in a state of near nudity.

"Open up, German police!" they shouted, running up the kitchen stairwell to the Laurents' bedroom.

Twelve men burst in on Maude in her flimsy, see-through slip, revolvers backed up by machine guns. "Hands up!"

Maude did as she was told, fuming at the violation, fearful for her life.

With commotion inside the house, Andrée jumped up from her work. There were two sets of stairs, one leading to the walled garden and one onto the street. The noise was coming from the back, toward the kitchen. She might still make a break out the other side of the house, the street-facing side. The night was so dark she could dash straight to the *bois* and get lost, hidden by the blackout and the bushes. Andrée was quick and nimble, athletic and young.

Grabbing the PROSPER organization's master list, she shoved it in her mouth. A Nazi threatened to shoot if she swallowed.

At 84 Avenue Foch, only a short walk from the Laurents' home, Andrée was marched to an upstairs interrogation room and questioned through the night and into the morning.

There was a security rule for agents, repeated in the training rooms of Beaulieu: In the likely and typical event of capture, say nothing for forty-eight hours. Take the beating, withstand any torture, two days is not a lifetime. It will not be the end.

But two days was enough time for word to get around a network, for the implicated and connected members to disappear, to destroy evidence, hide weapons, vacate safe houses, change passwords, retreat to an isolated *cachette,* signal to London, save other lives, spare the hard work of the Resistance.

The German interrogators stared down Andrée. They mocked her with her code names—Monique, Denise—demanding her real identity. Andrée's sister lived in Paris; they saw each other often. Léone was pregnant and would be in immediate peril if Andrée said a word. She offered only a false name.

The Nazis knew so much: Andrée and Gilbert were shown photographs of their colleagues. Just hours before, they had been sitting amid those same pictures, cobbling together identity cards. Now the information was in Nazi hands.

Andrée revealed nothing but contempt.

Working in shifts, Germans peppered her with questions: Where were Gilbert's radio sets hidden, and how many were there? Where were the weapons stored? She was asked questions about Buck and Vera, her training at Beaulieu. Interrogators even pronounced the name correctly: Bew-lee.

While secretaries took notes on her every response, Andrée was accused of "wicked and bestial premeditated acts that resulted in many [German] casualties." A mantel clock counted down the hours on Andrée's interrogation: Did she know the date of the Allied invasion?

In the cellar, champagne was chilling.

AFTER A LONG NIGHT of waiting for an airdrop that never came, Francis arrived in Paris on the morning train from Normandy, on June 24. It was the last night of the June moon, there were no more deliveries for another two weeks, and then the pressure would be even more intense. One moon of the summer was gone. The Allied landing was one moon closer to the shores of Europe.

With the posture of a man who had the weight of the war on his shoulders, he walked from the metro to his hotel, through progressively narrow streets. Buildings were squeezed together like books on a tight shelf; pigeons winged low between them. It was as ugly a quartier as Paris was likely to tolerate, a warren of peeling paint and dark shadows, fading propaganda posters, coiffeurs and *tabacs*. Trash lined the seams of the cobbles, bicycles rusted against doorjambs, laundry hung on wires between garrets, even in the rain.

Francis climbed the tumbledown stairs at the Hôtel Mazagran, every move closer to a much-needed bed. It was a short trip to the countryside, and before that his week had been long and met with failure: Pierre and Yvonne were scheduled to come into town but had not arrived. Two new agents, Pick and Mack, also never showed. After three days of missed rendezvous in Paris, with no word, Francis could only conclude his lieutenants were under arrest.

A dark cloud hung over the network. "It's not my health," he told a colleague as he boarded the train back to Paris. "It's much worse. I have not the right to tell you the trouble which weighs on my mind."

At the hotel, his arrival did not rouse the interest of Madame Fèvre, the obliging proprietress; no one met him, nor took any notice. There were no messages.

When Francis opened the heavy door to room 15, a gang of men in civilian clothes was waiting inside. Thugs rushed at him. Boot falls rumbled down from the stairwell above, taking three or four stairs at a time. Still more men came up from below. Francis was trapped, caught, cut down, *abattu*. He was beaten, punched, kicked. His room was "destroyed"; his face was "disfigured." His arm was fractured in the fight. In a hotel stairwell, Paris's sadistic collaborators bloodied and broke Francis.

In twelve hours, Avenue Foch decapitated the British-backed Resistance in the north of France.

It was high summer in Paris, and the Gestapo commanders at Avenue Foch—like the brass at Baker Street—were confident the invasion of Europe was near. In the eyes of those who survived, it is a marvel PROSPER's leadership had not been rounded up by Herr Bömelburg earlier. According to their captors, Andrée, Francis, and Gilbert had long been in view.

The PROSPER network had the misfortune of rebelling early, organizing fast, landing behind the lines before there was a large army of partisans to shield them from sight. Baker Street was now professionalizing the force of agent trainees with a view toward the imminent assault. Such epic catastrophes might be better avoided going forward.

None of this mattered for Francis in that moment. The ultimate cause of his downfall will never be known, only suspected, but the catalysts were everywhere: An armed underground of amateurs was scrambling for D-Day and plagued by breaches; the very nature of the rebel network was insecure. They were hunted by professionals.

Far across Paris, where the streets were wide and tree limbs stretched toward the sky in a generous embrace of light and air, in the upper rooms of the mansion at 84 Avenue Foch, Andrée, Gilbert, and Francis withstood days of questioning by the counterintelligence arm of the Gestapo.

The interrogators extended an offer: If the leaders came clean, no one subsequently caught would be tortured or killed or even treated like a spy. Prisoners would be viewed as soldiers, with deference, jailed in accordance with international law. The Nazis would suspend the criminal *Nacht und Nebel*—Night and Fog—policies of secret executions in exchange for transparency, for complete cooperation, for the slim chance to see sunlight again.

Francis was interrogated continuously for three days, allowed neither food, nor drink, nor sleep. In that small office on the fourth floor of the mansion at No. 84, the contents of the most treasured vault in the building were revealed: Photographed materials collected from the mail over the previous months were "put to very good use in the interrogation of Prosper."

Francis Suttill was shown a copy of his own letter to his wife, Margaret, his "darling child."

CHAPTER 19

When the Hour of Action Strikes

France, London

In Norgeby House on Baker Street, room 52, a FLASH arrived from Station 53: Monique, Prosper, and Archambaud were gone.

In the dark moon of June, the black cars of the Gestapo fanned out to the suburbs and countryside surrounding Paris, to the Atlantic and Channel coasts, through Normandy and Touraine, and to the forests along the Belgian border. German soldiers in groups of tens and twenties arrived at hay barns, cellars, homes, châteaus, sheds, hotels, shops, schools, and churches. In packs, the police came hunting for weapons; they returned to Paris with freedom fighters. Seemingly overnight, said Colonel Buckmaster, "man after man was picked up, the Germans cleverly synchronising their arrests so that no one could give the alarm."

The first new moon after Andrée, Gilbert, and Francis were captured was a bloodbath for the Resistance in northern France—in particular, those networks established along the Channel coast. One arrest led to the next until at least 240 partisans from the PROSPER subcircuits were caught. With a summer invasion coming, the rebel army was decimated in the very place it was needed most.

Buck believed the responsible move was to pull agents from the field. He radioed what was left of the networks in the North.

Compromised agents were to return to England. Paris was too hot to touch. So many agents were missing, not just in F Section, but in RF Section too. General de Gaulle's representative in France, Jean Moulin, was captured with local French Resistance leaders on the same night as Yvonne and Pierre. All lieutenants who had contact with the organizations were contaminated. All addresses were suspect, every café; each password was blown; everyone was likely being tailed.

Lise, who sent messages through Andrée, got recalled to London. From Bordeaux, her brother Claude and his courier, Mary Herbert, were also ordered to return. An airplane would be fetching them back to England in the coming full moons.

Locally recruited partisans who survived the roundups did not go; they couldn't. They were French. Paris was home. They hoped to regroup and rebuild. "Not one of us thought of stopping or running away: if we had wanted to save our skins we wouldn't have continued to work; on the contrary it encouraged us to redouble our activities when Suttill and the others had disappeared," said a PROSPER lieutenant. There had to be a rebel army waiting when the Allies came back to France.

"But we all knew, hour after hour, that it would be a miracle if we weren't arrested."

Lise had no idea why she was ordered to go, only that she had to leave Poitiers quickly. She abandoned her beautiful furnished flat, rent fully paid, shoved a pile of money into a bookcase—it was so much as to be incriminating—and took the opportunity to roam the country as a casual sightseer. She took long wandering walks and "led a different life" until the airplane took her home.

London in late June was fair, dry, and balmy, but the mood in Baker Street was nothing but gloom. "Thinking about captured agents had become a June preoccupation," said a young sergeant.

At last, the FANYs at Station 53 decoded a message from France with relief and joy. F Section's best coder, Gilbert Norman, was back on the air. His radio was operating.

He was alive.

Gilbert wrote that he was in hiding. He confirmed that Andrée and Francis were under arrest.

Vera Atkins received the FLASH in room 52. In those bleak days of bad news, she was over the moon; there was barely a moon in the sky, just a fingernail. Gilbert was a champion radio operator, a signals officer would recall, "inserting his true checks and bluff checks in every message." In all his time in France, Gilbert never once failed to let the FANYs know, via two prearranged identity confirmations, that he was not sending under duress, in enemy hands. He always made certain to tell them.

When Gilbert's hoped-for message arrived, it seemed to be a legitimate transmission, but one of his identity checks was missing. For the first time in eight months, he cocked up. One of the FANYs receiving the message suggested to her superiors that Gilbert might be captured. She knew his fist, his personal Morse signature, and said the traffic was "unusual, hesitant—quite easily the work of a flustered man doing his transmission under protest."

Buck dismissed her concerns. He trusted Gilbert, saying "he'd rather have shot himself" than betray the Firm. He was outraged by Gilbert's mistake in forgetting his true check and said so in his return message:

```
[THAT WAS] A SERIOUS BREACH OF SECURITY WHICH
MUST NOT REPEAT MUST NOT BE ALLOWED TO HAPPEN
AGAIN.
```

From that moment forward, radio specialists on the third floor of 84 Avenue Foch would make sure to always include Gilbert's identity checks when transmitting to London on his personal frequencies and schedules while using his unique codes.

At Avenue Foch, Gilbert was shown Buck's return message and was incredulous. He had deliberately left out the security signal in order to raise the alarm in London. What was the point of having the fail-safes when HQ ignored them? When most critical, Gilbert's identity confirmations meant nothing to the Firm. Absent any apparent support from his Baker Street spymasters, he capitulated.

Gilbert agreed to work for the Nazis of Avenue Foch.

THE PROSPER NETWORK was finished. Andrée was removed to Fresnes Prison. Gilbert was held in the garrets of 84 Avenue Foch to send radio messages on his assigned schedules. Francis would be dispatched to Berlin for further interrogation. He was the mastermind of the very important Paris network, the Nazis believed, so he would certainly know the date of the invasion.

Gilbert grew comfortable in the attic. Bömelburg's men kept British agents around the top floors of Avenue Foch like pets, to psychologically tease new prisoners during interrogations, to confirm identity questions in the radio game, and to serve as talismans, proof of German power in a losing war. For Gilbert, life on Avenue Foch was far easier than life in Fresnes: Prisoners ate the same food as the ranking officers, and at the headquarters of the chief of the Paris Gestapo there was ample butter, eggs, steaks, chocolate, real coffee. There were rewards, too, for active collaboration: cakes, cognac, cigars, and gentleness. Favored prisoners were brought out to restaurants and treated like friends, given flowers and presents on their birthdays. By cooperating, Gilbert believed he was sparing his underground helpers the cruel fate of a military tribunal, "which would condemn them to death by the hundreds." Gilbert revealed details of nearly all the British-backed networks stretching from the Atlantic across the Channel coast to the Belgian border and reaching deep into the Loire valley. Landing zones were identified and torn up, arms caches unveiled. Gilbert helped make organizational charts of the Firm's leaders, the circuits and subcircuits, all of which were ultimately sent to Berlin.

Once Gilbert instructed Avenue Foch where to look, the locals who were not already in hiding got rounded up. Or killed.

In the days that followed, as circuit members were brought to the interrogation rooms at Avenue Foch, Gilbert sat in on their questioning. He had always been "enthusiastic," with "plenty of dash." Now he urged partisans to talk at length to the enemy, to turn over each tiny mote of information down to the very last. "It serves no purpose to deny the truth," he said. "They know absolutely everything, in the most minute detail. If you persist, it will only aggravate the situation and other people will be charged too, but if you tell the truth, the little people will not be accused." He told each new prisoner about his pact with the Gestapo, that in exchange for the information he was saving their lives, that the Nazis gave their word of honor as officers. He predicted a rapid end to the occupation: "We will see each other after the war, if not before."

Despite the FANYs' initial doubts about Gilbert's capture, Baker Street kept transmitting to Gilbert's radio. The Firm's strategy was to keep a conversation going even once a radio was suspect, to always act as if the operator were free, in the hopes that he might be an ongoing source of useful information to the Nazis, that each day the radio game continued was one more day he might be kept alive. Even a losing game could be the difference between life and death for an imprisoned agent—time enough to organize an escape.

"I'm not sure," a German spy chief is reported to have said once Gilbert revealed the extent and depth of the secret sabotage operations in northern France, "whom we shall hang first when we get to London. Winston Churchill or Colonel Buckmaster."

WEEKS LATER, a telegraph signal sparked through shafts of sunlight into an evergreen forest in Bavaria. It was picked up by antenna; then the electric signals pulsed deep through the earth, down into an underground bunker.

In Obersalzberg, Germany, surrounded by three separate belts of barbed wire and minefields, in his steel-and-concrete cocoon, Adolf Hitler was encouraged by information on the progress of the war in France.

The multi-encrypted report was from the Paris security services on Avenue Foch, containing details about the arrest of Jean Moulin, General de Gaulle's ambassador in France. It also gave updates on the state of British terrorism in Paris, which amounted to an almost total victory for the Reich.

In the summer of 1943, fresh off defeat in Stalingrad, the führer remained confident his Reich would reign immortal for a millennium or more. The Germans were preparing for the largest tank battle in history against the Soviets at Kursk. Hitler paid little mind to the Allies' air raids against German targets; a bombing in Hamburg killed more than forty thousand people in one night, nearly as many civilians as the British who died in the Blitz. "A catastrophe, the extent of which simply staggers the imagination," Goebbels wrote in his diary, with no apparent irony.

The führer savored news of the Paris Gestapo's triumph:

> AN IMPORTANT BRITISH TERRORIST ORGANISATION HAS ALSO BEEN DISCOVERED WHICH WAS ENGAGED IN THE ESTABLISHMENT OF STORES OF SABOTAGE MATERIAL AND AUTOMATIC ARMS IN THE VICINITY OF COMMUNICATION CENTRES TO BE USED TO INTERRUPT TRAFFIC IN WESTERN FRANCE IN THE EVENT OF A LANDING AND THE CUTTING OFF OF BRITTANY AND NORMANDY.

In his windowless war chamber, Herr Hitler read on. It was a delightful report:

> THESE ARMS HAD BEEN DELIVERED BY AIR AND AT A GIVEN MOMENT WERE TO BE DISTRIBUTED TO THE CIVILIAN POPULATION WHO SUPPORTED BY BRITISH

PARATROOPS WOULD THEN HAVE PROCEEDED TO DISORGANISE GERMAN COMMUNICATIONS.

The German security services understood the D-Day strategy of the underground—interrupt the telephones and isolate Normandy and Brittany—and the Gestapo had just unraveled the largest espionage organization in France. In the arrests, they captured radio sets and codes that could be played back to London, directed by Berlin. It was a triumph for the Reich.

ONE OF THE HEADS OF THE ORGANISATION WAS A MAJOR IN THE BRITISH ARMY WHO WAS BORN IN FRANCE AND SPOKE PERFECT FRENCH. THE HEADS OF THE NORTH AND NORTH-WEST SECTORS HAVE ALSO BEEN ARRESTED, ONE OF THEM IS A NEPHEW OF CHURCHILL.

Hitler did not know the name of the French-born British major, Francis Suttill, or that his code name was Prosper, but he understood the utility of a prisoner who was a close member of the Churchill family.

The next sentence was intoxicating:

MORE ARRESTS ARE EXPECTED TO BE MADE.

The telegram affirmed Hitler's confidence in the inevitable dominance of the Nazis over Continental Europe:

THIS ORGANISATION WHICH WAS ESTABLISHED QUITE RECENTLY PRESENTED A SERIOUS DANGER IN THE EVENT OF A LANDING (IN ONE DUMP ALONE 240 SUBMACHINE GUNS WITH THE CORRESPONDING AMMUNITION WAS FOUND).

It was a downfall of the gods, a Götterdämmerung.

Hitler never smiled, it was said. But he knew his war was winnable, and he had an infectious sense of conviction. The Reich still possessed 800,000 square miles of Aryan "living room"—*Lebensraum*—and with it a continent of slave labor. He was building an impenetrable wall along the length of his Atlantic shores.

Hitler declared to his generals that the arrests in Paris would set back the Allied invasion of France by at least a year.

CATHEDRAL BELLS CHIMED the hours across the Loire. Swallows wheeled out from buttresses under a Gothic spire in Blois. In the hospital next door, housed in a former abbey and attended by nuns, Yvonne Rudellat lay with a bullet in her head.

Yvonne was wan and hollow-cheeked, her skin papery and lifeless. She was a believer in Oriental medicine, a woman who had put more faith in raw foods and Transcendental Meditation than in the Holy Father; now she was nursed back from death by sisters, in a room overlooking the pathway of pilgrims. She sank into the linens of her bed, but her heart kept beating and her eyelids fluttered.

One day after Yvonne was shot, she regained consciousness. At seventeen hundred miles per hour, the bullet had ripped past her hair, punctured her scalp, slammed into her skull, and stopped there, lodged in a solid box of bone. The projectile did not perforate or exit her head, and it did not penetrate the soft and semiliquid brain; it did not damage the spinal cord; it merely sheared nerve fibers and shredded blood vessels. She lost blood and then consciousness. The bullet was a sledgehammer to the head, her small frame absorbing shock waves that dissipated the energy of the assault.

Surgery could wait, the hospital decided. Dr. Maurice Luzuy chose to leave the bullet in Yvonne's head; the flesh and sinew would heal around it, and at some point in the future the shrapnel could be surgically removed. Yvonne was bandaged, the wound cleaned every few hours; sepsis was the thing most likely to kill her. Within the exigencies of Nazi captivity, thought the doctor, a bullet to the head "might be to her advantage."

Recovery from a bullet wound and head trauma is slow, agonizing, and uncertain. The doctor's prognosis was that Yvonne could expect a range of symptoms: Seizures, mental disorders, paralysis, and speech loss. Her senses would be altered; she would see anomalies—stars and darkness, flashes of light—her ears would ring; she might lose her sense of taste or smell. The best current medical thinking predicted Yvonne would be in pain; she would suffer seething headaches that radiated down her chin and neck into her shoulders and sternum. It was not a pretty future, but she would live. As Yvonne came back to the world from the mists of coma, Dr. Luzuy declared she was likely to regain almost all her faculties except her memory, "which I thought under the circumstances would be no bad thing."

Yvonne was a patient, and she was also a prisoner of the Reich. For members of her circuit, there was hope to be found in Yvonne's precarious health. It was far easier to visit a prisoner in a hospital than in a jail. The surviving members of the network came often to sit at the bedside of "our Jacqueline," undeterred by Nazis standing watch. "I was not sure if there were not even some undercover agents inside, paid by the Germans," said a local who made regular visits, wondering about the true illness of other patients in the ward. He whispered to Yvonne, "Soon you'll be up and we will have tea together again."

She was bewildered, but he believed she recognized him. Yet she did not speak.

In acts large and small, the hospital staff and Yvonne's compatriots conspired to keep her from her fate as an enemy of the Reich. The women of Yvonne's network brought her a new nightgown and smuggled in pastries, rich in butter, sugar, and jam. Said a local woman, "We tried to soften her days." It was not merely that Yvonne was beloved by those who worked for her, who were moved by her "dedication to her companions, her courage, firmness, and spirit of resistance"; there were practical reasons to monitor her as she recovered:

Yvonne was among the last people in the neighborhood who had been able to make reliable contact with London. Also, if the Nazis were ever able to question Yvonne, remaining arms caches might get captured, and other network members would be arrested. She must not be interviewed.

In the days after Yvonne was shot, the Gestapo came to interrogate her several times. Young men in high boots and cinched uniforms arrived at the hospital entrance on the river and marched through the maze of wards to her room. When the receptionists saw them at the entrance, they alerted the isolation ward, sounding an alarm far in the back of the hospital, where Yvonne rested, so that her doctors could administer Pentothal, a fast-acting general anesthetic. By the time the Nazis shouldered their way in and reached her bedside, Yvonne was fast asleep.

Yvonne's days of illness settled into something approaching routine as the spectral figure gained strength and health. A series of rescue plans took shape as she improved, some schemes more viable than others. Hospitals are vulnerable: There are points of transfer, nodes in a chain of possession, very few professional jailers, a compassionate staff, and plenty of opportunities to buy off someone in power. The police were German; the hospital was French.

There were supposedly tunnels between the crypts of the church and the eight-hundred-year-old vaults of the original abbey. Yvonne could be smuggled out on a gurney or wheelchair through underground passageways, and into a car, if anyone could remember where the secret tunnels were; no one knew.

When Yvonne was strong enough to walk, she could hypothetically leave in a nun's nursing habit, hiding her wounds, exiting via a locked door used only by medical staff. She could then be spirited across the river to a safe house. Circuit members got to work making a wax impression of the iron key to the lock, in order to pour a new one, a substitute to use on the day of her escape.

As rescue plans were shared within the network, the maelstrom of tragedy in the PROSPER-connected circuits came into clear view:

Pierre Culioli had described the location of arms dumps and drop zones around Blois and sent letters to his lieutenants instructing them to cooperate. When the Nazis poured back into the countryside, they swept up many of Yvonne's would-be rescuers.

The few remaining agents in Paris got word of Yvonne's capture and sent a large bribe to the countryside to secure her release, one million francs, the going rate for a British agent. At a time when communication between London and northern France was restricted by a dearth of radios, paying for Yvonne's freedom with money from the remaining coffers was a long shot with bad odds.

To the degree that Yvonne understood there was a rescue afoot, she discouraged it. Any breakout put more partisans at risk, extending the tragedy of her capture. She knew there was a torrent of disaster waiting.

Her presence in the Blois hospital was an open point of pride in those restless, humid days. She became a local celebrity, an honored guest, the lady saboteur, the little old woman from England who fought against Germany for France. The hospital staff developed a sense of ownership over Yvonne. Protecting her was a way to express support for the Resistance. It was an act of patriotism to keep her alive and away from the Nazis.

One night a young doctor at a nearby pub delighted in Yvonne's story after too many glasses of wine and was overheard by German soldiers. Abruptly orders came down to the hospital: Yvonne was to be transferred to a prison hospital in Paris.

THE HUNDRED MILES of country road between Blois and Paris sizzled on a summer day, and Yvonne's ambulance was a tin can of moisture and sickness. She was accompanied by the chief of the local health department, who monitored the patient. Hours into the ride, Yvonne's condition destabilized, her heartbeat grew irregular, her breathing labored.

The doctor insisted that the driver stop and pull over. The patient was failing, he said. He had to deliver an injection, or she would die long before she arrived at the Paris hospital.

The ambulance slowed to a stop on the side of the road. Insects hummed in fields, and the German on guard, cradling his gun, stepped out of the vehicle.

"If you will allow me, I would like to get out," the Nazi said, taking a deep breath of heady summer air.

"I can't stand the sight of blood."

THE MOON KEPT GROWING. France's twenty-eight-day cycle of nightly anticipation repeated in the middle of July. Wood radio cabinets were set in the middle of sitting rooms, far from walls, windows, and curious neighbors. The evening BBC ritual was by now a national joke. "Did you hear at 9:20 a Jew killed a German soldier and ate his heart?" someone would ask. "Impossible for three reasons: Germans have no heart, Jews don't eat pork, and at 9:20 everyone is listening to the BBC."

The French-language broadcast was preparing the country for one single piece of news in the summer of 1943: the announcement of the Allied invasion. Summertime and milder weather had made Channel crossings easier. As the July moon period began, the BBC French military correspondent laid out explicit details of the coming assault:

> The English and American armies wish to land as soon as possible on European soil. The occupied countries wait with impatience, but such a massive and important expedition requires long and difficult preparations.

A sigh was shared as the French digested the cautious information: Europe was witnessing an "air battle of unprecedented proportions." Virtually no corner of Hitler's Europe was now beyond the range of Allied aircraft. Anglo-American armies were at that moment being trained to land on beaches from the water.

The whole world waits impatiently for the day when it will at last be possible to begin the final attack.

In London, the spymasters at Baker Street were all on standby, for they too were listening when the BBC announcer said,

The chances of success grow every day.

On Saturday night, July 10, 1943, a waxing quarter moon rose behind the Eiffel Tower, while Parisians gathered *en famille* around the radio.

There was a special report, directed at France:

The United Nations armed forces have today launched an offensive against Sicily. It is the first stage in the liberation of the European continent. There will be others.

The news was wonderful and terrible, encouraging and sad. The Allies had landed in Europe, but they had not come to France. Liberation was so close, yet half a continent away.

Across a hundred miles of hazardous Mediterranean beachfront, Sicily saw the first invasion of Allied troops in Europe, in "an amphibious assault of peculiar complexity."

Yet in France, so many partisans risked their lives; so many young men were in the hills. So many had already died, and many more were joining the maquis daily. Though the PROSPER network had been destroyed, France had thousands of rebels at arms, waiting and ready. She wanted to liberate herself but could not do so without an Allied armada. Freedom went to Italy first, the country that invented fascism and then so eagerly signed on to Herr Hitler's brand.

It was not lost on Allied Force Headquarters that the announcement would be met with outrage in France.

In formal and measured tones, the radio presenter continued:

> I call on the French people to remain calm, not to allow themselves to be deceived by the false rumors which the enemy might circulate. The Allied radio will keep you informed on military developments.

Morale was about to break. How does one maintain hope after years of occupation? There were no reserves upon which resistance might draw. Can rebellion sustain itself in disappointment? The return of French colonies in North Africa was not enough; nightly words of inspiration from General de Gaulle were not the same as sovereignty. The future of France rested on its freedom, yet the Allies had chosen Italy instead.

The decision was six months old. At the Casablanca conference in January, the war chiefs declared they would open the line of assault against Hitler in Europe in 1943. One plan was named Operation Husky: With Sicily as the bridgehead, the Allies would launch the first major offensive in Europe. The island was only ten miles from the Continent. Winston Churchill called it an "attack against the soft under-belly of the Axis." British and American troops could bash their way up the boot, sever Italy from Hitler, and seize control of the Mediterranean, all the while diverting Wehrmacht firepower away from the Russian front.

> I count on your sangfroid and on your sense of discipline. Do not be rash, for the enemy is watching.

At 84 Avenue Foch, the fates of newly captured "terrorists"—Andrée and Gilbert among them—at once changed. There would be no further point in torturing Andrée for the date of an invasion that wouldn't take place that summer. Berlin knew as well as London and Washington that Allied forces were not strong enough to mount simultaneous side-by-side campaigns in Italy and France in 1943.

> When the hour of action strikes we will let you know. Till then help us by following our instructions. That is to say: keep calm, conserve your strength.

If the French people fought back now, they could expect no Allied support for an uprising. There would be no victory parade marching to the "Sambre-et-Meuse" in the summer of 1943.

France was instructed to wait. *Attentisme.*

We repeat: when the hour of action strikes we will let you know.

Hitler was given one more summer to reinforce his Atlantic Wall.

Part III

CHAPTER 20

Kisses

Fresnes Prison

In the prison yard at Fresnes, Andrée Borrel could hear occasional bars of the "Marseillaise," though the German officials there forbade all singing. News got around the prison; information was whispered through pipes, passed along in notes by cellmates, tapped out in Morse code. Every prisoner knew the Allies had landed in Italy.

Andrée always believed she would survive the war, that Hitler would lose. She told her colleagues so and insisted they cheer up and pass it on.

Andrée was sunny, all things considered, in contact with the outside world again as 1943 became 1944. She charmed or inveigled a way to pay a prison wardress to send her laundry to her sister. In dainty handwriting on the thinnest of cigarette paper, Andrée tucked messages into the lining of her lingerie and gloves, quotidian requests for necessities, news, and intricately coded information for the few members remaining in the Paris-based underground.

"*Chère Lily,*" Andrée's letters began. Her sister Léone had been pregnant the previous summer, and now there was a baby, a nephew—what was his name? In the cascade of the PROSPER disaster, Léone's husband, Robert, had been captured too, so the family must need money: Andrée urged her sister to sell everything—all of Andrée's possessions. Léone should not deny herself or their mother. (And certainly not on this prisoner's account, Andrée snarked; with her new "military situation" she didn't need much.) The only thing she didn't want Léone to sell was the gold necklace; she might want that after the war. There was still money to be had in Paris through the British organization: Andrée continued earning a salary in London; all IOUs would be backed up. The inmates of Fresnes were convinced that 1944 would be the year of their freedom.

Andrée made requests for food: tea, oil, jam. There should be supplies left from the British airdrops, she wrote. If Léone would put some sugar cubes in the bottom of the jam jar, Andrée would find them. She needed soap too, toothpaste, sanitary napkins. And cigarettes. She reminded Léone to never forget matches, either. At Christmas, the Red Cross supplied prisoners with gingerbread—too much really, Andrée wrote, she was stuffed. Andrée worried their mother might learn she was in jail, so please, she begged, don't send any packages if *Maman* might find out.

There were errands for Léone to perform: Andrée was having clothes made in Paris. Would her sister mind going around to the tailor to get the suits? The dressmaker just happened to be connected to the underground network. "Tell her I regret not having been able to invite her for lunch," was the message, "but it will happen soon and be better than at the Tavern deGenève." Mentioning your last meal together was an identity check, a way to confirm the veracity of the sender. The seamstress would understand any deeper connotations.

Andrée continued working for the Firm, even from prison. She had a coat for winter, so didn't need one, but she had no boots or warm pants in prison. The winter gear was stored with a rebel colleague in Trie-Château who would also understand Andrée was checking in as a professional when Léone delivered her message. As her sister instructed, "You will say that Andrée is very happy, let him have the provisions, she hopes that it will last." The so-called provisions were likely supplies from containers that had not been rooted out by Nazis in the collapse of the circuit. Andrée asked that Léone relay any messages back through the laundry.

The list went on: Could Léone send rabbit fur slippers to the Tambour sisters, also in Fresnes? Andrée tried to stay clean and hygienic, she wrote, she wore a slip under her suit so as not to dirty it, but she hadn't taken the right outfits to prison; when instructing an armed Nazi on what to collect from your apartment, it was hard to think. Avenue Foch interrogators found Andrée's address in Pierre Culioli's briefcase. From Gilbert they discovered where Léone's in-laws lived; he had hidden a wireless set there. (She wrote that it might, however, be insensitive to mention Gilbert's perfidy to the in-laws, whose son had just been imprisoned in the sweep.) Andrée's lover Maurice Dufour had never surrendered a word under torture; Maurice had been unmoved even by threats of Andrée's gang rape.

Now Gilbert had betrayed an entire network to Avenue Foch.

So, too, had the other Gilbert, Henri Déricourt.

Andrée wrote she was making use of the time on her hands. She was knitting a sweater and needed fine-gauge needles, scissors, zippers, trimmings. She was also studying English and asked for a textbook.

Andrée's prison letters are awkward, reading as if they are written in a subtle code, understood only by sisters and members in on the subterfuge. It is hard to imagine she was really having suits professionally made when all French fabric was shipped to Germany in occupation payments; or that an English textbook would be an anodyne request, smuggled into a prison controlled by Germans.

If anyone were to find Andrée's hidden missives, they might not know precisely what was intended by her requests. Four years into the occupation, it was a habit of the French to put few specifics into writing, to say things via allusion and implication—everything was censored. Andrée's notes were high risk to deliver, the penalties severe if captured. Her instructions to Léone feel like cryptic riddles.

The big and obvious appeals were tucked into the enciphered and mundane. She told her sister to burn her papers in the suitcases. She added that any trace of wireless messages obviously had to go. She wanted to know who came around asking about Andrée's rented room. And she warned that if anyone were to say they had a message from Fresnes Prison, Léone was not to believe them. Most important,

Andrée admonished, her sister was not to trust anyone else to pass a message back: It would only be a trap.

Take care of yourself, she said. *Bon Noël.* She wished happy birthdays to both her sister and her mother.

"I think I am going to Germany."

Baisers.

CHAPTER 21

A Patriotic Profession

Poitiers

The rent was paid, the moon was waning, and in the wee hours of February 18, 1944, the agent Mary Herbert sat in bed feeding her newborn daughter, Claudine, two months old.

Mary had taken up residence in Lise de Baissac's comfortable and now empty flat next door to the Gestapo headquarters. Lise and Mary had been friendly colleagues—they were graduates of the same class at Beaulieu—and after Mary arrived in France on *Seadog,* alongside Odette, she became the courier for Claude's SCIENTIST network on the coast.

Now Lise and Mary were family: Claude de Baissac was both Mary's commanding officer and the father of her child. At first, he had not wanted a woman under his command, since "their nerves were not usually strong enough for the job." But Mary's discreet intellectualism convinced him otherwise. They were a reliable team, close and confiding (closer than advisable by military standards; the baby was intentional).

"Claude and I are doing the necessary to have a baby," Mary announced to Lise one night the previous spring.

"You are completely crazy," said Lise. "What are you going to do with a baby during the war?"

"I want a baby," said Mary. She was forty years old, she came from an old recusant family—the line of British Catholics who refused to convert after the Reformation—and the family was small. She wanted to be a mother.

"Please, give me a child?" Mary said to Claude.

So he did.

Mary "didn't want a husband, she wanted a child," said Lise. "Things happen."

Claude's circuit in Bordeaux had been a "powerful organization" in a region full of Vichy sympathizers, many of them former soldiers from the military Right, the *anciens militaires*. Claude was "one of the most capable organizers we ever sent to France," said his commanders. The SCIENTIST network was twenty thousand paramilitary men strong. Claude also mobilized thirty thousand sympathizers who might be put to use during the Allied invasion. In his first year in the field, his teams received 121 dropping operations: 1,600 containers, 350 packages, containing 18,400 pounds of high explosives, 7,500 Sten submachine guns, 300 Bren machine guns, 1,500 rifles, and 17,200 grenades.

Claude, like his sister, was an overachiever who grew into a multipurpose espionage agent. He was dispatched for sabotage, but he doubted the value of Bangs before the Allied landing; when the time came, his men were ready to deny the Germans use of all railway lines between Bordeaux and Spain. Until then, Claude provided key intelligence to the Allies about shipping in and out of France. "It is the ground intelligence from Bordeaux which has virtually put an end to blockade-running between Europe and the Far East this year. The stoppage of this traffic is of the highest importance as the supplies ordered are vital to the Japanese."

Mary worked continuously for Claude through her first two trimesters. Her impending motherhood was reasonable cover—what pregnant woman would work for the underground?

Mary's work ended long before she went into labor. Lise and Claude were exfiltrated back to London on the same flight in the summer of 1943, and Mary vanished into France. They all had to go, their network was rocked by arrests, and they were familiar faces to so many of the captured Paris agents—Andrée, Yvonne, Gilbert, and Francis—but it was believed Mary could not go in her condition. Also, if Mary returned to London, what kind of life could she hope for? Pregnancy meant instant demobilization. What job would she find as an unmarried mother, alone in England?

France, at least, had a reverence for mothers. It was considered a patriotic profession. Philippe Pétain had blamed France's fall to Hitler on "too few children," the idea being that babies grow up to become soldiers and France would have had the strength to resist the German assault. For the Vichy regime, childbirth was championed as a collaborative act; reproduction was a service to the *Patrie*—so much so that birth control and abortion were criminalized under Vichy law, punishable with both fines and imprisonment, up to 120,000 francs and twenty years. Abortionists were guillotined. (Abortion was treason; prostitution was legalized.)

Mary preferred France, though war was no happy time for babies. She had money from the Firm and a safe home that was paid in full. By 1944, the coastlines were under constant Allied bombardment. In Poitiers, there were only a few hundred German soldiers compared with the many divisions stationed along the coast. Lise's apartment was so warm and inviting that at one point the Gestapo tried to requisition it for themselves. Said Mary, "Life in Bordeaux was too uncomfortable with a very young baby." It would have been a lousy place to raise Claude's daughter: There was a price on his head. He was among the Gestapo's most wanted men.

In the winter of 1944, the coming invasion of France was a near certainty. Though the Italy campaign was deadlocked at Monte Cassino—the Allies had yet to reach Rome—between Nazi command and Allied chiefs, there was shared conviction that the Anglo-American fleet would cross the Channel in the spring or summer. The whole world expected it.

In Britain, Lise and Claude were briefed on their roles in the Allies' D-Day battle plans. A new scheme paired British and American special operatives with French officers, who would parachute in uniform after the landings to provide a command structure for the amateur French Resistance: Operation Jedburgh. When the Jeds arrived, Claude would be there waiting, a key maquis commander in northern France.

If Mary and Claude survived the war, he promised to someday make her his wife, to legitimize the child. He would do the proper and correct thing by his new family, and before leaving France, he testified in writing that the baby was his, with witnesses from the Firm, on the type of document that might get everyone killed. Put nothing on paper, security rules dictated, but the letter was a necessity; though detailing Claudine was born a bastard, if either Mary or Claude died in action, it was the little girl's only hope at a war pension.

No one at Baker Street knew what had become of Mary. She had slipped away from Bordeaux without a trace. Armed with passwords for Lise's young maid, Mary took over the charming apartment, the pile of money in the bookshelf, as well as the "heating and an easier life." There was no further contact with London.

Formerly so thin, Mary had filled out from the pregnancy but was frail from giving birth. That February day, during Claudine's morning feeding, Mary was in bed when the doorbell rang. She hoped it might be one of the partisans with news of Claude from London; she had no idea when he would return.

The charwoman let in two men from the Gestapo, asking for Madame Irène Brisée, Lise's cover name.

Madame Brisée was in Paris, Mary said.

How friendly were the two women, such that a new mother might reside in her home while the other was away in Paris?

They had met via a mutual friend, Mary responded. With a newborn, Mary didn't know where else to go. There was no father. She had looked to Madame Brisée for help.

With the Gestapo in the flat and a baby in her arms, Mary asked if it might be possible to send her maid out to shop for a few basics such as bread, formula, diapers, and, if it could be found, soap. Newborns had so many needs.

If the young maid had any sense at all, Mary thought, she would warn someone in Lise's network, get the word out, sound the alarm.

Mary clutched her baby daughter and in her mind invoiced the contents of the apartment: There was a piece of British-labeled chocolate in the cupboard. In the uncut sheaves of a book, there was the note testifying to Claudine's paternity and an inexplicably large sum of money, damning evidence in so many directions.

The Gestapo inspectors told Mary that she would have to come to headquarters for questioning. Her baby would stay behind.

Mary refused: No infant can be left alone. What kind of mother does that? What Frenchwoman would consider it? What cretin even demands it?

The Germans agreed to wait until the maid returned.

Under the circumstances, Mary explained, it was a mother's job to leave instructions for her baby's care. She scribbled out a note about diets, bedtimes, changing, and perhaps what to do with Claudine should Mary never return from prison.

Would she be in jail for very long? Mary asked. The German inspectors were nonresponsive.

The maid returned and in whispers let Mary know that Lise's network helpers were at that moment getting rounded up too; throughout Poitiers, at least five were taken into custody.

Mary was arrested.

She surrendered her baby girl.

Resistance had the attention of France in the winter of 1944. So many agents were captured in the deadly summer of 1943 that at least a third of the arms dumps in the North of France were now in the hands of the Nazis—in what would become the combat zone. Despite this, much had been accomplished: There were Bangs. Factories were put out of action, boats were sunk, locomotive axles got fouled with sand, and at a French shirt factory a consignment of navy uniforms destined for Nazi submarines was treated with itching powder.

The Firm's tactics now looked only toward the invasion. Baker Street no longer sanctioned small, violent acts of inconvenience for morale boosting and recruitment, but was instead coordinating synchronized countrywide efforts to hobble infrastructure during the largest seaborne assault the world had ever seen. Battle plans for underground uprisings in Europe stretched two thousand miles, from Scandinavia to Spain.

In France, the aim was to weaken the Wehrmacht on all sides. The BBC French service declared a national goal in the spring of 1944 to "prepare the mass of French for the responsibilities that devolve to them at the time of the landing." Announcers began calling for attacks "disrupting transport of the enemy by harassing his troops, eliminating militia, organizing sympathy strikes." During the invasion, if the Germans could be forced to use radios instead of telephones, the Allies could anticipate enemy movements via Ultra decrypts of the Enigma code.

Mary did not know it yet, but Claude was already back in France for his second mission, assigned to Normandy. He was arming a rebel band to harry the German army from the rear, to prevent reinforcement troops from ever reaching the front. Where a year earlier Claude sent angry wires to Baker Street about the dearth of weapons, by the fourth year of the war in France air operations were frantic, rising from 107 in the final three months of 1943 to 759 in the first quarter of 1944 and to 1,969 between April and June. Petty concerns about morale no longer obsessed Claude; instead, he focused on massing sufficient men for his maquis. The Firm was now supplying weapons to a rebel army 125,000 strong; 75,000 would be armed by F Section, 50,000 by de Gaulle's RF Section.

At secret training schools in England and Scotland, Lise was now a seasoned agent, working as a conducting officer for a new class of female recruits, all with missions tailored to the invasion. But one day as she was practicing her parachute jumps, she broke her leg. The injury laid her up many more months than she would have liked; she wanted back in on the fight.

Still, nobody knew where the Allies would land: Calais? Brittany? Normandy? All areas in northern France were waiting for the flotilla.

All action bent toward the target date: May 1944.

Mary was interrogated every ten days. As rehearsed at Beaulieu, she recounted her cover story: She had spent most of her life in Alexandria, she said. Her father was an archaeologist; she studied art in Florence. Now she had to improvise around the baby. Her husband was an engineer, she told the Nazis, but they were separated, and she took up a lover in Paris. When she discovered she was pregnant, she went to the capital to announce the news and found him in bed with a blonde. He "told her to get out," handed her 100,000 francs to go away and "never trouble him again." It was a pitiable tale that explained both her lonely status and the quantities of cash sitting around the apartment.

On its face, the Gestapo accepted Mary's story. They were targeting Lise.

Did Mary know Lise had a lot of lovers? Or were all those men who went in and out of her home actually British agents? Did she know that Lise was a British spy?

Mary professed innocence. She had only ever been introduced to Lise's Spanish teacher, a university professor. She was very weak from her cesarean, she explained. The surgery was debilitating; she was too unwell to socialize.

Did Mary know that Lise spoke fluent English?

Mary said no, she did not.

The interrogator held a quizzical beat. Mary did not sound French. You have a queer accent, she was told.

For this too, Mary had a practiced and ready response: If you'd spent your life in Egypt, speaking Arabic, French, English, Spanish, and Italian, you, too, would have an odd accent.

Mary did not tell her captors she spoke excellent German; it was her sixth language.

"I don't think we shall get anything out of this woman," the interrogator confided to his superior *auf Deutsch*.

"We will keep her while she thinks it over."

As part of the interrogations, the Gestapo showed Mary organizational charts and photos of F Section agents such as Andrée, Yvonne, and Odette, with addresses she recognized. She'd had a duplicate key to Andrée's apartment for when she passed through Paris.

Mary declared her ignorance. She was just a single mother who was missing her baby daughter.

One day an air raid interrupted the endless hours of repetitive questioning. The Allied bombing campaign was intensifying at every point, strategically pummeling France in advance of the summer offensive.

A panicking German asked his superior officer, should they leave for the shelter?

The interrogator was sanguine: "We will all be dead shortly." Even hardened Nazi commanders believed the Reich was fighting a losing war in France in 1944.

Why was the baby called Claudine? the Gestapo asked. Did Mary know there was an agent Claudine in Bordeaux? Was there any connection?

Claudine was Mary's alias.

No, she answered, it is just a pretty name. A pious name. The little girl was born near the feast of Saint Claude, a midwinter saint's day.

Would she ever see her daughter again? she wanted to know.

Only if she told the truth.

Mary signed seven copies of her testimony, in French and in German.

Just before Easter, after two months' imprisonment, Mary was released from Gestapo custody. The wardens returned her belongings, but not her ring; she was asked to come back to the jail the following day to see if it could be found. With Holy Week near, the ring was returned with apologies.

While Mary was in prison, air raids burned through Poitiers, terrifying Lise's little maid. She had brought baby Claudine to a local orphanage and fled the small city for safer—less populated and less strategic—ground.

The sisters at the Hôtel-Dieu were kind to Mary's baby, "who had been very well looked after." It was against church policy to return foundlings to mothers who had abandoned them, but Mary explained that the Nazis had arrested her, and the nuns were compassionate.

Throughout her captivity, Gestapo interrogators and Vichy collaborators never accepted that a frail new mother might also be a British spy.

Motherhood saved Mary's life.

CHAPTER 22

A Little Braver

Paris

At 84 Avenue Foch, on May 13, 1944, Andrée Borrel and Odette Sansom stepped into the drawing room with six other women, all from F Section. Belle epoque mirrors angled down on the room: Odette and Andrée had been in prison for almost a year; the others had mostly just arrived and had the fresh, healthy look of women for whom captivity was a new inconvenience rather than an established hell.

They sat under the diffident and hard watch of German soldiers.

"Why don't you make us some tea?" Odette demanded. "You've got a lot of English tea, I know."

It was an imperious, dangerous command, but she was right: The Nazis had been receiving British containers for nearly a year thanks to the radio games of Avenue Foch.

As if by rote, the Nazi sentries followed Odette's orders. Tea came on a platter, in bone china teacups patterned on the rim. The women marveled at the simple human pleasure of a good brew in a delicate cup. They hadn't seen anything like it in a long time.

A chipper British man whom Odette recognized came into the room. John Starr, Avenue Foch's newest pet agent, had replaced Gilbert once his radio was confirmed to have been captured. John wandered in from his workroom, where he helped the Nazis, and offered the women chocolate. Odette had met him on her very first day in France: His brother had sailed on the felucca *Seadog* alongside Odette and Mary, and they had passed briefly on the rock-strewn beach in the middle of the night. During one of her Avenue Foch interrogations, he even sat in and listened. Odette was furious any British agent would side with his captors. John was translating messages for the radio game and checking the grammar of non-native English speakers, using phrases that would only be understood by a Briton. He rationalized that he never actively gave information away, only received it, that if he kept up friendly conversation, the Gestapo might tip its hand and give up some intelligence, some key thing that might help win the war. He believed he might escape in a stray and careless moment and be useful again to the Allies with all he had overheard. But when John helped the Nazis at Avenue Foch with their radio games, Baker Street sent seventeen agents to parachute grounds controlled by Hitler.

Odette greeted John with a cool "How are you?" then taunted him. She announced his brother had been sent to Germany. (Odette was wrong; she mixed up secret identities. John's brother George Starr was instead in Toulouse, allegedly torturing collaborators by setting their feet on fire.) She memorized the details of John's face, what he was wearing—flannel trousers, blue jacket, beret—so that when the war was over, she could report his treachery to Baker Street.

But Odette did not expect to survive. She had tuberculosis. Upon leaving Fresnes, she left a package with the prison chaplain intended for her daughters. It contained a letter and handmade rag dolls stitched in prison from scraps of clothing.

Andrée, though, had faith she would live. The Allies were winning. She could hear bombs from her prison window. It was only a matter of time.

Each woman carried with her a few precious possessions: One had a large fur coat, despite the summer heat; Andrée had all that winter clothing from her sister. Another had lipstick in a pretty and flirtatious shade; she passed it around so that everyone could take a turn. They thought it was such a treat.

In the gracious environment, such a contrast to their cells, they were happy to see one another, to be among colleagues, said Odette. They "talked and talked and talked." In Fresnes, they had to maintain cover with other prisoners—there were stool pigeons everywhere—but here at Avenue Foch all was revealed. Every woman was a secret agent; "everybody was more or less in the same position."

Over tea, the women reflected on their service. All were lucky to be alive. Many of their colleagues were not. Some blamed themselves: Counting their own errors, they rehearsed their missions, listing the things they might have done otherwise, with the accumulated wisdom, hindsight, and regret of a prisoner.

They shared suspicions that there was a mole actually inside London headquarters—so much had gone wrong for so many. One woman had been apprehended at touchdown, a victim of the radio games. Another was pregnant, married to an agent but determined to be helpful, even in a fragile state. One young agent was a great laugh, even fun, especially for a prisoner; she had been captured just six weeks before, and her incarceration was a novelty. There was an older French businesswoman; some terribly stiff English girl with a tartan ribbon in her hair; and a German-born Jew, the girlfriend of a lieutenant in the Jewish network who got swept up in the dragnet that followed the PROSPER arrests.

However unique their lives and histories, what struck Odette were their commonalities, why they had taken up spy craft in the first place. "We all had the feeling in the beginning that we were going to be—helpful."

They tried to keep their spirits up by talking about what would happen after the war. Conversations about the far future skipped over the proximate one: Teutonic formality yielded little information, only that they would be transferred from a French prison to a German one.

There was a sense of confidence in numbers, in togetherness, after the lonely days of Fresnes. In a lavish mansion in a summery Paris, the women were considerate and supportive, talking up a promising future over English tea. "Everybody tried to be a little braver than they felt."

Sunlight spilled in through tall windows, past heavy drapes. Every woman was beautiful and courageous; each took her turn to cry. They wept for what lay ahead.

The women were handcuffed to each other as they got into the police van and drove away from 84 Avenue Foch to a train bound for Germany.

Paris blinked past. On the streets, women were wearing light dresses and big round sunglasses, men were in shirtsleeves; couples chatted on café terraces, sipping coffees. Everybody seemed to be holding hands. It was a glimpse of the life they knew and loved, of the France for which they had fought.

Tomorrow was all night and fog.

CHAPTER 23

The Sighing Begins

France

On June 1, 1944, a strawberry moon waxed full over the English Channel when the 9:15 BBC French broadcast began—as it had for four years—by pounding out victory notes, demanding the attention of occupied France.

Ici Londres!

Following the news, in the endless stream of puerile phrases and throwaway nursery rhymes, a personal message aired, repeating a signal that had also sounded on May 1:

When a sighing begins
In the violins
Of the autumn-song.

It was the first three lines of "Autumn Song" by Verlaine, one of the best-known poems in the French language: This was the "A" message, the "standby" order. It played again on June 2, June 3, and June 4.

Resistance cells throughout France had received orders by telegraph:

MAJOR OPERATION SCHEDULED IN THE NEXT FEW DAYS
STOP YOU WILL BE NOTIFIED BY THE BBC TWENTY
FOUR HOURS BEFORE OPERATIONS COMMENCE STOP THE
RELEVANT MESSAGE WILL BE

MY HEART IS LULLED
IN THE SLOW SOUND
LANGUOROUS AND LONG.

This was the second half of the Verlaine stanza—slightly mangled—the so-called B message. The "action" order.

YOUR TASK WILL BE TO SABOTAGE RAILWAY LINES
DESTROY PETROL DUMPS AND MAXIMIZE DISRUPTION TO
THE ENEMY'S LINES OF COMMUNICATION STOP EXECUTE
WELL-TIMED GUERRILLA OPERATIONS BUT AVOID
ANY LARGE SCALE ACTION THAT COULD EXPOSE THE
CIVILIAN POPULATION TO REPRISALS.

Targeting instructions had gone out to all networks in France. Plan Green was a two-week operation to sabotage the rails. Plan Blue ordered destruction of electrical plants. Plan Violet aimed to destroy enemy telephone and teleprinter wires, forcing the Nazis to broadcast their battle plans by radio. Plan Turtle called for a stalling operation, to keep Hitler's reinforcements away from the beaches.

The invasion would necessarily be in the North, but General Eisenhower believed it was important to notify circuits everywhere to prepare for mass sabotage, to mask the specific D-Day landing site.

In Indre, around Valençay and Châteauroux, rebels were listening for

Quasimodo est une fête.
Quasimodo is a party.

In the Dordogne, rebels expected to hear

La girafe a un long cou.
The giraffe has a long neck.

On June 5, 1944, at 9:15, when the second broadcast of the nightly *Les Français parlent aux Français* program began, the weather over the English Channel was chilly with high winds, ugly squalls, and fractured, confused seas.

A little before 10:00 p.m., at 84 Avenue Foch, all radios were tuned in. Gestapo officers listened for the personal messages at the end of the variety show. Hitler believed the invasion would "decide the issue not only of the year but of the whole war. . . . If we don't throw the invaders back we cannot win a static war in the long run." Germany had exhausted itself over five years of fighting, and France was too large for a massive countrywide opposing front line in a war of attrition. "Therefore, the invasion must be thrown back on [its] first attempt."

In the thread of *messages personnels,* the announcer read in French the "B" message:

Bercent mon coeur
D'une langueur
Monotone.

The Paris Gestapo recognized the "action" call for D-Day. Between captured radio sets and imprisoned agents, the code phrase had been in German hands all spring. Avenue Foch had noted an increase in radio activity and understood the invasion was near; Sergeant Hugo Bleicher, the notorious "Colonel Henri" who arrested Odette and Peter, said he got information about "action" codes from two of his double agents, men recruited by André Marsac, the CARTE lieutenant.

Avenue Foch believed the Verlaine poem was the "action" call to all rebel forces, everywhere in France. Once the message sounded, Nazi leadership of *Gross-Paris* sent urgent telegrams to the German high command.

The Allied invasion was arriving within forty-eight hours.

Upon hearing the alerts, the German military did nothing. With every moon, it seemed, the Nazis on the Channel coast had been told to stand ready; with each false start, they became more frustrated. At Calais, on the Cotentin Peninsula, the German Fifteenth Army heard the known BBC code words and was placed on alert, but in Normandy it was decided the German Seventh Army should take no action whatsoever. "I'm too old a bunny to get too excited about this," sniffed a Nazi commander as he resumed his bridge game. General Rommel received no warning at all; he was home celebrating his wife's birthday. Field Marshal von Rundstedt, commander of German forces on the western front, balked: "As if General Eisenhower would announce the invasion over the BBC."

Within minutes of the last words—*langueur monotone*—the rebels were neither languorous nor dull; they were fully engaged. Allied tacticians hoped for action in phases, but the people were so hungry for freedom that the Resistance stepped out all at once.

At sunrise on June 6, on a rusty bicycle on a back road west of Paris, Lise de Baissac's leg was aching. It smarted from the bad break she had received during her follow-up training jump between missions. Bicycles were the true weapon of the Resistance, it was said. A daily convenience before the war, they now cost as much as a new car and were as closely regulated with license plates. Lise cycled away from the capital, toward Normandy.

In the vast farm country below the Channel coast, Lise was working for Claude as his second-in-command. She operated south of beaches that would forever be known as Omaha, Utah, Gold, Juno, and Sword.

Lise had been in Paris on a recruiting trip when the "B" message sounded. She did not yet know where the Allies would strike, only that the SCIENTIST network's territory was located between crucial deepwater ports in the Channel and the Atlantic.

In France, D-Day action began before the first ship landed. Once Lise's maquis heard their message on the night of June 5, her "soldiers" demolished the train junction in the town of Avranches, at the base of the Cotentin Peninsula; it was left "completely unusable." As she rode in the darkness, the teenagers she had been training and arming that spring were cutting subterranean telephone and teleprinter cables all along the Normandy coast. Seven of her men got arrested that night, but not before they took down two aerial power lines and felled trees across the main roads.

Throughout France on the night of June 5, 1944, there were some 950 cuts on the railways using explosives dropped by the Firm.

At daybreak, June 6, the whole of Normandy was isolated.

Lise was on only the first day of what would be a three-day bicycle ride over small back roads "through thick enemy formations" to the combat zone. She slept in ditches when she tired, then picked up her *vélo* and began traveling again to her headquarters.

She was nowhere near a radio when the communiqué from General Dwight D. Eisenhower, supreme commander of Allied forces, aired for the people of Normandy:

> The lives of many of you depend on the speed with which you obey. Leave your towns at once—stay off the roads—go on foot and take nothing with you that is difficult to carry. Do not gather in groups which may be mistaken for enemy troops.

The largest armada the world had ever known was minutes away from landing on the northern beaches of France.

> The hour of your liberation is approaching.

Bombers flew over villages dotting the Normandy coast—Saint-Lô, Avranches, Cherbourg, Caen—dropping leaflets to warn locals of the incoming assault.

At 6:20 a.m., the Nazi garrison stationed on Pointe du Hoc reported the presence of four battle cruisers.

At 6:30 a.m., H-Hour arrived. (Just as the *D* in "D-Day" stands for nothing, merely signaling the day of attack, the *H* in "H-Hour" is the appointed hour of assault.)

Operation Overlord would "go."

American troops were the first to disembark in France, on Omaha and Utah Beaches.

Eighteen minutes later, at 6:48 a.m., Berlin Radio, Transocean, declared that Allied paratroopers were landing at the mouth of the Seine, that Havre, Calais, and Dunkirk were getting heavily bombarded by air, and that German naval forces were engaged with Allied landing craft.

The Associated Press picked up the news from Germany. It flashed around the planet.

Following H-Hours on Sword, Gold, and Juno, at 9:00 a.m. General Eisenhower authorized release of a terse update. Sounding at 9:32 a.m., the statement was played on a gramophone in London and blasted to everyone with a radio, the globe over. The message revealed nothing of strategic detail yet contained the most important piece of military intelligence in the war:

> Under the command of General Eisenhower, Allied naval forces, supported by strong air forces, began landing Allied armies this morning on the Northern coast of France.

It was everything France had been waiting years—four awful, occupied years—to hear.

The world stood by in somber attention.

At noon in Paris, June 6, from the third floor of 84 Avenue Foch, a Morse transmission was tapped out in un-encrypted text on a stolen British wireless set. The radio message was prepared weeks in advance, on orders from Himmler, Göring, and Hitler; it had been a matter of strategic debate throughout the spring, with the Nazi command arguing about the precise moment to unmask the captured Allied radios. At what point in the war should the Reich's clever *Englandspiel* be revealed to the English? Adolf Hitler thought the unveiling would so unnerve Allied generals they would wonder just how deeply the underground had been penetrated. He assumed the deception would be so powerful and destabilizing that the SHAEF commanders might reconsider and recall attack orders. They would assume Nazi forces were about to spring a trap.

On the day of the invasion, the Gestapo ended its long-played game:

TELEGRAM FROM BARBER BLUE

MANY THANKS LARGE DELIVERIES ARMS AND AMMUNITIONS SENT DURING LONG PERIOD ALL OVER FRANCE STOP HAVE GREATLY APPRECIATED GOOD TIPS CONCERNING YOUR INTENTIONS AND PLANS STOP.

On D-Day, Hitler's armies possessed thousands of tons of matériel air-dropped into France by SOE, captured from the rebels.

UNAVOIDABLE WE HAD TO TAKE UNDER THE CARE OF GESTAPO YOUR FRIENDS OF FRENCH SECTION SUCH AS MAX PHONO THEODORE ETC ETC STOP ANTOINE AND TELL IN EXCELLENT HEALTH STOP.

The Gestapo was preening: Phono and Antoine were code names for Emile Garry and France Antelme, agents who worked alongside the PROSPER network.

VERY PLEASED TO HAVE YOUR VISIT FOR WHICH WE HAVE PREPARED EVERYTHING.

When the message was received in London, on June 6, 1944, the weather was unsettled, dull, and cool. In the neon-lit sterility of the Baker Street headquarters, all hands were on deck and every last nerve was tried.

Colonel Buckmaster ordered broadcast of a reply to his opposite numbers, the spymasters at 84 Avenue Foch:

TO NIGHT BARBER

SORRY TO SEE YOUR PATIENCE IS EXHAUSTED AND YOUR NERVES NOT SO GOOD AS OURS STOP SORRY WE GAVE YOU SO MUCH TROUBLE IN COLLECTING CONTAINERS BUT WE HAD TO CARRY ON UNTIL OUR OFFICERS HAD BEEN ABLE [TO] MAKE BIGGER AND BETTER FRIENDS YOUR AREAS STOP EXPENSE AND STORES NO OBJECT STOP WE SUGGEST YOU BEGIN ORGANISING FURTHER EAST STOP GIVE US GROUND NEAR BERLIN FOR RECEPTION ORGANISER AND WT OPERATOR BUT BE SURE YOU DO NOT CLASH WITH OUR RUSSIAN FRIENDS STOP INCIDENTALLY SUGGEST YOU CHANGE YOUR S PHONE OPERATOR WE DON'T THINK MUCH OF HIS ENGLISH STOP WE ARE CLOSING YOUR PLAN DOWN NOW AS WE WANT IT FOR SOMEONE ELSE AUF WIEDERSEHEN.

Allied forces were six hours into Europe and 750 miles from Berlin.

CHAPTER 24

Death on One Side, Life on the Other

Normandy

A German officer stood in the middle of Lise de Baissac's new apartment in the Norman village of Saint-Aubin-du-Désert and delivered an order.

"Move out," he said.

In northern France, far from her previous base in Poitiers, Lise was again living undercover as a Parisian widow, the lonely refugee who fled to the countryside to find food. According to her fictitious biography, she was weak and vulnerable. This flat was all of two rooms, "one table, a bench and not a bed, [but] a mattress on the floor." The landlady was a cripple who occupied the ground floor; she was bedridden and so did not protest when the German army arrived to take possession of her house.

D-Day was only one day in the Allied battle for Europe. Anglo-American armies had captured the beaches, but throughout the summer of 1944 they were still fighting on the landing grounds, in the fields, on the streets, and in the hills. By D+45, the situation in Normandy was "very much war," Lise said. The Wehrmacht was stationed throughout Claude de Baissac's new SCIENTIST area: German divisions were in the big cities and the small hamlets; Hitler's troops swelled town squares. Horse convoys, trucks, and troop columns clogged the winding, muddy roads. The war was still precarious and "very hot."

The SCIENTIST network covered the farm fields below Caen, Saint-Lô, and Avranches. It was not good maquis territory: more pasture and orchards than bush or mountains. But Lise's men were adapted to the terrain; sleeping rough in the woods, they were mobile and difficult to find, attacking by surprise, in small groups with light arms. The Wehrmacht, by contrast, could not easily live outdoors. The skies were crowded with Allied bombers, and canvas cities turned soldiers into sleeping targets. Germans were hesitant to construct mass military encampments. The BBC said the air campaign was trying to avoid bombing French villages, to minimize civilian casualties. So Hitler's forces moved in, commandeering old women's ivy-clad houses for billets, without permission and without payment.

Now the enemy filled Lise's small home. Rifles and helmets littered the floor. The ranking Nazi was flanked by forty Russian soldiers, draftees from the eastern front who preferred killing in France to starvation in a German concentration camp. "Will you move?" the lieutenant said, standing amid his corps of dirty conscripts. "We need your rooms, you must go."

The German officer was polite, scrupulous, and correct, but nevertheless commanding.

"Take your belongings and leave your room to us."

LISE WAS IN NORMANDY at a pregnant hour of history. The Wehrmacht fought for their lives, for Hitler, and for Europe. If the führer lost France, he would lose his grip on *Festung Europa*—the Fortress of Europe, his whole citadel of hate. Once the Reich lost Europe, Germany would vanish forever. The Allies' "unconditional surrender" policy made it clear: Postwar plans for Germany included division, occupation zones, and disarmament. Hitler understood the stakes from his earliest days, writing in *Mein Kampf,* "Germany will either be a world power or it will not exist at all."

For the Anglo-American alliance, the battle for Normandy was not merely a war against Nazism; it was a defense of liberal democracy and would determine the global balance of power. Britain and America were racing the Soviets: On the eastern front, the Red Army had decimated Hitler's troops, and now 1.6 million Russian soldiers were marching into Poland and Lithuania on their way to Germany. If the Anglo-American armed forces could not also attack Hitler from the west, there was every good chance Stalin would claim Berlin for himself, replacing one dictator with another.

Britain was also fighting for her own future. If the Allies were routed in Normandy and beaten back into the sea, the Americans could redirect efforts to the Pacific theater and Japan. Their war might stretch on for a few more years. The United States would recover. Great Britain would not.

The invasion of France would be decisive for all. The war was far from over; there was at least one year to go. An ending had yet to be written. General Eisenhower's strategy called for a massive landing on the Continent to secure a wide corridor from which to launch an overpowering forward assault on the Reich.

The French were wary. In Normandy, they remembered the last time the blitzkrieg came through, in the summer of 1940. It was cataclysmic. Every family was still mourning someone. Now on Sundays, in gray stone churches, widows thought of their husbands and sons and lit candles for a happier outcome.

This time, France met the challenge. To reinforce the front lines in Normandy, the Wehrmacht had to travel through an entire nation teeming with belligerent rebel fighters, "most of whom had been trained and practically all of whom had been armed by SOE," said Michael Foot, historian of the Special Operations Executive in France.

This was the war for which the Firm was built; the years of agent organizing, recruitment, evasion, and suffering, all crescendoed to one epic finale. The moonlit nights Lise and her colleagues spent in the fields, waiting for explosives, were now amply justified. General Eisenhower said in July, "These multiple and simultaneous cases of sabotage, coordinated with the Allied effort, have delayed considerably the movement of German reserves to the combat zone."

Hitler's panzers failed to achieve a counter-blitzkrieg in the summer of 1944. When the railways were cut all over France, the elite SS tank divisions traveled by road instead—mined with explosives and blocked with felled trees. Bridges were blown out. Unending harassment held down the Reich's armor and delayed its arrival in Normandy by almost three weeks. Said Foot, "When they did eventually crawl into their laagers close to the fighting line, heaving a sigh of relief that at last they would have real soldiers to deal with and not these damned terrorists, their fighting quality was much below what it had been when they started. The division might be compared to a cobra which had struck with its fangs at the head of a stick held out to tempt it; the amount of poison left in its bite was far less than it had been."

Nazi reinforcements traveled straight through Claude de Baissac's SCIENTIST territory. When and if Hitler called for a retreat, it would be back through Claude's maquis too.

At the war's zenith, Lise and Claude were a successful team in Normandy. She was too sensible to be bent by nepotism, yet she still considered Claude's performance "really first class." Their work was hard, their closest lieutenants were captured and died in shoot-outs, but Lise "enjoyed" the pairing as second-in-command to her older brother.

The SCIENTIST maquis were busy every day. Claude had permitted no sabotage before D-Day, and now, after years in the shadows, the network engaged in open battle. The circuit was "extremely active in that type of small-scale activity, which, if repeated often enough, hamstrings an army." Claude expected the invasion to bring other partisan fighters into active service, but when he looked for demolitions in his zone by other locally controlled rebels, Gaullists or Communists, he found none at all. The French-organized French Resistance seemed to be *introuvable,* he said. "The secret army is so secret that it's impossible to find it!"

Allied commanders were more complimentary of France's army of the shadows. In an early post–D-Day report, the chiefs declared the

Resistance "far surpassed" expectations and "displayed unity in action and a high fighting spirit."

Then the Allied offensive got stuck.

If the invasion was "much the greatest thing we have ever attempted," as Churchill said, the six weeks that followed were a great deal less impressive. In the fight to break past the Normandy beachheads, progress was grim and grinding. By the end of June, the Americans had captured the Cotentin Peninsula; it was a thumb sticking out into the Channel, with the port of Cherbourg at its tip, but the harbor was so damaged and booby-trapped as it was abandoned that it was worthless to the fight. The American front line was held up on the peninsula and did not move for weeks. The British and Canadian armies failed to seize Caen, the city closest to the beaches, on D-Day. It was not captured until D+44.

By July, the invasion of Europe was stymied. The stalemate was a problem inherent in Operation Overlord planning: Favoring surprise and secrecy, the Allies landed on a coast with no deepwater port for ferrying troops and supplies. They could not off-load enough food and gas onto the Continent to keep armies moving forward. From England, artificial harbors were floated across the Channel, but the weather was uncooperative; so-called once-in-a-lifetime storms routinely pasted the coast and destroyed the installations. Squalls also delayed the cross-Channel fuel lines. If the Germans couldn't hold back the Allies, the tempests did.

The invasion was in the mud, in a very literal way. Normandy was tough country for an assault: Fields of cow pasture and apple grove were separated by thick, seven- to ten-foot-high hedgerows, deep-rooted and built up over centuries. The *bocages* were a picturesque problem; the steep ditches and high nettles hid German snipers and stopped Sherman tanks in their tracks. Military planners had considered that the Wehrmacht would "die hard," but the *bocage* died harder.

The Allies were trapped. For weeks, the expeditionary forces peered over the edge of Europe and were dying—by the thousands—to get in. The self-proclaimed liberators had a beach and a peninsula but could not move the fight inland. Hitler held his ground. The Normandy coast was not France.

Confined to the outskirts of the Continent, Allied chiefs planned a breakout, a way to smash past the Atlantic Wall: Operation Cobra called for saturation bombing and a tight, four-mile-wide push down from the peninsula and into the rest of Europe.

Cobra was concentrated in SCIENTIST territory.

In a summer of merciless rain, Lise was on her bicycle every day. For months, the SCIENTIST maquis bedeviled the Germans in the rolling dairy land, hoping to tip the balance of the invasion. Claude slept in a different hayloft each night, reeking of manure. "I was to know no rest," he said. Some nights they would receive as many as sixty containers. But he could not be everywhere. What her brother could not command, Lise could. She took his "place, as head of the circuit, when [he] was away 'on *tournée.*'"

One night, as Lise and a small party traveled toward the Somme to coordinate with other rebel groups, she encountered a German patrol. From the *bocage,* a hail of fire opened on her men. Said the report, "Our automatic weapons did wonders against the mausers." Several Germans died that night, but not one of Lise's "soldiers" fell.

Among the most pernicious threats to Lise was her network's newly arrived radio operator, Ensign Phyllis Latour, who was "very brave and very willing, but such a mess of a girl." At twenty-three, she was among the youngest and last women recruited by SOE and infiltrated into France. Old enough to deploy as an agent, she both looked and acted much younger than her years. Immaturity and neurosis are strong correlates for failure undercover: Phyllis scored high on both. Her cover story was that she fled the coast to live with relatives, that she was a fourteen-year-old schoolgirl on summer holidays. She tried to chat with German soldiers like a giddy teenager. They conversed, in her words, "about anything and everything, [as if I were] trying to be helpful." She mindlessly left coded messages behind in her safe houses. Once, when Lise gave Phyllis an English candy, a sweet from the parachuted containers, Phyllis ate the treat with relish, balled up the wrapper, then pitched it into the middle of the street. Phyllis was completely "unreasonable," Lise thought. Working with the girl was like juggling a loaded gun.

Phyllis accomplished her radio work "with stupidity, but also with courage," reported Claude. She tried to prove she wasn't hopeless: Like most girls in France, Phyllis was a knitter, so she translated her Morse messages into scarves and sweaters, taking advantage of the binary nature of knit and purl stitches. "An ordinary loop knot can make the equivalent of a dot, and a knot in the figure-eight manner will give you the equivalent of a dash," she said.

But ingenuity could not change the bare facts of a radio operator's job. As Phyllis transmitted, Nazi direction finders were tuned to her messages, dialing in to her frequencies; she could hear the interference on the line. The vans circled ever nearer, triangulating her signal, disguised sometimes as ambulances or bakers' trucks. They were only ever an hour or so behind. At last, Lise's maquis lobbed a grenade into a stalking van; a German woman and two children died in the attack. In defiance of all sense or security, Phyllis attended the public funerals as a mourner: "I heard I was responsible for their deaths. It was a horrible feeling."

Phyllis was traumatized by war and a menace to her commanding officers. Residents of Normandy were instructed to bunk in place as the German army repositioned behind the front. With the "prohibition on movement in the area," Lise cycled with Phyllis to help keep her safe. Their days consisted of travel between scheduled transmissions; their midnights were flurries of parachute receptions. Phyllis would daydream as she rode, watching Allied planes overhead, picturing the young pilots as they passed "patting each other on the back and offering congratulations after a strike." Normandy was all sky and field pockmarked by craters from the air campaign. The bombers never saw the devastation that followed, "the carnage that was left." She always saw it. Lise assigned other partisans to move Phyllis's transmitter and batteries. Lise, meanwhile, tucked the radio crystals under her own dress.

One midsummer day, as they were pedaling toward a hideout, split skirts splashed with mud, blouses clammy from exertion, they arrived at a German checkpoint. The sentry waved Phyllis and Lise aside for an interview, to see their papers, to assert his dominance. He wore his gun slung over his shoulder like some swashbuckler, his hand loose on the stock.

Nazis were mostly well behaved to French civilians, but as their hold on France slipped, so too did their manners. Just west of Lise's territory, a female agent couriering documents was gang-raped with her skirt on. "One held me down," she said. "My first instinct was to put up a fight and then I thought, no, I can't. I've got these papers. If I put up a fight they're going to overpower me and then they'll probably strip me and we'd be in a worse mess than we already are in."

Lise squinted in the summer light, but did not flinch when the German felt around her waist, up and down her skirt, and over the bulky bits of radio. She was a role model for the little wireless operator girl with "no head." ("Had [Phyllis] been searched she would probably have been arrested," said Lise.)

In the summer of 1944, German propaganda repeated that all partisans were now to be treated as *francs-tireurs,* traitors, dissidents, guerrillas, subversives, irregulars, spies. The rising citizens of France would not be extended the rights of prisoners of war; they would be executed without trial. Hitler's illegal and secret *Kommando* order of 1942 was now openly promulgated on the radio; it expanded to cover as many as 150,000 French patriot forces.

The Wehrmacht soldier frisked Lise under her rib cage; he patted around her hips for a gun, running a hand around her middle and down her thighs. It was as close as she had yet come to her own unmasking, to losing her cover and revealing herself as a member of the Resistance. "He touched everything."

You're free to go, the German said.

Phyllis and Lise got back astride their bikes.

As Lise pedaled away, a spare radio part fell out of her skirt and clunked onto the road.

She leaned over, picked up the crystal, pocketed it, and rode on.

On July 25, 1944, D+49, the Allies launched Operation Cobra, the breakout. Targeting the German defenses at Saint-Lô, an epic bombing campaign was followed by a narrow concentration of firepower that at last pierced the Nazi fortification of Normandy. Hitler's defensive stronghold shattered. Overnight, the four-mile corridor expanded into an American freeway. What had been a slow and tortured Allied tiptoe through the hedgerows was now a sluice of American tanks and trucks. The quick thrust was good for France; the offensive moved fast enough to leave most villages and ancient churches intact. As a Wehrmacht general had predicted, "All France [will be] lost following the rupture of the German front containing the invasion."

At once, the Americans were on their very own lightning strike. The forward attack was so swift and unyielding that Allied commanders suffered from lack of information, a "woeful insufficiency in Signal troops," according to General Eisenhower. As ever, there were never enough radios in the field.

No one could see what was happening. The Allies could not pinpoint where the action was, to a depth of fifty miles beyond the German front lines. "At a moment like this it is a mortifying experience for a war correspondent not to be able to say who is doing what, nor precisely where they are," wrote *The Times* of London. Lise cycled through anti-aircraft and antitank artillery installations; she knew more about conditions in the combat zone than did SHAEF, the Supreme Headquarters Allied Expeditionary Force in London. On sunny days, dust thrown up by convoys signaled to farmers whence the Wehrmacht came, and by turn deep mud tracks led to where they were going. Telephone wires were suspended on crucifixes at crossroads pointing in the enemy's direction; sniper fire repeated through the hedgerows; rotting horses and human bodies were stacked along the road like logs.

COMMUNICATION FROM INSIDE enemy territory was critical. Lise was a linchpin: She received a parachute agent just ahead of the push, Captain Jack Hayes, brother of Claude's former lieutenant in Bordeaux. He was tasked with signaling to commanders during the thrust of the Cobra offensive. Lise and Claude helped assign local guides to Captain Hayes, some thirty-one runners who could sneak up to the fighting, cross into Allied territory to contact commanders, and supply "news of what was happening behind enemy lines." Lise's maquis runners were key to locating the front as it drove into France, modern-day Pheidippides at Marathon.

In retreat, the German army fell apart. The Wehrmacht were "sporadic, disorganized and chaotic." The Reich was now six years into Hitler's war: Its guns and supplies were tired and inferior to the shiny fresh equipment out of America, the world's newest industrial powerhouse. German soldiers had not seen home leave in two years. The troops slogging through Normandy were either "starveling" boys as young as fifteen, wizened soldiers exhausted by winters bashing against the Red Army, or the "East Battalions" of POWs drafted from distant Soviet theaters such as Armenia, Georgia, and Azerbaijan. The elite SS were no longer the leading professional military in the world; they were a humiliated defensive force in retreat. The July 20, 1944, assassination attempt on Hitler's life by senior officers of the Abwehr made all Nazi commanders fearful for their futures, compounding the anarchy of withdrawal.

"We had all the German army coming from the sea, retreating faster and faster in my village," recalled Lise. SCIENTIST headquarters were set up in a local schoolhouse, which doubled as the town hall. It was a summer of war, and the schoolmaster gave the place over to the Resistance.

As the German evacuation approached the town of Saint-Mars-du-Désert, the Wehrmacht also commandeered the simple two-story building for a field station. While the maquis snuck in and out of the kitchen from the back of the building, Hitler's commanders took over the classrooms and refectory in the front.

Outside the schoolhouse, there was a sign stamped with the official German *Kommandantur* seal: Farmers were told "that nothing must be left outside their houses and all women folk must be taken care of as the German NCOs and officers could not hold themselves responsible for any damage done by the Russians." Nazis had disavowed Russian barbarism.

The schoolmistress was a "very simple person, a housekeeper who liked to make sure that things were done properly," said Lise. The scruffy, polyglot German army of 1944 anticipated their bleak future by indulging in a bender of Norman dairy products: milk, butter, and soft cheeses. When the soldiers helped themselves to the offerings of the school kitchen and fixed a meal of eggs, the schoolmaster's wife was mortally offended.

"You don't do it like that," she scolded. This was her kitchen, and she was a French cook. She instructed the savages on how to prepare an omelet.

THE WAVE OF Nazi disengagement from Normandy was tidal by August 1944. When the Wehrmacht took over the schoolhouse, they also claimed Lise's small apartment for billets. Now forty surly Russians with muddy boots were rooting through Lise's meager possessions, rummaging in her larder, eyeing her underwear, declaring that the rough inspection was a mere "attempt to take her things to a place of safety." The same Red Army reputation for cruelty that was a winning trait in Stalingrad was a moral abomination in France. The captured Soviet troops "behaved very badly," said Claude, "pillaging houses and raping women."

Lise appealed to the officer in charge, the ranking German. This was her home. She was a widow. Could he not control his conscripts?

He shrugged, saying he "could not do much about it." Then, in a show of military discipline and Aryan superiority, he set an example for the Russians under him: He walked over to the cabinet and, without examining its contents, shut the door, turned the lock, and handed over the key. There, he said, "I've shut your cupboard door."

Inside, Lise had a packet of English tea.

One lazy soldier lay down across Lise's lumpy mattress on the floor. Others squatted beside him, bunched up on her sleeping sack sewn from an old silk parachute.

"Please," Lise asked, would they mind getting off the bed? "Let me take my sleeping bag."

With the Nazi officer standing watch, the Russians acquiesced. Lise collected her few items of clothing, a skirt, a jacket, hurrying about the room. "I tried to keep my dignity," she said. She rolled everything into the Allied parachute that might otherwise kill her if recognized and excused herself from her own home.

WITH THE AMERICAN breakout in Normandy, France was on a path to liberation.

In the first week of August, Hitler made one last stand. The Allies were on the move, and each day the Americans' fuel and food had to travel a greater distance to reach advancing troops. Hitler aimed to cut the supply lines. His generals counseled that a counteroffensive was doomed to failure, that the Nazi fight for France was already lost. It was time to evacuate. There could be no defensive answer to the overwhelming Allied airpower. The führer nevertheless struck hard at the American armies between Avranches and Mortain, in SCIENTIST territory.

It was a decisive mistake. The Allies were reading Hitler's communications via the Enigma decrypts, anticipating his moves. On the first day of his attack, the Germans reclaimed the town of Mortain. Then a week of intense, close-range fighting followed; the town was captured and retaken seven times. Between the advance intelligence and the sheer might and diligence of the air campaign, Mortain became, in the words of Prime Minister Churchill, a "slaughter."

The German front collapsed. The American army's battle historian Forrest Pogue said of that turning point, "We had gone from inch-by-inch battles in the hedgerows to a great battle of maneuver with the whole of Normandy and Brittany for the battleground."

Hitler's counterassault was a bloodying catastrophe at a pivotal moment. By August 8, 1944, D+63, the Allies were rolling in Lise's direction: General George Patton took Le Mans, then Alençon. The American army swung at the Nazis from the left, while the British and Canadian armies punched down from Caen. The Wehrmacht was surrounded—"pocketed"—in the town of Falaise. "This is an opportunity that comes to a commander not more than once in a century," said the American general Omar Bradley. "We're about to destroy an entire hostile army and go all the way from here to the German border."

In only a matter of days, Lise and Claude would be overrun by the Americans, advancing now almost unopposed. Along the Orne River, the SCIENTIST maquis were still smoking out the last wasp's nests of German fighters. They were joined now by late-coming collaborating and accommodating French, known as mothball men for their ancient uniforms—dusty from four years in a closet—who were chanting retributive the slogan: "To each, his own German." A region that was Nazi-held territory since 1940 would be French again in the summer of 1944, but until that happened, Lise still had to maintain cover and command over the true secret soldiers in a moment of increasing lawlessness.

The weather was finally hot, and Lise cycled through plagues of mosquitoes. Smashed trucks and disabled tanks littered the roads, dead horses lay beside toppled wagons, prisoner cages overflowed, wood crosses popped up like daisies with helmets dangling off the top.

A German soldier stopped Lise for yet another inspection. She straddled the frame of her bicycle and prepared to produce her papers.

Get off your *vélo,* the German ordered.

With thick and dirty hands, he grabbed the frame, shook hard, and tried to muscle her off. Among the many things the enemy requisitioned in its final days in France, the soldier was demanding her bicycle. His army was withdrawing; better to go on wheels, he thought, than to hoof it all the way back to the Kitzinger Line.

Without a bicycle, Lise could not fulfill her mission.

She held her ground with all her strength. Then she pulled rank.

"No! I'll call your officer," she said.

He froze at the threat. Stealing was against orders. Even in retreat, Nazis had an instinctive reaction to authority.

"I'm going to see your officer and tell him."

The German let Lise have her bicycle.

On August 13, 1944, D+68, the SCIENTIST headquarters were overtaken by the American army advance.

Two days later, Nazi command made the "Big Decision" to evacuate from the Normandy front. That very same day, General Eisenhower launched his second offensive in France, striking up from the Mediterranean; 151,000 Allied soldiers landed on the Côte d'Azur in Operation Dragoon.

Hitler called August 15, 1944, D+70, the worst day of his life.

Claude was picked up and flown back to England on August 17, 1944, D+72. Lise remained in Normandy, waiting for him to return and collect her.

In a free Paris on August 26, 1944, D+81, the bells of Notre Dame, Sacré-Coeur, and every other church in the city pealed without end.

General de Gaulle strode tall on the Champs-Élysées. He waved, shook hands—survived at least two assassination attempts with cameras rolling—and celebrated his public homecoming, thronged by Parisians chanting the "Marseillaise."

Allons enfants de la Patrie,
Le jour de gloire est arrivé!
Arise, children of the nation,
The day of glory has arrived!

Lise waited for the Firm to return to France to find her. She visited the scenes of a firefight in which two of her closest colleagues had been captured and killed. "I looked at this house which was destroyed," she said of the charred foundations and blackened walls, "and the country around it was ravishing, a field all green, covered with pink mushrooms which you could eat." Normandy was already returning to itself, to a lush and pastoral cow country.

"And it was sad because it was death on one side, life on the other."

Two years after she parachuted into a moonlit field beside Andrée Borrel, Lise's secret mission to France was complete.

CHAPTER 25

Your Mind Goes On Thinking

Ravensbrück, Germany

Odette cracked her knuckles, one at a time, pulling each finger out of its socket, listening for the satisfying click after the pop. It occupied her days. In the dark of her cell, she could sleep only two hours out of every twenty-four. It never mattered when those two hours arrived; she had been alone with no lights at all, or windows, for three months and eleven days. But she had inner defenses even for this. She was sickly as a little girl when the poliovirus raged through France, blinded and paralyzed for three years, so she told herself now what she had learned as a child: She was not afraid of the dark. For one week, no one brought any food at all. The concentration camp forgot her.

In those long empty days—or were they nights?—Odette made patterns for little girls' dresses in her mind, matching fabrics, sewing cottons, attaching ribbons, stitching pleats and plackets for her daughters' Sunday outfits. "Your mind goes on thinking," she said.

Odette focused on her girls: Françoise, Marianne, and Lily. "I thought about them all the time. All the time. It made me stronger."

She strained to recall lines of poetry and phrases of music. "You'd think it was easy to find something to think about, but it wasn't."

In a cell ten feet long, six feet wide, without leaving her bed, Odette walked through other houses in her mind: her grandparents' home, the flats she shared with her husband when she was first married, a villa in the Côte d'Azur with Peter Churchill, all while sleeping on a wooden plank. In the hot summer months, the heat on in her cell at full blast, she soaked her sleeping sack in the constantly running tap to stay cool while unspooling imaginary Oriental rugs onto hardwood floors somewhere else. She filled invisible bud vases with wildflowers, "refurnished every house I ever knew."

Odette lived anywhere but where she was: Ravensbrück, Germany, in the largest women's prison in history. It was not a camp for Jews: Heinrich Himmler declared Ravensbrück *judenfrei* since 1942.

The lights were never on, but the sounds around Odette were loud and gruesome. She was in the basement of the punishment block, the *Strafblock*, and heard screams from nearby cells every evening. Odette saw nothing; she listened to everything. "On written instructions from Himmler, inmates were whipped with [a] leather whip about 75 cm in length for disciplinary offenses," said the camp commandant, Fritz Suhren. "I could count every stroke," Odette recalled. Wardresses tallied the blows in German, *eins, zwei, drei*. Sometimes screams were followed by gunshots. Then smoke filled the air of the camp.

Once a month, it was Odette's turn for special attention. As the alleged niece of Prime Minister Winston Churchill, she was believed to be a VIP: The commandant came to her cell door to ask after her well-being.

Have you anything to say?

No, Odette would respond.

Suhren was always accompanied by a cruel wardress. If Odette complained of anything at all, the *Aufseherin* and her police dog would exact revenge once the commandant went away. Prisoners recalled the female guards of Ravensbrück as "hard, awful women."

It was 1945, and in her second year in prison Odette weighed eighty-five pounds. Ill and undernourished, she was a living skeleton, a *Muselweib*. (The term meant Muslim girl—concentration camp shorthand for the walking dead.) She had tuberculosis, a broken back, and a bleeding rash that ran across her body; her hair fell out in clumps; her glands were so swollen it hurt to breathe; she suffered unending headaches. "I was one minute away from death so often. It would have been so easy to die. It would have been a pleasure." She carried a razor blade with her and became seduced by the thought she might deprive the *Boches* of her slow suffering. The notion of suicide made her happy, she said. "I confess, I reached the bottom of the abyss."

At that point, Odette was taken to the sick bay and given what derisory care prisoners got when there was little incentive to keep them alive. The sunlight blinded her, and the fresh air made her stomach turn over. But in the hospital she heard word that France had been liberated by the Allies.

On the day Odette left the hospital ward, a leaf blew past her feet in the wind. She stood in wonder at the miracle of a dry leaf on a winter's day: "There were no trees at Ravensbrück." She took it as a sign from God.

Upon her limited recovery, Odette was relocated from underground cell No. 42 to an aboveground cell, a room with an open window at the top of the wall, a crack of light. It was enough: The sun rose every morning, and it restored hope that "something extraordinary would happen tomorrow." Every night, cinders blew in with the odor of charred meat, an "overbearing smell."

By April 1945, in all the cities of Germany, Nazis were surrendering. Hitler would lose his fatherland. Ravensbrück sat between advancing armies, the Americans and the Soviets, and the thunder of bombs grew ever closer. The commandant bargained with his inmates: War trials were coming, and he needed a good word from those who would otherwise testify against him. He turned Ravensbrück into a show camp, a *Musterlager,* and began acting as if he and his Nazi colleagues were "mother's darlings [who] have never done anything nasty to anybody." There were other VIP prisoners who had arrived wearing diamonds. They now disappeared from their housing blocks and Frau Suhren's sparkling new necklaces were simultaneously hidden from view. The politically favored inmates who might speak unkindly of their incarceration were transported out of camp by the Red Cross.

The commandant aimed to "give the impression that he was the headmaster of a very select girls school or pleasure resort."

By the spring of 1945, while the Allies marched toward Berlin, victory in Europe was at last assured. But the end of World War II brought the peculiar problem of women in war to the attention of the brass once again. It was at least possible for male agents to end up on prison lists under their own names; they had commissions in the regular services. Captured male agents might have given themselves away to the enemy, revealing they were officers in hopes of claiming the rights of prisoners of war. But that was not a privilege of which Odette or other captured women could avail themselves: The FANYs were a civilian organization. The *Corps féminins*' status as combatants was never clear to begin with; it became less so once they went missing in action.

The boys in khaki would soon head home. Some troops wouldn't make it back; condolence letters would be posted to mothers and fathers announcing the sad death of their sons, the date and place of their passing, thanking them for their service in the victory against tyranny. But the process of locating missing soldiers was hardly straightforward. The many branches of Allied armed services were circulating lists of the missing to the Red Cross, to the Vatican, and to SHAEF, Supreme Headquarters Allied Expeditionary Force. The Germans had a legal duty to notify the Red Cross if any listed name appeared in their camps, but there was no corresponding obligation to report every name on the Nazi rolls. Only prisoners who were explicitly requested were even looked for. It was a game of diplomatic Go Fish with POW lives.

Searching for agents out of uniform was more complicated yet. In London, the status of more than a hundred F Section operatives became a matter of growing alarm. Families deserve to know what happened, and when a clandestine government department loses agents, it too has to notify dependents. The government was not previously equipped to handle pensions and disability benefits for jobs that never officially existed. Even in a winning war, militaries seek to maintain strict classification of covert operations. A good agent leaves no trace, no documentation, and SOE aimed to keep agents undercover to the end. If Baker Street alerted the Red Cross, it would give up clues about their missions, which could provide the enemy with top secret intelligence in a war that was yet unfinished. The information would also be available to the Soviets, the newest rivals waiting in Europe's wings.

On both sides of the conflict, there was a heavy incentive to keep agents' names far from ink and paper. Berlin risked criminal exposure. SOE feared leaving public footprints of secret actions and foolish blunders behind enemy lines.

While the Allies bowled through Germany, memos flew back and forth to London about the coming influx of returnees. If Baker Street was reluctant to put men's names on the Red Cross lists, to say that women were among the missing meant acknowledging that the fairer sex was deployed in a dirty war and that they had been sacrificed. It was not an admission that came easily.

By the end of the winter of 1945, the case for publishing agents' names was acute: Russians were liberating the concentration camps in Poland. Allied forces would have every reason to doubt the story of anyone who was not on combatant lists but who claimed military status. Man or woman, there would be few immediate ways to certify that a so-called secret soldier was not, in fact, a fraud. A decision had to be made.

At first, Colonel Buckmaster was certain that there would be few casualties for his team. "We have every reason to believe that they will be recovered at the cessation of hostilities," he said. Mounting evidence to the contrary, Buck kept faith in the decorum of military commanders on all sides. But by March, information reached London suggesting something altogether more sinister under the Reich.

Records would show there were no records. Agents' names—code or Christian—were seldom on prison registers at all; they were lost in the methodical clouds of Nazi war crimes. In an inscription found in Fresnes Prison files, there was a notation in the remarks column:

N plus N. Ständig gefesselt
Nacht und Nebel.
Night and Fog. Constantly shackled.

The war in Europe ground to its gruesome conclusion eleven months after D-Day. On April 16, 1945, Commandant Suhren received orders from Heinrich Himmler to execute all prisoners within his command. Odette was among several captives considered VIPs in Ravensbrück, women who might be useful as bargaining chips. Of those who remained, Fritz Suhren was obliging and solicitous: How was their health? Were they short of clothing? Of food? Would the women bearing torture scars be willing to testify in writing that it was a work accident in a factory? The war was ending, the Allies were in Germany, so Suhren acted "like a shopkeeper offering his goods," where before he had been a monster.

On Odette's thirty-third birthday, she was "1000 years old." But she was alive on April 28, 1945, when, just after midnight, Suhren came to her cell to tell her to gather her belongings, that she would be leaving in the morning at 6:00. A handsome man, with bright red hair and pale gray eyes framed by lashes so blond they seemed invisible, Suhren "stood at the door and made a gesture indicating a throat being cut." The Russians were advancing, and the commandant believed "Mrs. Churchill," married to the nephew of the prime minister, was leverage: A prisoner of the Americans would see a happier future than a captive of the Soviets.

At 8:00 the following morning, an SS officer came to Odette's cell to escort her out. She hobbled to the parade grounds of Ravensbrück on her heels; her feet still festered from the removal of her toenails, and her ankles were swollen from starvation. Odette was packed into a black prison van with other VIPs and driven some 350 miles toward the Belgian border, to a detention camp at Neustadt. There was no food there, nor water. The prisoners were raving, and the guards fired into crowds with abandon. When a woman fell dead at Odette's mangled, septic feet, other prisoners descended to eat the body.

On April 30, 1945, Adolf Hitler swallowed a cyanide capsule and shot himself in the head in his underground bunker in Berlin. His staff poured gasoline over the body and set fire to the remains.

A Neustadt *Kapo* came to Odette on the afternoon of May 2, 1945, and told her to meet Commandant Suhren outside the camp. In a white Mercedes-Benz, Suhren sat with two Polish girls who worked for him, one a governess to his children. Odette's soiled skirt and matted brown hair pressed in against the soft leather upholstery as Suhren drove westward through the night and into the next day, accompanied by an SS motorcade.

"Do you want to know where we are going?" he asked Odette.

She did not care. The commandant believed she was someone of importance, and she had no idea what he might expect of her.

"Well I am taking you to the Americans," he announced. At a picnic lunch, he plied Odette with red wine and told her he expected a positive report of her treatment under his command, that it had been humane, even kind, that she got medical care when she needed it and had a clean cell with light and air. From a Churchill family member, the report would have moral weight.

At 10:00 p.m., the car was stopped at an American checkpoint.

"This is Frau Churchill, she has been my prisoner," Suhren said in surrender.

"This is the Commandant of Ravensbrück, you make him a prisoner!" said Odette.

Suhren was led out of his car; his pistol was confiscated, broken down, and thrown onto the driver's seat. Odette was left alone in a magnificent new Mercedes.

The young GIs said they would find her somewhere to sleep, but Odette declined.

"No, if you don't mind, I have not seen the sky for a very long time and the stars. I would like to sit in this car until the morning."

It was a romantic request. But it was also a strategic one: The paper bonfires at Ravensbrück had not yet destroyed all evidence of Fritz Suhren's crimes; there were documents in the trunk of the Mercedes, three albums of photos. Some rosy-cheeked American doughboy brought Odette a clean blanket, and she fell asleep in her jailer's limousine.

It was her first night of freedom in two years.

Odette was repatriated to England on May 8, 1945, on the day of the Victory in Europe celebration, V-E Day. She arrived carrying Fritz Suhren's suitcase, his pistol, his diary, and his pajamas.

Her daughters were waiting.

EPILOGUE

A Useful Life

London

"God Save the King" trumpeted through a Buckingham Palace reception hall on the morning of November 17, 1946. The palace had been bombed nine separate times in the Blitz; still it was primed for the pomp and show of an investiture ceremony. King George VI stood in uniform on the dais.

The gilded room was chilly with a damp that seeped into the bones. Off to the side of the hall, leading the procession, was Odette Sansom in her FANY cap and bush jacket, her wounded feet still in cotton bandages and oversize men's shoes. She would be the only woman to receive a national honor that day, she recalled. The George Cross (GC) was the British Empire's highest civilian award for gallantry.

As the anthem marched to its coda, Odette shuffled forward on tender feet.

"Mrs. Odette Sansom," called the lord chamberlain, reading her citation to the assembled courtiers and family members:

> Mrs. Sansom was infiltrated into enemy-occupied France and worked with great courage and distinction until April, 1943, when she was arrested with her Commanding Officer.

Two of Odette's daughters were seated in a front row, in their finest dresses.

"Is the George Cross the best thing you could do?" Marianne asked when she was tucked into bed the night the Honors List was published.

"I don't know but it seems to be an important thing," cooed Odette. It was this recognition by her daughter at bedtime that she would remember as her "best moment."

Women were new to war, and the George Cross was a brand-new medal, created for this conflict, the first to hit home soil in some two hundred years. The Second World War demanded grit from ordinary Britons, a kind of valor that had not previously been asked for or required. Civilians displayed daily courage on an island under siege; they faced a shared common danger on the home front. The nerve, pluck, and spirit of regular citizens had to be recognized.

Odette was among the first women awarded the George Cross, the first—and at that point only—woman to receive it for serving behind enemy lines. (Two other female agents from French Section, Ensign Noor Inayat Khan and Ensign Violette Szabo, would be decorated with posthumous GCs.) By the terms of the award, they were civilians. Yet their service to the British Empire was undeniably military.

The George Cross was not Odette's first honor. Upon her immediate return from Germany, she received a lesser award, Member of the Most Excellent Order of the British Empire, MBE (Civil). It was the same medal that would be awarded to other women agents in F Section.

When the war ended and the bodies were counted, new information out of France revealed the extent of Odette's service, the way she had saved Peter Churchill's life as well as the life of her radio operator, even under torture. At that point, she was recommended for the George Cross. The Crown now acknowledged her two years in enemy hands during which "she displayed courage, endurance and self sacrifice of the highest possible order."

Men won different laurels for their fight. By the end of the war, such sex segregation was a familiar story: Male agents performing the same tasks might be recommended for the Victoria Cross, created by Queen Victoria, the highest honor for military gallantry. While the

Corps féminins did much of the same work in the same places, they were not technically soldiers and so not eligible for military honors—only civil decorations. It was one of the many ways women were denied equal status. Their salaries and ranks were lower; so too were their war pensions. When it took five parachute jumps to receive paratrooper wings, women were only ever assigned to four jumps and so never received their wings. And though the women of F Section served in combat, government chauvinism dictated they were not eligible for military recognition.

"There was nothing remotely civil about what I did. I didn't sit behind a desk all day," said Lieutenant Pearl Witherington, refusing her MBE (Civil) for her work arming, training, and commanding a maquis force of fifteen hundred men, while presiding over the surrender of more than eighteen thousand German prisoners after D-Day.

Odette's story generated international attention. Two days after she arrived in England from Germany, her commanding officer returned from Italy. Peter Churchill's experience in prison was gentler, though by no means easy. Odette's giant Churchillian fable spared him the worst of Nazi ferocity:

> For mutual protection they agreed to maintain that they were married. She adhered to this story and even succeeded in convincing her captors in spite of considerable contrary evidence and through at least fourteen interrogations. She also drew Gestapo attention off her Commanding Officer and on to herself by saying that he was completely innocent and had only come to FRANCE on her insistence.

Odette curtsied and took three steps toward the king.

The monarch appended the medal to Odette's FANY uniform, then took her hand and held it for longer than felt proper or perfunctory. "He would not let go."

"I asked that you should lead the procession, Madam," stuttered the king, "as no woman has done so before during my reign."

Odette flashed a smile, backed up three paces facing the sovereign, and curtsied one last time. Some two hundred royal handshakes later, a tall and smiling Peter Churchill strode across the red carpet to receive his Distinguished Service Order (Military):

> Organized a number of parachute dropping operations and the reception of agents by sea on the Mediterranean coast.

By the time their honors were gazetted, Odette and Peter were living together in a cottage in Culmstock, recovering from the traumas of war and the illnesses of imprisonment. On Odette's immediate return, she had resumed the use of her maiden name, Brailly, then got a quick and discreet divorce from Roy Sansom. One week after the GC was made public, the press ran the headline "British Heroine to Wed Spy She Saved in France: Suffered Torture to Protect Him."

In newsreels and papers, Peter said he intended to live as they had pretended in France: "I hope to marry Mrs. Sansom."

"Tell me, Churchill," said the king, "to what do you attribute Mrs. Sansom's power in overcoming the fearful things she had to face?"

"I am convinced," said Peter, "that in her case it was the power of the spirit that overcame the handicaps of a fragile physique."

Odette was fragile because her body was the site of atrocities. Soon after the investiture, in December 1946, Odette would travel with a delegation to Hamburg to give testimony at the war crimes trial for the women's prison at Ravensbrück.

Odette and Peter married in 1947. Five years after landing in Vichy France, she became Odette Churchill; the name that had once saved her life was now hers for life.

At least until her divorce.

The women of F Section did not have an easy reintegration after the victory in Europe. The economy and ego of Great Britain wrestled with the peace, under the heavy burden of war debts and the emotional tolls of Hitler's extremism.

Odette was one of three women from F Section to survive the concentration camps. She was placed under military medical supervision, and although nothing "organic" could be diagnosed beyond malnourishment, tuberculosis, torture scars, "nails like cigarette papers," and an untreated broken back, the Firm's own doctor noted that Odette was "suffering from psychological symptoms which undoubtedly have been brought on by [her] service in the field." He wrote, "These symptoms interfere to a considerable extent with [her] efficiency for future employment and it is likely that [they] may continue to do so for some time to come." Like soldiers the world over, she was shell-shocked. Odette was recommended for 70 percent disability compensation, the doctor said. "It is felt that these agents come under a class of their own and that they should be given preferential treatment."

In her lifetime, Odette became a British national phenomenon, a one-word household name, the Diana of her day. Much of the Firm's activities remained secret until SOE personnel files were declassified in 2003, but immediately on her return the War Office publicity department collaborated on her authorized biography, *Odette,* to tell the story of her service, love, capture, and escape. It became part of the received history of the Special Operations Executive; in 1950, a film of the same name was produced. Buck, Vera, and the king and queen attended the gala opening. In the dismal postwar years, the young mother's heroic tale united two bruised and victimized countries that had not always fought on the same side: France and Britain.

The women of F Section were symbols of Britain's lost innocence, its pain, strength, and sacrifices in the worst war abroad and the first war at home. Their collective achievements helped pave over some of F Section's most heinous errors—notably, the parachuting of agents into enemy control at the request of Nazi-captured radio sets, the radio games.

Loving two countries, committed to a single cause of freedom, each woman was given the chance to remain in England, and each signed on for the fight in France. Women seldom make it into big, official war documents; their war experiences are about families, bombardment, shortages, work, and loss. Where men are celebrated as heroes, women's wars are quiet and forgotten. When the *Corps féminins* went to war, they broke barriers, smashed taboos, and altered the course of history: Among their many firsts, they were the first women in organized combat, the first women in active-duty special forces, the first women paratroopers infiltrated into a war zone, the first female commando raiders, the first female signals officers behind enemy lines; they were first to write women into the history of war.

The "total war" of 1939–1945 was a modernizing force in the story of women at every level of society, not just for FANYs and other auxiliaries. It was an engine for social change. At war, women were encouraged to take on a "man's job," the highly skilled, well-compensated tasks fueled by the industrial demands of battle. But it did not effect a permanent economic revolution. Many of women's gains dissipated as men demobilized and returned to the workforce. In the postwar boom, more women worked outside the home than ever before, but their participation was not met with a corresponding rise in wages. In the immediate peace, women were again relegated to "soft" jobs—nursing and clerking—with lower pay and a "marriage bar" that prohibited cashing a check after tying the knot.

To some of the more favored women of the Firm, Vera served as an informal headhunter. F Section hoped to keep track of its most successful agents, in case there was another conflict and a renewed need for seasoned clandestine operatives. Some women were put on an unofficial "white list" and set up in careers.

"I was going back to nothing. I had no home, I didn't know what . . . I [was] going to do in the future," said Lise de Baissac. In London, she was recommended to the French service of the BBC and became a radio journalist.

Lise had been crucial to the liberation of France. For her MBE (Civil) it was noted,

> It was usual for this officer to cycle sixty to seventy kilometers daily carrying compromising material at the imminent risk of her life. On one occasion when the maquis HQ were attacked

she used firearms with great skill. Her work, carried out under most difficult conditions, did much to assist the maquis preparations prior to the break-through at MAYENNE [*département* of Normandy].

But she felt she could not go back after the war. Her Paris life was over. After Lise fled in 1940, a friend commandeered her furniture and told the owner of the flat she would not be returning. "I had no more house, no money, no nothing. I had nowhere to go."

Lise married in her forties—the artist whom her mother had rejected when Lise was a teen—and returned to live in the South of France.

"I was very happy that France had been delivered and that I had a little help that I had been able to give." Lise received the Croix de Guerre and the Legion of Honor and at age ninety-one was finally awarded her paratrooper wings. "My life has been worth something. That gives me pleasure."

Mary Herbert, after her release by the Gestapo, fled to the countryside and hid with her infant daughter until the cessation of hostilities in France. Four months after the liberation, the principals of F Section traveled around France on a victory tour, Operation Judex, where they found Mary living outside Poitiers:

> 20th December, 1944: We saw the youngest member of the Resistance group, Mlle Claudine de Baissac, aged one year.

Mary and Claude got married, legitimizing their daughter, but never lived together as husband and wife.

Once Mary became a mother, she was no longer of use to the Firm, and her immediate postwar years were anxious ones. Concerned about finding decent work with a young daughter in tow, she returned to England and became a language teacher.

THIRTY-NINE WOMEN FROM French Section went to war, and fourteen died in action. While the casualty rate seems high, war is always deadly—for forward units in particular.

On April 15, 1945, when the hospital camp in Belsen, Germany, was liberated by the British army, Yvonne Rudellat was registered as a French patient under the name Jacqueline Gauthier.

A census of the hospital was taken ten days later: On April 25, 1945, Jacqueline Gauthier was no longer on the Bergen-Belsen rolls.

Yvonne, the first female sabotage agent, died from typhus, starvation, and dysentery, with a bullet in her head.

She lived long enough to witness her own liberation.

ANDRÉE BORREL DIED as she lived: fighting.

Retaliation was on the collective mind of the Reich in the weeks after D-Day. One month to the day after the Allied invasion of France, July 6, 1944, at Natzweiler, in the high and foggy pine forests of the Vosges Mountains in Alsace—the only concentration camp on French soil—Andrée was injected with poison.

It is said Andrée woke up just as her feet were placed in the crematorium oven. She clawed at her jailer, digging her nails deep, "severely" scratching his face to the point of drawing blood.

As he closed the door, Andrée screamed, "*Vive la France!*"

THE SPECIAL OPERATIONS Executive was indeed special—remarkable—for it was largely new under the sun. In the battle for Europe, the women and men of F Section were a key fighting force. Some 429 agents went behind the lines, suffering 104 casualties; together with de Gaulle's RF Section, they armed the whole of occupied France. In total, Allied-backed resistance forces were counted as worth fifteen divisions in France, or about 200,000 troops.

The special agents were all heroic, determined, and human: Their mistakes were grave—more than fifty agents in Europe would be captured as the result of the Nazi radio game deceptions, the *Funkspiele*—but these men and women hastened the end of the war. The record of sabotage in France stands up favorably against the riskier, costlier, and more deadly (at least for civilians) strategy of sending bombers to target enemy installations.

Like its female agents, the Firm heralded plenty of historic firsts: It was the first government agency devoted to irregular combat, acts of sabotage, and political and economic warfare. (It provided a model for James Bond's many adventures. Vera is said to be the prototype for Miss Moneypenny; Ian Fleming would have known about SOE in his wartime role as a naval intelligence officer.) The Firm is gone, but its methods and techniques became blueprints for the OSS in America, predecessor to the CIA, and the Mossad in Israel, among many others. The special operations pioneered in Europe and the Far East in World War II remain essential tactics for any modern power.

The Special Operations Executive was shuttered in 1946, and rival spy shops—the various MIs—claimed the Cold War and beyond. The SOE war records were selectively edited, and many burned in a fire. The Firm simply ceased to exist.

Yet its heroic legacy lives. In the occupied countries of Europe, guerrilla warfare did at least as much to promote postwar self-respect as it did to speed the downfall of Hitler.

Military historians debate whether *la Résistance* racked up strategic wins or if it was only ever a useful symbol. Let them argue. The Allied air chief said, "Its greatest victory was that it kept the flame of the French spirit burning through the dark years of Occupation." But General Eisenhower, supreme commander of Allied forces in Europe, paid the Firm the highest compliment, saying that the strategic acts of sabotage by this irregular bunch of amateurs shortened the war by as much as six months, saving thousands of lives.

When General Charles de Gaulle marched victorious through the streets of Paris, he reclaimed his country from the Reich. But the general also had to reconcile disquieting truths in the national conscience: France was no mere victim; France had actively collaborated with Hitler. By the end of the war, half the German airplanes that bombed the Allies had been manufactured in France; Marshal Pétain and the Vichy regime sent 650,000 French workers to Nazi war factories and 76,000 Jews to their deaths in extermination camps.

De Gaulle crafted a new France from the ashes of war. The Resistance was critical to his argument; it became the narrative vehicle by which he maneuvered a fresh and free country. He said there was an unbroken thread linking the Third Republic to the Fourth. The Vichy years were not an aberration; they did not exist at all. "The Republic has never ceased," he said. "Vichy always was and still remains null and void." When France's rebel armies played a role in the emancipation, they linked one republic to the next, erasing four years of cooperation, complicity, and consent.

Once the German army was defeated on French soil and de Gaulle claimed credit for the win, France was suddenly "a nation of resisters."

Everyone was in the French Resistance.

Except women.

The role women played in the liberation is not celebrated in the founding fable of the Resistance. When France tallied its maquis forces after the war, women constituted only between 10 and 15 percent of the foot soldiers, though they were more than 51 percent of the population given the various conscription policies and high mortality of men at war. Historically, women's labor goes uncounted, and women's war work was also in the shadows. They were forgers, couriers, and quartermasters; feeding a rebel is resistance work too.

In order to canonize de Gaulle's self-liberation coup, the Resistance had to be perceived as strong, a legitimate ruling force. Traditional feminine frailty weakened de Gaulle's argument for a virile nation. Women were not yet considered political actors; Frenchwomen didn't even get the vote until 1946. And so women were undercounted and unappreciated in the final census of France's freedom fighters.

The general was a leader for his moment—strong-willed, egotistical, the last great Frenchman—but a poor colleague: His was the only voice in the room. Yet with no resources, no army, no bargaining power whatsoever, he resurrected a nation. To have a seat at the global table, to claim a share of the new world order, he insisted France had built its own chair. So the Allies, too, were sidelined by de Gaulle. The Churchillian epic of arming French rebels ran counter to Gaullist triumphalism. The fact of Anglo-American aid was a narrative inconvenience to the Fourth Republic, as it reduced France to a colonial satellite of great powers.

So France freed herself.

There was little space for thanks in the general's new national mythology. Shortly after D-Day, the F Section networks were marginalized, their organizers recalled and replaced with Gaullist commanders. Some agents were kicked out of France entirely. The new government was "extremely touchy" about SOE. For the Allied-backed rebel leaders, there were few honors in de Gaulle's new country.

The men and women of F Section spoke mostly without bitterness of those dismissive years after the war; they recognized France's new national story as reasonable, necessary, and perhaps even just. They fought undercover; they did not expect glory.

C'était la guerre.

Author's Note

The war historian Max Hastings says that what gets published about the female agents of SOE is "romantic twaddle." As a journalist, as a storyteller, and as a woman, I believe that twaddle matters. It is the stuff of human experience. What we feel, whom we love, how we mourn—this is the matrix in which we exist and act, even as armies blitz across continents. To twaddle or not to twaddle is a false choice. The framing itself hints at the original sin of women at war. See it as a rhetorical game: It silences women's stories while privileging everything else in a conflict. Were it not for oral histories, most of women's history would be lost forever. So the call to empiricism gets trumpeted in bad faith: misogyny wrapped in pieties. It is the rare historian, from Thucydides to Tuchman, whose stories would be remembered at all without the romance or the twaddle.

This book is not fiction. It was built from archives in Britain, France, and the United States and from the memories, both written and oral, of those fortunate enough to survive. As we lose the survivors and as governments grapple with their roles in the war, new documents continue to be declassified and released. Everything that appears in quotation marks is from original sources, spoken, written, or reported by the principals. Sources might, intentionally or otherwise, have narrated events in a self-serving way. (We are all the heroes of our own lives.) But if a story is true to the subject, if it was the story she had to tell, then that is truth. It will always break my heart that Andrée Borrel did not live to tell us herself.

Such is the machinery of history; it is how writing the past works. I have tried to square the gaps and tensions in what we know against the broader context of the occupation, guided by the historian's toolbox: the criteria of multiple attestation, embarrassment, plausibility, coherence, and other judgment calls. Taken together, the whole story had to make sense. I hope it does.

In the end, as Colonel Buckmaster said, "*Tant pis,* it had to be told."

Acknowledgments

Words are not enough to express my gratitude to Larry Weissman, Sascha Alper, and Amanda Cook, but words are all I have. Larry and Sascha advocate for me, read me, and inspire me, as agents and as friends. I have never wanted any editor's approval more than Amanda Cook's—thank you so much, Amanda, for letting me try. The support and diligence of the entire team at Crown has been a persistent pleasure and motivation: Thanks to Claire Potter, Zachary Philips, Rachel Rokicki, Julie Cepler, Penny Simon, Rachel Aldrich, Courtney Snyder, Chris Brand, Elena Giavaldi, Craig Adams, Andrea Lau, Heather Williamson, Mark Stutzman, Annsley Rosner, David Drake, and Molly Stern. I am indebted to the community of veterans, families, and scholars who shared time, energy, archival materials, and insights with me, with special thanks to Dr. Juliette Pattinson at the University of Kent for her interview transcripts; to Martyn Cox, who made the introductions and maintains the memories; and to Steven Kippax, whose command of the archives is a gift to researchers. I could not be more grateful to my first readers, who provided sterling insight, necessary corrections, and informed guidance from the global to the anorak: Anne Whiteside, Francis J. Suttill, Colonel (Retired) Nick Fox, OBE, David Harrison, and Saul Austerlitz. For warm beds, hot tea, and cold champagne in Paris and in London, my love to Elizabeth Austin and Tory and Henry Asch, and to Richard Heelas. I would not be here were it not for Joel Derfner and Kim Binsted; thank you for everything ever. For acts of friendship large and infinite, thank you Gabriela Shelley; Charles Coxe; Peter Grant; Diane Selkirk; Maria Smilios; Michael Zola, Shea Grimm, and Lola Nagata; Maria, Sergio, and Pieralberto Deganello; Jeff and Betsy Garfield; Jennifer Baker and Jason (Big Red) Jestice; Kenny Longenecker and Tammy Castleforte; Darlene McCampbell; Steven Dickstein; Michael Combs; Maya Kron, Lauren Coleman, and Esther Saskin; Erik Larson; Laurie Gwen Shapiro; Susannah Cahalan; Richard Ford; Maia Selkirk and Evan Gatehouse; Mary O'Dowd, Meagan O'Dowd O'Malley, and Ed O'Malley; Oliver and Rob Tannenbaum; Stephanie, Adam, Jacob, and Lily Brown; Katherine Austin and Sy Bortz; Elissa and Erin Labbie; Jason, Beth, Will, Cora, Lorelei, Bill, and Barbara Myers; Talia, Laila, Mia, and Marco Veissid and Phyllis Bieri; Amanda Gadziak and Douglas Pulver; Julian Land; Shai Ingber; Miriam Nabarro; Heather Massart; Josh Marshall; Charity Thomas; Peter Greenberg; Duncan Black; Nina Combs; Scott Anderson; Joy Tutela and David Black; Lieutenant Colonel Brian N. Sabowitz; Edward Readicker-Henderson; Église Française du Saint-Esprit for the French classes; and bless the entire heroic staff of Village Care at 46/10th. I am staggered by the love and forbearance of my family; thank you, Barney, Gerald, and Helen Cohen Rose.

Notes

CHAPTER 1: GOD HELP US

3 **"fresh complexion":** Odette Hallowes, HS 9/648/4, National Archives, Kew.

4 **smiled in French:** Leo Marks, *Between Silk and Cyanide: A Codemaker's Story, 1941–1945* (New York: Touchstone, 1998), 95.

4 **"Dear Madam":** Jerrard Tickell, *Odette: The Story of a British Agent* (1949; London: Chapman & Hall, 1952), 69.

Odette's surviving personnel file does not contain a copy of Captain Jepson's original letter. This text comes from the authorized version of Odette's story, written by a man, Jerrard Tickell, who was a member of the War Office Public Relations Department. We do, however, have the surviving text of one of Captain Jepson's letters sent June 5, 1942, to the recruit Jacqueline Nearne, a member of Odette's training class. When one compares the texts, it reads almost identically to the one quoted in Tickell's biography. To my mind, it suggests that Tickell had access to Odette's files as he wrote. The full Nearne letter is reproduced here for the doubting reader: "Your name has been passed to me as that of someone possessing qualifications which may be of value in a phase of the war effort. If you are available for interview I would be glad to see you at the above address at 3.30 p.m. on Thursday 25th June, 1942. I would be glad if you would let me know whether you can come or not. Yours truly, Selwyn Jepson, Captain." Susan Ottaway, *A Cool and Lonely Courage: The Untold Story of Sister Spies in Occupied France* (New York: Little, Brown, 2014), 26.

4 ***Mrs. Miniver:*** *Mrs. Miniver* debuted in June 1942. It was the top box-office attraction for the U.K. in 1942.

5 **She was not too old to type:** Odette Marie Celine Sansom, Oral History, 1986, Imperial War Museum, London.

5 **Instead, she dragged her mother:** Valerie Grove, "Life Wisdom Learnt in the Darkness of a Torture Cell—Odette Hallowes, GC," *Sunday Times* (London), Oct. 14, 1990.

5 **She was only four:** In late-in-life interviews, Odette says she was two when her father died. But the Battle of Verdun was in 1916, so she was four.

6 **As an adult, married:** Odette's personnel file on July 11, 1942, gives her address as 11 Comeragh Road, W4, which is in Hammersmith. Her authorized biography and her lifelong oral accounts suggest she had left London for Somerset. Documentary evidence doesn't always match her oral reports. As an author, I have had to choose between versions. Where possible, I note which account I use and the reasons why.

6 **"Austerity Clothes":** Even the smallest pleasures were censured: "It is quite wrong and improper to see comfortable housewives—young and old—still gorging on buns and cakes in every one of the many restaurants in this city between 4 and 5 pm every day," decried women's magazines. "But it's time this wasteful frivolity stopped." S. A. Thompson, Court Hey Avenue, Bowring Park, Liverpool, *Picture Post,* Sept. 12, 1942.

6 **room 055a:** Ottaway, *Cool and Lonely Courage,* 26.

6 **Victoria Hotel, room 238:** Shrabani Basu, *Spy Princess: The Life of Noor Inayat Khan* (London: Sutton, 2006), ebook.

6 **He wanted nothing:** Jepson, Imperial War Museum, London.

7 **"Full Christian Names":** Hallowes, HS 9/648/4, National Archives, Kew.

7 **The announcement was one:** Keith Grint, *Leadership, Management, and Command: Rethinking D-Day* (London: Palgrave Macmillan, 2007), 46; Paul Winter, ed., *D-Day Documents* (London: Bloomsbury, 2014), 76.

8 **The ISTD built:** Allison Lear, "Report on Suzanne Kyrie-Pope, an ISTD Employee," WW2 People's War: An Archive of World War Two Memories, BBC, 2005, online.

9 **a man who was eternally constipated:** Nancy Wake, *The Autobiography of the Woman the Gestapo Called the White Mouse* (South Melbourne: Macmillan, 1985), 104.

9 **What did Odette think:** Jepson, Imperial War Museum, London.

9 **Oh, she figured she might:** Sansom, Imperial War Museum, London.

9 **The captain understood:** Jepson, Imperial War Museum, London.

9 **"You would not know":** Sansom, Imperial War Museum, London.

10 **"Well, what do you mean?":** Sansom, Imperial War Museum, London.

10 **Vichy ships in North Africa:** "The French Ships in Egypt," *Times* (London), July 17, 1942.

10 **"What do you think I am?":** Sansom, Imperial War Museum, London.

10 **He was willing to risk:** Jepson, Imperial War Museum, London.

11 **Her chances of returning:** Gordon Nornable, as quoted in Roderick Bailey, ed., *Forgotten Voices of the Secret War: An Inside History of Special Operations During the Second World War in Association with the Imperial War Museum* (London: Ebury Press, 2008), 43.

11 **"Oh, they won't bother":** Jepson, Imperial War Museum, London.

11 ***Am I supposed to accept*:** Sansom, Imperial War Museum, London.

11 **"Train me":** Ibid.

11 **"God help us along the way":** Jepson, Imperial War Museum, London. In Tickell's biography *Odette,* the inscription reads, "Direct minded and courageous. God help the Nazis if we can get her near enough to them. S.J." The book was published soon after the war, and Jepson was not interviewed for the archives until more than forty years later, in 1986. Though I believe Odette's biographer had access to original and unedited personnel files, because some documents are reproduced faithfully, the book is notable for being written by a man and fictionalized and for containing easy-to-spot inaccuracies. It was conceived as a public relations tool of the War Office to celebrate a secret government agency at a time when actions behind enemy lines remained classified, and so it tends toward propaganda. In the era before declassification, Odette served as an unofficial spokeswoman for SOE, and she seldom (if ever) contradicted the party line. While Odette stood by the book until she died, I lean on the side of first-person accounts over the Tickell biography for the simple reason that the principal characters were there and Tickell was not.

CHAPTER 2: UNGENTLEMANLY WARFARE

12 **"the Firm":** In oral interviews archived at the Imperial War Museum, London, former agents casually refer to the Special Operations Executive as "the Firm." Some stated they did not know the actual name SOE until after the war.

12 **"the Org":** C. Wretch, Private Papers, Imperial War Museum, London.

12 **often enough "Bedlam":** Marks, *Between Silk and Cyanide,* 5.

13 **"Western Europe is favoured":** CHAR 20/52/30/73, Sir Winston Churchill Archive Trust, 2002.

13 **April 1, 1943:** The earliest possible date is named as April 1, 1943, and if shipping from America was delayed, it would be postponed to "late summer" 1943. Ibid.

14 **Adolf Hitler had captured:** In descending order of time taken to surrender, not in chronological order.

14 **"We have got to organize":** Hugh Dalton to Lord Halifax, July 2, 1940, daltondatabank.org.

15 **July 22, 1940:** In *The Fateful Years,* Hugh Dalton puts this conversation with Churchill on July 16, 1940, which maps to the same day as Hitler's inception of Operation Sea Lion, a nice bit of narrative symmetry. William Mackenzie says, "The Prime Minister wrote formally to Mr. Dalton acquainting him of these proposals and asking him to accept the task" on July 16, 1940, and says the letter was formerly contained in SOE Archives file 2/340/3.0, which has since been destroyed. Dalton's diaries, however,

suggest the date of the conversation was actually July 22, 1940, which is reflected here.

15 **"Brave and desperate men":** To defense committee, Churchill chairing, with Attlee, Eden, Lyttelton, Grigg, Sinclair, Pound, Brooke, Portal, Mountbatten, and Ismay; Selborne, Hambro, Cadogan, Morton, and three secretaries in attendance, as quoted in M. R. D. Foot, *SOE in France: An Account of the Work of the British Special Operations Executive in France, 1940–1944* (London: Frank Cass, 2004), ebook.

16 **"the most potent weapons":** Lieutenant Colonel Stanley Woolrych's opening address to new students, Group B Training Syllabus, HS 7/52, National Archives, Kew.

16 **global political conventions:** The prevailing Geneva Conventions had four criteria for any combatants to be recognized as soldiers by an opponent: They had to be commanded by an officer responsible for his subordinates, wear a "fixed distinctive emblem recognizable at a distance" (that is, be in uniform), carry arms openly, and conduct operations within the laws of war. SOE's agents would qualify on only one count: They were subject to command and control.

16 **code name: D-Day:** The *D* stands for nothing more than "day," just as the *J* in *Jour J* stands for nothing more than *jour.*

16 **July 16, 1940:** The Führer and Supreme Commander of the Armed Forces, Führer Headquarters, July 16, 1940, "Directive No. 16: On Preparations for a Landing Operation Against England."

17 **Britain had simply run out:** A substantial portion of men of service age in World War II were born during World War I's demographic "baby bust," when birthrates collapsed. At the moment when Europe needed soldiers most, the supply of male recruits could not meet the demand for military labor, so women were drawn into service.

17 **Putting women in the line:** Jepson, Imperial War Museum, London.

17 **not to destroy it:** Pearl Witherington, interview with Kate Vigurs, May 2003, as quoted in "The Women Agents of the Special Operations Executive F Section: Wartime Realities and Post War Representations" (PhD thesis, University of Leeds, 2011).

17 **into Hitler's hands: rape:** To be sure, there has been homosexual rape on the battlefield since the beginning of time. For this purpose, because we are speaking of women, we are speaking of heterosexual rape only.

17 **uniquely exposed:** The fear was of rape by opposing forces. We now know that in practice women in combat are as—or more—likely to be raped by men in their own military.

17 **their bodies become war bounty:** Historically, attempts had been made to address the problem of rape in war. The social activist Jane Addams argued for rape's inclusion among war crimes at the 1915 International Congress of Women in The Hague: "Worse than death . . . is the defenselessness of women in warfare and their violation by the invading soldier." Her campaign was not successful. Rape was not listed among war crimes in the governing Geneva Conventions.

18 **what killing and dying actually meant:** The National Service (No. 2) Act, which extended the previous act of 1939 to 1941 to include women, stated, "No woman who is called up for service under the principal Act shall be required actually to use any lethal weapon or to take part in the actual use of any lethal weapon unless she has signified in writing her willingness to use lethal weapons or, as the case may be, to take part in the use thereof." National Archives, National Service (No. 2) Act, as cited in Juliette Pattinson, *Behind Enemy Lines: Gender, Passing, and the Special Operations Executive in the Second World War* (Manchester, U.K.: University of Manchester Press, 2007), 26.

18 **days of the Blitz:** The first time a mixed-sex regiment fired in action was in November 1941, and the first successful "kill" came in April 1942. D'Ann Campbell, "Women in Combat: The World War II Experience in the United States, Great Britain, Germany, and the Soviet Union," *Journal of Military History* 57, no. 2 (April 1993): 301–23.

18 **(ack-ack) artillery:** James Moore, "The Blitz Spirit—75 Years On!," *Express* (London), Sept. 6, 2015.

18 **They lit up the night sky:** What we now know as the Blitz was composed of two different air-raid cycles. The first followed the fall of France and lasted about eight months, from September 7, 1940, to May 11, 1941. The second cycle began in January 1944 and lasted until March 29, 1945. Following D-Day in 1944, the second cycle included Hitler's secret weapons: the V1 cruise missiles and the V2 ballistic missiles. The number of women manning ack-ack defenses is a total for the entire war.

18 **Winston Churchill's own daughter:** Churchill was so enthusiastic about using women on gun sites he declared that any general who could save over forty thousand fighting men for the field gained the equivalent of a victory. Campbell, "Women in Combat."

18 **"A gunner is a gunner":** The original sourcing for this quotation seems to have been lost to history. It is repeated so often and in so many places as to be canon. See Pattinson, *Behind Enemy Lines,* as well as Duncan Barrett and Nuala Calvi, *The Girls Who Went to War: Heroism, Heartache, and Happiness in Wartime Women's Forces* (London: Harper Element, 2015), ebook.

18 **"cool and lonely courage":** Jepson, Imperial War Museum, London.

19 **In that mournful summer:** By most reports, very few heard de Gaulle's first *Appel du 18 juin* on the day of broadcast, but as a piece of propaganda it got repeated so often on BBC radio that it became its own myth early in the war.

20 **But the Firm found the Cross:** "Of all the crosses I have had to bear, the Croix de Lorraine is the heaviest," said Churchill of de Gaulle. Michael Mould, *The Routledge Dictionary of Cultural References in Modern French* (London: Routledge, 2011).

21 **Prime Minister Churchill needed:** It was said working with General de Gaulle was "like trying to live amicably with a jealous, touchy and domineering wife." Keith Jeffery, *MI6: The History of the Secret Intelligence*

Service (London: Bloomsbury, 2010), as cited in Max Hastings, *Winston's War: Churchill, 1940–1945* (New York: Vintage, 2011), 273.

21 **"Every time I have to decide":** Translated from the French, in Charles de Gaulle, *Mémoires de guerre: L'Unité, 1942–1944* (Paris: Librarie Plon, 1956), 224.

21 **with RF Section:** The Free French created the BCRA (Bureau Central de Renseignements et d'Action) for covert operations in France. RF Section was always part of SOE and remained under its command. It was "the daily interlocutor and the obligatory intermediary with the French secret services," according to Jean-Louis Crémieux-Brilhac in his book *La France libre: De l'appel du 18 juin à la Libération* (Paris: Gallimard, 1996).

21 **F Section:** F Section refers to the working of the French Section alone. When I use "the Firm" or "SOE," I am mostly referring to the broader organization that oversaw covert operations in Europe, North Africa, and the Far East. Other times, "the Firm" is used from an agents' perspective, because many agents did not know it was called SOE until they returned from war. But on occasion, I revert to the "elegant variation" so that there aren't echoes of SOE or F Section too often in the same place.

21 **"army of the shadows":** *L'armée de l'ombre.*

21 **"right type":** History of SOE, HS 7/121, National Archives, Kew.

21 **Virginia Hall, an American:** "A mother to all the F Section agents with whom she came into contact (and many with whom she didn't). She was a banker, guide, philosopher, and friend to at least fifteen of our men." History of F Section, HS 7/121, National Archives, Kew.

22 **"What are you doing?":** Jepson, Imperial War Museum, London.

22 **"manpower bottleneck":** *Times* (London), Aug. 8, 1942.

22 **"And good luck to you":** Jepson, Imperial War Museum, London.

22 **"Would you mind talking":** Ibid.

CHAPTER 3: A FIRST-CLASS AGENT

24 **"a dull flat noise":** Colonel André Passy as quoted in Foot, *SOE in France,* ebook.

24 **"Apache-type":** Phyllis Bingham, FANY staff commander, quoted in Stella King, *Jacqueline: Pioneer Heroine of the Resistance* (London: Arms and Armour Press, 1989), 127.

24 **easy to share a smoke:** Elizabeth Nicholas, *Death Be Not Proud* (London: Cresset Press, 1958). Mme. Le Chêne, Andrée's Beaulieu colleague, noted that she smoked and that it was considered unbecoming of a young woman.

24 **"She knew little":** Le Chêne, quoted in Nicholas, *Death Be Not Proud,* 134.

24 **No man could stomach:** Robert Ferrier, interview, Imperial War Museum, London.

24 **Instructors shouted to all students:** Andrée did not speak fluent English.

All secret instruction was said to be in French, but she was also trained at Ringway, where instructors were as likely to be English speakers.

24 **"Where is the prince":** Franklin to Jan Ingenhousz, Jan. 16, 1784, Founders Online.

25 **the first wartime operation:** From the 1920s onward, parachute jumping had mixed with popular entertainment at fairgrounds and flight shows throughout the Continent. The interwar years saw the perfection of combat technique—in battle exercises with the Red Army, for nurses in France.

25 **a British airborne company:** First Airborne Division, C Company, Second Battalion of the First Parachute Brigade, about 120 men.

25 **radar equipment in Bruneval:** Capture of the Reich's radar technology helped the Allies develop and deploy countermeasures, such as a jamming strategy.

25 **"Parachutists in Action":** *Times* (London), March 2, 1942.

25 **"To be dropped in Occupied France":** Eric Piquet Wicks, *Four in the Shadows* (London: Jarrolds, 1957), 142, cited in Foot, *SOE in France,* ebook.

25 **helping some sixty-five:** Maurice H. Dufour, HS 9/455/565, National Archives, Kew. Sixty-five is the combined number of assists attributed to Andrée's boyfriend, Captain Maurice Dufour, and I apply this number to Andrée in the belief—supported by government documents and personal diaries—that they were working together. On one night, they helped as many as fifty evaders according to documents on Dufour.

26 **one in every three humans:** U.S. Census, international population, historical, www.census.gov.

27 **"She was entirely wonderful":** Le Chêne, quoted in Nicholas, *Death Be Not Proud,* 135.

27 **stalag and oflag detention camps:** "Stalag" was the general term for a POW camp; oflags were for officers.

27 **"an attitude of masterly":** Maurice Dufour, HS 9/455/5, National Archives, Kew.

28 **One daring night:** Ibid.

28 **"If [the Nazis] knew how many":** Pat O'Leary as quoted in Brian Stonehouse Diary, unpublished. Courtesy of Steven Kippax.

28 **"France is down":** Winston Churchill, *The Second World War,* 6 vols. (Boston: Houghton Mifflin, 1948–1953), vol. 4, *The Hinge of Fate,* 483.

28 **Maurice was collared:** Dufour, HS 9/455/5, National Archives, Kew.

29 **Meanwhile, Andrée's railway stop:** Ibid.

29 **with the Free French:** The interviews took place just before de Gaulle changed the name, so the Free French would have yet to become the Fighting French.

30 **"an excellent type":** Andrée Borrel, HS 9/183, National Archives, Kew.

30 **"an essential link":** Dufour, letter, July 18, 1942, HS 9/455/5, National Archives, Kew.

30 **the French secret service:** Both Wybot and Passy worked under aliases

to spare their families in France retaliation. Colonel Wybot was really Roger Warin. Passy was the name of a Paris metro station; he was André Dewavrin by birth.

31 **"most intelligent and made":** Dufour, HS 9/455/5, National Archives, Kew.

32 **"Better that nine innocents":** U.S. embassy report as quoted in Michael Bilton, "Dirty War on Our Doorstep," *Sunday Times* (London), March 15, 2009.

32 **"they kept hitting me":** King's Bench Division Folios 23. Writ issued on August 6, 1943, between Maurice Henri Dufour, Plaintiff, and General Charles de Gaulle, Lieutenant Colonel André Passy, Captain Roger Wybot, Captain François Girard, Colonel Louis Renouard, Commandant de Person, Commandant Etienne Cauchois, and Commandant Pierre Simon, Defendants.

32 **"One of the French officers":** King's Bench Division Folios, Aug. 6, 1943.

32 **"unquestionably third degreed":** Dufour, HS 9/455/5, National Archives, Kew.

32 **"We have arrested Mademoiselle":** King's Bench Division Folios, Aug. 6, 1943.

33 **"Of sound intelligence":** Borrel, HS 9/183, National Archives, Kew.

33 ***Quatorze Juillet* was forbidden:** Nevertheless, tens of thousands marched defiantly in France. "France's National Day," *Times* (London), July 14, 1942; "Le Quatorze Juillet: Celebrations," *Times* (London), July 15, 1942; "July 14 in France," *Times* (London), July 16, 1942.

33 **"You are not free":** "French ATS: New Chief Appointed in England," March 25, 1942, reprinted in *Auckland Star.*

34 **only female parachutist:** Nigel West, ed., *The Guy Liddell Diaries: MI5's Director of Counter-Espionage in World War II,* vol. 1, *1939–1942* (London: Routledge, 2005), ebook.

34 **the only woman combat:** Andrée was the first woman to be trained for parachuting in combat and would be the first deployed. No one else from her class at Beaulieu went by parachute. (The other women in her training class were considered too old to jump.) Other women in the auxiliaries would get trained for parachuting—such as those needed for aircraft delivery—but they were not deployed in combat operations.

35 **"She is expected":** Dufour, HS 9/455/5, National Archives, Kew.

35 **"position that the FF":** Dufour, HS 9/455/5, National Archives, Kew. In the summer of 1942, de Gaulle changed the name of his movement from Free French to Fighting French. Both are abbreviated "FF" in documents.

35 **"jollied into":** Ibid.

35 **subject to military justice:** Notably, it was a Frenchman, Georges Clemenceau, who said that military justice was to justice as military music was to music.

35 **Andrée Borrel's love saved:** "In the circumstances, quite irrespective of the merits or demerits of Dufour's case, we hope that you will be able to take steps to see that he is not returned to the FF and, if necessary, is detained in

a safe place until such time as he is no longer in a position to compromise our agent." Dufour, HS, 9/455/5, National Archives, Kew.

35 **"The proper course would be":** Ibid.

CHAPTER 4: THE QUEEN OF THE ORGANIZATION

37 **Special Training School 31:** Special agent training on the Beaulieu estate occurred in smaller houses on the property—such as the Rings and the House in the Woods. The Beaulieu area was collectively considered STS 31 or STS 27b. At the time of Lise's class, the common name for the Beaulieu area on documents seems to have been STS 31. The number "27" was the Firm's code for things pertaining to France, "27Land."

37 **"*The stately homes of England*":** Noël Coward, "The Stately Homes of England," lyrics from *Operette* (1938), with permission.

38 **Major Maurice Buckmaster:** Buckmaster was promoted to lieutenant colonel in April 1943, so he's a major for this part of the story.

38 **the Beaulieu area:** Maurice Buckmaster, F Section History and Agents, HS 7/121, National Archives, Kew.

38 **five women:** There might have been more students who are not reflected in the National Archives' SOE files. There was also a conducting officer for this class. The five students of whom we have confirmed documentary knowledge are Lise, Mary, Odette, Hélène, and Jacqueline.

38 **Lieutenant Colonel Woolrych:** Cyril Cunningham, *Beaulieu: The Finishing School for Secret Agents* (South Yorkshire, U.K.: Pen & Sword Military, 1998), 57.

39 **Lieutenant Lise de Baissac:** Lise de Baissac, HS 9/77/1, National Archives, Kew.

39 **With a bright light shining:** In late-in-life interviews, Lise dismissed the usefulness of the mock interrogation, but it also seems she barely remembered it (Pattinson interview in *Behind Enemy Lines*). She was in her nineties when the personnel files were declassified. Audio interviews with other agents, such as those archived at the Imperial War Museum, London, suggest the hostage-taking playacting was fairly transparent. Some agents found it useful, in retrospect. Odette testified to the usefulness of the practice in her Imperial War Museum sound recording. In the years before declassification, Odette served as an unofficial spokeswoman for the Firm; she seldom (if ever) contradicted the party line.

39 **"*Allez! Bougez!*":** Come on, come on, go, move, and so on.

39 **"I was really more":** Lise Villemeur, née de Baissac, interview by Juliette Pattinson, Marseilles, France, April 17, 2002. Dr. Pattinson provided transcripts of her interviews conducted with male and female SOE agents for her doctoral dissertation, published as Pattinson, *Behind Enemy Lines;* hereafter cited as Pattinson interview.

39 **"ordinary everyday":** Harry Ree, in *School for Danger* (1947). This propaganda film was produced at the end of the war by SOE and starred

the agents Jacqueline Nearne and Harry Ree. The training in the film is considered by Michael Foot, official historian of SOE, an accurate reflection of an agent's education at the Special Training Schools.

40 **"Pétain was awful":** Lise de Baissac, interview with Darlow Smithson, June 1, 2002, for the film *Behind Enemy Lines: The Real Charlotte Grays,* directed by Jenny Morgan (London: British Film Institute, 2002); hereafter cited as *Real Charlotte Grays* interview.

40 **came to spy craft:** There is debate about use of the term "spy" applied to SOE's agents. There is a distinction between intelligence work and the work of organizing guerrillas; many argue that SOE employed not spies but saboteurs. The agents themselves, however, used the word "spy" to describe the jobs they performed in France. Lise said, "We listened to a wireless together and that sort of thing. And when I h— I had special messages, and he—once he told me, you know, 'That is for the spy!' *[LAUGHS]* And—and I am one of them!" Lise, *Real Charlotte Grays* interview.

40 **like her brother:** "She perhaps suffered from the family faults (excess of personal ambition and touchiness), but she is always ready to see reason and invariably put her work first. Is 'difficult' but devoted." This was Buckmaster's evaluation. Lise de Baissac, HS 9/77/1, National Archives, Kew.

41 **"I went to England":** Lise, Pattinson interview.

41 **"crap in the corner":** Robert Ferrier, Sound Archives, Imperial War Museum, London.

41 **Harold "Kim" Philby:** Philby helped design the Beaulieu course for clandestine propaganda but was not Lise's instructor.

41 **Officers from the infamous:** William E. Fairbairn and Eric Anthony Sykes taught in the Scottish training schools, which Lise did not attend for her first mission. She was, however, instructed in the Firm's fighting techniques, which were derived from their all-in methods.

41 **"knee kick to the testicles":** William E. Fairbairn, *All-In Fighting* (London: Faber and Faber, 1942; repr., Naval and Military Press in association with the Royal Armouries, 2009), 30.

42 **"at least 100 ways":** "He knew at least 100 ways to kill people without shooting them. He was a knife fighter and an alley fighter. It was said that he had killed dozens of people in hand to hand combat. . . . Fairbairn had us throwing each other all over the place. Fortunately none of us killed any of our classmates. We all survived." Edgar Prichard, "Address to Historical Prince William, Inc.," National Park Service, typescript of talk, Jan. 16, 1991. Cited in John Whiteclay Chambers II, *OSS Training in the National Parks and Service Abroad in World War II* (Washington, D.C.: National Park Service, 2008).

42 **Lise came from a family:** Claude de Baissac's personnel files, HS 9/75 and 9/76, National Archives, Kew, say he was accustomed to shooting in France as a hobby prior to the war.

42 **"They took up, funnily enough":** Jepson, Imperial War Museum, London.
43 **"I didn't want to be a courier":** Lise, Pattinson interview.
43 **Buck and Vera listened:** We know Buck and Vera listened because Lise was assigned not as a courier but instead to launch her own network as a liaison agent.
43 **"I didn't want to get married":** Lise, Pattinson interview.
44 **"In a sense, you see":** Sara Helm, *A Life in Secrets: Vera Atkins and the Missing Agents of WWII* (New York: Anchor Books, 2007), 49.
44 **"Cover is the guise":** Training Lectures and Statistics, HS 8/371, National Archives, Kew.
44 **"I can be anything":** Lise, Pattinson interview.
44 **Lise was issued a false name:** Lise's nom de guerre was Odile, but she would not have used her code name for training.
45 **"feel like a different person":** Jean-Marc Dewaele, *Emotions in Multiple Languages* (London: Palgrave Macmillan, 2010).
45 **"Not my type of girl":** Lise, Pattinson interview.
45 **"Intelligent, extremely conscientious":** Lise de Baissac, HS 9/77/1, National Archives, Kew.
46 **Vera drew on her cigarette:** In interviews archived at the Imperial War Museum, London, you can hear Vera smoking nonstop; it was a lifelong habit.
46 **cross-continental march to Berlin:** Okay, so there was the Ardennes forest.
47 **"I should have been failing":** Maurice Buckmaster, *They Fought Alone: The Story of British Agents in France* (1958; repr., London: Biteback, 2014), 233.
47 **"It was no use":** Ibid., 134.
47 **"were deterred by old-fashioned":** History of F Section, HS 7/121, National Archives, Kew. It sounds uncomfortable to the modern ear, but "girls" was common parlance for the adult women of the Special Operations Executive. The word was widely used by female agents, commanders, coders, and pilots, in spoken communication and written.

PEARL WITHERINGTON

One girl who was training with me said, after a whole day of blowing up ammunition and shooting and all the rest of it, and she said "What are we doing here now?" I was just so amazed! I said "Don't you know?" and she said "No! I was asked to—to be a bilingual secretary." Well, I wasn't going to tell her what she was letting herself in for, so I went to the Commandant of the school and told him. But he said "That's the recruitment, I'm afraid." And, well, she stayed and she did the rest of the—of the er training, the three weeks' training with the paramilitary, and we trained with the boys.

NANCY WAKE

. . . my code. Well most girls used Shakespeare or the Bible and I'm not a, I'm a bit agnostic. So I thought well I'll have something, so I chose a little prose in my head. "She stood right there, in the moonlight fair. The moon shone through her nightie. It lit right on the nipple of her tit, oh Jesus Christ Almighty!"

LISE DE BAISSAC

Of course we were—were trying to—to help, and trying to do our best, to—to—to do something useful for the—for the war effort. We felt very much that. We were several of us, three or four girls. . . .

SONIA D'ARTOIS

I know we were taught it [training in unarmed combat] and we were supposed to know how to use it and I never had to use it. And er I'm just as glad I didn't. Probably some of the men did but I don't think many of the girls ever did have to use that. But we needed to know it anyway, it was part of the training and the training for the women was the same as the training for the men.

HUGH VERITY (SPECIAL DUTIES SQUADRONS, PILOT)

One girl I, I did fly in and out three times, I didn't actually get to know her, err on these occasions but, err . . . because they were so anonymous, they were just bods we [laughingly] carried, and umm she, she was Julienne Aisner and became Madame Besnard, and she was actually Dericourt's courier.

. . . [O]f the, err of 50 or more girls, umm put into France—mainly by parachute, I may say—erm, only a rather few were actually transported by Lysander, there was . . . most of them went in by parachute.

. . . [T]he girls we, we carried, the FANYs and WAAFs, were very welcome passengers, and err one of my pilots—Bunny Rymills—err, err he err seemed to have a particular corner (?) in carrying gorgeous girls, although it was pure chance that he got them because, err we, we didn't really know what gender our passengers would be, err until they arrived.

LESLIE FERNANDEZ (SOE TRAINER AND THEN DECORATED AGENT)

I grew up with the FANYs if you know what I mean in the training schools, I mean the girls were brought in first as wireless operators, you know that, that was the idea that started it all, but some of them, there's no doubt about it, were exceptionally good clandestine operators, in many cases it's easier for a woman to move about clandestinely with phoney papers and so on provided she had the basic language. . . . Some of them were excellent, no doubt about that. They made better spies if you know what I mean.

(Quotations courtesy of Martyn Cox, founder of the Secret WW2 Learning Network.)

47 **the Battle of Britain:** Ultimately, some twenty thousand civilian deaths were counted in the Battle of Britain; this includes the Blitz bombings of 1940–1941 and 1944–1945.

47 **Stalin and Hitler:** The clash would ultimately claim two million civilian lives.

48 **"I understand you are":** Lise, Pattinson interview.

48 **Buckmaster would take the theatrical:** Tickell spoke with both Buckmaster and Odette for his book. He seems to have had access to unedited personnel files, and both Buck and Odette signed off on the story, standing by it publicly for the rest of their lives. Tickell, *Odette.*

CHAPTER 5: *MERDE ALORS!*

49 **full moon—Charlotte:** Benjamin Cowburn, *No Cloak, No Dagger* (London: Frontline, 2009), ebook.

49 **Andrée waited for Charlotte:** "For at least two years the moon was as much of a goddess as she ever was in a near eastern religion." Brook to Foreign Office, Nov. 16, 1964, as quoted in Foot, *SOE in France,* ebook.

49 **"Now the time has come":** Lise de Baissac, Legasee Project interview, Legasee Educational Trust, 2011, legasee.org.uk, hereafter cited as Lise, Legasee interview.

50 **"If you're frightened":** Lise, *Real Charlotte Grays* interview.

50 **"very charming, very simple":** Lise, Pattinson interview.

50 **"to expand our various organizations":** History of F Section, HS 7/121, National Archives, Kew. In "pyramiding," several organizations become connected to a single node or commander, like a pyramid. Keeping

networks independent and running in parallel to one another was thought to prevent this and promote security.

51 **"talked at and talked at":** Suttill to his wife, Sept. 22, 1942, courtesy of Francis Suttill.

51 **"showing off":** Suttill to his wife, Oct. 1, 1942, courtesy of Francis Suttill.

52 **"*Now, God be thanked*":** Rupert Brooke, "Peace," *Poetry Magazine* 6, no. 1 (April 1915), poetryfoundation.org.

52 **Each was a girl:** "If—," by Rudyard Kipling. "If you can keep your head when all about you / Are losing theirs and blaming it on you . . . And—which is more—you'll be a Man, my son!"

52 **gold cigarette case:** Lise, Pattinson interview.

52 **"remind them that":** Maurice Buckmaster, *Specially Employed* (London: Batchworth, 1952), 73.

53 **at least thirty-nine times:** We don't have an exact number of parting gifts; Lise went on two missions, as did Virginia Hall. For Lise's second, she was given a gold pencil. "If I sold that, I wouldn't live a very long time with money I get from that." Lise, Pattinson interview.

53 **"She was the soul of SOE":** Lise, *Real Charlotte Grays* interview.

53 **"Tid Bits":** Vera Atkins, Sound Archives, Imperial War Museum, London.

53 ***Josephine ressemble à sa grand-mère:*** Josephine looks like her grandmother.

53 **Joseph looks like his grandfather:** *Joseph ressemble à son grand-père.*

53 **for a boy:** In interviews, Vera had several plays on this code, such as Jean/Jacqueline or Clément/Clémentine.

53 **"Fairy Godmother":** Maurice Buckmaster, Sound Archives, Imperial War Museum, London.

54 **Ballyhoo or Bunnyhug:** Max Hastings, "Agent Blunderhead: The British Spy Who Was Left Out in the Cold," *Times* (London), Aug. 31, 2015.

54 **"an ecclesiastical air":** Lise de Baissac, HS 9/77/1, National Archives, Kew.

55 **Andrée had some 250,000 francs:** Borrel, HS9/183, National Archives, Kew.

55 ***Merde alors!:*** Marks, *Between Silk and Cyanide,* 45.

55 **It was illegal to listen:** On May 10, 1940, Germany threatened French citizens with prison, hard labor, or death if they listened to non-German radio broadcasts. Olivier Wieviorka, *The French Resistance,* trans. Jane Marie Todd (Cambridge, Mass.: Harvard University Press, 2016).

55 **half the nation:** There were four or five million wireless receivers in France. Michael Stenton, *Radio London and Resistance in Occupied Europe: British Political Warfare, 1939–1943* (Oxford Scholarship Online, 2011). The population of France was then forty million. "Half the nation" is based on an assumption of about four people listening to any one radio, on average. Families were large, few could afford to live alone, and radios were expensive. The notion of "pass-along circulation" in media is well established.

57 **"*Jean a des cors*":** Claude de Baissac, HS 9/75, National Archives, Kew.

This is reproduced from an archival document in which the grammar and accents are not technically correct.

57 **"L'arc en ciel":** Telegram from Actor, Dec. 24, 1942, in J. A. F. Antelme, HS 9/43, National Archives, Kew.

57 **the signaling sentences:** The method is now known as "blind-transmission broadcasting."

58 **"the joy of hearing":** Armel Guerne, interview in John Vader, *The Prosper Double-Cross* (Mullimbimby, Australia: Sunrise Press, 1977), 59.

58 **"perfidious Albion":** This is a commonly used phrase in England and in France. The diplomatic phrase can be traced to the thirteenth century, though it is conventionally attributed to Augustin Louis de Ximénès, a French playwright who wrote it in a poem titled "L'ère des Français," published in 1793:

> *Attaquons dans ses eaux la perfide Albion.*
> Let us attack perfidious Albion in her waters.

58 **give cover to the aircraft:** For Andrée and Lise's operation, the pamphlets were potentially scattered after they had to abort the jump, not before, according to Colonel (Retired) Nick Fox, MBE.

59 **"We can't drop you":** Lise, Legasee interview.

60 **"worry about no-essentials":** Maurice Buckmaster, "They Went by Parachute," reprinted online by Steven Kippax, from a series of eight articles published in *Chambers's Journal,* 1946–1947.

60 **With so much produce diverted:** Marcel Ophuls, dir., *Le chagrin et la pitié* (*The Sorrow and the Pity*), Télévision Rencontre, 1969.

61 **Andrée, Lise, their suitcases:** HS 7/244, National Archives, Kew.

61 **"Everything ok":** "Report on Operations Undertaken by 138 Squadron on Night 24/25th September 1942."

61 ***Well, now I am living:*** Lise, Pattinson interview.

62 **"It wasn't quite free":** Lise, *Real Charlotte Grays* interview.

62 **Monique and Odile arrived safe:** Andrée was Monique Urbain on her documents, Denise in communications, and Whitebeam was her call name. In the F Section War Diary of July 1942–September 1942, HS 7/244, Andrée is Monique in the narrative and Whitebeam in the notes. Lise was Irène Brisée on her documents, and in the War Diary, she was Odile and Artist.

CHAPTER 6: TO THE VERY LAST MAN

63 **Those pleasant pastures:** William Blake, "Jerusalem." "And was the holy Lamb of God, / On England's pleasant pastures seen!"

64 **"Helped by some blows":** Fritjof Saelen as quoted in Eric Lee, *Operation Basalt: The British Raid on Sark and Hitler's Commando Order* (Stroud, U.K.: History Press, 2016), ebook.

64 **He blew the prisoner's head:** The number of Germans shot in the raid remains a controversy, according to Lee, author of *Operation Basalt*.

65 **"the Geneva Conventions":** "Prisoners of war are in the power of the hostile Government, but not of the individuals or formation which captured them. They shall at all times be humanely treated and protected, particularly against acts of violence, from insults and from public curiosity. Measures of reprisal against them are forbidden." Part I: General Provisions—Art. 2, Convention Relative to the Treatment of Prisoners of War, Geneva, July 27, 1929.

66 **"*Nacht und Nebel*":** *Das Rheingold,* scene 3, when the dwarf Alberich puts on the gold helmet of invisibility, the Tarnhelm. Composition and libretto by Richard Wagner, 1869.

66 **"Night and fog":** Author's translation. The agent Bob Shepherd suggested in a televised interview in the limited-distribution documentary *Brian, You're Dreaming* that the N+N phrasing of the order has a much earlier source: the Middle High German epic poem *Parzival,* by Wolfram von Eschenbach. The poet describes the mourning of Parzival's mother, Herzeloyde: "*In ihrer Trauer, da ihr aller Glanz der Welt in Nacht und Nebel versunken, und die Sonne selbst verdunkelt, die Nacht aber ein wacher Tag des Grauens und der Sorgen geworden war.*" Herzeloyde paints a dim view of what would be in store for anyone subjected to N+N. "In her sorrow, in which the whole world was night and fog, the sun was shadow, the night was a living day of grief and suffering [author's translation]." Between Wagner and von Eschenbach, the competing sources can be reconciled: Wagner was in the middle of reading von Eschenbach as the source text for his opera *Parsifal* when he put the manuscript down to compose the *Ring Cycle.* That Bob Shepherd could cite the medieval origins testifies to the kind of classical education and upper-class upbringing that agents possessed.

CHAPTER 7: A THOUSAND DANGERS

69 **home at No. 84:** The full arrival of SD counterintelligence at Avenue Foch occurred in early 1943. Nazi war crime testimonies put the radio counterintelligence unit at No. 84 as of April 1943.

70 **He decorated his personal apartments:** Jacques Delarue, *Histoire de la Gestapo* (1962), as quoted in David Drake, *Paris at War, 1939–1944* (Cambridge, Mass.: Harvard University Press, 2015), 316.

70 **"Millions are looking upon":** *"Es shau'n aufs Hakenkreuz voll Hoffnung schon Millionen, / Der Tag für Freiheit und für Brot bricht an."* (Author's translation.)

71 **plump blond secretaries:** The secretaries of Avenue Foch were nicknamed the mice, *souris;* they were German women assigned to Paris and not collaborating French. The Nazi occupiers were well fed; Parisians were not.

72 **The letters *j, k, q*:** Beker and Piper table, as reproduced in Simon Singh, *The Code Book: The Science of Secrecy from Ancient Egypt to Quantum Cryptology* (New York: Anchor Books, 2000), 19.

72 **"a large city like Paris":** "We must defer the decision to continue toward the west of Paris," the führer said. "A large city like Paris can hide a thousand dangers: the enemy can throw at us between four hundred thousand and five hundred thousand men at any moment. Our tanks cannot carry on an intense combat in the streets. It's a trap. . . . On the contrary, our armies east [of the city] must be ready for an important armored force to take Paris quickly, but only if necessary." Hitler to military leaders, May 26 or 27, 1940, as quoted in Ronald C. Rosbottom, *When Paris Went Dark: The City of Light Under German Occupation, 1940–1944* (New York: Little, Brown, 2014), 30.

73 **simple word-replacement codes:** This was known as a "Simple Word Code" in SOE textbooks:

A simple word code is the arrangement by conventions of certain words or phrases to mean other words or phrases.

> . . . e.g. The name "John" might mean—"I am going into hiding immediately."
>
> . . . NO NEWS RECEIVED FOR AGES ARE YOU WELL
>
> might be agreed to mean
>
> CARRY ON WITH THE SCHEME AS ARRANGED

(SOE Group B Training Syllabus, HS 7/52, National Archives, Kew.)

73 **He was in contact:** There are stories that Bömelburg and the SOE agents Nicholas Bodington and Henri Déricourt knew each other socially before the war, but these seem to have cropped up long after the conflict. The language expert at Avenue Foch said Déricourt was approached to become an agent for the Luftwaffe and, in order to avoid flying for them, asked to be introduced to Bömelburg. Francis J. Suttill, *Shadows in the Fog: The True Story of Major Suttill and the Prosper French Resistance Network* (Stroud, U.K.: History Press, 2017), note in French edition. Procès Verbal, Nov. 29, 1945, dossier Z6 NL 17339, Archives Nationales.

73 **four million francs:** "£20,000 was the current sterling equivalent. Goetz replied that was just the price of an estate that Déricourt wanted to buy in the Midi; and the latter admitted to the French that he had been interested in a property worth three-quarters of that sum where he and some friends had proposed to start a chicken-farm." Placke interrogation by DST, April 10, 1946, as cited in Foot, *SOE in France,* ebook.

73 **"This is not a peace":** Ferdinand Foch at the signing of the Treaty of Versailles, 1919; Paul Reynaud, *Mémoires* (1963), vol. 2 (Paris: Flammarion 1960), as cited in the *Oxford Dictionary of Quotations*.

74 **"as from the 21st of March":** J. A. F. Antelme, HS 9/43, National Archives, Kew.

CHAPTER 8: THE DARK YEARS

77 **"She was antimilitarist":** Guerne interview, in Vader, *Prosper Double-Cross,* 72.

77 **"*de la part de Charlot*":** Andrée Borrel, HS 9/183, National Archives, Kew.

77 **"We count on you":** Author's translation. Oct. 9, 1943, broadcast, in *Les Français parlent aux Français,* ed. Jacques Pessis, with historical commentary by Jean-Louis Crémieux-Brilhac (Paris: Omnibus, 2010), 2:1487. This meeting between Andrée and Francis likely took place between October 3 and 5, 1943.

78 **He was always on time:** Claude de Baissac, HS 9/75 and 9/76, National Archives, Kew.

78 **"Where might one find":** *"Où peut-on avoir de l'essence à briquette?"* Borrel, HS 9/183, National Archives, Kew.

79 **"The crayfish walk":** "*Les écrevisses marchent de travers,*" as cited in Suttill, *Shadows in the Fog,* ebook. A reference to a fable by La Fontaine that every schoolchild in France would have memorized.

81 **"With PROSPER's arrival":** Jacques Bureau, interview with Robert Marshall, Feb. 24, 1986, in *All the King's Men* (London: Bloomsbury, 2012), ebook.

82 **"We were all young":** Roger Landes, interview in King, *Jacqueline,* 238. Agent Roger Landes, code name Actor, was the radio operator for Claude de Baissac's SCIENTIST circuit in Bordeaux.

82 **"Experience as an agent":** Guerne, in Vader, *Prosper Double-Cross,* 58.

82 **"perfect in all ways":** Gilbert Norman, HS 9/110/5, National Archives, Kew.

83 **an agricultural region:** "Generally speaking the people in France, particularly in the provinces, have weathered the storm wonderfully well. They help each other and with the exception of fats, they have everything they need such as eggs, poultry, meat and vegetables," reported the agent France Antelme, HS 9/43, National Archives, Kew.

83 **"They felt this was the way":** Harry Ree, "Experiences of an SOE Agent in France, Henri Raymond, Alias César" (courtesy of Steven Kippax).

83 **listening to rebels' needs:** Field reports from organizers such as Francis Suttill, Claude de Baissac, and Peter Churchill report extensively on the needs and emotions of their French colleagues.

83 **in exchange for cooperation:** Shane Harris, "Do Women Make Better Spies? CIA Director John Brennan Is Considering Whether to Put a Woman in Charge of the National Clandestine Service," *Washingtonian,* April 2, 2013.

83 **"Everybody was very friendly":** King, *Jacqueline,* 238.

83 **"She cycles about at night":** Pierre Culioli, HS 9/379/8, National Archives, Kew.
84 **"Here's to the King":** King, *Jacqueline,* 273.
84 **"We had to be very careful":** Buckmaster interview, Imperial War Museum, London.
84 **"old maidish look":** Buckmaster, "They Went by Parachute."
84 **"The secret to being secret":** Training Lectures and Statistics, HS 8/371, National Archives, Kew.
85 **"She lives *en ménage*":** PROSPER's Lieutenants, report May 18, 1943, in Culioli, HS 9/379/8, National Archives, Kew.
85 **"It was much easier":** King, *Jacqueline,* 281.
86 **"It would be the first time":** Ibid., 79. On this, Buckmaster seems to have forgotten that Virginia Hall was already in the field. Virginia was American and had been working undercover as a journalist in France since 1941. She seems to have held a special status within F Section at the time and was not generally regarded as being in the same class of agents trained for the *Corps féminins.*
86 **"We wondered how tough":** Ibid., 160.
86 **village of Montrichard:** Pierre Culioli does not give a specific date for this operation in his interviews with Stella King, only winter 1942–1943, which would make Yvonne the first female sabotage agent in combat. The Prosper reports of April and May say that Yvonne "is also becoming, *and by personal participation in sabotage,* a demolition expert like MONIQUE." April 18, 1943. In J. Agazarian, HS 9/11/1, National Archives, Kew. And "Suzanne has become a first class demolition expert." May 18, 1943. In Culioli, HS 9/379/8, National Archives, Kew.
87 **"She looks fifteen years":** Culioli, HS 9/379/8, National Archives, Kew.
88 **Indemnities claimed 50 percent:** Filippo Occhino, Kim Oosterlinck, and Eugene N. White, "How Much Can a Victor Force the Vanquished to Pay? France Under the Nazi Boot," *Journal of Economic History* 68, no. 1 (March 2008).
88 **In total, some 55 percent:** Jonathan Fenby, *France: A Modern History from the Revolution to the War with Terror* (New York: St. Martin's Press, 2016), ebook.
88 **"Let them deliver":** Ian Ousby, *Occupation: The Ordeal of France, 1940–1944* (New York: Cooper Square Press, 2000), 103.
88 **"After all," she said:** King, *Jacqueline,* 282.
89 **She had been home:** "Major Attack on London," *Times* (London), April 17, 1941; "Germans Gloat over London Raid," *Times* (London), April 18, 1941.
89 **In the Blitz, London:** Moore, "Blitz Spirit–75 Years On!"
89 **"We shall go out":** Baron Gustav Braun von Stumm, a spokesman for the German Foreign Office, is reported to have said this on April 24, 1942.

CHAPTER 9: ALONE IN THE WORLD

90 **Richard the Lionheart:** Lise, *Real Charlotte Grays* interview. "There was plenty to see, older antiques and things like that and I was interested in archaeology and architecture."

91 **"as if I was going to":** Ibid.

91 **"I was just an ordinary":** Ibid.

91 **"You'd say good morning":** Lise, Legasee interview.

91 **"The German troops":** Claude de Baissac, HS 9/75, National Archives, Kew.

91 **"afraid of being killed":** Ibid.

91 **enough to eat:** *Tout pour la bouche* (Everything for the mouth). Ibid.

92 **"The chief concern":** Ibid.

92 **The Vatican itself remained neutral:** In his Christmas Eve 1942 radio broadcast, Pope Pius XII announced European society should go "back to its immovable center of gravity in divine law." Without mentioning the Jews by name, he claimed, "Humanity owes this vow to those hundreds of thousands who, without any fault of their own, sometimes only by reason of their nationality or race, are marked down for death or gradual extinction." Over the course of the war, it was the Vatican's most direct statement on Hitler's Final Solution.

92 **One Jesuit priest:** Father Jean Fleury was named a "Righteous Gentile" by Yad Vashem, Israel's Holocaust museum.

92 **"spontaneous and autonomous":** Henry du Moulin de Labarthète testimony, Oct. 26, 1946, cited in Michael Curtis, *Verdict on Vichy* (New York: Arcade, 2002), 111, quoted in Robert Satloff, *Among the Righteous* (New York: PublicAffairs, 2006), 31.

94 **Only eight:** This list includes Marie-Thérèse Le Chêne, Andrée Borrel, Blanche Charlet, Yvonne Rudellat, Lise de Baissac, Odette Sansom, Mary Herbert, and Virginia Hall. Jacqueline Nearne, who trained with Lise, Odette, and Mary, would not deploy until January 1943.

94 **She had completed the training course:** There were two parts to the Party No. 27.OB course for women: The earliest included Yvonne Rudellat and Andrée Borrel and was held in June of 1942; the second was held in August 1942 and included Odette Sansom, Lise de Baissac, Mary Herbert, Jacqueline Nearne, and Hélène Aron.

94 **dismal final reports:** The remarks from instructors at Beaulieu could be cutting, such as "mentally slow and not very intelligent," the assessment received by one of Hélène and Lise's classmates, Jacqueline Nearne, to which there is a penciled response, "O.K. I think her one of the best we have had."

94 **"wanted to kill":** Hélène B. Aron, HS 9/55/6, National Archives, Kew.

95 **Fleet Street splashed stories:** "Espionage in U.S.," *Times* (London), Oct. 19, 1940; "German Spy Shot at the Tower," *Times* (London), Aug. 16, 1941; "My Husband Never Was a Spy," *Times* (London), July 31, 1940.

95 **"In my opinion":** To Buckmaster's credit, it looks as if F's response to this

in pencil was double-underlined, double-exclamation-pointed "nonsense!!" Aug. 1942, in Charles Hayes, HS 9/681/3, National Archives, Kew.

95 **"girls who were very obviously":** Yvonne Baseden, Pattinson interview.

95 **Baker Street did employ:** Later in the war, other Jewish women were recruited. Of the women SOE seconded to France, Denise Bloch and Muriel Byck were Jewish. They both died in service.

95 **an all-Jewish network:** The ROBIN/JUGGLER circuit.

95 **Some Jewish recruits:** The firm kept recruiting Jewish agents throughout the war, but October 1942 was a watershed moment for Vichy roundups of Jews. Once Hitler took over all of France in November 1942, Jewish deportations became less enthusiastic.

95 **"Without going so far":** Aron, HS 9/55/6, National Archives, Kew.

96 **"The money evidently":** It was always assumed any *agent* taken into custody by Nazis was "turned" if he was released or escaped. But in this instance, Hélène was a private citizen. SOE made no such noises about possible double-dealing by other agent candidates who had previously been imprisoned, such as Claude de Baissac and Frank Pickersgill, both of whom escaped prisons, immigrated to Britain, and joined SOE.

97 **"She tells me she is":** In other words, she was greedy, a label long attributed to Jews.

97 **"She is unlikely to be":** Aron, HS 9/55/6, National Archives, Kew.

97 **"repatriated to France":** Ibid. It was, at the time, known to be a death sentence. See "Jews' Plight in France," *Times* (London), Aug. 22, 1942; "More Deportations of French Jews," *Times* (London), Sept. 9, 1942; "Vichy's Jewish Victims," *Times* (London), Sept. 7, 1942; "Round-Up of Jews in France," *Times* (London), Sept. 1, 1942.

97 **"the Forgetting School":** Peter Churchill, *Of Their Own Choice* (London: Hodder & Stoughton, 1953), 32.

98 **a government does not spy:** For this reason, secret agencies and liberal civilizations tend to be at cross-purposes, at least in peacetime.

98 **It was suggested:** Though the name of de Gaulle's movement was officially changed, in documents it is here referred to as "Free French."

98 **Let the Gaullists struggle:** *Mein Kampf* means "my struggle."

99 **The "Amazons":** This training class was referred to as Amazons throughout Hélène's personnel file.

99 **Other women's auxiliaries:** The combatant versus noncombatant debate would plague the women of SOE throughout the war and long after, affecting many aspects of their wartime performance and postwar fate. At the same time the *Corps féminins* were recruited, the Soviets began sending female soldiers to the eastern front, where they were categorized immediately as combatants. Campbell, "Women in Combat."

100 **"*amour propre*":** Aron, HS 9/55/6, National Archives, Kew.

100 **"This war is not":** Pessis, *Les Français parlent aux Français,* 2:1459.

100 **"It will not be the Aryan":** Hitler, Berlin Sportpalast speech, Sept. 30, 1942, as cited in Robert S. Wistrich, *A Lethal Obsession: Anti-Semitism from Antiquity to the Global Jihad* (New York: Random House, 2010).

100 **"The German Record":** *Times* (London), July 10, 1942.
100 **At the highest levels:** Robert Louis Benson, "SIGINT and the Holocaust," *Cryptologic Quarterly,* www.nsa.gov, released by FOIA in 2010. Also see Robert J. Hanyok, "Eavesdropping on Hell: Historical Guide to Western Communications Intelligence and the Holocaust, 1939–1945," Center for Cryptologic History, National Security Agency, 2005.
100 **women at Bletchley:** The workforce at Bletchley was overwhelmingly women, about 75 percent.
101 **"From all the occupied countries":** Persecution of the Jews: Allied Declaration, House of Lords debate, Dec. 17, 1942, read by the lord chancellor, Viscount John Simon.
101 **Hélène had a new job:** We do not know in what capacity de Gaulle hired her, only that she was not infiltrated to France as an agent.
102 **"some of the members":** Claude de Baissac, HS 9/75, National Archives, Kew.
102 **"object was to have":** Lise de Baissac, HS 9/77/1, National Archives, Kew.
102 **"I had to take some interest":** Lise, Pattinson interview.
102 **"You have false papers":** Liane Jones, *A Quiet Courage: Heart-Stopping Accounts of Those Brave Women Agents Who Risked Their Lives in Nazi-Occupied France* (London: Corgi Books, 1990), 75.
102 **"I arrived [in Poitiers]":** Lise, Pattinson interview.
102 **Claude was drawing up:** Lise de Baissac, HS 9/77/1, National Archives, Kew.
102 **"Contrary to his expectation":** Circuit and Mission Reports—B, Baissac, HS 6/567, National Archives, Kew.
103 **"Two friends meeting":** Lise, *Real Charlotte Grays* interview.
103 **"extremely French and volatile":** Claude de Baissac, HS 9/76, National Archives, Kew.
103 **"He was a vital":** Claudine Pappe interview with author, Sept. 15, 2017.
103 **"He is conscientious":** Claude de Baissac, HS 9/76, National Archives, Kew.
103 **"I think in the family":** Lise, Pattinson interview.
103 **"I thought it wasn't enough":** Lise, *Real Charlotte Grays* interview.
104 **"They agreed or they didn't":** Lise, Legasee interview.
104 **"They *knew* what they":** Lise, *Real Charlotte Grays* interview.
104 **"Everything will turn 'round":** Lise, Pattinson interview. Full quotation: "I think that everything will turn 'round all right. I'm not a pessimist," which was cut to make the tense less awkward.

CHAPTER 10: *ROBERT EST ARRIVÉ*

105 **postboxes:** *Boîtes aux lettres.*
106 **Odette Sansom arrived in France:** Of our principal female agents, Odette is the only one for whom we don't see a full training report in the book's

text. For fairness' sake, and because it is interesting, here is what Odette's Beaulieu trainers thought of her:

Has enthusiasm and seems to have absorbed the teaching given on the course. She is, however, impulsive and hasty in her judgments and has not quite the clarity of mind which is desirable for subversive activity.

She seems to have little experience of the outside world. She is excitable and temperamental, although she has a certain determination.

A likable character and gets on well with most people.

Her main asset is her patriotism and keenness to do something for France; her main weakness is a complete unwillingness to admit that she could ever be wrong.

(Odette Hallowes, HS 9/648/4, National Archives, Kew.)

106 **no bathroom:** Men and women relieved themselves in the ocean.

106 **"dozen German foreskins":** King, *Jacqueline,* 198.

107 **Odette was dressed for function:** Foot, *SOE in France,* ebook.

107 **Gibraltar by destroyer:** M.-T. Le Chêne, HS 9/304/1, National Archives, Kew.

108 **"All around the mighty":** André Girard, *Bataille secrète en France* (Paris: Brentano's, 1944), 292. Author's translation.

108 **"is engaged in the organisation":** Nicholas Bodington report, Sept. 1942, France-Missions-Carte, HS 6/382, National Archives, Kew.

109 **"the pinnacle of his power":** Peter Churchill, *Duel of Wits* (New York: G. P. Putnam's Sons, 1955), 206.

109 **"She will never die!":** *Elle ne mourra pas!* Girard, *Bataille secrète en France,* 292.

109 **"I now feel the old":** Peter Churchill, HS 9/314, National Archives, Kew.

110 **"one thousand pounds":** Ibid.

110 **"like a Bank Holiday crowd":** P. Churchill, *Duel of Wits,* 196.

110 **This was the tragedy:** The occupation was an age of Cain.

110 **"I close my peepers":** P. Churchill, *Duel of Wits,* 197.

111 **"a question mark with a mustache":** Marks, *Between Silk and Cyanide,* 17.

111 **"publicity, metallurgy":** P. Churchill, *Duel of Wits,* jacket copy.

111 **"a quality of strangeness":** Agent George Hiller as quoted in Max Hastings, *Das Reich: The March of the 2nd SS Panzer Division Through France, June 1944* (Minneapolis: Zenith Press, 2013), ebook.

112 **"We sell tourism":** Janet Flanner, "Guinea Pigs and the Mona Lisa," A Reporter at Large, *New Yorker,* Oct. 31, 1942.

112 **"hot from the rolls":** Peter Churchill, HS 9/314, National Archives, Kew.

112 **"hidden depths":** P. Churchill, *Duel of Wits,* 225.

112 **"I observed a telltale expanse":** Ibid.
113 **"This reception is all":** Ibid., 226.
114 **"Security just doesn't exist":** Ibid., 188.
114 **"flashy characters":** Peter Churchill, HS 9/314, National Archives, Kew.
114 **"happy-go-lucky meetings":** P. Churchill, *Duel of Wits,* 238. This quote is almost certainly taken from Peter Churchill's personnel files, in a note dated November 30, 1942, where he wrote, "You remember the happy-go-lucky meetings on park benches with anything up to half a dozen characters sitting around and scribbling with pencil and paper." This sentence indicates that Peter had access to his personnel files as he was writing his memoirs, and lends additional credibility to his published account.
114 **"I challenge you all":** Peter Churchill, HS 9/314, National Archives, Kew.
114 **"He was rather rude":** Hallowes, HS 9/648/4, National Archives, Kew.
114 **"I don't need any rest":** P. Churchill, *Duel of Wits,* ebook.
115 **"Because you seemed":** Tickell, *Odette,* 175. (Ellipsis in original text.)
115 **Odette was "dynamite":** P. Churchill, *Duel of Wits,* 229.
115 **"complete and absolute victory":** *Times* (London), Nov. 7, 1942.
115 **The Allied forces recognized it:** Lise de Baissac, who reported hearing the alert, did not know what it was an alert for. It sounded many times, whereas BBC *messages personnels* alerts sounded on two broadcasts but not in repetition.
116 **They crossed the Atlantic:** "Operation Torch: Invasion of North Africa, 8–16 November 1942," Naval History and Heritage Command, www.history.navy.mil, citing Robert J. Cressman, *The Official Chronology of the U.S. Navy in World War II* (Annapolis, Md./Washington, D.C.: U.S. Naval Institute Press/Naval Historical Center, 1999); Samuel Eliot Morison, *History of United States Naval Operations in World War II,* vol. 2, *Operations in North African Waters, October 1942–June 1943* (Boston: Little, Brown, 1947).
116 **"The Valkyries will go back":** Benoîte Groult and Flora Groult, *Journal à quatre mains* (Paris: Livre de Poche, 1962), translated in Drake, *Paris at War,* 292.
116 **"Now this is not the end":** Winston Churchill, Lord Mayor's Luncheon, Mansion House, Nov. 10, 1942.
116 **Remembrance Day:** "40,000,000 Poppies for Remembrance Day," *Times* (London), Nov. 5, 1942.
117 **"took the action":** "German Troops Occupy Vichy France," *Times* (London), Nov. 12, 1942.
117 **"disturb as little":** In the same speech, Hitler threatened, "Where blind fanaticism, or agents in the pay of England, oppose our troops, there decisions will be made by force."
117 **"*Radio Paris ment*":** Pessis, *Les Français parlent aux Français,* 1:viii.
117 **he raised France's occupation payments:** "Plunderers of Europe," *Times* (London), April 28, 1943; "Hitler Turns the Screw," *Times* (London), Feb. 9, 1943.

118 **"It seems most important":** W. Churchill to M. Selborne (minister of economic warfare), Nov. 13, 1942, CAB 120/827, cited in Mark Seaman, *Special Operations Executive: A New Instrument of War* (London: Routledge, 2013), ebook.

118 **Mussolini's troops pressed in:** Mary Herbert was still in Cannes on the day of the invasion, November 11, 1942. "She was, however, in CANNES when the Italians arrived there, and the population seemed to her to be worried about the change of living conditions, which might be brought about by the occupation." Circuit and Mission Reports—B, HS 6/567, National Archives, Kew.

118 **"A lovely house":** Peter Churchill, HS 9/314, National Archives, Kew.

118 **"She smiled":** P. Churchill, *Duel of Wits,* 227.

119 **"husband and wife":** Hallowes, HS 9/648/4, National Archives, Kew.

CHAPTER 11: THE PARIS OF THE SAHARA

120 **Anglo-American military chiefs:** Stalin refused to attend the Casablanca conference as he was launching the winter campaign against Hitler. "Front business absolutely prevents it, demanding my constant presence near our troops," he wrote to Churchill, rejecting the invitation. W. Churchill, *Hinge of Fate,* 667.

120 **"fortune-tellers, snake-charmers":** Ibid., 694.

121 **"You cannot come":** Ibid.

122 **Hitler and Tojo:** General Hideki Tojo was the Japanese prime minister who ordered the attack on Pearl Harbor. He was tried for war crimes and, in 1948, was hanged.

122 **The North African colonies:** They would not be restored to the people of North Africa for many years.

122 **"French Africa is the only":** "Darlan in Algiers," *Times* (London), Nov. 28, 1942.

123 **"much the greatest thing":** Churchill to FDR, telegram, Oct. 23, 1943. "My dear friend, this is much the greatest thing we have ever attempted." Roosevelt Papers, U.S. Department of State, Office of the Historian.

124 **"pull yourself back together":** Jochen Hellbeck, ed., *Stalingrad: The City That Defeated the Third Reich* (New York: PublicAffairs, 2015), ebook.

124 **"Is it really to be":** W. Churchill, *Hinge of Fate,* 649–50.

124 **July 12, 1943:** Discussion of dates, summer 1943. W. Churchill, *Hinge of Fate,* 648–52; Churchill minute to Chiefs of Staff, Nov. 29, 1942, Churchill Archives, CHAR 20/67/9, as cited in Hastings, *Winston's War,* 283.

124 **The balance of power:** Hastings, *Winston's War,* 289.

124 **"We came, we listened":** General Albert Wedemeyer, U.S. Army, quoted in John Keegan, *The Second World War* (New York: Basic Books, 2017), ebook.

125 **"unconditional surrender":** W. Churchill, *Hinge of Fate,* discussion begins on 685.

CHAPTER 12: OUR POSSIBILITIES

126 **the agent Prosper:** When the code name Prosper refers to Francis Suttill, it is in initial caps as a proper name. When it refers to his network, PHYSICIAN/PROSPER, it is in all caps.

127 **"February 1, 1943":** Annex of Telegrams, HS 6/338, National Archives, Kew. The telegrams in this chapter come from the same document, but not all of them would have been from the PROSPER network.

127 **Grendon Hall, Station 53:** It would become Station 53a within the year as a second receiver was built to handle traffic for SOE.

127 **"talcum powder and dry rot":** Marks, *Between Silk and Cyanide,* 138.

127 **The FANYs of Station 53:** The term used for the female coders and wireless operators was "cypherenes."

128 **"Each W/T transmission":** Agents' Ciphers, HS 7/45, National Archives, Kew.

128 **"one of those rare agents":** Marks, *Between Silk and Cyanide,* 326.

128 **"at all times conduct":** Brigadier Gammell as quoted ibid., 37.

128 **call themselves "girls":** Use of the word "girls" was also common parlance for female SOE coders, not just agents:

PADDY SPROULE (CYPHERENE, MASSINGHAM. SPEAKING ABOUT CHRISTINE GRANVILLE)

She was a fascinating. . . . I literally just taught her how to do her particular code and she was very bright, I mean she didn't need a lot of tuition as it were. I think it was just a sort of half a day almost, and she was just one of the agents that went through Massingham. Presumably she took off from Blida, and . . . into France and . . . but I think she was the only female agent that I remember, that I had anything to do with, but no—she was a great girl. She was lovely.

. . . [I]n Massingham there were quite a few what we called "post office girls" . . . because they knew about wireless and cable and this sort of thing, they'd been recruited specially and they were from all sorts of walks of life.

BETTY NORTON (CYPHERENE, MASSINGHAM)

Colonel Anstey gave me this message and um I encoded it and of course I mean I handed it in at the signals office and um then we had a signal back from Avignon and one of the girls who was doing coding said "hey this is for you."

(Quotations courtesy of Martyn Cox, founder of the Secret WW2 Learning Network.)

The body of literature on the women's auxiliaries at war also includes multiple examples of women celebrating the word "girl." See Joan Miller's memoir *One Girl's War: Personal Exploits in MI5's Most Secret Station* (Dingle, Ire.: Brandon, 1986). Also see Dorothy Brewer Kerr, *The Girls Behind the Guns: With the ATS in World War II* (London: Robert Hale, 1990).

128 **They were generally in their twenties:** The presence of women in the workplace was a challenge to many of the young men in the signals directorate. Sergeant Leo Marks said he could not, for instance, understand why his best coders were unreliable at intervals, why deciphering accuracy fell apart with clockwork regularity. He reported that he was taken aside to learn the mechanics of the female body, whereupon he discovered his coders got erratic in time with their menstrual cycles. Once a month when accuracy dipped, he said, he offered FANYs less taxing duties.

129 **"*Is de Gaulle's prick*":** Marks, *Between Silk and Cyanide,* 38.

130 **Only two airdrop operations:** Suttill, *Shadows in the Fog,* ebook.

130 **"February 21, 1943":** Annex of Telegrams, HS 6/338, National Archives, Kew.

130 **"hitherto unknown Germanophobia":** Allan Mitchell, *Nazi Paris: The History of an Occupation, 1940–1944* (New York: Berghahn Books, 2008), 94–95, as quoted in Drake, *Paris at War,* 294.

131 **"Germans are killed daily":** J. A. F. Antelme, HS 9/43, National Archives, Kew.

131 **"Anyone committing acts":** Posters of ordinances can be found at the Musée de la Résistance Nationale, Champigny, online.

132 **"The blood of the martyrs":** As quoted in Foot, *SOE in France,* ebook.

132 **inflation had risen 50 percent:** Drake, *Paris at War,* 288.

132 **Paris had the lowest rations:** Ibid., 332.

133 **2 ounces of margarine:** Virginia d'Albert-Lake, *An American Heroine in the French Resistance: The Diary and Memoir of Virginia d'Albert-Lake,* ed. Judy Barrett Litoff (New York: Fordham University Press, 2006), ebook.

133 **slip through the hole:** Larry Collins and Dominique Lapierre, *Is Paris Burning?* (New York: Warner Books, 1991).

133 **one-third of the children:** Hanna Diamond, *Women and the Second World War in France, 1939–1948: Choices and Constraints* (London: Routledge, 1999), 156.

133 **only one in five:** Flanner, "Guinea Pigs and the Mona Lisa."

133 **the "redcoats" have landed:** *Les Anglais sont débarqués.*

133 **whisking away 650,000 men:** This is the generally accepted number, repeated everywhere. See Stenton, *Radio London and Resistance in Occupied Europe.*

133 **The STO brought the war:** Between January and March 1943, 250,000

Frenchmen were packed off to Germany, 70,000 from Paris alone; another 220,000 were demanded by June. (Drake, *Paris at War,* 303.) "*Pas un homme pour l'Allemagne!*" cried the announcers nightly on the BBC—not one man for Germany! (Jan. 23, 1943, Jean-Louis Crémieux-Brilhac, *Ici Londres, 1940–1944: La voix de la liberté,* 5 vols. [Paris: Documentation Français, 1975], 3:81.)

134 **"March 2, 1943":** Annex of Telegrams, HS 6/338, National Archives, Kew.

134 **"inseparable friends":** Guerne interview, in Vader, *Prosper Double-Cross,* 99.

134 **"As a general rule":** J. Agazarian, HS 9/11/1, National Archives, Kew.

134 **"Suttill was like a father":** Guerne quoted in Vader, *Prosper Double-Cross,* 100.

134 **Django Reinhardt:** Reinhardt (1910–1953) was a French guitarist of Gypsy (Romany) origins, considered one of the greatest musicians of the twentieth century as well as Europe's leading jazz composer.

134 **"were veritable gods":** Guerne quoted in Vader, *Prosper Double-Cross,* 50.

134 **"had a perfect understanding":** Andrée Borrel, HS 9/183, National Archives, Kew.

135 **"You couldn't sort of openly":** Sonya d'Artois, Pattinson interview.

135 **played the part of a gamine *zazou:*** The word *zazou* comes from the Cab Calloway song "Zah, Zuh Zaz," recorded in 1934.

135 **Guinea pigs too:** Food was so scarce that even rabbits couldn't multiply. Guinea pigs also became a source of homegrown animal protein. "Guinea pig meat, thank God, is excessively fat," wrote one American gourmet. "Most of the cats, even the favorites, have been eaten. If you still have a pet dog, a butcher in Marseilles will sell you dog food made from other pets." Flanner, "Guinea Pigs and the Mona Lisa."

136 **"For the enemy":** Mme. Guepin, quoted in Nicholas, *Death Be Not Proud,* 171.

136 **some eighty thousand French mothers:** Diamond, *Women and the Second World War in France,* 83.

136 **"She is the best":** Borrel, HS 9/183, National Archives, Kew.

137 **The so-called Carlingue:** J. O. Fuller, *The German Penetration of SOE* (London: Kimber, 1975), 61.

138 **"Nothing would deflect her":** Mme. Guepin as quoted in Nicholas, *Death Be Not Proud,* 171.

138 **"March 9, 1943":** Borrel, HS 9/183, National Archives, Kew.

139 **"March 12, 1943":** Annex of Telegrams, HS 6/338, National Archives, Kew.

139 **"March 19, 1943":** Ibid.

139 **"March 21, 1943":** Ibid.

140 **By that winter, some eighty thousand:** Foot, *SOE in France,* ebook.

141 **"March 22, 1943":** Annex of Telegrams, HS 6/338, National Archives, Kew.

141 **"March 23, 1943":** Ibid.

141 **"March 24, 1943":** Ibid.

141 **"March 28, 1943 RUSH ALL":** Ibid.
142 **"March 28, 1943 OWING NO":** Ibid.

CHAPTER 13: THE DEMOLITION MUST NEVER FAIL

143 **Andrée Borrel bicycled:** There were at least two attacks on the Chaingy transformer stations as well as an attack on the Chevilly station. The SOE files give dates in both March and early April. We have ample evidence that Andrée attended her network's sabotage operations. (Progress Report to SOE Executive Committee, April 26, 1943; Agazarian report, June 23, 1943. Prosper mentions in dispatches that Andrée took part in recent sabotage: She "shares all the dangers." National Archives, Kew.) The scene for this chapter comes from *Pin-Stripe Saboteur: The Story of "Robin," British Agent and French Resistance Leader* (London: Odhams, 1959) by Charles Wighton, which appears to be the pen name for Jacques Weil, a member of the ROBIN/JUGGLER circuit in Paris, the Jewish network affiliated with Andrée's PHYSICIAN network. M. R. D. Foot, the official historian of SOE, says *Pin-Stripe Saboteur* includes "imaginative reconstructions," casting doubt on the accuracy of Jacques Weil's memories. Weil was a Jewish Swiss businessman who survived the war, helped fund the Resistance, and was decorated for his service, but his book, published fifteen years after the war, is a mishmash of truth and elaboration. Weil elides his role in the circuit with that of the organizer Jean Worms, a Beaulieu-trained SOE agent and French Jew who was executed at Flossenbürg. Weil puts the location of this attack near Orléans. There were also attacks during the same time period at Chaingy, south of Nantes, in March and/or April 1943. We know these assaults occurred and that Andrée participated. I cannot confirm that Jean Worms was her partner on this operation or if it was the March or April attack, or if it was at Chevilly or Chaingy—or what they saw—because neither survived the war. When *Pin-Stripe Saboteur* was published, information on SOE remained classified, and a novelized narrative under a pseudonym treads the edges of what was legally permissible given Britain's tight libel and secrecy laws. As a source, I take information from *Pin-Stripe Saboteur* sparingly and note where I can't square it with contemporaneous accounts. But I cannot discount Weil's memories entirely. *Pin-Stripe Saboteur* remains an agent's personal story, however colorful.
143 **"left the bodies":** J. A. F. Antelme, HS 9/43, National Archives, Kew.
144 **The two thousand miles:** Foot, *SOE in France,* ebook.
144 **"took up the hunt":** Antelme, HS 9/43, National Archives, Kew.
144 **"She hoisted it":** Léone Arend, née Borrel, quoted in Nicholas, *Death Be Not Proud,* 176.
144 **"a perfect lieutenant":** Andrée Borrel, HS 9/183, National Archives, Kew; extract from Prosper letter.
144 **pretended to be "sweethearts":** Wighton, *Pin-Stripe Saboteur,* 158.

144 **"In our business":** Training Lectures and Statistics, HS 8/371, National Archives, Kew.

145 **"100 percent Jew":** Circuit and Mission Reports: Carte, HS 6/382, National Archives, Kew.

145 **"He seems to have one":** Jean Worms, HS 9/1621/4, National Archives, Kew.

145 **"Do not handle":** Pierre Lorain, *Secret Warfare: The Arms and Techniques of the Resistance,* adapted by David Kahn (London: Orbis, 1983), 154.

145 **"20-odd" charges:** Antelme, HS 9/43, National Archives, Kew. Antelme Report on Butcher and Prosper, March 25, 1943, says "20 odd charges" was a typical load.

145 **"THE DEMOLITION MUST":** Syllabus of Lectures, HS 7/56, National Archives, Kew, H.2. Nov. 1943.

146 **All around the region:** Antelme, HS 9/43, National Archives, Kew.

146 **Partisans were also laying:** Power lines were immobilized from Eguzon, Chevilly, and L'Épine.

146 **"loving pair":** Wighton, *Pin-Stripe Saboteur,* 158.

146 **Carbon dioxide:** When detonated, plastic explosives decompose to release nitrogen and carbon oxides as well as other gases. The detonation proceeds at an explosive velocity of 8,092 meters per second (26,550 feet per second).

147 **"sparking and spitting blue flame":** Wighton, *Pin-Stripe Saboteur,* 158.

147 **"Incomplete detonation":** Syllabus of Lectures, HS 7/56, National Archives, Kew, H.2. Nov. 1943.

147 **"there were priests":** Ree, "Experiences of an SOE Agent in France, Henri Raymond, alias César."

147 **It was reported:** These German deaths are not confirmed in French records or newspapers in Chaingy or Chevilly. Because I can't locate the date with precision, or the place, there is no way of checking casualty records. For the same reason, I have not found detailed corroboration in newspapers, but also the French press was tightly controlled. Globally, however, there is ample confirmation: The British and international press described partisan attacks in the PROSPER network's regions in the March/April 1943 time period, broadcast as part of a public relations push demonstrating to the world there was successful local opposition to Hitler within France and that it was coalescing around de Gaulle. It is also important to note that most acts of sabotage were not communicated from the field to London for the very good reason that body counts, if found, would be inculpatory documents. Agents reported details of their sabotage mostly when safe back in Britain, as Buckmaster notes in a November 1943 report: "It was not until the return to this country of [our agents] that we learned anything of what they had done" (F Section History and Agents, HS 7/121, National Archives, Kew). Other officers noted organizers were "not good at reporting on . . . activities. This is one of the facts of life with which we have to cope and is almost entirely due to a most laudable desire to limit W/T [wireless] traffic as far as possible to operational needs" (Robert Bourne-Patterson on Claude de Baissac, HS 9/76, National

Archives, Kew). Further, it was during this time period that the "volume of attacks grew so great that individual recordings became impossible," noting "continual sabotage ever since April, but details too voluminous to send by W/T" (History of SOE, 1938–1945, HS 7/1, National Archives, Kew).

147 **"to smithereens":** Wighton, *Pin-Stripe Saboteur,* 159.

147 **The story of Andrée's demolition:** Because Wighton confabulates the experiences of two agents, Weil and Worms, there is no certainty over who attended demolitions with Andrée. SOE records cannot confirm, and Worms did not survive the war. Worms, however, was trained in demolitions in Britain; Weil was not.

148 **"The record of achievement":** Claude de Baissac, HS 9/75, National Archives, Kew.

148 **And by that spring:** F Section History and Agents, HS 7/121, National Archives, Kew.

148 **Between December 1942:** Robert Bourne-Patterson, British Circuits in France, HS 7/122, National Archives, Kew.

148 **"A train taking foodstuffs":** Antelme, HS 9/43, National Archives, Kew.

149 **"blasted off the rails":** "French Guerrillas Wreck Train," *Times* (London), March 12, 1943.

149 **"It was decided":** F Section History and Agents, HS 7/121, National Archives, Kew.

149 **In Blois:** Antelme, HS 9/43, National Archives, Kew.

149 **"The rate of 'density'":** F Section History and Agents, HS 7/121, National Archives, Kew.

CHAPTER 14: AN OBSTINATE WOMAN

150 **An Obstinate Woman:** "I still think you should have gone. You're an obstinate woman. My God, you're an obstinate woman." Peter Churchill to Odette, in Tickell, *Odette,* 236.

150 **his days in Fresnes Prison:** Depictions of Fresnes Prison from Fresnes and Avenue Foch, WO 311/103, National Archives, Kew. Also HS 9 files, National Archives, Kew, including Odette Hallowes and Andrée Borrel, as well as from agents' published memoirs, including Christopher Burney, *Solitary Confinement* (London: Macmillan, 1951); Peter Churchill, *The Spirit in the Cage* (New York: G. P. Putnam's Sons, 1955); and Hugo Bleicher, *Colonel Henri's Story* (London: Kimber, 1954).

151 **He was a dandy:** Descriptions of Bleicher come from Odette Sansom's and Peter Churchill's personnel files; Bleicher's KV file, KV 2/2127; and Bardet, KV 2/1175, National Archives, Kew. For books, see Tickell's biography, *Odette;* Bleicher's autobiography, *Colonel Henri's Story;* and Peter Churchill's books, notably *Spirit in the Cage.* Also see Fuller, *German Penetration of SOE* and private papers.

151 **"shut up like a trap":** Bleicher, *Colonel Henri's Story,* 77.

151 **"not only with handcuffs":** Bleicher, KV 2/2127, National Archives, Kew.

152 **"I cannot believe":** Bleicher, *Colonel Henri's Story,* 78.
152 **"Can't we arrange":** KV 2/165, Hugo Ernst Bleicher, alias Verbeck, Castel, Heinrich, National Archives, Kew.
153 **"I would be in a position":** Bleicher, *Colonel Henri's Story,* 81.
153 **"But I must proceed":** Ibid., 91.
153 **"Do you really believe":** Ibid.
154 **"But I can give my word":** Ibid.
154 **"My success surprised me":** Ibid., 92.
155 **The Riviera networks splintered:** The CARTE network did not end with the exfiltration of André Girard, but was reconstituted under new leadership.
156 **"a very strange looking man":** Odette Hallowes, HS 9/648/4, National Archives, Kew.
156 **"prominent veins":** Bleicher, KV 2/2127, National Archives, Kew.
156 **"dark and sparkling":** Bleicher, *Colonel Henri's Story,* 89.
156 **"ten or fifteen young people":** F. C. A. Cammaerts, HS9/258/5 National Archives, Kew.
156 **"Men who come to fight":** Ousby, *Occupation,* ebook.
157 **The man ordered:** Bleicher, *Colonel Henri's Story,* 88.
157 **One British agent:** Captain Sydney Jones.
157 **"talking in a very silly way":** Hallowes, HS 9/648/4, National Archives, Kew.
157 **"very hard and smiled":** Ibid.
157 **"quite all right":** Ibid.
157 **"I would bless the day":** Ibid. Author's translation.
158 **The plan was stupid:** Ibid.
158 **When Rabinovitch heard:** Bleicher, KV 2/2127, National Archives, Kew; Tickell, *Odette.*
159 **"HENRI HIGHLY DANGEROUS":** P. Churchill, *Duel of Wits,* 345. This telegram from Churchill's postwar memoir does not square with information in Odette's 1945 interrogation, yet we know that Peter had access to SOE files as he wrote his book, seemingly before the files were culled, as some of his more colorful letters and telegrams are reproduced word for word in his books. Odette says in her 1945 interrogation she was told to "act according to [her] discretion with regard to the German Colonel." However, a report from the interrogation also says that from Baker Street's side HQ insisted she "lay off the German Colonel" (Hallowes, HS 9/648/4, National Archives, Kew). Reports from war crimes documents suggest she was acting against orders: "SOE very understandably instructed the agents concerned with the message to have nothing whatever to do with the obviously dangerous project" (Bardet, KV 2/1131, National Archives, Kew).
159 **London said it was a trap:** Hallowes, HS 9/648/4, National Archives, Kew.
159 **buried cryptograms:** *"Voici maintenant quelques messages personnels."*
159 **"The gold bug":** *"La scarabée d'or fait sa toilette de printemps."* P. Churchill, *Duel of Wits,* ebook.

159 **Peter was on his way:** Rabinovitch told Odette the date of Churchill's arrival. We know that Baker Street told Odette via Rabinovitch's radio to cut off contact with the colonel. Independently, Baker Street also told Rabinovitch to receive Peter Churchill. (The two events were not necessarily logically connected, only temporally.) By all reports, Odette made the independent decision to be on the mountain to receive Peter. One year later, Buckmaster seems to have decided it was Churchill's own fault he got caught. F letter, March 28, 1944, Peter Churchill, HS 9/315, National Archives, Kew.

160 **"If you take a step":** P. Churchill, *Duel of Wits,* 356.

160 **There was a knock:** According to Rabinovitch's interrogation on the arrest of Odette and Peter, the proprietor was "threatened with death" if they ever told the French police what happened. Bleicher, KV 2/2127, National Archives, Kew.

160 **"There is a strange man":** Peter Churchill, HS 9/315, National Archives, Kew.

160 **"My reflex action":** Ibid.

160 **"I think a lot of you":** Hallowes, HS 9/648/4, National Archives, Kew.

160 **"You have done a very good job":** Ibid.

161 **"There is the Gestapo":** Ibid.

161 **"Your other names":** Peter Churchill, HS 9/315, National Archives, Kew. Bleicher also claims he knew Peter's true identity at the time of his arrest. Bleicher, KV 2/2127, National Archives, Kew.

161 **seventy thousand francs:** P. Churchill, *Spirit in the Cage,* 12.

161 **five incriminating messages:** Hallowes, HS 9/684/4, National Archives, Kew.

161 **Do you want to go:** Ibid.

162 **"went about it as though":** P. Churchill, *Spirit in the Cage,* 13.

162 **"war names":** Peter Churchill, HS 9/315, National Archives, Kew.

162 **It could have been worse:** In *Duel of Wits,* Peter also says he was carrying new codes for radio operators. Around this time, SOE's poem codes were phased out in favor of single-use codes that could not be memorized before they were destroyed.

162 **"Take good care":** P. Churchill, *Spirit in the Cage,* 13.

CHAPTER 15: AN ENDLESS CALVARY

163 **"as a man would":** Odette Hallowes, HS 9/648/4, National Archives, Kew.

163 **"as much as we liked":** Interrogation, in Peter Churchill, HS 9/315, National Archives, Kew.

164 **"As long as there is life":** Jones, *Quiet Courage,* 295.

164 **"It was I who told them":** P. Churchill, *Spirit in the Cage,* 31.

164 **The gambit seemed:** There was apparently no obvious or immediate way for the Italian government or Nazi command to check Winston Churchill's extended ancestry in the middle of the war. Once Odette's lie was accepted,

it seems to have been repeated throughout Axis command, at each point of the chain of possession. Odette's citation for the GC (George Cross) notes, "She adhered to this story and even succeeded in convincing her captors in spite of considerable contrary evidence" (Hallowes, HS9/648/4, National Archives, Kew). Instead of being doubted, the story got reified. The Nazis seemed to desire a high-value prisoner to exchange for Deputy Führer Rudolf Hess, then imprisoned in Scotland. In August 1943, telegrams would go all the way to Hitler testifying that the Paris Gestapo had captured Winston Churchill's nephew.

164 **"the Germans are the most frightful snobs":** P. Churchill, *Spirit in the Cage,* 31.

164 **"I always thought it":** Ibid., 32.

164 **"sixty-second cousin":** Peter Churchill, HS 9/315, National Archives, Kew.

164 **"Wrong psychology altogether":** P. Churchill, *Spirit in the Cage,* 32.

165 **"If I ever get the chance":** Ibid., 33.

165 **"an endless Calvary":** P. Churchill, *Duel of Wits,* 364.

166 **Hugo Bleicher ascended:** Bleicher interrogation, Aug. 15, 1945, KV 2/165, National Archives, Kew.

166 **swirling staircase:** Avenue Foch Paris, WO 208/4675, National Archives, Kew.

167 **While both served in intelligence:** Bömelburg's Sipo-SD—*Sicherheitspolizei/Sicherheitsdienst,* commonly called the *Sicherheitsdienst* or just SD—contained five subsections: Anti-Communism, Counter-Sabotage, Anti-Jew, False Papers and Workers Evading Compulsory Labor, and Counterespionage. He answered to *SS-Standartenführer* Dr. Helmut Knochen, who was in charge of not just Sipo-SD but also Administration, Propaganda, Liaison with French Police, Criminal Police, Espionage, and Ideology.

167 **Paris Gestapo:** The contraction for secret police GESTAPO—*GEheime STAatsPOlizei*—originated in the 1930s when a postal clerk got cranky about overly long, compound German nouns.

167 **Paris saw an administrative tangle:** There was also a Vichy antiterrorism police as of 1943, the *Milice,* fighting "the enemies within."

167 **"The exact nature":** Foot, *SOE in France,* ebook.

167 **named BOE48:** Joseph August Peter Placke statement to Vera Atkins, Aug. 13, 1946.

168 **assassinate Adolf Hitler:** The plot would fail: Canaris died at Flossenbürg concentration camp, garroted with a short length of violin string.

168 **After two weeks:** I have condensed the timing of interrogations because I found it impossible to map Odette's recollection of her repeat visits and many interrogators to the cast of employees in war crimes testimony on Avenue Foch. Odette's postwar debriefs are inconclusive, and Odette's story was then filtered through a ghostwritten biography. Her citation says she was interrogated fourteen times. Her postwar interrogations cite ten to twelve times. These episodes happened between May 1943 and May 1944. I have left names blank with only general reference to her recollection

of scenes and actors. Ernest Vogt was the French-language speaker and interrogator at 84 Avenue Foch during the period when some of her interrogations would have taken place; at the time Captain John Starr was in residence. War Crimes Avenue Foch Paris, WO 311/933; Fresnes and Avenue Foch, WO 311/103; Hallowes, HS 9/648/4; John Starr, HS 9/1406/8, National Archives, Kew.

169 **carbon "quintuplicate":** P. Churchill, *Spirit in the Cage,* 67. In Peter's postwar interrogation, he said he was shown "several sheets of closely-typed" information from Marsac and letters he had sent while an agent.

169 **The source of betrayal:** Hallowes, HS 9/648/4, National Archives, Kew.

170 **She knew she could endure:** Odette Hallowes, interview, Imperial War Museum, London.

170 **"Have a look":** Hallowes, HS 9/648/4, National Archives, Kew.

170 **"Are you doing this":** Ibid.

170 **"very beautiful eyes":** Ibid.

170 **she had no idea:** In Odette's immediate postwar interrogation, she said she didn't know if it was a hot poker or a cigarette. In later years, she only said it was a hot poker.

170 **The stench of burning flesh:** Years after the war, Odette's torture was publicly questioned in the press and by historians of SOE. It became the object of a publicity backlash when the British government was less than forthcoming about the fate of its missing female agents, those who died in the concentration camps. Critics claimed Odette invented everything, it never happened, she was histrionic. Selwyn Jepson goes so far as to suggest she survived Ravensbrück only by sleeping with the concentration camp commandant, Fritz Suhren (Jepson, interview, Imperial War Museum, London). While Odette prevailed in a defamation trial against SOE's historian, Michael Foot, a whispered suspicion that she invented the atrocities persists among some experts today. Odette, then and now, comes under fire for being SOE's most public agent, for being a symbol of an agency that kept dark secrets from the British public, and for her dramatic personality. Nevertheless, medical reports reflect physical evidence of war crimes: "Some nails on her toes were missing; there was on her back a rounded scar about half an inch diameter" (T. Markowicz, M.D., May 31, 1946, in Hallowes, HS 9/648/4, National Archives, Kew; also see Christopher J. Murphy, "Whitehall, Intelligence, and Official History: Editing *SOE in France,*" in *Intelligence Studies in Britain and the US: Historiography Since 1945,* ed. Christopher R. Moran and Christopher J. Murphy [Edinburgh: Edinburgh University Press, 2013]). Further, a captured British pilot from 41 Squadron, Hugh Lawrence Parry, witnessed Odette immediately after a torture session in 1944 when they were both in the Rue des Saussaies, site of another Nazi interrogation chamber. By any modern standard, the two years Odette spent in prison—largely in solitary confinement and denied medical care—constitute cruel and inhumane treatment of the highest order. It is true that Odette was dramatic and her recollection of details could be slippery, but she was consistent on the point

of her torture throughout her lifetime. (Indeed, on all major elements of her story. It is the petite details that shift.) Women's pain is often silenced, and it is hard not to recognize that element in the campaign against Odette. Male agents seldom endured such criticisms.

171 **"You would have thought":** Hallowes, Imperial War Museum, London.

171 **"If I am going to die":** Ibid.

171 **"Of course you don't love":** Hallowes, HS 9/648/4, National Archives, Kew.

171 **"any little thing":** Ibid.

172 **"You are not the sort":** Ibid.

172 **"in danger of death":** War Crimes Avenue Foch Paris, WO 311/933, National Archives, Kew.

172 **"Her weakness was extreme":** Hallowes, HS 9/648/4, National Archives, Kew.

172 **"one tin finger":** Fresnes and Avenue Foch, WO 311/103, National Archives, Kew.

172 **fourteen interrogations:** In Odette's earliest postwar reports, the number of Nazi interrogations ranges from ten to twelve; her citation says fourteen.

172 **"how fine it was":** Starr affidavit, May 1, 1946, "In the Matter of Ill Treatment of British and Allied Nationals and Prisoners of War at Gestapo Headquarters in the Avenue Foch in 1943 and 1944," in Avenue Foch Paris, WO 208/4675, National Archives, Kew.

173 **"the cold water cure":** Avenue Foch Paris, WO 208/4675, National Archives, Kew.

173 **"Really all they wanted":** Hugh Lawrence Parry, interview, Imperial War Museum, London. Of note here, Parry was shot down September 24, 1943, well after the invasion of Sicily. From Parry's report, it seems the Paris Gestapo never let go of the idea that captive Britons might know more about the time and date of the invasion. Reports from Claude de Baissac in the summer of 1943 also suggest he believed an autumn landing might be possible, as do Buckmaster's 1943 reports. Standby alert messages were sent to the French Resistance in September–October 1943 but were never followed up by action messages. This might have been part of the decoy invasion, a deception plan named Operation Cockade, set to take place from September to November 1943. It seems there remained at least reasonable belief within Allied forces that an invasion might take place—or that Hitler might be fooled into believing the invasion of France was still likely—late into 1943.

173 **The secretaries kept typing:** Yvonne Burney, née Baseden, Pattinson interview. Burney speaks about how odd it was to see German women in interrogations: "There were four or five German women in uniform nattering away in the corner and two other men talking there and they didn't even look up! Or turn around! You know, it was all normal to see someone in the state that I was in being dragged up a bit further up."

173 **"Do you like":** Jones, *Quiet Courage,* 299.

173 **"clean game":** Hallowes, Imperial War Museum, London.

174 **"a wreck, unkempt":** Parry, Imperial War Museum, London.
174 **"In every tragedy":** Hallowes, Imperial War Museum, London.
174 **A woman can only die once:** Hallowes, HS 9/648/4, National Archives, Kew.

CHAPTER 16: THE SWAP

176 **the main radios in Paris:** At least two were on their way: Gaston Cohen would go to JUGGLER/ROBIN, the Jewish network in Paris, on June 13, 1943. Noor Inayat Khan would arrive by Lysander on June 16/17, 1943, and was promised to a PROSPER sub-circuit to be called PHONO.
176 **Ultra decrypts:** German Penetration of SOE SIS and Allied Organizations, KV 3/75, National Archives, Kew.
176 **"These were the important":** Ree, "Experiences of an SOE Agent in France, Henri Raymond, Alias César."
176 **"He is not being":** J. Agazarian, HS 9/11/1, National Archives, Kew.
177 **"I am a friend":** *"Je suis un ami de Roger Dumont. Il y a plus d'un mois que je ne l'ai vu."* Suttill, *Shadows in the Fog,* ebook.
177 **He was stout:** Anton Pierrefeu, KV 2/946, National Archives, Kew.
177 **"looks and behaves like a waiter":** Foot, *SOE in France,* ebook.
178 **"The defeat of Japan":** "Prime Minister's Speech to Congress: Good Allies in the Cause," *Times* (London), May 20, 1943.
178 **the Admiralty rarely announced:** "Increased Sinkings of U-Boats," *Times* (London), May 15, 1943.
179 **Only the highest levels:** The Allies were trying to dupe the world. At that moment, double agents were misinforming Berlin, hinting that D-Day would arrive in July in the Pas-de-Calais. The goal was to convince Germany that the British fleet was gathering in Kent and Hampshire and that Americans were setting their sights on an invasion in Brittany.
179 **"in June, July, August":** Danièle Lheureux, *La Résistance "Action-Buckmaster": Sylvestre-Farmer, avec le captaine "Michel"* (Roubaix: Geai Bleu, 2001), as quoted in Suttill, *Shadows in the Fog,* ebook.
179 **secret government budget:** The SOE budget was known to be extravagant. In London, the Firm had a corporate apartment in Orchard Court decked out in the height of Art Deco excess, with a bathroom in black tile with a giant marble tub, a bidet, and peach-pink mirrors engraved with dancing maidens.
179 **"to 'do their duty'":** Special Report, April 1943–September 1943, dated Oct. 1, 1943, in F Section History and Agents, HS 7/121, National Archives, Kew.
179 **His safe houses:** By chance, a man living next to Gilbert was actually a wireless operator working for de Gaulle's RF Section—until he, too, was arrested. J. A. F. Antelme, HS 9/42, National Archives, Kew.
180 **most "perturbed":** Gilbert Norman, HS 9/110/5, National Archives, Kew.
180 **Every agent descended:** The Tambour family instructed British arrivals

on the newest regulations and rules imposed by the Nazis: what time curfew started, which night meat was available in what restaurants, where one might get a good fake identity card.

180 **"organization in Paris":** Buckmaster puts this in direct quotation marks in his F Section history (HS 7/121, National Archives, Kew).

180 **Buck—now promoted:** Buckmaster was promoted on April 29, 1943.

180 **Andrée and Yvonne were working:** J. Agazarian, HS 9/11/1, National Archives, Kew.

180 **"Please, please, please":** Ibid.

181 **a CARTE member:** Henri Frager had been second-in-command of CARTE and later launched DONKEYMAN.

181 **"Life for him":** Guerne, in Vader, *Prosper Double-Cross,* 63.

181 **"terribly headstrong and firm":** Ibid., 99.

181 **He commanded an army:** F Section History and Agents, HS 7/121, National Archives, Kew.

181 **set to grow to eighty operators:** Ibid.

181 **One would go to the Jewish circuit:** Gaston Cohen, infiltrated June 13, 1943.

181 **an Indian woman:** Noor Inayat Khan, infiltrated June 17, 1943.

182 **"I cannot praise them":** Agazarian, HS 9/11/1, National Archives, Kew.

182 **"ACTION FOR 'D' DAY":** J. A. F. Antelme, HS 9/42, National Archives, Kew.

183 **The plan would call for:** These are the D-Day numbers for 1944. 1943–1944 would have seen massive increases in production and troops. I have no hard numbers for this period, in part because the invasion was going to Italy instead. It is why I used the subjunctive mood. Data from www.history.com.

183 **"alert" message:** "In the middle of 1943 we had a top secret message telling us that D-Day might be closer than we thought. This message had been tied up with international politics on a level far above our knowledge and we, of course, acted upon it without question" (Buckmaster, *They Fought Alone,* 225). "His orders, as he remembered them many years afterwards, had been to accelerate his section's preparations to support an invasion, in case it turned out possible to mount one after all later in the year. This possibility was widely canvassed at the time, for it was politically attractive, especially on the far left; but it turned out logistically impracticable. Suttill, in any event, was sent back to Paris from London in late May 'with an "alert" signal, warning the whole circuit to stand by'" (Foot, *SOE in France,* ebook). However, in subsequent research, Francis Suttill's son, also Francis, now suggests these were not "standby" orders but targeting messages for the Le Mans area.

183 **"Darling Child":** Francis Suttill to his wife, late May 1943, courtesy of Francis Suttill.

184 **"sipping a tasteless":** Wighton, *Pin-Stripe Saboteur,* 131.

185 **"knew too much":** Guerne, in Vader, *Prosper Double-Cross,* 73.

185 **"Awful PM":** Buckmaster Diary, March 26, 1943, courtesy of Tim Buckmaster.

185 **"You are not the Salvation Army!":** Guerne, in Vader, *Prosper Double-Cross,* 73. The quotation suggests Francis should not have been bartering for rebel lives and/or that he is offering too much money. Records show that funds sent to the PROSPER circuit in May 1943 were many millions more than in previous months. It could mean that Baker Street signed off on the deal. (And, also, they were anticipating increased expenses ahead of a landing.) F Section Diary, HS 7/121, National Archives, Kew.

185 **"It isn't cricket":** "From Army Orderly to Secret Service Lady" on Dee Gallie, Stratford upon Avon Society web page.

186 **"rather tired looking blondes":** Wighton, *Pin-Stripe Saboteur,* 132.

186 **"young ladies of doubtful virtue":** Ibid.

186 **The French inspectors apologized:** Antelme, HS 9/43, National Archives, Kew.

187 **"like a storm of confetti":** Wighton, *Pin-Stripe Saboteur,* 138.

187 **Parisian networks:** By the spring of 1943, several networks were at work in Paris, not just Andrée's PHYSICIAN/PROSPER. Jean Worms, Andrée's demolition partner, was leader of the Jewish JUGGLER/ROBIN circuit, also in Paris. The reconstituted CARTE network was at work in Paris under new leadership after André Girard was exfiltrated to London. Agent France Antelme was also in Paris, as the BRICKLAYER circuit.

CHAPTER 17: THE DOG SNEEZED ON THE CURTAINS

191 **"amphibious operations":** "Prime Minister on the Fight Ahead," *Times* (London), June 9, 1943.

191 **death toll rose:** Robert Gildea, *Fighters in the Shadows: A New History of the French Resistance* (Cambridge, Mass.: Belknap Press of Harvard University Press, 2015), ebook.

191 ***Paris-Soir* published pictures:** In February 1943, German authorities in France banned photographs of fashion and couture, not wanting to seed sartorial desires that could not be satisfied when there was no fabric to be had.

191 **Across the dissident spectrum:** Under de Gaulle's umbrella, on May 23, 1943, Jean Moulin formed the sixteen-member National Council of Resistance, a confederacy that included representatives from eight resistance groups, five political parties, and two trade unions.

192 **"light of victory":** "Prime Minister on the Fight Ahead."

192 **205 containers:** Suttill, *Shadows in the Fog,* ebook.

192 **"The resistance terrorists":** SS Colonel Mersch, in E. H. Cookridge, *Inside S.O.E.: The First Full Story of Special Operations Executive in Western Europe, 1940–45* (London: Arthur Barker, 1966), 205.

192 **"The dog sneezed":** Suttill, *Shadows in the Fog,* ebook.

192 **"We find ourselves":** Guerne, in Vader, *Prosper Double-Cross,* 60.
193 **"A blinding glare":** La République du Centre, Sept. 13/14, 1947, as translated and quoted in Suttill, *Shadows in the Fog,* ebook.
193 **"We are betrayed":** King, *Jacqueline,* 297.
194 **"I thought she was marvelous":** Ibid.
194 **Go back as you came:** Yvonne was not in charge of the reception that night, but she was an attendant.
194 **The little house was booby-trapped:** King, *Jacqueline,* 276.
196 **Duke of Windsor:** Edward VIII, Prince of Wales, took on the title Duke of Windsor after his abdication.
196 **It was unusual:** Pierre Culioli, HS 9/379/8, National Archives, Kew.
196 **"Whatever happens":** King, *Jacqueline,* 309.
197 **Instead, it held un-encrypted messages:** Not all messages were encrypted. Encryption was always used for telegraph traffic. Messages with a known chain of possession—couriered from an agent to London or vice versa—were often sent *en clair,* in plain text, or with prearranged codes buried within the text, or in a cipher known as PLAYFAIR.
197 **"Do not be afraid":** Culioli, HS 9/379/8, National Archives, Kew.
197 **"Charcuterie," he was told:** Ibid.
198 **"I have often seen him around":** Ibid.
198 **And that tall blond Canadian:** "Speaks 27 with a Canadian accent," said a training report; "27" was the Firm's code for things pertaining to France, "27Land." F. H. D. Pickersgill, HS 9/1186/2, National Archives, Kew.

CHAPTER 18: HUNTED

202 **"came and went":** Interrogations, Extracts on Prosper, HS 6/440 SPU, National Archives, Kew.
202 **Gilbert never transmitted:** Nicolas handed the keys to Gilbert. "He was our leader," Maude said by way of helpless explanation.
202 **"It is impossible":** Philippe de Vomécourt, *Who Lived to See the Day: France in Arms, 1940–1945* (London: Hutchinson, 1961), 74.
202 ***cartes d'identité:*** Suttill, *Shadows in the Fog,* ebook.
203 **"the fake fake papers":** *Les faux faux papiers.* Circuit and Mission Reports—B, Baissac, HS 6/567, National Archives, Kew.
203 **"true fakes":** *Les vrais faux papiers.*
203 **Paris police were demanding:** J. A. F. Antelme, HS 9/43, National Archives, Kew.
203 **"arms and money":** M. R. D. Foot as quoted in Lois Gordon, *The World of Samuel Beckett, 1906–1946* (New Haven, Conn.: Yale University Press, 1996), ebook.
203 **"quantity of false papers":** Guerne, in Vader, *Prosper Double-Cross,* 95.
203 **"She never tired":** Léone Arend, née Borrel, as quoted in Nicholas, *Death Be Not Proud,* 175.

203 **last name, first name:** *Nom, prénom, profession, nationalité, naissance, adresse.*

204 **"Open up, German police!":** *Ouvrez, la police allemande!*

206 **"wicked and bestial":** Swiss chief of consulate in Paris to his foreign minister, Feb. 1944, on Armel Guerne and his wife—both members of Andrée's circuit, in Vader, *Prosper Double-Cross,* 95.

206 **"It's not my health":** Fuller, *German Penetration of SOE,* 72.

207 **His room was "destroyed":** "Some two hours later he appeared to me all disfigured, having the appearance of being beaten and totally miserable," the proprietress said. "When I got my room back the following Sunday, I realized that the Germans had destroyed everything. The marble slab of the fireplace had been torn off and broken. The mirror in my wardrobe was shattered. Chairs and armchairs damaged all over the place." From Suttill, *Shadows in the Fog,* French-language version, in manuscript, courtesy of Francis Suttill.

207 **Paris's sadistic collaborators:** This gang was known as the Sion Gang, commonly known as the French Gestapo, according to Francis Suttill, author of *Shadows in the Fog.*

207 **The ultimate cause:** There are good reasons to believe it was Pierre Culioli's arrest that triggered the downfall. Upon his capture, he was tortured and interrogated in Blois, then brought to Avenue Foch on June 24, 1943, for more questioning. Nevertheless, any number of mistakes could have pulled on the threads that unraveled PROSPER: In November, Marsac, the CARTE lieutenant, fell asleep on a train with a list of names connecting the dots of the British networks. Once Marsac was captured in March, he pointed the Germans to Germaine Tambour.

Francis likely could not know, but seems to have suspected, that Marsac introduced the Germans to other British agents who worked in parallel to Francis's network (Roger Bardet and Henri Frager); they too were double-crossing the Resistance in the Paris vicinity, still interacting with the PROSPER circuit—however much Francis tried to insulate his team.

Andrée's flat was a crossroads for couriers in other networks: Mary Herbert in Bordeaux had her own key; Lise de Baissac got messages from Andrée. Police had snooped around. Andrée lived above a café frequented by other members of the French Gestapo, the notorious Rue Lauriston gang.

The crisis could have come later that spring, while Francis was exfiltrated back to London and that mysterious Dutch agent was arrested in the Café Capucines. The latter had seen the network leadership up close—Andrée and Gilbert—during the poker game and perhaps tipped off the Gestapo; he was already on their team as an agent of the Abwehr. The radio operator Jack Agazarian, who escaped the *rafle* at the café, might have been followed when he went to meet Andrée; it was he who then infected the rest of the Parisian crew.

There were so many elements that went awry: Pierre and Yvonne were missing, arrested, only three days before. The Avenue Foch goons likely pinpointed Francis's location only in the last few hours, after Pierre was taken to Paris for questioning. Pierre was shot in the leg, in pain, and watched his partner take a bullet to the head; he might have given up the entire PROSPER network under torture—or to save himself. Pierre knew where Nicolas and Maude Laurent lived, where Andrée and Gilbert worked on forgeries. Pierre wrote letters to four of his own deputies in the Loire, telling them to give up arms dumps, promising the Gestapo would not hurt them if they cooperated.

When Andrée was captured the previous night at the Laurents' house, she left a desk full of paperwork that implicated the extended circuit, with pictures, fake names, false addresses, and details for nearly everyone involved, her signature on every single one. The knock-on effects of Andrée and Gilbert's arrest could have led the Gestapo to the Hôtel Mazagran and to Francis.

There were other directions from which the storm might have blown: Henri Déricourt was delivering mail bound for England to the Germans headquartered on Avenue Foch. A ranking officer at Baker Street seemed to understand—and perhaps even consent to—this perfidy; on a note distributed that day around the offices in London, a senior officer in French Section wrote of Déricourt, "We know he is in contact with the Germans and also how and why."

208 **"put to very good use":** Prosper Press Cuttings Correspondence, HS 6/426, National Archives, Kew; Deposition of Hans Kieffer Statement to Vera Atkins, Jan. 19, 1947, Atkins Papers.

CHAPTER 19: WHEN THE HOUR OF ACTION STRIKES

209 **"man after man":** Buckmaster, *They Fought Alone,* 229. Also see Prosper Press Cuttings Correspondence, HS 6/426, National Archives, Kew.

209 **at least 240 partisans:** Suttill, *Shadows in the Fog,* ebook. Suttill has evidence for 240 arrests. Earlier estimates put the toll much higher. Foot suggests the range was between 400 and 1,500 arrests.

210 **"Not one of us":** Guerne, in Vader, *Prosper Double-Cross,* 86. Late in life, Guerne said the French rebels never wanted to leave. In the immediate aftermath of the PROSPER disaster, he begged to be exfiltrated to London. Gilbert Norman, HS 9/1110/5, National Archives, Kew.

210 **"But we all knew":** Guerne, in Vader, *Prosper Double-Cross,* 87.

210 **"led a different life":** Lise, Legasee interview.

210 **"Thinking about captured agents":** Marks, *Between Silk and Cyanide,* 328.

211 **"inserting his true checks":** Ibid., 326.

211 **"unusual, hesitant":** Punctuation added for clarity. J. A. F. Antelme, HS 9/43, National Archives, Kew.

211 **"he'd rather have shot":** Norman, HS 9/110/5, National Archives, Kew.

211 **"[THAT WAS] A SERIOUS BREACH":** Marks, *Between Silk and*

Cyanide, 326. All caps added for stylistic consistency because telegrams were transmitted in Morse and represented by capital letters. We do not have the original text for this message; Marks's memoir was published almost fifty years after the war. Yet telegrams that survive in files and that appear in Marks's book are strikingly similar. To back up Marks, we have the immediate postwar report of the agent Maurice Southgate, who spoke to Gilbert Norman at Avenue Foch: "Time after time, for different men, LONDON sent back messages saying 'my dear fellow, you only left us a week ago. On your first message you go and forget to put your true check.' You may now realise what happened to our agents who did *not* give the true check to the Germans, thus making them send a message that was obviously phoney. After putting them through the worst degrees of torture these Germans managed—sometimes a week later—to obtain the true check and send another message to LONDON with the proper check in the telegram and LONDON saying 'Now you are a good boy, you have remembered to give both of them!!!' " SOE Activities in France, HS 8/422, National Archives, Kew.

212 **Nazis of Avenue Foch:** "Subsequently the work becomes, technically, quite normal," Baker Street noted following that first stilted signal. "Home Station operators accept [Gilbert's] messages without query or comment." Antelme, HS 9/43, National Archives, Kew.

212 **Bömelburg's men kept British agents:** Known as *agents de la maison.*

212 **Favored prisoners:** For a description of Avenue Foch life as a British agent working for the Nazis, see J. Starr, HS 9/1406/8, National Archives, Kew, and Jean Overton Fuller, *The Starr Affair* (London: Victor Gollancz, 1954), as well as war crimes testimonies from the Nazis of Avenue Foch, Goetz, Placke, Stork, and others. War Crimes Avenue Foch, WO 311/933, National Archives, Kew.

212 **"which would condemn":** Reported speech, Gilbert Norman to Armel Guerne in prison, Guerne interview, in Vader, *Prosper Double-Cross,* 99. Also see Kieffer war crimes testimony, Prosper Press Cuttings and Correspondence, HS 6/426, National Archives, Kew.

213 **"plenty of dash":** Norman, HS 9/110/5, National Archives, Kew.

213 **"It serves no purpose":** Balachowski interrogation, in SPU 24 Interrogations—Extracts on Prosper, HS 6/440, National Archives, Kew.

213 **He told each new prisoner:** Conversations with Gilbert Norman about his collaboration with Nazis are recorded in multiple postwar interviews with agents who were captured and survived, including Balachowski, Southgate, Guerne, Arend, Culioli, Starr, and Rousset. Gilbert was a radio operator, so there is a preponderance of evidence against him in the wireless traffic he sent on the Nazis' behalf and in that he revealed the whereabouts of his radio sets. It has long been suggested that not only Gilbert but also Francis Suttill capitulated in what was called "the famous Prosper/Archambaud pact." Returned agents did not report having similar conversations with Francis, who was not held at Avenue Foch but sent to Berlin. Evidence against Francis seems either to be British hearsay or to

come directly from Nazis in war crimes testimonies. During the war at least, the Nazis of Avenue Foch would have had an interest in spreading disinformation, letting prisoners believe the circuit leader had flipped as a tool of psychological coercion.

213 **"We will see each other":** Guerne interview, in Vader, *Prosper Double-Cross,* 92.

213 **"I'm not sure":** "Couriers of Churchill's Order Who Set Europe Ablaze," reprinted in *Ottawa Journal,* June 25, 1949.

213 **Weeks later:** August 11, 1943.

214 **"A catastrophe, the extent":** Lochner, *Goebbels Diaries,* 404, cited in Milan Hauner, *Hitler: A Chronology of His Life and Time* (London: Macmillan, 1983), ebook.

214 **"AN IMPORTANT BRITISH":** "Most Secret" sources report No. 121.21.8.43, German Penetration of SOE SIS and Allied Organizations, KV 3/75, National Archives, Kew. Capitalization added for stylistic consistency because telegrams were transmitted in Morse.

215 **"ESTABLISHED QUITE RECENTLY":** At the time of this telegram, Hitler had been at war for four years, since 1939. The PROSPER network in Paris was a relative newcomer to Nazi commanders; it was established in October 1942.

216 **Hitler declared to his generals:** "French Hero Is Questioned on D-Day Betrayal," *Daily Graphic* (London), June 9, 1947, Atkins Papers.

216 **Cathedral bells chimed:** In much of Europe, church bells went silent during World War II, but not in France by most reports. In Britain, bells were silenced out of mourning. On the Continent, Nazis seized an estimated 175,000 church bells; some were confiscated for their copper and tin, smelted for war industries; a few were looted for aesthetic reasons, as fine instruments. Generally, one small bell would be left in a tower to ring in emergencies. In France, the bells continued to sound. France evaded the worst of Nazi bell theft, just as Paris was left largely intact as a conquered emblem of European civilization. Notre Dame's bells pealed every fifteen minutes without fail between 1856 and 2012, when they were replaced.

216 **At seventeen hundred miles per hour:** The average bullet travels at twenty-five hundred feet per second. *MythBusters.*

216 **The projectile did not perforate:** Summary of doctor's report in King, *Jacqueline,* 323; "How Explosive Shock Waves Harm the Brain," *Neuroscience News,* Feb. 23, 2016. Also, thanks to Dr. Steven Dickstein for medical explanation of brain injury.

217 **"might be to her advantage":** King, *Jacqueline,* 323.

217 **"which I thought":** Ibid.

217 **"our Jacqueline":** *Notre Jacqueline.*

217 **"I was not sure":** King, *Jacqueline,* 338.

217 **"We tried to soften her days":** Ibid., 337.

217 **"dedication to her companions":** Yvonne Rudellat, 16P-115050, Service Historique de la Défense, Vincennes, Paris.

218 **administer Pentothal:** King, *Jacqueline,* 327.

219 **one million francs:** Antelme, HS 9/43, National Archives, Kew.

219 **the little old woman from England:** Yvonne was not in fact English. Born in France, she had moved to London young, where she got married to an Italian and gave birth to a daughter.

220 **"If you will allow me":** King, *Jacqueline,* 339.

220 **"The English and American armies":** Author's translation. "L'Europe attend," July 7, 1943, in Crémieux-Brilhac, *Ici Londres,* 3:204.

221 **"The United Nations":** "Call to France," *Times* (London), July 12, 1943.

222 **"attack against the soft":** Churchill's phrase comes up again and again, in both General Montgomery's and General Eisenhower's war memoirs. Also see "Mr. Churchill's War-Time Policy," *Times* (London), Aug. 20, 1946.

222 **"I count on your sangfroid":** "Call to France," *Times* (London), July 12, 1943.

222 **"When the hour of action":** Ibid.

223 **"We repeat: when the hour":** Ibid.

CHAPTER 20: KISSES

227 **Fresnes Prison:** This is constructed from Andrée's five prison letters, written between November 1943 and January 1944, in Andrée Borrel, HS 9/183, National Archives, Kew.

227 **She told her colleagues:** Borrel, HS 9/183, National Archives, Kew.

228 **"military situation":** Ibid.

228 **At Christmas, the Red Cross:** Judging from Andrée's letters, a GI doctor might suspect she had celiac disease. Bread made her ill; she begged not to be sent bread in a prison where reports say there was never enough food. "I do not like flour!!"

228 **There were errands:** *Commissions.*

228 **The seamstress would understand:** Andrée's sister Léone was involved in the Resistance; she would understand many common word replacements used routinely by the underground. We have seen "sweets and toys" as stand-ins for "guns and matériel," according to SOE training handbooks; additionally, agents were known as "lambs." Other prison letters from agents survive in which we see similar gaps in implicature: Maurice Pertschuk, a Jewish agent and poet, writes from Buchenwald about the eggs he received as a present. ("Next time, wrap them more carefully.") It is possible somebody sent eggs from occupied France to a German concentration camp, but unlikely. Pertschuk letter, courtesy of Anne Whiteside.

229 **So, too, had the other Gilbert:** In the long history of SOE scholarship, there has been at least half a century of debate over who is the Gilbert to whom Andrée refers in her prison letters: Gilbert Norman or the agent Gilbert, Henri Déricourt. In my read of these letters, she is speaking of her boyfriend, Gilbert Norman. She would have known in prison about his perfidy because he got her brother-in-law arrested when he revealed the whereabouts of the radio sets. However, it had already been reported that

Andrée also believed that Henri Déricourt's air pickups and landings were suspect.

230 **"I think I am going to Germany":** *"Je pense aller en Allemagne."*

CHAPTER 21: A PATRIOTIC PROFESSION

231 **"their nerves were not":** Claude de Baissac, HS 9/75, National Archives, Kew.

232 **"Things happen":** Lise, Pattinson interview.

232 **"powerful organization":** Bourne-Patterson, British Circuits in France, HS 7/122, National Archives, Kew.

232 **"It is the ground intelligence":** History of F Section and Agents, HS 7/121, National Archives, Kew.

233 **rocked by arrests:** Claude was exfiltrated not only because of the PROSPER network collapse. The SCIENTIST network was also betrayed by a double agent in 1943.

233 **"Life in Bordeaux":** Circuit and Mission Reports—B, HS 6/567, National Archives, Kew.

236 **"prepare the mass of French":** Author's translation. Audrey Bonnéry-Vedel, "La BBC a-t-elle jamais été la voix de la France libre?," *Le Temps des Médias,* no. 11 (2008).

236 **The Firm was now supplying:** "All this air effort amounted, by the middle of May, to the arming of about 75,000 men by F section and 50,000 by RF, at the most optimistic estimates; and these figures took no account of the arms captured in any of the Gestapo triumphs that had disfigured 1943, which probably reduced the totals of available armed men by something like a third." Foot, *SOE in France,* ebook.

236 **May 1944:** Foot says it was specifically May 17, 1944, but that was a waning quarter moon, the dark moon before D-Day. Dark moons were useful for small-scale raids but a questionable choice for mass mobilization.

239 **"who had been very well":** Circuit and Mission Reports—B, HS 6/567, National Archives, Kew.

CHAPTER 22: A LITTLE BRAVER

240 **"Why don't you":** Rita Kramer, *Flames in the Field* (London: Michael Joseph, 1995), ebook.

241 **George Starr was instead:** George Starr was accused of torturing the *Milice,* the Vichy security police. He was cleared of all charges in a court of inquiry. SOE maintained George Starr was one of the best organizers in the field, recommending him for the DSO (Distinguished Service Order) and the MC (Military Cross); he was one of only three agents to be promoted to the rank of colonel. One accusation came from a female agent, Anne-Marie Walters, who wrote the book *Moondrop to Gascony*

(1947; repr., Wiltshire, U.K.: Moho Books, 2009). Walters reported to her superiors: "It was also quite wrong in my opinion to lower oneself to the standards of the Gestapo by torturing milicients [French Secret Police] and collaborators to make them reveal the whereabouts of their colleagues—some were beaten until blood spurted all over the walls, others were horribly burnt: one man's feet were held in the fire 20 minutes and his legs were slowly burnt off to the knees; other tortures are too horrible to mention." French Section denied the allegations, condemning Walters for being excitable and "romantic minded." Starr also gave a speech to SOE trainers soon after his return that left officers with the impression he oversaw torture under his command in France. Colonel Woolrych, commandant of Beaulieu, gave sworn testimony about Starr's lecture. "He said that in the case of the Gestapo man he had been hung by one foot for several hours. He also stated that a steel knitting pin had been inserted in his penis, and heat applied to the other end." George Reginald Starr, HS 9/1407/1, National Archives, Kew; Court of Enquiry re Lt. Col. G. R. Starr (SOE), Feb. 1945, courtesy of David Harrison.

242 **"everybody was more or less":** Odette Sansom, Imperial War Museum, London.

242 **Over tea, the women reflected:** The other women reported to be in the room that day were Yolande Beekman, Madeleine Damerment, Vera Leigh, Eliane Plewman, Diana Rowden, Sonia Olschanezky—all of whom died.

242 **"We all had the feeling":** Kramer, *Flames in the Field,* ebook.

242 **"Everybody tried to be":** Ibid.

243 **Tomorrow was all night and fog:** On the train to Germany, the SS officer from Avenue Foch told Odette and other F Section women that "none of us would come back alive and that we would be made to suffer before they got rid of us." Odette Sansom affidavit, "In the Matter of War Crimes and the Matter of the Ill-Treatment of Allied Personnel and Atrocities Committed at Ravensbruck [*sic*] Concentration Camp," signed May 20, 1946, Atkins Papers. Only Odette survived.

CHAPTER 23: THE SIGHING BEGINS

244 **a personal message aired:** English translation by Arthur Symonds. BBC listeners in France heard:

Les sanglots longs
Des violons
D'automne

245 **"MAJOR OPERATION":** Jacques R. E. Poirier, *The Giraffe Has a Long Neck,* trans. John Brownjohn (Barnsley, U.K.: Pen & Sword, 1995), 137.

245 **"THE RELEVANT MESSAGE WILL BE":** In French:

Bercent mon coeur
D'une langueur
Monotone

The couplet as reported by de Vomécourt says, "*Bercent mon coeur*" (Lull my heart) as opposed to the actual phrase by Verlaine, "*Blessent mon coeur*" (Wound my heart).

245 **so-called B message:** In Francis Suttill's 1943 reports, the substitute code for A and B messages was "Apple" and "Beer" messages.

245 **"YOUR TASK WILL BE":** Poirier, *Giraffe Has a Long Neck*, 137.

245 **The invasion would:** In Nantes, on the Loire, there were A and B messages for railway targets and for telephone targets.

For railway targets:

A: *C'était le sergent qui fumait sa pipe en pleine campagne.*
It was the sergeant who smoked his pipe in the open country.

B: *Il avait mal au coeur mais il continuait tout de même.*
He was queasy, but continued anyway.

For telephone targets:

A: *La Corse ressemble à une poire.*
Corsica looks like a pear.

B: *L'Italie est une botte.*
Italy is a boot.

(R. Benoist, HS 9/127/128, National Archives, Kew.)

245 **"*Quasimodo est une fête*":** Pearl Witherington Cornioley, *Code Name Pauline: Memoirs of a World War II Special Agent* (Chicago: Chicago Review Press, 2013), app., interview with Pearl Cornioley. There is a play on words in this message: While it translates literally to "Quasimodo is a party," it sounds similar to *quasiment un fait* or *quasiment fait,* either "nearly a fact" or "nearly done"—a fairly direct reference to the landings. Imagine what it would have sounded like over the crackle of the airwaves. More than that, Quasimodo Sunday is, in the Catholic Church, the name given to the Sunday after Easter. *Quasi* and *modo* are the first two Latin words of the Mass that week and indicated that day in popular language; in this way, the message pointed to a certain date when something might happen. As a D-Day action message, it would have sounded many weeks too late for Quasimodo Sunday, but as a standby message sounding on May 1, 1944, it would have been nearly on time.

246 **"*La girafe a un long cou*":** From Poirier, *Giraffe Has a Long Neck*. There is wordplay in this message too: The French word *cou* has homonyms and phonetically similar words, many of which are sexual in nature. For the giraffe, it is likely long.

246 **"decide the issue":** D. K. R. Crosswell, *Beetle: The Life of General Walter Bedell Smith* (Lexington: University Press of Kentucky, 2010), 669.

247 **"I'm too old a bunny":** David Kahn, *Hitler's Spies: German Military and Intelligence in World War II* (New York: Da Capo Press, 1978), 513.

247 **"As if General Eisenhower":** Paul Carell, *Invasion—They're Coming,* trans. E. Osers (New York: Dutton, 1963), online.

248 **Once Lise's maquis heard:** In the Manche—part of SCIENTIST territory—some action messages are known to us in English:

Alert: The hour of combat will come.

End of alert (railways): Children become bored on Sundays.

Plan Vert: The dice are on the rug.

Guerilla: It is hot at Suez.

(France Resistance and Secret Army, June–July 44, HS 6/377, National Archives, Kew.)

248 **"through thick enemy formations":** Claude de Baissac, HS 9/76, National Archives, Kew.

248 **"The lives of many of you":** "D-Day: June 6th 1944 as It Happened," *Telegraph* (London), June 6, 2014.

249 **Operation Overlord would "go":** General Eisenhower's simple command: "Ok. Let's go." June 5, 1944, National Archives and Records Administration, www.archives.gov.

249 **American troops were the first:** British troops were the first boots on the ground in France in Operation Deadstick. On the night of June 5, led by Major John Howard, 181 men left the U.K. in six gliders to capture two bridges near Sword Beach. The first glider landed at 0016 on June 6, 1944, six hours before H-Hour.

249 **Omaha and Utah Beaches:** Martha Gellhorn was the only woman to report on the D-Day landings from Normandy. Women were prohibited from the front, but Gellhorn stowed away on a hospital ship to get across the Channel, locked herself in a toilet, and hit the beach disguised as a stretcher bearer. She even beat her husband, Ernest Hemingway, to the beaches after he had usurped her press credentials.

249 **at 6:48 a.m.:** "D-Day: June 6th 1944 as It Happened," June 6, 2014, Telegraph.co.uk.

249 **"Under the command":** Digital Collections, Brigham Young Library, Eisenhower Communiques, June 6, 1944, No. 1, lib.byu.edu.

250 **"TELEGRAM FROM BARBER BLUE":** "Telegram from BARBER BLUE, dated 6.6.44," France Maquis Jan.–June 44, HS 6/597, National Archives, Kew.

250 **"SUCH AS MAX":** It's worth noting that Max was also the alias of Jean Moulin, General de Gaulle's emissary to France, who spent the last two tortured weeks of his life in the private villa of *SS-Sturmbannführer* Karl Bömelburg. But this telegram refers only to F Section agents in Nazi

hands: Max is the agent Jean Bougennec/Butler, Tell is Gustave Bieler/Musician, and Theodore is Jacques de Guélis/Facade.

251 **"VERY PLEASED":** The following section was omitted for clarity: "COMPARATIVELY EASY TO WIN OVER TO US MEMBERS OF THE BUREAU D'OPERATIONS AERIENNES AND THE DELUGE MILITAIRE LIAISON VAUTRIN AND COMET ALIAS PIQUIER DETAINED AS THEY FAILED TO UNDERSTAND US STOP."

251 **"TO NIGHT BARBER":** France Maquis Jan.–June 44, HS 6/597, National Archives, Kew. The reference to "trouble in collecting containers" refers to the deception of the parachute operations. The "bigger and better friends" suggests that the operations were gathering steam as the Grand Alliance—England, America, and Russia—grew stronger; it also seems to reference the arming of the French population. "Give us ground near Berlin" suggests they will be landing in the German capital. "Do not clash with our Russian friends" is a reference to the feared Soviet army. And the "S Phone" was a new radio technology by which a pilot overhead could communicate with the parachute team on the ground; this advance in technology required the Germans to have prisoners who could be at radio game receptions to dupe the flight crews overhead. "We don't think much of his English" suggests that Baker Street knew they were German plants (or an agent working under duress). "We are closing your plan down" refers to the schedule of radio transmissions, when the FANYs at Station 53 would know to listen in for a certain radio.

CHAPTER 24: DEATH ON ONE SIDE, LIFE ON THE OTHER

252 **According to her fictitious:** For this assignment, Lise traveled under the false identity of Jeanette Bouville.

252 **"one table, a bench":** Lise, Pattinson interview.

252 **Anglo-American armies:** Reference to Churchill's "never surrender" speech after the fall of Dunkirk, June 4, 1940. "We shall fight in France. We shall fight on the seas and oceans . . . we shall fight on the beaches, we shall fight on the landing grounds, we shall fight in the fields and in the streets, we shall fight in the hills, we shall never surrender."

252 **"very much war":** Lise, Pattinson interview.

252 **new SCIENTIST area:** Claude's networks were named after his code name, Scientist, but are broken up by historians into SCIENTIST I and SCIENTIST II, reflecting his two missions—the first in Bordeaux in 1942–1943, and the second in Normandy in 1944.

253 **The ranking Nazi was flanked:** Lise tells this story in several late-in-life interviews; it maps closely to the report Claude de Baissac gives in his interrogation of 1944.

253 **"Will you move?":** Lise, Pattinson interview.

253 **"Take your belongings":** Lise, Legasee interview.

253 **"Germany will either be":** Adolf Hitler, *Mein Kampf* (Munich: Franz Eher Nachfolger, 1925).

254 **"These multiple and simultaneous":** Dwight D. Eisenhower Special Communiqué No. 1, June 17, 1944; "French Forces of Resistance," *Times* (London), June 19, 1944.

255 **"When they did eventually":** Foot, *SOE in France,* ebook.

255 **"really first class":** Lise, Pattinson interview.

255 **died in shoot-outs:** Maurice Larcher and Jean Marie Renaud-Dandicolle.

255 **Lise "enjoyed":** Lise, Pattinson interview.

255 **"extremely active in that type":** Bourne-Patterson, British Circuits in France, HS 7/122, National Archives, Kew.

255 **"The secret army":** Claude de Baissac, HS 9/76, National Archives, Kew.

256 **"far surpassed":** Report, SFHQ to SHAEF, 10th Monthly Report (for June 1944), July 10, 1944, SHAEF SGS 319.1/10 Monthly SOE/SO Reports (SFHQ). Also see The French Forces of the Interior, prep in French Resistance Unit, Hist Sec, ETOUSA, 1944, MS, pt. 2, chaps. 1–2, OCMH files. As quoted in Forrest C. Pogue, *United States Army in World War II: European Theater of Operations: The Supreme Command* (Washington, D.C.: Office of the Chief of Military History, Department of the Army, 1954), online.

256 **From England, artificial harbors:** Code name Mulberry.

256 **cross-Channel fuel lines:** Code name Pluto.

257 **SCIENTIST territory:** "A brief summary of SCIENTIST network's post–D-Day accomplishments in the combat zone:

Between 5th–8th June numerous objectives attacked and the Caen-Vire line cut. The beginning of an extremely valuable series of tactical Intelligence messages by Verger [Jean Marie Renaud-Dandicolle], Scientist's [Claude de Baissac's] second-in-command from the Thury Harcourt area.

15th June Paris–Granville line cut near Tessy s/Vire.

18th June Reported taking command of a group of 600 men near Laval.

22nd June Reported his Foret de Monaye Maquis re-forming in the Domfront–Mayenne–Pré-en-Pail triangle.

23rd June Attempted to provide guides to assist patrols of British Airborne Troops between the Rivers Orne and Dive. This was unsuccessful.

30th June Telephone lines and underground cables cut S. of the Cotentin Peninsula. Reported himself as able to receive paratroops on five "controllable" grounds.

30th July Convoys blocked on roads: hundreds of lorries destroyed: infantry columns attacked: trains derailed: communications cut.

(Bourne-Patterson, British Circuits in France, HS 7/122, National Archives, Kew.)

257 **"I was to know no rest":** Claude de Baissac, HS 9/76, National Archives, Kew.

257 **Some nights they would receive:** Lise, Legasee interview.

257 **"Our automatic weapons":** Claude de Baissac, HS 9/76, National Archives, Kew. Mausers were the common infantry rifle in service in the German army in World War II.

257 **"very brave and very willing":** Lise, Pattinson interview.

257 **"about anything and everything":** Judith Martin, "Pippa's War," *New Zealand Army News,* July 21, 2009.

258 **completely "unreasonable":** Lise, Pattinson interview.

258 **"with stupidity":** Claude de Baissac, HS 9/76, National Archives, Kew.

258 **"An ordinary loop knot":** Martin, "Pippa's War."

258 **"I heard I was responsible":** Ibid.

258 **Phyllis was traumatized:** She was nevertheless brave: When Phyllis couldn't get around the Wehrmacht controls to her next hideout, she had to send scheduled messages from the middle of pastures, her antenna wire slung over fences or hedgerows. Soldiers walked in on her safe house once as she was sending; she screamed that she had scarlet fever, and the Germans fled the contagion. On another occasion when she was targeted while transmitting, a farmer's daughter wooed the direction finders away with glasses of fiery home-brewed cider.

258 **"prohibition on movement":** Claude de Baissac, HS 9/76, National Archives, Kew.

258 **"the carnage that was left":** Martin, "Pippa's War."

259 **"One held me down":** Sonia d'Artois (née Butt), Pattinson interview.

259 **"Had [Phyllis] been searched":** Lise, Pattinson interview.

259 **"He touched everything":** Ibid.

260 **"All France [will be] lost":** Joachim Ludewig, *Rückzug: The German Retreat from France, 1944* (Lexington: University Press of Kentucky, 2012), ebook.

260 **"woeful insufficiency":** Eisenhower, as quoted in Crosswell, *Beetle,* 679.

260 **The Allies could not pinpoint:** Bourne-Patterson, British Circuits in France, HS 7/122, National Archives, Kew.

260 **"At a moment like this":** "Americans Cross River into Brittany," *Times* (London), Aug. 2, 1944.

260 **Lise cycled through:** "Her missions were always of a very dangerous nature, because of the difficulty of moving around, and the danger of contacting people active in the resistance," Claude reported. Claude de Baissac, HS 9/76, National Archives, Kew.

261 **Lise's maquis runners:** The success of this, Operation Helmsman, was such that these types of maneuvers are still called Helmsman missions, according to Foot, *SOE in France,* ebook.

261 **"sporadic, disorganized":** "US Forces Break Through West of St. Lô," *Times* (London), July 28, 1944.
261 **"starveling" boys:** A. J. Liebling, Letter from France, *New Yorker,* July 29, 1944.
261 **"East Battalions":** S. J. Lewis, "Jedburgh Team Operations in Support of the 12th Army Group, August 1944" (Fort Leavenworth, Kans.: U.S. Army Command and General Staff College, 1991).
261 **July 20, 1944:** D+44.
261 **"We had all the German army":** Lise, Legasee interview.
262 **"very simple person":** Lise, Pattinson interview.
262 **"attempt to take her things":** Claude de Baissac, HS 9/76, National Archives, Kew.
263 **"could not do much":** Ibid.
263 **"I tried to keep my dignity":** Lise, *Real Charlotte Grays* interview.
264 **a "slaughter":** W. Churchill, *Second World War,* vol. 6, *Triumph and Tragedy,* 33.
264 **"We had gone from inch-by-inch":** Crosswell, *Beetle,* ebook.
264 **"This is an opportunity":** Bradley to Secretary of Treasury Henry Morgenthau, Aug. 8, 1944, in Omar N. Bradley, *A Soldier's Story* (New York: Henry Holt, 1951), 375–76.
264 **mothball men:** *Napthalinards.*
264 **"To each, his own German":** *Chacun son boche.*
265 **"I'm going to see":** Lise felt pity for the scrambling Germans. "When you have been the winner and then you become the loser, it's sad," she said. "A man is a man. The enemy, even if he is the enemy, he can't do otherwise." Lise, Pattinson interview.
266 **Lise waited for the Firm:** Operation Judex in 1944 was a victory tour for F Section. Commanders went to meet the local circuits in France and to take notes on what had occurred behind the lines.
266 **two of her closest colleagues:** Jean Marie Renaud-Dandicolle and Maurice Larcher.
266 **"And it was sad":** Jones, *Quiet Courage,* 291.

CHAPTER 25: YOUR MIND GOES ON THINKING

267 **Odette cracked her knuckles:** Odette Hallowes, interview, Imperial War Museum, London.
267 **For one week, no one brought:** Sansom affidavit, "In the Matter of War Crimes and the Matter of the Ill-Treatment of Allied Personnel and Atrocities Committed at Ravensbruck [*sic*] Concentration Camp," signed May 20, 1946.
267 **"You'd think it was":** Grove, "Life Wisdom Learnt in the Darkness of a Torture Cell."
268 **"refurnished every house":** Ibid.
268 **"On written instructions":** Fritz Suhren deposition, June 15, 1945, Atkins Papers.

268 **"I could count":** Hallowes, Imperial War Museum, London.

268 **As the alleged niece:** Odette's lie that she was married to Peter, the nephew of Winston Churchill, was sustained throughout the war. Ravensbrück held a collection of VIPs. General Charles de Gaulle's niece Geneviève de Gaulle was also a prisoner there for her work in the Resistance; her imprisonment overlapped Odette's. The Nazis seemed to desire high-value prisoners who might be considered in exchange for Rudolf Hess or as bargaining chips in coming war crimes trials. In the August 1943 telegram to Hitler decrypted by Ultra, the story that Peter Churchill was a nephew of Winston Churchill was repeated for the führer himself. Over the course of the war, Odette's story seemed to get concretized more than critiqued.

268 **Have you anything to say?:** Odette interview, in Jones, *Quiet Courage,* 306.

268 **"hard, awful women":** Yvonne Burney, *Real Charlotte Grays* interview.

268 **She had tuberculosis:** Sansom affidavit, "In the Matter of War Crimes and the Matter of the Ill-Treatment of Allied Personnel and Atrocities Committed at Ravensbruck [*sic*] Concentration Camp," signed May 20, 1946.

269 **"I was one minute":** Odette Hallowes, *London Dispatch,* Nov. 30, 1958, as quoted in Penny Starns, *Odette: World War II's Darling Spy* (Stroud, U.K.: History Press, 2009), 104.

269 **"I confess, I reached":** *"J'avoue que j'ai touché le fond de l'abîme du désespoir."* O. Sansom, in French, Atkins Papers.

269 **"There were no trees":** Hallowes, *London Dispatch,* Nov. 30, 1958, as quoted in Starns, *Odette,* 103.

269 **"something extraordinary":** "Imaginary Hobbies in Prison: Odette Churchill's Remedy," *Guardian* (Manchester), Dec. 16, 1953.

269 **"overbearing smell":** Sansom affidavit, "In the Matter of War Crimes and the Matter of the Ill-Treatment of Allied Personnel and Atrocities Committed at Ravensbruck [*sic*] Concentration Camp," signed May 20, 1946.

269 **"mother's darlings":** Vera Atkins to Odette, Nov. 3, 1949, Atkins Papers.

271 **SOE aimed to keep agents:** The institutionalized use of clandestine operatives was effectively a national secret in 1945, one that the West expected to deploy against the Soviets. The desire for secrecy was so acute that SOE's personnel files would not be declassified until 2003, some sixty years after the first female agents were infiltrated.

271 **a fraud:** This happened to the agent Eileen Nearne. Upon liberation, she announced she was an agent working for the British, but the American peace forces decided she was mad and put her in prison—alongside the same wardresses who had held her captive at Ravensbrück.

271 **"We have every reason":** Buckmaster, as cited in Helm, *Life in Secrets,* ebook.

272 **"*N plus N*":** March 12, 1945, from J/Comd SKOYLES, London, in HS 6/439, SPU 24 Paris Interrogation of Returned Agents, National Archives, Kew.

272 **VIPs:** *Sonderhäftlinge.*

272 **"like a shopkeeper":** Karolina Lanckoronska, *Michelangelo in Ravensbrück: One Woman's War Against the Nazis,* trans. Noel Clark (Cambridge, Mass.: Da Capo Press, 2007), 275.

272 **"1000 years old":** Hallowes, Imperial War Museum, London.

272 **"stood at the door":** Sansom affidavit, "In the Matter of War Crimes and the Matter of the Ill-Treatment of Allied Personnel and Atrocities Committed at Ravensbruck [*sic*] Concentration Camp," signed May 20, 1946.

272 **When a woman fell dead:** Sansom interview, Imperial War Museum, London.

273 **"Do you want to know":** Hallowes, *London Dispatch,* Nov. 30, 1958, in Starns, *Odette,* 103.

273 **"This is the Commandant":** Sansom interview, Imperial War Museum, London.

273 **"No, if you don't mind":** Ibid.

273 **there were documents:** O. Sansom in French, Atkins Papers. Author's translation.

EPILOGUE: A USEFUL LIFE

275 **A Useful Life:** Lise, Pattinson interview. "I'm glad to have been able to lead a useful life."

276 **"best moment":** Odette Sansom interview, Imperial War Museum, London.

276 **her radio operator:** Captain Adolphe Rabinovitch did not survive the war, but that outcome was independent of his mission alongside Odette. Because Odette refused to surrender information on his whereabouts during her interrogations, Rabinovitch survived the roundups that followed the arrest of Marsac. For a subsequent mission, Rabinovitch was dropped to a German-controlled landing ground as a result of the radio games deceptions and was executed at Gross-Rosen concentration camp in 1944.

277 **When it took five parachute jumps:** "War Heroine Honoured 63 Years On," BBC News, April 11, 2006, news.bbc.co.uk.

277 **four jumps:** Three training jumps and the fourth operational.

277 **"There was nothing remotely":** Witherington's award was later changed to an MBE (Military).

277 **Peter Churchill's experience:** He was interned at Fresnes, Sachsenhausen, Flossenbürg, and Dachau.

277 **"For mutual protection":** The following has been omitted: "In addition the Gestapo were most determined to discover the whereabouts of the wireless operator who had been working with her Commanding Officer and of another senior British officer whose life was of the greatest value to the Resistance Movement. Ensign SANSOM was the only person who knew their whereabouts. The Gestapo tortured her most brutally to try to make her give away this information. They seared her back with a red-hot iron and, when that failed, they pulled out all her toe-nails; but Ensign

SANSOM continually refused to speak and by her courage, determination and self-sacrifice, she not only saved the lives of these two officers [Adolphe Rabinovitch and Francis Cammaerts, members of F Section] but also enabled them to carry on their most valuable work." Odette Hallowes, HS 9/648/4, National Archives, Kew.

277 **"He would not let go":** Grove, "Life Wisdom Learnt in the Darkness of a Torture Cell."

277 **"I asked that you should lead":** P. Churchill, *Spirit in the Cage,* 296.

278 **the press ran the headline:** "British Heroine to Wed Spy She Saved in France: Suffered Torture to Protect Him," *Chicago Daily Tribune,* Aug. 26, 1946.

278 **"I hope to marry":** Ibid.

278 **"Tell me, Churchill":** P. Churchill, *Spirit in the Cage,* 296.

278 **Soon after the investiture:** Eleven death sentences were passed, but Commandant Fritz Suhren had escaped Allied custody and so was found guilty in absentia. He was later arrested by German police and executed for crimes against humanity in 1950.

278 **At least until her divorce:** Peter Churchill and Odette dissolved their marriage after ten years. He continued to relive his wartime past, and she hoped for a quieter life. Odette subsequently married another SOE agent, Geoffrey Hallowes.

279 **Odette was one of three:** The other two were Eileen Nearne and Yvonne Baseden. Each of them was appointed MBE (Member of the Most Excellent Order of the British Empire).

279 **"suffering from psychological symptoms":** Odette Hallowes, HS 9/648/4, National Archives, Kew.

279 **Odette was recommended:** Eileen Nearne was recommended for disability compensation at 50 percent. She was the little sister of Lise's Beaulieu classmate Jacqueline Nearne, MBE. Jacqueline held a glamorous public profile for a time. As the "pretty one," she starred in the official documentary film about SOE along with the agent Harry Ree, *Now It Can Be Told,* or *School for Danger.* The film, like Odette's romance with Peter Churchill, constituted the public legacy of a previously secret government agency. With Jacqueline's knowledge of languages, experience in covert operations, and public relations background, she got a job as liaison officer for a new peace organization built on the site of a former slaughterhouse in New York City: the United Nations.

279 **In her lifetime, Odette became:** For the rest of her life, Odette said she accepted the George Cross not for herself, but on behalf of the women agents who never returned. "I had a voice to answer with so the best thing I could do was try to give them some kind of publicity," she said.

Everyone should know the story of

Yolande Beekman
Denise Bloch
Andrée Borrel

Muriel Byck
Madeleine Damerment
Noor Inayat Khan
Cecily Lefort
Vera Leigh
Sonia Olschanezky
Éliane Plewman
Lilian Rolfe
Diana Rowden
Yvonne Rudellat
Violette Szabo

(Odette Sansom, Imperial War Museum, London.)

279 ***Odette*, to tell the story:** "The story of a woman agent facing danger and bringing home the goods or being tortured makes the media drool. Odette, who was the first one to do this, was seized on and there, I suppose, you could say there's a hint of exploitation if you like. It was realized that it would make very good propaganda to parade this pretty woman who'd been in love with the man she met, you know when she touched ground they sort of ran in slow motion [laughs] and so she was given a sort of promotional tour." Gervase Cowell, ex–adviser to the Foreign Office, Pattinson interview.

280 **first women in organized combat:** This is a heavily parsed definition. The first women to serve in modern combat served in Russia during World War I: Between 1914 and 1916, at least forty-nine women served as family attached to military men or in subterfuge—that is, dressed as men. They were not a mobilized force. The very first women in organized combat would appear to be Russia's "Women's Battalion of Death" (*Zhenski batal'on smerti*), which fought in the Bolshevik Revolution of 1917, the civil war. Nitpicking differences between adversary combat and combat within a state seems petty—in Russia, World War I and the Revolution elide—but I want to recognize the challenge to the claim of "first women in combat." SOE's female agents were in special forces, not regular forces; guerrilla action is not organized combat, but they answered to military command. At some point, we draw a line somewhere: By World War II, there were women in combat; the women of SOE were among those very first. Let us celebrate and acknowledge all these trailblazers. Beate Fieseler, M. Michaela Hampf, and Jutta Schwarzkopf, "Gendering Combat: Military Women's Status in Britain, the United States, and the Soviet Union During the Second World War," *Women's Studies International Forum* 47, Part A (Nov.–Dec. 2014).

280 **history of war:** The female agents of SOE tie Russian women for first units to see action: As of 1942, the Soviet army began deploying female soldiers. Some 800,000 women would serve in the Red Army during World War II, over half in frontline duty units, constituting 8 percent of total Russian combat forces. Ibid.

280 **Firm, Vera:** For her service, in 1997 Vera Atkins was appointed CBE (Commander of the Most Excellent Order of the British Empire).

280 **"I was going back":** Lise, *Real Charlotte Grays* interview.

280 **"It was usual for this officer":** Lise de Baissac, HS 9/77/1, National Archives, Kew.

The following has been omitted:

> This officer was dropped into France by parachute in September 1942 as a courier and to provide a centre for help and information for resistance workers. She accomplished this task and, in addition, organised a number of supply drops and receptions of agents at a time when the Gestapo were extremely active. By her outstanding work in difficult conditions she made an important contribution to the organisation of resistance in N.W. France.
>
> In July 1943, being seriously compromised, she returned to the U.K. In April 1944 she went back to the field as liaison officer to an important circuit in southern France. A month later she was transferred to Normandy to act as assistant to an organiser in that area, and worked there with diligence, skill and success until the liberation.
>
> Her commanding officer reports that she successfully handled delicate contacts which he was unable to deal with himself, and when he was away she took his place. Twice she was sent to Paris through the German lines and on one occasion she was arrested and searched when carrying W/T plans and crystals. By her calm and sang froid she hoodwinked her captors and thus enabled her circuit to maintain contact with the U.K. at a critical time.

Lise's dossier on the French Resistance states,

> She was the inspiring-force for the groups in the Orne [*département* of Normandy] and through her initiatives she inflicted heavy losses on the Germans thanks to anti-tire devices scattered on the roads near Saint-Aubin-du-Désert, Saint-Mars-du-Désert, and even as far as Laval, Le Mans and Rennes. She also took part in armed attacks on enemy columns.

281 **"I had no more house":** Lise, *Real Charlotte Grays* interview, edited for clarity. Original wording: "I had no—nowhere to go in France! I had no more—no house, no—no money, no nothing! And I had nothing—nowhere to go to."

281 **"I was very happy":** Ibid.

281 **"My life has been worth":** Lise, Pattinson interview.

281 **Mary living outside Poitiers:** "She appears to be perfectly happy in France and ardently to desire to stay there." Mary de Baissac-Herbert, HS 9/77/2, National Archives, Kew.

281 **"20th December, 1944":** Report on Judex Mission, HS 7/134, National Archives, Kew.

281 **Mary and Claude got married:** Claude received the DSO (Military) and bar.

281 **Concerned about finding:** Phyllis Latour, Lise's radio operator, lives in New Zealand.

282 **Yvonne:** For her service, Yvonne Rudellat was posthumously appointed MBE (Member of the Most Excellent Order of the British Empire).

282 **the first female sabotage agent:** F Section already had a woman on the ground in France when Yvonne was infiltrated, Virginia Hall, who worked as a liaison agent on her first mission. For the purposes of this definition, drilling down: Yvonne Rudellat was the first woman to perform combat demolitions; she was the first female sabotage agent, or commando raider.

282 **bullet in her head:** Pierre Culioli, Yvonne's colleague, survived the war after internment in Buchenwald. He was tried twice for betraying his network, found guilty at the first trial, and acquitted at the second. He died in 1994.

282 **Andrée Borrel died:** After her death, Andrée was awarded the KCMB (King's Commendation for Brave Conduct). The proposal for Andrée's decoration reads, "Acted as courier and lieutenant to PHYSICIAN until arrested—took part in reception committee in December 1942. Reported by PHYSICIAN to be a perfect lieutenant, cell chiefs being useless without her owing to his (PHYSICIAN's) accent; shared all dangers. Worked in Paris and Normandy section of his circuit."

282 **"*Vive la France!*":** The jailer's testimony is unclear on this. Four women died that day; the quotation has been ascribed to Andrée as well as to the other women. I'd be happy to credit them all.

282 **Some 429 agents:** As files continue to be released, new names are added to the total; 429 is the current count.

282 **suffering 104 casualties:** Francis Suttill was executed at Sachsenhausen concentration camp on March 23, 1945. He was awarded the Distinguished Service Order after his death. Gilbert Norman died at Mauthausen on September 6, 1944.

282 **fifteen divisions in France:** "Eisenhower credited the French section with shortening the war by six months. 'It was,' he said, 'the equivalent of 15 Divisions.'" Vera Atkins obituary, *Daily Telegraph* (London), June 26, 2000.

283 **more than fifty agents:** The exact number of agents who died as a result of the radio games remains in dispute. According to the Dutch government, at least fifty-four agents were parachuted into the Dutch radio games, which were played for years. In France, at least seventeen were captured.

283 **Ian Fleming would have known:** Fleming would certainly have known about SOE as a naval intelligence officer, but his role would not have required agent training. It is often repeated that Fleming got agent training at an SOE Special Training School, yet no contemporary evidence of this survives.

283 **"Its greatest victory":** Lord Tedder, in Vomécourt, *Who Lived to See the Day,* 13.

283 **But General Eisenhower:** Foot, *SOE in France,* ebook. The French Resistance "had been of inestimable value in the campaign. They were particularly active in Brittany, but on every portion of the front we secured help from them in a multitude of ways. Without their great assistance the liberation of France and the defeat of the enemy in Western Europe would have consumed a much longer time and meant greater losses to ourselves." Dwight D. Eisenhower, *Crusade in Europe* (Garden City, N.Y.: Doubleday, 1948), 296.

284 **"The Republic has never ceased":** De Gaulle, reportedly spoken from the Hôtel de Ville on the liberation of Paris, quoted everywhere. See Thomas R. Christofferson and Michael S. Christofferson, *France During World War II: From Defeat to Liberation* (New York: Fordham University Press, 2006), ebook.

284 **When France tallied its maquis forces:** Gildea, *Fighters in the Shadows,* ebook.

284 **In order to canonize:** Toward this end, the battalions of black African soldiers were also written out of de Gaulle's mythmaking and not allowed to march beside him in the liberation of Paris while cameras were rolling.

284 **Traditional feminine frailty:** The sexism in the origin myth of the Fourth Republic is emotionally overdetermined. It was said that France was emasculated by Germany. In this vein, homosexuality was also a popular explanatory metaphor: Pétain "bottomed" Hitler's "top."

284 **Women were not yet:** Citizenship and military service have become inextricably linked in the modern mind; denying women's combat roles suggests a denial of women's full citizenship status.

284 **Frenchwomen didn't even get the vote:** A two-hundred-year-old law forbidding Frenchwomen to wear trousers was not repealed until 2013.

285 **So France freed itself:** "Gen. de Gaulle Enters Paris," *Times* (London), Aug. 26, 1944.

285 **"extremely touchy":** SPU 24 Paris Interrogation of Returned Agents, HS 6/439, National Archives, Kew.

AUTHOR'S NOTE

287 **"romantic twaddle":** "Most accounts of wartime SOE agents, particularly women and especially in France, contain large doses of romantic twaddle," according to Max Hastings, in *The Secret War: Spies, Codes, and Guerrillas* (London: William Collins, 2015). Hastings is an extraordinary historian upon whose scholarship I have often relied, but I suggest this posture is an example of a prevailing attitude within the community of World War II researchers.

288 **"*Tant pis,* it had to be told":** Buckmaster, *Specially Employed,* 148.

Bibliography

MEMOIRS AND CONTEMPORARY ACCOUNTS

Albert-Lake, Virginia d'. *An American Heroine in the French Resistance: The Diary and Memoir of Virginia d'Albert-Lake*. Edited by Judy Barrett Litoff. New York: Fordham University Press, 2006.

Amicale de Ravensbrück and Association des Déportées et Internées de la Résistance. *Les Françaises à Ravensbrück*. Paris: Gallimard, 1965.

Aubrac, Lucie. *Outwitting the Gestapo*. Lincoln: University of Nebraska Press, 1994.

Bailey, Roderick, ed. *Forgotten Voices of the Secret War: An Inside History of Special Operations During the Second World War in Association with the Imperial War Museum*. London: Ebury Press, 2008.

Bleicher, Hugo. *Colonel Henri's Story*. London: Kimber, 1954.

Bourne-Patterson, Robert. *SOE in France, 1941–1945: An Official Account of the Special Operations Executive's French Circuits*. Barnsley, U.K.: Frontline Books, 2016.

Bradley, Omar N. *A Soldier's Story*. New York: Henry Holt, 1951.

Buckmaster, Maurice. "Prosper," *Chambers's Journal*, Jan. 1947.

———. *Specially Employed*. London: Batchworth, 1952.

———. *They Fought Alone: The Story of British Agents in France*. London: Biteback, 2014. First published in 1958 by Odhams Press.

———. *They Went by Parachute*. Reprinted online by Steven Kippax, 2011, from a series of eight articles published in *Chambers's Journal*, 1946–1947.

Bureau, Jacques. *Un soldat menteur*. Paris: Laffont, 1992.

Burney, Christopher. *Solitary Confinement*. London: Macmillan, 1951.

Carré, Mathilde-Lily. *I Was the Cat*. London: Four Square, 1961.

Chevrillon, Claire. *Code Name Christiane Clouet: A Woman in the French Resistance.* College Station: Texas A&M University Press, 1995.

Churchill, Peter. *Duel of Wits.* New York: G. P. Putnam's Sons, 1955. Combining British editions of *Duel of Wits* and *Of Their Own Choice.*

———. *Of Their Own Choice.* London: Hodder & Stoughton, 1953.

———. *Spirit in the Cage.* New York: G. P. Putnam's Sons, 1955.

Churchill, Winston. *The Second World War.* 6 vols. Boston: Houghton Mifflin, 1948–1953.

Gathering Storm
Their Finest Hour
The Grand Alliance
The Hinge of Fate
Closing the Ring
Triumph and Tragedy

Coleville, John. *The Fringes of Power: 10 Downing Street Diaries, 1939–1955.* New York: Norton, 1985.

Cornioley, Pearl Witherington. *Code Name Pauline: Memoirs of a World War II Special Agent.* Chicago: Chicago Review Press, 2013.

Cowburn, Benjamin. *No Cloak, No Dagger.* London: Frontline, 2009.

Crémieux-Brilhac, Jean-Louis, ed. *Ici Londres, 1940–1944: Les voix de la liberté.* 5 vols. Paris: Documentation Français, 1975.

Crosswell, D. K. R. *Beetle: The Life of General Walter Bedell Smith.* Lexington: University Press of Kentucky, 2010.

Dalton, Hugh. *The Fateful Years.* London: Muller, 1957.

de Gaulle, Charles. *The Complete War Memoirs of Charles de Gaulle.* Translated by Jonathan Griffin and Richard Howard. New York: Carroll and Graf, 1998.

de Gaulle-Anthonioz, Geneviève. *God Remained Outside: An Echo of Ravensbrück.* New York: Arcade, 1998.

Dodds-Parker, Douglas. *Setting Europe Ablaze.* Windlesham, U.K.: Springwood Books, 1983.

Dourlein, Pieter. *Inside North Pole.* Translated by F. G. Renier and Anne Cliff. London: Kimber, 1953.

Dreux, William. *No Bridges Blown.* Notre Dame, Ind.: University of Notre Dame Press, 1971.

Drummond-Hay, Peggy. *The Driving Force: Memoirs of Wartime WAAF Drivers 1665 HCU and 81 OTU.* Lewes, U.K.: Book Guild, 2005.

Dufournier, Denise. *Ravensbrück: The Women's Camp of Death.* London: George Allen & Unwin, 1948.

Eisenhower, Dwight D. *Crusade in Europe.* Garden City, N.Y.: Doubleday, 1948.

Fairbairn, William E. *All-In Fighting.* London: Faber and Faber, 1942. Reprint, Naval and Military Press in association with the Royal Armouries, 2009.

Fermor, Patrick Leigh. *Abducting a General: The Kreipe Operation in Crete.* London: John Murray, 2014.

Garby-Czerniawski, Roman. *The Big Network*. London: George Ronald, 1961.

Girard, André. *Bataille secrète en France*. Paris: Brentano's, 1944.

Giskes, H. J. *London Calling North Pole*. New York: British Book Centre, 1953.

Goldsmith, John. *Accidental Agent*. London: Leo Cooper, 1971.

Guéhenno, Jean. *Diary of the Dark Years, 1940–1944: Collaboration, Resistance, and Daily Life in Occupied Paris*. Translated by David Ball. New York: Oxford University Press, 2016.

Hart, B. H. Liddell. *The German Generals Talk: Startling Revelations from Hitler's High Command*. New York: Quill, 1979.

Harvie, John D. *Missing in Action: An RCAF Navigator's Story*. Montreal: McGill-Queen's University Press, 1995.

Hillary, Richard. *The Last Enemy*. London: Macmillan, 1942.

Humbert, Agnès. *Résistance: A Woman's Journal of Struggle and Defiance in Occupied France*. New York: Bloomsbury, 2008.

Inkster, Marjorie. *Bow and Arrow War: From FANY to Radar in World War II*. Studley, U.K.: Brewin Books, 2005.

Kerr, Dorothy Brewer. *The Girls Behind the Guns: With the ATS in World War II*. London: Robert Hale, 1990.

Khan, Noor Inayat. *Twenty Jātaka Tales*. Rochester, Vt.: Inner Traditions International, 1985.

Lanckoronska, Karolina. *Michelangelo in Ravensbrück: One Woman's War Against the Nazis*. Translated by Noel Clark. Cambridge, Mass.: Da Capo Press, 2007.

Langelaan, George. *Knights of the Floating Silk*. London: Hutchinson, 1959.

Le Chene, Evelyn. *Watch for Me by Moonlight*. London: Corgi, 1974.

Mackenzie, William. *The Secret History of SOE: Special Operations Executive, 1940–1945*. London: St. Ermin's Press, 2000.

Marks, Leo. *Between Silk and Cyanide: A Codemaker's Story, 1941–1945*. New York: HarperCollins, 1998.

Millar, George. *Maquis*. London: Heinemann, 1945.

———. *Road to Resistance*. London: Bodley Head, 1979.

Miller, Joan. *One Girl's War: Personal Exploits in MI5's Most Secret Station*. Dingle, Ire.: Brandon, 1986.

Montgomery, Bernard. *The Memoirs of Field Marshal Montgomery*. Barnsley, U.K.: Pen & Sword, 2016.

Neave, Airey. *Saturday at M.I.9*. London: Pen & Sword Military, 2010.

Osmont, Marie-Louise. *The Normandy Diary of Marie-Louise Osmont, 1940–1944*. Translated by George L. Newman. New York: Random House/Discovery Channel Press, 1994.

Pessis, Jacques, ed. *Les Français parlent aux Français*. 3 vols. With historical commentary by Jean-Louis Crémieux-Brilhac. Paris: Omnibus, 2010.

Pickersgill, Frank. *The Pickersgill Letters*. Toronto: Ryerson Press, 1948.

Pogue, Forrest C. *Pogue's War: Diaries of a WWII Combat Historian*. Lexington: University Press of Kentucky, 2001.

———. *United States Army in World War II: European Theater of Operations: The Supreme Command.* Washington, D.C.: Office of the Chief of Military History, Department of the Army, 1954.

Poirier, Jacques R. E. *The Giraffe Has a Long Neck.* Translated by John Brownjohn. Barnsley, U.K.: Pen & Sword, 1995.

Rigden, Denis. *SOE Syllabus: Lessons in Ungentlemanly Warfare, World War II.* Richmond, U.K.: Secret History Files, National Archives, 2001.

Riols, Noreen. *The Secret Ministry of Ag. & Fish: My Life in Churchill's School for Spies.* London: Macmillan, 2013.

Sweet-Escott, Bickham. *Baker Street Irregular.* London: Methuen, 1965.

Tickell, Jerrard. *Odette: The Story of a British Agent.* 1949. London: Chapman & Hall, 1952.

Verity, Hugh. *We Landed by Moonlight: Secret RAF Landings in France, 1940–1944.* London: Crécy, 2013.

Vomécourt, Philippe de. *Who Lived to See the Day: France in Arms, 1940–1945.* London: Hutchinson, 1961.

Wake, Nancy. *The Autobiography of the Woman the Gestapo Called the White Mouse.* South Melbourne: Macmillan, 1985.

Walters, Anne-Marie. *Moondrop to Gascony.* 1947. Reprint, Wiltshire, U.K.: Moho Books, 2009.

Webb, A. M., ed. *The Natzweiler Trial.* London: Hodge, 1949.

West, Nigel, ed. *The Guy Liddell Diaries: MI5's Director of Counter-Espionage in World War II.* Vol. 1, *1939–1942.* London: Routledge, 2005.

Wighton, Charles. *Pin-Stripe Saboteur: The Story of "Robin," British Agent and French Resistance Leader.* London: Odhams, 1959.

Winter, Paul, ed. *D-Day Documents.* London: Bloomsbury, 2014.

Zucca, André. *Les Parisiens sous l'Occupation: Photographies en couleurs d'André Zucca.* Paris: Gallimard, 2000.

HISTORIES, SOE

Basu, Shrabani. *Spy Princess: The Life of Noor Inayat Khan.* London: Sutton, 2006.

Beavan, Colin. *Operation Jedburgh: D-Day and America's First Shadow War.* New York: Penguin Books, 2007.

Binney, Marcus. *The Women Who Lived for Danger.* London: Morrow, 2003.

Brome, Vincent. *The Way Back.* London: Cassell, 1957.

Cookridge, E. H. *Inside S.O.E.: The First Full Story of Special Operations Executive in Western Europe, 1940–45.* London: Arthur Barker, 1966.

Cunningham, Cyril. *Beaulieu: The Finishing School for Secret Agents.* South Yorkshire, U.K.: Pen & Sword Military, 2005.

Foot, M. R. D. *SOE: An Outline History of the Special Operations Executive, 1940–46.* London: British Broadcasting Corporation, 1984.

———. *SOE in France: An Account of the Work of the British Special Operations Executive in France, 1940–1944*. London: Frank Cass, 2004.

Fuller, Jean Overton. *Déricourt: The Chequered Spy*. London: Michael Russell, 1989.

———. *Double Agent?* London: Pan Books, 1961.

———. *Double Webs*. London: Putnam, 1958.

———. *Espionage as a Fine Art by Henri Déricourt*. Translated from (previously unpublished) French original stories with an introduction and commentary. London: Michael Russell, 2002.

———. *The German Penetration of SOE*. London: George Mann, 1996.

———. *Horoscope for a Double Agent*. London: Fowler, 1961.

———. *Noor-un-nisa Inayat Khan (Madeleine)*. Rotterdam: East-West Publications; London: Barrie & Jenkins, 1971.

———. *The Starr Affair*. London: Victor Gollancz, 1954.

Gleeson, James. *They Feared No Evil: The Stories of the Gallant and Courageous Women Agents of Britain's Secret Armies, 1939–45*. London: Robert Hale, 1976.

Guillaume, Paul. *L'abbé Émile Pasty, prêtre et soldat*. Baule, France: Comité Abbé Pasty, 1946.

———. *Les martyrs de la Résistance en Sologne*. Orléans, France: Lodde, 1945.

———. *La Sologne au temps de l'héroïsme et de la trahison*. Orléans, France: Imprimerie Nouvelle, 1950.

Helm, Sara. *A Life in Secrets: Vera Atkins and the Missing Agents of WWII*. New York: Anchor Books, 2007.

Irwin, Will. *The Jedburghs: The Secret History of the Allied Special Forces, France 1944*. New York: PublicAffairs, 2006.

Jakub, Jay. *Spies and Saboteurs: Anglo-American Collaboration and Rivalry in Human Intelligence Collection and Special Operations, 1940–1945*. London: Palgrave Macmillan, 1999.

Jones, Liane. *A Quiet Courage: Heart-Stopping Accounts of Those Brave Women Agents Who Risked Their Lives in Nazi-Occupied France*. London: Corgi Books, 1990.

King, Stella. *Jacqueline: Pioneer Heroine of the Resistance*. London: Arms and Armour Press, 1989.

Kramer, Rita. *Flames in the Field*. London: Michael Joseph, 1995.

Lorain, Pierre. *Secret Warfare: The Arms and Techniques of the Resistance*. Adapted by David Kahn. London: Orbis, 1983.

Maloubier, Bob, and Jean Lartéguy. *Triple jeu: L'espion Déricourt*. Paris: Robert Laffont, 1992.

Marshall, Bruce. *The White Rabbit*. London: Evans, 1952.

Marshall, Robert. *All the King's Men*. London: Bloomsbury, 2012.

McCue, Paul. *Brighton's Secret Agents: The Brighton and Hove Contribution to Britain's WW2 Special Operations Executive*. Chicago: Uniform Press, 2017.

Nicholas, Elizabeth. *Death Be Not Proud*. London: Cresset Press, 1958.

Ottaway, Susan. *A Cool and Lonely Courage: The Untold Story of Sister Spies in Occupied France*. New York: Little, Brown, 2014.

Pattinson, Juliette. *Behind Enemy Lines: Gender, Passing, and the Special Operations Executive in the Second World War*. Manchester, U.K.: University of Manchester Press, 2007.

Rabino, Thomas. *Le réseau Carte*. Paris: Perrin, 2008.

Richards, Brooks. *Secret Flotillas*. London: Her Majesty's Stationery Office, 1996.

Seaman, Mark. *Bravest of the Brave: The True Story of Wing Commander "Tommy" Yeo-Thomas, SOE Secret Agent, Codename "the White Rabbit."* London: Michael O'Mara Books, 1997.

———. *Secret Agent's Handbook of Special Devices*. Richmond, U.K.: PRO, 2000.

———. *Special Operations Executive: A New Instrument of War*. London: Routledge, 2006.

Seymour-Jones, Carole. *She Landed by Moonlight: The Story of Secret Agent Pearl Witherington, the Real "Charlotte Gray."* London: Hodder & Stoughton, 2013.

Stafford, David. *Secret Agent: The True Story of the Special Operations Executive*. London: BBC, 2000.

———. *Ten Days to D-Day: Countdown to Liberation of Europe*. London: Abacus, 2004.

Starns, Penny. *Odette: World War Two's Darling Spy*. London: History Press, 2010.

Stenton, Michael. *Radio London and Resistance in Occupied Europe: British Political Warfare, 1939–1943*. Oxford Scholarship Online, 2011.

Suttill, Francis J. *Shadows in the Fog: The True Story of Major Suttill and the Prosper French Resistance Network*. Stroud, U.K.: History Press, 2017.

Téllez Solá, Antonio. *The Anarchist Pimpernel: Francisco Ponzán Vidal: The Anarchists in the Spanish Civil War and the Allied Escape Networks of WWII*. Translated by Paul Sharkey. Hastings, U.K.: ChristieBooks, 2012.

Tickell, Jerrard. *Moon Squadron*. London: Endeavour Media, 2013.

Vader, John. *The Prosper Double-Cross*. Mullimbimby, Australia: Sunrise Press, 1977.

Waller, Douglas. *Wild Bill Donovan: The Spymaster Who Created the OSS and Modern American Espionage*. New York: Free Press, 2012.

Ward, Irene. *F.A.N.Y. Invicta*. London: Hutchinson, 1955.

West, Nigel. *Secret War: The Story of SOE, Britain's Wartime Sabotage Organization*. London: Hodder & Stoughton, 1992.

Wilkinson, Peter, and Joan Bright Astley. *Gubbins and SOE*. Barnsley, U.K.: Pen & Sword Military, 2010.

Wylie, Neville. *The Politics and Strategy of Clandestine War: Special Operations Executive, 1940–1946*. London: Routledge, 2007.

Yarnold, Patrick. *Wanborough Manor: School for Secret Agents*. Puttenham, U.K.: Hopfield, 2009.

HISTORIES, FRANCE

Adams, Christine. *Poverty, Charity, and Motherhood: Maternal Societies in Nineteenth-Century France*. Urbana: University of Illinois Press, 2010.

Ambrose, Stephen. *D-Day, June 6, 1944: The Climactic Battle of World War II*. New York: Simon & Schuster, 1993.

Aron, Robert. *The Vichy Regime, 1940–1944*. London: Putnam, 1958.

Atkin, Nicholas. *The Forgotten French: Exiles in the British Isles, 1940–1944*. Manchester, U.K.: Manchester University Press, 2003.

Beevor, Antony. *D-Day: The Battle for Normandy*. New York: Viking, 2009.

Boyd, Douglas. *Voices from the Dark Years: The Truth About Occupied France, 1940–1945*. London: Sutton, 2007.

Burrin, Philippe. *France Under the Germans: Collaboration and Compromise*. New York: New Press, 1996.

Caron, Vicki. *Uneasy Asylum: France and the Jewish Refugee Crisis, 1933–1942*. Stanford, Calif.: Stanford University Press, 1999.

Cobb, Matthew. *The Resistance: The French Fight Against the Nazis*. London: Simon & Schuster, 2009.

Collins, Larry, and Dominique Lapierre. *Is Paris Burning?* New York: Warner Books, 1991.

Collins Weitz, Margaret. *Sisters in the Resistance: How Women Fought to Free France, 1940–45*. New York: Wiley, 1995.

Davies, Peter. *France and the Second World War: Occupation, Collaboration, and Resistance*. London: Routledge, 2001.

Diamond, Hanna. *Fleeing Hitler: France, 1940*. New York: Oxford University Press, 2008.

———. *Women and the Second World War in France, 1939–1948: Choices and Constraints*. London: Routledge, 1999.

Drake, David. *Paris at War, 1939–1944*. Cambridge, Mass.: Harvard University Press, 2015.

Fenby, Jonathan. *France: A Modern History from the Revolution to the War with Terror*. New York: St. Martin's Press, 2016.

———. *The General: Charles de Gaulle and the France He Saved*. New York: Simon & Schuster, 2010.

Fishman, Sarah. *We Will Wait: Wives of French Prisoners of War, 1940–1945*. New Haven, Conn.: Yale University Press, 1991.

Gildea, Robert. *Fighters in the Shadows: A New History of the French Resistance*. Cambridge, Mass.: Belknap Press of Harvard University Press, 2015.

———. *Marianne in Chains: In Search of the German Occupation, 1940–1945*. London: Macmillan, 2002.

Hastings, Max. *Overlord: D-Day and the Battle for Normandy*. New York: Simon & Schuster, 1984.

———. *Das Reich: The March of the 2nd SS Panzer Division Through France, June 1944*. Minneapolis: Zenith Press, 2013.

Jackson, Jeffrey H. *Making Jazz French: Music and Modern Life in Interwar Paris*. Durham, N.C.: Duke University Press, 2003.

Jackson, Julian. *France: The Dark Years, 1940–1944*. Oxford: Oxford University Press, 2001.

Jones, Benjamin. *Eisenhower's Guerrillas: The Jedburghs, the Maquis, and the Liberation of France*. New York: Oxford University Press, 2016.

Kedward, Harry R. *In Search of the Maquis: Rural Resistance in Southern France, 1942–1944*. Oxford: Clarendon Press, 1994.

———. *Occupied France: Collaboration and Resistance, 1940–1944*. London: Wiley-Blackwell, 1991.

———. *Resistance in Vichy France: A Study of Ideas and Motivation in the Southern Zone, 1940–1942*. New York: Oxford University Press, 1978.

Kershaw, Alex. *Avenue of Spies: A True Story of Terror, Espionage, and One American Family's Heroic Resistance in Nazi-Occupied France*. New York: Crown, 2015.

Ludewig, Joachim. *Rückzug: The German Retreat from France, 1944*. Lexington: University Press of Kentucky, 2012.

Man, John. *The D-Day Atlas: The Definitive Account of the Allied Invasion of Normandy*. New York: Facts on File, 1994.

Marnham, Patrick. *Resistance and Betrayal: The Death and Life of the Greatest Hero of the French Resistance*. New York: Random House, 2002.

Marrus, Michael R., and Robert O. Paxton. *Vichy France and the Jews*. New York: Basic Books, 1981.

Mayo, Jonathan. *D-Day Minute by Minute*. New York: Atria Books, 2014.

Messenger, Charles. *The D-Day Atlas: Anatomy of the Normandy Campaign*. New York: Thames and Hudson, 2014.

Michel, Henri. *The Shadow War: European Resistance, 1939–1945*. Translated by Richard Barry. New York: Harper and Row, 1972.

Michlin, Gilbert. *Of No Interest to the Nation: A Jewish Family in France, 1925–1945*. Detroit: Wayne State University Press, 2004.

Milward, Alan S. *The New Order and the French Economy*. Oxford: Clarendon Press, 1970.

Moorehead, Caroline. *A Train in Winter: An Extraordinary Story of Women, Friendship, and Resistance in Occupied France*. New York: HarperCollins, 2011.

———. *Village of Secrets: Defying the Nazis in Vichy France*. New York: HarperCollins, 2014.

Mould, Michael. *The Routledge Dictionary of Cultural References in Modern French*. New York: Routledge, 2011.

Muel-Dreyfus, Francine. *Vichy and the Eternal Feminine: A Contribution to a Political Sociology of Gender*. Translated by Kathleen A. Johnson. Durham, N.C.: Duke University Press, 2001.

Ottis, Sherri Greene. *Silent Heroes: Downed Airmen and the French Underground*. Lexington: University Press of Kentucky, 2001.

Ousby, Ian. *Occupation: The Ordeal of France, 1940–1944*. New York: Cooper Square Press, 1999.

Paxton, Robert. *Vichy France: Old Guard and New Order, 1940–1944*. New York: Columbia University Press, 1972.

Perrault, Gilles, and Jean-Pierre Azéma. *Paris Under the Occupation*. New York: Vendome Press, 1989.

Pollard, Miranda. *Reign of Virtue: Mobilizing Gender in Vichy France*. Chicago: University of Chicago Press, 1998.

Porch, Douglas. *The French Secret Services: A History of French Intelligence from the Dreyfus Affair to the Gulf War*. New York: Farrar, Straus and Giroux, 1995.

Potter, Charles B. *The Resistance, 1940: An Anthology of Writings from the French Underground*. Baton Rouge: Louisiana State University Press, 2016.

Pryce-Jones, David. *Paris in the Third Reich: A History of the German Occupation, 1940–1944*. New York: Holt, Rinehart and Winston, 1981.

Rees, Siân. *Lucie Aubrac: The French Resistance Heroine Who Outwitted the Gestapo*. Chicago: Chicago Review Press, 2016.

Rosbottom, Ronald C. *When Paris Went Dark: The City of Light Under German Occupation, 1940–1944*. New York: Little, Brown, 2014.

Rossiter, Margaret. *Women in the Resistance*. New York: Praeger, 1986.

Rousso, Henry. *The Vichy Syndrome: History and Memory in France Since 1944*. Translated by Arthur Goldhammer. Cambridge, Mass.: Harvard University Press, 1991.

Schoenbrun, David. *Soldiers of the Night: The Story of the French Resistance*. New York: New American Library, 1980.

Shakespeare, Nicholas. *Priscilla: The Hidden Life of an Englishwoman in Wartime France*. New York: HarperCollins, 2014.

Spotts, Frederic. *The Shameful Peace: How French Artists and Intellectuals Survived the Nazi Occupation*. New Haven, Conn.: Yale University Press, 2008.

Sweets, John F. *Choices in Vichy France: The French Under Nazi Occupation*. New York: Oxford University Press, 1994.

Thiébaud, Eric, and Olivier Corpet. *Collaboration and Resistance: French Literary Life Under the Nazi Occupation*. New York: Five Ties, 2010.

Vinen, Richard. *The Unfree French: Life Under the Occupation*. London: Allen Lane, 2006.

Wieviorka, Olivier. *Divided Memory: French Recollections of World War II from the Liberation to the Present*. Translated by George Holoch. Stanford, Calif.: Stanford University Press, 2012.

———. *The French Resistance*. Translated by Jane Marie Todd. Cambridge, Mass.: Harvard University Press, 2016.

Zucotti, Susan. *The Holocaust, the French, and the Jews*. New York: Basic Books, 1993.

HISTORIES, WORLD WAR II

Ambrose, Stephen. *The Supreme Commander: The War Years of General Dwight D. Eisenhower*. New York: Doubleday, 1970.

Bambery, Chris. *The Second World War: A Marxist History*. London: Pluto Press, 2014.

Bassett, Richard. *Hitler's Spy Chief: The Wilhelm Canaris Betrayal: The Intelligence Campaign Against Adolf Hitler*. New York: Pegasus Books, 2013.

Bennett, G. H. "Women and the Battle of the Atlantic, 1939–1945: Contemporary Texts, Propaganda, and Life Writing." In *Gender and Warfare in the Twentieth Century: Textual Representations.* Edited by Angela K. Smith. Manchester, U.K.: Manchester University Press, 2004.

Christofferson, Thomas R., and Michael S. Christofferson. *France During World War II: From Defeat to Liberation.* New York: Fordham University Press, 2006.

Crémieux-Brilhac, Jean-Louis. *La France libre: De l'appel du 18 juin à la Libération.* Paris: Gallimard, 1996.

Donnelly, Mark. *Britain in the Second World War.* London: Routledge, 1999.

Feigel, Lara. *The Love-Charm of Bombs: Restless Lives in the Second World War.* London: Bloomsbury Press, 2013.

Gilbert, Martin. *Churchill: A Life.* New York: Henry Holt, 1991.

———. *Road to Victory: Winston S. Churchill, 1941–1945.* London: Minerva, 1989.

Gluckstein, Donny. *A People's History of the Second World War: Resistance Versus Empire.* London: Pluto Press, 2012.

Gordon, Lois. *Nancy Cunard: Heiress, Muse, Political Idealist.* New York: Columbia University Press, 2007.

Grint, Keith. *Leadership, Management, and Command: Rethinking D-Day.* London: Palgrave Macmillan, 2007.

Hastings, Max. *Inferno: The World at War, 1939–1945.* New York: Vintage, 2012.

———. *The Secret War: Spies, Codes, and Guerrillas, 1939–45.* London: William Collins, 2015.

———. *Winston's War: Churchill, 1940–1945.* New York: Vintage, 2011.

Hauner, Milan. *Hitler: A Chronology of His Life and Time.* London: Macmillan, 1983.

Hellbeck, Jochen, ed. *Stalingrad: The City That Defeated the Third Reich.* New York: PublicAffairs, 2015.

Hinsley, F. H. *British Intelligence in the Second World War.* With E. E. Thomas, C. F. G. Ransom, and R. C. Knight. Vols. 1–3. London: Her Majesty's Stationery Office, 1979.

Hitler, Adolf. *Hitler's Table Talk, 1941–1944.* Translated by Norman Cameron and R. H. Stevens. London: Weidenfeld & Nicolson, 1953.

Keegan, John. *The Second World War.* New York: Penguin Books, 1989.

Kremer, Lillian. *Women's Holocaust Writing: Memory and Imagination.* Lincoln: University of Nebraska Press, 1999.

Larson, Erik. *In the Garden of Beasts: Love, Terror, and an American Family in Hitler's Berlin.* New York: Crown, 2011.

Laska, Vera, ed. *Women in the Resistance and in the Holocaust.* Westport, Conn.: Greenwood Press, 1983.

Lee, Eric. *Operation Basalt: The British Raid on Sark and Hitler's Commando Order.* Stroud, U.K.: History Press, 2016.

Macintyre, Ben. *Agent Zigzag: A True Story of Nazi Espionage, Love, and Betrayal.* New York: Crown, 2007.

———. *Double Cross: The True Story of the D-Day Spies.* New York: Crown, 2012.

———. *Rogue Heroes: The History of the SAS, Britain's Secret Special Forces Unit That Sabotaged the Nazis and Changed the Nature of War.* New York: Crown, 2016.

Manchester, William. *The Last Lion: Winston Spencer Churchill.* New York: Little, Brown, 2012.

Morrison, Jack G. *Ravensbrück: Everyday Life in a Woman's Concentration Camp, 1939–45.* Princeton, N.J.: Markus Wiener, 2000.

Nicholson, Mavis. *What Did You Do in the War, Mummy?* London: Pimlico, 1995.

Noakes, Lucy. *Women in the British Army: War and the Gentle Sex, 1907–1948.* London: Routledge, 2006.

Norman, Jill. *Make Do and Mend: Keeping Family and Home Afloat on War Rations: Reproductions of Official Second World War Instruction Leaflets.* London: Michael O'Mara Books, 2007.

Olson, Lynne. *Last Hope Island: Britain, Occupied Europe, and the Brotherhood That Helped Turn the Tide of War.* New York: Random House, 2017.

Roberts, Andrew. *The Storm of War: A New History of the Second World War.* New York: Harper, 2012.

Shirer, William L. *The Rise and Fall of the Third Reich: A History of Nazi Germany.* New York: Simon & Schuster, 1960.

Summerfield, Penny. *Reconstructing Women's Wartime Lives: Discourse and Subjectivity in Oral Histories of the Second World War.* Manchester, U.K.: Manchester University Press, 1998.

Tec, Nehama. *Resilience and Courage: Women, Men, and the Holocaust.* New Haven, Conn.: Yale University Press, 2003.

Westerfield, L. Leigh. *"This Anguish, Like a Kind of Intimate Song": Resistance in Women's Literature of World War II.* New York: Rodopi, 2004.

Wood, Ian. *Britain, Ireland, and the Second World War.* Edinburgh: Edinburgh University Press, 2010.

Zeiger, Susan. *Entangling Alliances: Foreign War Brides and American Soldiers in the Twentieth Century.* New York: New York University Press, 2010.

OTHER WORKS CONSULTED

Abernethy, David B. *The Dynamics of Global Dominance: European Overseas Empires, 1415–1980.* New Haven, Conn.: Yale University Press, 2000.

Axinn, Sidney. *A Moral Military.* Philadelphia: Temple University Press, 2009.

Blaetz, Robin. *Visions of the Maid: Joan of Arc in American Film and Culture.* Charlottesville: University of Virginia Press, 2001.

Churchill, Winston. June 16, 1940, Great Britain, Parliament, *Parliamentary Debates,* 5th Series, vol. 365. *House of Commons Official Report Eleventh Volume of Session 1939–40* (London: His Majesty's Stationery Office, 1940), cols. 701–2.

Dewaele, Jean-Marc. "Pavlenko, Aneta Multilingualism, and Emotions." In *The Encyclopedia of Applied Linguistics,* edited by Carol A. Chapelle, 1–7. Oxford: Wiley-Blackwell, 2013.

Goldstein, Joshua S. *War and Gender: How Gender Shapes the War System and Vice Versa*. Cambridge, U.K.: Cambridge University Press, 2001.

Gordon, Lois. *The World of Samuel Beckett, 1906–1946*. New Haven, Conn.: Yale University Press, 1996.

Macrakis, Kristie. *Prisoners, Lovers, and Spies: The Story of Invisible Ink from Herodotus to al-Qaeda*. New Haven, Conn.: Yale University Press, 2014.

Moran, Christopher R., and Christopher J. Murphy, eds. *Intelligence Studies in Britain and the US: Historiography Since 1945*. Edinburgh: Edinburgh University Press, 2013.

Rejali, Darius. *Torture and Democracy*. Princeton, N.J.: Princeton University Press, 2007.

Singh, Simon. *The Code Book: The Science of Secrecy from Ancient Egypt to Quantum Cryptology*. New York: Anchor Books, 2000.

Soloway, Richard A. *Demography and Degeneration: Eugenics and the Declining Birthrate in Twentieth-Century Britain*. Chapel Hill: University of North Carolina Press, 1995.

Suisman, David, and Susan Strasser, eds. *Sound in the Age of Mechanical Reproduction*. Philadelphia: University of Pennsylvania Press, 2010.

Wistrich, Robert S. *A Lethal Obsession: Anti-Semitism from Antiquity to the Global Jihad*. New York: Random House, 2010.

ARTICLES

Adler, Jacques. "The Jews and Vichy: Reflections on French Historiography." *Historical Journal* 44, no. 4 (2001).

Aldrich, Richard J. "Policing the Past: Official History, Secrecy, and British Intelligence Since 1945." *English Historical Review* 119, no. 483 (2004): 922–53.

Almond, Harry H., Jr., Donald Blackburn, James Ward, W. T. Mallison, and R. W. Gehring. "Irregular Warfare: Legal Implications of the Facts, Policies, and Law from World War II to Vietnam." *Proceedings of the Annual Meeting (American Society of International Law)* 70 (1976): 154–59.

Ambrose, Stephen. "Eisenhower and the Intelligence Community in World War II." *Journal of Contemporary History* 16, no. 1 (1981).

Andrieu, Claire. "Women in the French Resistance: Revisiting the Historical Record." *French Politics, Culture, and Society* 18, no. 1 (Spring 2000).

Anfilogoff, R., P. J. Hale, M. Nattrass, V. A. Hammond, and J. C. Carter. "Physiological Response to Parachute Jumping." *British Medical Journal* 295, no. 6595 (1987): 415.

Belot, Robert. "Intelligence Considered as a War Weapon and a Global Power Tool: About the Birth of US Secret Services (1942–1945)." *Icon* 8 (2002).

Ben-Mos, T. "Winston Churchill and the 'Second Front': A Reappraisal." *Journal of Modern History* 62, no. 3 (1990): 503.

Benson, Robert Louis. "SIGINT and the Holocaust." *Cryptologic Quarterly*, www.nsa.gov, released by FOIA 2010.

Boldorf, Michael, and Jonas Scherner. "France's Occupation Costs and the War in the East: The Contribution to the German War Economy, 1940–4." *Journal of Contemporary History* 47, no. 2 (2012).

Bonnéry-Vedel, Audrey. "La BBC a-t-elle jamais été la voix de la France libre?" *Le Temps des Médias,* no. 11 (2008).

Bowles, Brett. "German Newsreel Propaganda in France, 1940–1944." *Historical Journal of Film, Radio, and Television* 24, no. 1 (2004): 45–67.

———. "Résistance Oblige? Historiography, Memory, and the Evolution of *Le silence de la mer,* 1942–2012." *French Politics, Culture, and Society* 32, no. 1 (Spring 2014).

———. "'La Tragédie de Mers-el-Kébir' and the Politics of Filmed News in France, 1940–1944." *Journal of Modern History* 76, no. 2 (2004): 347–88.

———. "*Vichy's Afterlife: History and Counterhistory in Postwar France* by Richard J. Golsan; *The Papon Affair: Memory and Justice on Trial* by Richard J. Golsan." *SubStance* 31, no. 1 (2002): 125–28.

Bracher, Nathan. "Remembering the French Resistance: Ethics and Poetics of the Epic." *History and Memory* 19, no. 1 (2007).

Campbell, D'Ann. "Women in Combat: The World War II Experience in the United States, Great Britain, Germany, and the Soviet Union." *Journal of Military History* 57, no. 2 (April 1993): 301–23.

———. "Women in Uniform: The World War II Experiment." *Military Affairs* 51, no. 3 (1987): 137–39.

Card, Claudia. "Rape as a Weapon of War." *Hypatia* 11, no. 4 (1996).

Caron, Vicki. "The Politics of Frustration: French Jewry and the Refugee Crisis in the 1930s." *Journal of Modern History* 65, no. 2 (1993): 311–56.

Carter, Ross S. "How Tranquil the Desert." *Prairie Schooner* 22, no. 1 (1948): 57–61.

Cassin, René. "Vichy or Free France?" *Foreign Affairs* 20, no. 1 (1941).

Charney, David L., and John A. Irvin. "The Psychology of Espionage." *Intelligencer: Journal of U.S. Intelligence Studies* 22, no. 1 (Spring 2016).

"Darlan and After: The Significance of North Africa." *Commonwealth Journal of International Affairs* 33, no. 130 (1943).

de Jong, Louis. "The 'Great Game' of Secret Agents: Was It 'Treason'—or Sheer Incompetence—Which Enabled the Ingenious German 'Englandspiel' to Cripple Resistance Forces in World War II? A Dutch Historian Investigates the Charges." *Encounter Magazine,* Jan. 1980.

Deutsch, Harold C. "The Historical Impact of Revealing the Ultra Secret." Reprinted, with permission from *Parameters: Journal of the U.S. Army War College,* approved for release by NSA on Oct. 26, 2006, FOIA case no. 51639.

Donohoe, Jerri. "The Kindness of Strangers: An Ohioan Escapes the Nazis' Timeline." Ohio Historical Society, Oct.–Dec. 2007.

Drapac, Vesna. "The Devotion of French Prisoners of War and Requisitioned Workers to Thérèse of Lisieux: Transcending the 'Diocese Behind Barbed Wire.'" *Journal of War and Culture Studies* 7, no. 3 (2014): 283–96.

Events Leading Up to World War II: Chronological History of Certain Major International Events Leading Up to and During World War II with the Ostensible

Reasons Advanced for Their Occurrence, 1931–1944. Washington, D.C.: U.S. Government Printing Office, 1944.

Feil, Alison. "Gendering the War Story." *Journal of War and Culture Studies* 1, no. 1 (2008).

Fette, Julie. "Apology and the Past in Contemporary France." *French Politics, Culture, and Society* 26, no. 2 (Summer 2008).

Fielding, Raymond. "The Nazi-German Newsreel." *Journal of the University Film Producers Association* 12, no. 3 (Spring 1960): 3–5.

Fieseler, Beate, M. Michaela Hampf, and Jutta Schwarzkopf. "Gendering Combat: Military Women's Status in Britain, the United States, and the Soviet Union During the Second World War." *Women's Studies International Forum* 47, Part A (Nov.–Dec. 2014).

Flanner, Janet. "Blitz by Partnership." A Reporter at Large. *New Yorker,* June 7, 1941.

———. "Come Down, Giuseppe!" A Reporter at Large. *New Yorker,* Jan. 17, 1942.

———. "The Escape of Mrs. Jeffries—I." A Reporter at Large. *New Yorker,* May 22, 1943.

———. "The Escape of Mrs. Jeffries—II." A Reporter at Large. *New Yorker,* May 29, 1943.

———. "The Escape of Mrs. Jeffries—III." A Reporter at Large. *New Yorker,* June 5, 1943.

———. "Ferox, Mendax, AC Praedator." A Reporter at Large. *New Yorker,* Aug. 1, 1942.

———. "La France et le Vieux: I—From the Empress Eugenie to the A.E.F." Profiles. *New Yorker,* Feb. 12, 1944.

———. "La France et le Vieux: II—Hero of Verdun." Profiles. *New Yorker,* Feb. 19, 1944.

———. "La France et le Vieux: IV—Marechal, Nous Voila!" Profiles. *New Yorker,* March 4, 1944.

———. "Führer—I." Profiles. *New Yorker,* Feb. 29, 1936.

———. "Guinea Pigs and the Mona Lisa." A Reporter at Large. *New Yorker,* Oct. 31, 1942.

———. "Ladies in Uniform." Profiles. *New Yorker,* July 4, 1942.

———. "Le Nouvel Ordre." A Reporter at Large. *New Yorker,* March 15, 1941.

———. "So You're Going to Paris." A Reporter at Large. *New Yorker,* June 21, 1941.

Foot, Michael R. D. "Was SOE Any Good?" *Journal of Contemporary History* 16, no. 1 (1981): 167–81.

Fox, Jo. "Careless Talk: Tensions Within British Domestic Propaganda During the Second World War." *Journal of British Studies* 51, no. 4 (2012): 936–66.

Fuchs, Rachel G. "Crossing Borders in Love, War, and History: French Families During World War II." *Pacific Historical Review* 79, no. 1 (Feb. 2010): 1–22.

Gildea, Robert. "Resistance, Reprisals, and Community in Occupied France." *Transactions of the Royal Historical Society* 13 (2003): 163–85.

Glantz, David. "Soviet Use of 'Substandard' Manpower in the Red Army, 1941–1945." In *Scraping the Barrel: The Military Use of Substandard Manpower, 1860–1960.* Edited by Sanders Marble. New York: Fordham University Press, 2012.

Goldin, Claudia. "The Role of World War II in the Rise of Women's Employment." *American Economic Review* 81 no. 4 (1991).

Goldin, Claudia, and Claudia Olivetti. "Shocking Labor Supply: A Reassessment of the Role of World War II on Women's Labor Supply." *American Economic Review* 103, no. 3 (2013): 257–62.

Gregory, Derwin. "Communicating with the European Resistance: An Assessment of the Special Operations Executive's Wireless Facilities in the UK During the Second World War." *Post-medieval Archaeology* 50, no. 2 (2016): 289–304.

Hacker, Barton C. "Engineering a New Order: Military Institutions, Technical Education, and the Rise of the Industrial State." *Technology and Culture* 34, no. 1 (Jan. 1993): 1–27.

Hale, Oron J. "World War II Documents and Interrogations." *Social Science* 47, no. 2 (1972).

Hanna, Martha. "Iconology and Ideology: Images of Joan of Arc in the Idiom of the Action Française, 1908–1931." *French Historical Studies* 14, no. 2 (1985).

Hanyok, Robert J. "Eavesdropping on Hell: Historical Guide to Western Communications Intelligence and the Holocaust, 1939–1945." Center for Cryptologic History, National Security Agency, 2005.

Harding, James M. "You Forgot Your Double Security Check." *Performance Research* 17, no. 3 (2012): 76–82.

Hawker, Pat. "John Brown and His S.O.E. Radios." *Bulletin of the Vintage British Wireless Society* 18, no. 1 (Feb. 1993).

Ho Davies, Peter. "Think of England." *Ploughshares* 26, nos. 2/3 (2000).

Hoffmann, Kay. "Propagandistic Problems of German Newsreels in World War II." *Historical Journal of Film, Radio, and Television* 24, no. 1 (2004): 133–42.

Horowitz, Milton W. "The Psychology of Confession." *Journal of Criminal Law, Criminology, and Police Science* 47, no. 2 (July–Aug. 1956): 197–204.

Jackson, Julian. "The Republic and Vichy." In *The French Republic: History, Values, Debates.* Edited by Edward Berenson, Vincent Duclert, and Christophe Prochasson. Ithaca, N.Y.: Cornell University Press, 2011.

Jeffords, Susan. "Performative Masculinities, or, 'After a Few Times You Won't Be Afraid of Rape at All.'" *Discourse* 13, no. 2 (Spring–Summer 1991): 102–18.

Johnson, William R. "Clandestinity and Current Intelligence." In *Inside CIA's Private World: Declassified Articles from the Agency's Internal Journal, 1955–1992.* Edited by H. Bradford Westerfield. New Haven, Conn.: Yale University Press, 1995.

Jones, Benjamin F. "Freeing France: The Allies, the Resistance, and the Jedburghs." Master's thesis, University of Kansas, 2008.

Judt, Tony. "In the Light of Experience: The 'Lessons' of Defeat and Occupation." In *Past Imperfect: French Intellectuals, 1944–1956*. New York: New York University Press, 2011.

"Jumping for Joy." *British Medical Journal* 2, no. 5511 (1966): 423–24.

Kedward, H. R. "Mapping the Resistance: An Essay on Roots and Routes." *Modern and Contemporary France* 20, no. 4 (2012).

———. "Patriots and Patriotism in Vichy France." *Transactions of the Royal Society* 32 (1982).

Kehoe, Robert R. "1944: An Allied Team with the French Resistance." www.cia .gov, 1997.

Kuisel, Richard F. "The Legend of the Vichy Synarchy." *French Historical Studies* 6, no. 3 (1970).

Lear, Allison. "Report on Suzanne Kyrie-Pope, an ISTD Employee." WW2 People's War: An Archive of World War Two Memories. BBC, 2005.

Lee, Janet. "FANY (First Aid Nursing Yeomanry) 'Other Spaces': Toward an Application of Foucault's Heterotopias as Alternate Spaces of Social Ordering." *Gender, Place, and Culture* 16, no. 6 (2009).

———. " 'I Wish My Mother Could See Me Now': The First Aid Nursing Yeomanry (FANY) and Negotiation of Gender and Class Relations, 1907–1918." *NWSA Journal* 19, no. 2 (Summer 2007): 138–58.

Lewis, S. J. "Jedburgh Team Operations in Support of the 12th Army Group, August 1944." U.S. Army Command and General Staff College, Fort Leavenworth, Kans., 1991.

Liebling, A. J. "Cross-Channel Trip." A Reporter at Large. *New Yorker,* July 1, 1944.

———. "Cross-Channel Trip—II." A Reporter at Large. *New Yorker,* July 8, 1944.

———. "Cross-Channel Trip—III." A Reporter at Large. *New Yorker,* July 15, 1944.

———. "Gloomy Meadow." A Reporter in France. *New Yorker,* June 15, 1940.

———. Letter from France. *New Yorker,* July 22, 1944.

———. Letter from France. *New Yorker,* July 29, 1944.

———. Letter from France. *New Yorker,* Aug. 26, 1944.

———. Letter from Paris. *New Yorker,* Sept. 23, 1944.

———. Letter from Paris. *New Yorker,* Sept. 30, 1944.

———. "Paris Postscript—I." A Reporter at Large. *New Yorker,* Aug. 3, 1940.

———. "Paris Postscript—II." A Reporter at Large. *New Yorker,* Aug. 10, 1940.

———. "Revisited: Normandy: The Chatelaine of Vouilly." Our Far-Flung Correspondents. *New Yorker,* Oct. 15, 1955.

Limore, Yagil. "Rescue of Jews: Between History and Memory." *Humboldt Journal of Social Relations* 28, no. 2 (2004): 105–38.

Lukacs, John. "The Importance of Being Winston." *National Interest,* Dec. 16, 2010.

Maddrell, Avril. "The 'Map Girls': British Women Geographers' War Work, Shifting Gender Boundaries, and Reflections on the History of Geography." *Transactions of the Institute of British Geographers,* n.s., 33, no. 1 (2007).

Martin, Judith. "Pippa's War." *New Zealand Army News,* July 21, 2009.

McDonagh, Eileen. "Political Citizenship and Democratization: The Gender Paradox." *American Political Science Review* 96, no. 3 (2002).

Michaels, Paula A. "Comrades in the Labor Room: The Lamaze Method of Childbirth Preparation and France's Cold War Home Front, 1951–1957." *American Historical Review* 115, no. 4 (2010).

Mitchell, Robert W. "The Psychology of Human Deception." *Social Research* 63, no. 3 (1996).

Mouré, Kenneth. "Black Market Fictions: 'Au Bon Beurre, La Traversée de Paris,' and the Black Market in France." *French Politics, Culture, and Society* 32, no. 1 (Spring 2014): 47–67.

———. "The Faux Policier in Occupied Paris." *Journal of Contemporary History* 45, no. 1 (2010).

Murphy, Christopher. "The Origins of SOE in France." *Historical Journal* 46, no. 4 (Dec. 2003): 935–52.

Neumaier, Christopher. "The Escalation of German Reprisal Policy in Occupied France, 1941–42." *Journal of Contemporary History* 41, no. 1 (Jan. 2006): 113–31.

Noakes, Lucy. "Gender, War, and Memory: Discourse and Experience in History." *Journal of Contemporary History* 36, no. 4 (Oct. 2001).

Occhino, Filippo, Kim Oosterlinck, and Eugene N. White. "How Much Can a Victor Force the Vanquished to Pay? France Under the Nazi Boot." *Journal of Economic History* 68, no. 1 (March 2008).

"Operation Torch: Invasion of North Africa, 8–16 November 1942." Naval History and Heritage Command, www.history.navy.mil, citing Robert J. Cressman, *The Official Chronology of the U.S. Navy in World War II*. Annapolis, Md./Washington, D.C.: U.S. Naval Institute Press/Naval Historical Center, 1999.

Osborne, Deirdre. "'I Do Not Know About Politics or Governments . . . I Am a Housewife': The Female Secret Agent and the Male War Machine in Occupied France (1942–5)." *Women: A Cultural Review* 17, no. 1 (2006): 42–64.

Ossian, Lisa L. "Fragilities and Failures, Promises and Patriotism: Elements of Second World War English and American Girlhood, 1939–1945." In *Girlhood: A Global History*. Edited by Jennifer Helgren and Colleen A. Vasconcellos. New Brunswick, N.J.: Rutgers University Press, 2010.

Ott, Sandra. "Duplicity, Indulgence, and Ambiguity in Franco-German Relations, 1940–1946." *History and Anthropology* 20, no. 1 (March 2009): 57–77.

———. "Undesirable Pen Pals, Unthinkable Houseguests: Representations of Franco-German Friendships in a Post-liberation Trial Dossier and *Suite Française*." *French Politics, Culture, and Society* 32, no. 1 (2014).

Padover, Saul K. "France in Defeat: Causes and Consequences." *World Politics* 2, no. 3 (1950): 305–37.

Panter-Downes, Mollie. "After the Men Have Gone." A Reporter at Large. *New Yorker*, April 11, 1942.

———. "Bundles from Britain." A Reporter at Large. *New Yorker*, Nov. 29, 1941.

———. "The Good Women of Grosvenor Street." A Reporter at Large. *New Yorker*, May 24, 1941.

———. "The Lancashire Way." A Reporter at Large. *New Yorker*, Nov. 22, 1941.

———. Letter from London. *New Yorker*, Jan. 13, 1940.

———. "Making It Dirty for Them." A Reporter at Large. *New Yorker,* Sept. 7, 1940.

———. "A Night at the Savoy." A Reporter at Large. *New Yorker,* Dec. 21, 1940.

———. "St. Thomas's Takes Four." A Reporter at Large. *New Yorker,* Feb. 8, 1941.

Pattinson, Juliette. " 'The Best Disguise': Performing Femininities for Clandestine Purposes During the Second World War." In *Gender and Warfare in the Twentieth Century: Textual Representations.* Edited by Angela K. Smith. Manchester, U.K.: Manchester University Press, 2004.

———. " 'Playing the Daft Lassie with Them': Gender, Captivity, and the Special Operations Executive During the Second World War." *European Review of History: Revue Européenne d'Histoire* 13, no. 2 (2006): 271–92.

———. " 'The Thing That Made Me Hesitate . . . ': Re-examining Gendered Intersubjectivities in Interviews with British Secret War Veterans." *Women's History Review* 20, no. 2 (2011): 245–63.

Pearl, Monica B. " 'What Strange Intimacy': Janet Flanner's Letters from Paris." *Journal of European Studies* 32 (2002).

Peniston-Bird, Corinna. "Of Hockey Sticks and Sten Guns: British Auxiliaries and Their Weapons in the Second World War." *Women's History Magazine* 76 (Autumn 2014).

Quataert, Jean H., and Leigh Ann Wheeler. "Gender, War, and Sexuality: Convergences of Past and Present." *Journal of Women's History* 26, no. 3 (2014): 7–11.

Reid, Donald. "Available in Hell: Germaine Tillion's Operetta of Resistance at Ravensbrück." *French Politics, Culture, and Society* 25, no. 2 (2007): 141–50.

———. "Everybody Was in the French Resistance . . . Now! American Representations of the French Resistance." *French Cultural Studies* 23, no. 1 (2012): 49–63.

Report of the Committee on Amenities and Welfare Conditions in the Three Women's Services. London: His Majesty's Stationery Office, 1942.

Rose, Sonya O. "Sex, Citizenship, and the Nation in World War II Britain." *American Historical Review* 103, no. 4 (1998): 1147–76.

Russell, Diana. "Rape and the Masculine Mystique." In *The Changing Experience of Women.* Edited by Elizabeth Whitelegg. Oxford: Martin Robertson, 1982.

Ryan, Isadore. "Between Detention and Destitution: The Irish in France During the Occupation." *History Ireland,* Sept./Oct. 2016.

Safran, William. "State, Nation, National Identity, and Citizenship: France as a Test Case." *International Political Science Review* 12, no. 3 (1991).

Schwartz, Paula. "*Partisanes* and Gender Politics in Vichy France." *French Historical Studies* 16, no. 1 (1989): 126–51.

———. "Redefining Resistance: Women's Activities in Wartime France." In *Behind the Lines: Gender and the Two World Wars.* Edited by Margaret R. Higonnet et al. New Haven, Conn.: Yale University Press, 1987.

———. "La répression des femmes communistes (1940–1944)." In *Identités féminines et violences politiques.* Edited by François Rouquet and Danièle Voldman. Paris: Centre National de la Recherche Scientifique, 1995.

Seaman, Mark. "A Glass Half Full—Some Thoughts on the Evolution of the Study of the Special Operations Executive." *Intelligence and National Security* 20, no. 1 (2006): 27–43.

———. "Good Thrillers but Bad History: A Review of Published Works on the Special Operations Executive Work in France During the Second World War." In *War, Resistance, and Intelligence: Essays in Honour of M. R. D. Foot.* Edited by K. G. Robertson. Barnsley, U.K.: Pen & Sword, 1999.

Segal, Mady Wechsler. "Women's Military Roles Cross-Nationally: Past, Present, and Future." *Gender and Society* 9, no. 6 (Dec. 1995): 757–75.

Seitz, Stephen S., Kelly M. Oakeley, and Francisco Garcia-Huidobro. *Operation Overlord and the Principles of War.* Norfolk, Va.: Joint Forces Staff College, Joint and Combined Staff Officer School, 2002.

"A Short History of Northumberland House, 8 Northumberland Avenue, London." Online publication.

Stafford, David. "The Detonator Concept: British Strategy, SOE, and European Resistance After the Fall of France." *Journal of Contemporary History* 10, no. 2 (1975): 185–217.

Stockdale, Melissa K. "'My Death for the Motherland Is Happiness': Women, Patriotism, and Soldiering in Russia's Great War, 1914–1917." *American Historical Review* 109, no. 1 (Feb. 2004): 78–116.

Sugarman, Martin. "Two Jewish Heroines of the SOE." *Jewish Historical Studies* 35 (1996–1998): 309–28.

Summerfield, Penny. "Public Memory or Public Amnesia? British Women of the Second World War in Popular Films of the 1950s and 1960s." *Journal of British Studies* 48, no. 4 (2009).

Suttill, Francis J., and M. R. D. Foot. "SOE's 'Prosper' Disaster of 1943." *Intelligence and National Security* 26, no. 1 (2011): 99–105.

Tegel, Susan. "Third Reich Newsreels—an Effective Tool of Propaganda? *Historical Journal of Film, Radio, and Television* 24, no. 1 (2004).

Thomas, Martin. "After Mers-el-Kébir: The Armed Neutrality of the Vichy French Navy, 1940–43." *English Historical Review* 112, no. 447 (1997).

Tillet, Pierre. "History of WWII Infiltrations into France." Self-published online.

Valliant, Derek W. "Occupied Listeners: The Legacies of Interwar Radio for France During World War II." In David Suisman and Susan Strasser, eds. *Sound in the Age of Mechanical Reproduction.* Philadelphia: University of Pennsylvania Press, 2010.

Vandenbroucke, Guillaume. "On a Demographic Consequence of the First World War." *Vox,* Centre for Economic Policy Research, 2012.

Vande Winkel, Roel. "Nazi Newsreels in Europe, 1939–1945: The Many Faces of Ufa's Foreign Weekly Newsreel (Auslandstonwoche) Versus German's Weekly Newsreel (Die Deutsche Wochenschau)." *Historical Journal of Film, Radio, and Television* 24, no. 1 (2004).

Vigurs, Kate. "Handbags to Hand Grenades: Preparing Women for Work Behind the Lines in Occupied France." *Women's History Magazine* 76 (Autumn 2014).

———. "The Women Agents of the Special Operations Executive F Section: Wartime Realities and Post War Representations." PhD thesis, University of Leeds, 2011.

Wallace, William. "Foreign Policy and National Identity in the United Kingdom." *International Affairs* 67, no. 1 (1991).

Weber, Eugen. "Of Stereotypes and of the French." *Journal of Contemporary History* 25, nos. 2/3 (1990).

Webster, Wendy. " 'Europe Against the Germans': The British Resistance Narrative, 1940–1950." *Journal of British Studies* 48 (Oct. 2009): 958–82.

Weisiger, Alex. "World War II: German Expansion and Allied Response." In *Logics of War: Explanations for Limited and Unlimited Conflicts*. Ithaca, N.Y.: Cornell University Press, 2013.

Wernick, Robert. "The Shadow of a Gunman from World War II." *Smithsonian,* Sept. 1993.

Wheeler, Mark. "The SOE Phenomenon." *Journal of Contemporary History* 16, no. 3 (1981): 513–19.

Wilkinson, James D. "Remembering World War II: The Perspective of the Losers." *American Scholar* 54, no. 3 (1985): 329–43.

Witte, Peter, and Stephen Tyas. "A New Document on the Deportation and Murder of Jews During 'Einsatz Reinhardt' 1942." *Holocaust and Genocide Studies* 15, no. 3 (2001).

World War II Military Intelligence Map Collection: Declassified Maps from the American, British, and German Militaries. Geography & Map Division, Library of Congress, Washington, D.C., 2015.

Zeiger, Susan. "GIs and Girls Around the Globe: The Geopolitics of Sex and Marriage in World War II." In *Entangling Alliances: Foreign War Brides and American Soldiers in the Twentieth Century*. New York: New York University Press, 2010.

ARCHIVES

Archives of Libre Résistance, Paris. Amicale Buck.

Atkins, Vera M. Private Papers. Imperial War Museum, London.

Buckmaster, Maurice. Diary. Unpublished. Courtesy of Tim Buckmaster.

Churchill, Winston. Papers. Churchill Archive, Churchill College, Cambridge, U.K. (online).

Dilks, Professor D. Private Papers. Imperial War Museum, London.

Fuller, Jean Overton. Private Papers. Imperial War Museum, London.

Jackson, M. W. Private Papers. Imperial War Museum, London.

Johnston, Lieutenant J. B. Letter, July 1, 1944. Unpublished. Courtesy of John Johnston.

National Archives of the United Kingdom, Kew, England. Material cited in accord with Britain's Open Government License. Records of the Special Operations

Executive, Series: HS 6 (Western Europe), HS 7 (Histories and War Diaries), HS 8 (Headquarters Records), HS 9 (Personnel Files), HS 13 (French Card Index); Records of the Security Service, MI5, Series: KV 2 (Personal Files), KV 3 (Subject Files); Records of the War Office and Successor, Series: WO 309 (Judge Advocate General's Office, War Crimes, British Army of the Rhine War Crimes Group), WO 311 (Judge Advocate General's Office, War Crimes files), WO 204 (Allied Forces, Mediterranean Theatre: Military Headquarters Papers), WO 219 (Papers of the Supreme Headquarters Allied Expeditionary Force, covering the invasion of Northern Europe), AIR 27 (Air Ministry Operations Record Books).

Ree, Harry. "Experiences of an SOE Agent in France, Henri Raymond, Alias César." Courtesy Steven Kippax.

Service Historique de la Défense, Paris. Series 16P (individual dossiers), 17P (networks, Buckmaster).

Standards Charges + French & Polish Rail Charges. Courtesy of Nick Fox.

Stonehouse, Brian. Private Papers. Imperial War Museum, London.

Suttill, Francis. Letters. Courtesy of Francis Suttill.

U.S. National Records and Archives, College Park, Md., and Washington, D.C.

Wretch, C. Private Papers. Imperial War Museum, London.

ORAL HISTORIES

Interview transcripts, courtesy of Dr. Juliette Pattinson:

Yvonne Burney
Pearl Cornioley
Sonia d'Artois
Sydney Hudson
Lise Villemeur
Nancy Wake

Sound Archives, Imperial War Museum, London.

VIDEO

Behind Enemy Lines: The Real Charlotte Grays. Directed by Jenny Morgan. London: British Film Institute, 2002.

Brian, You're Dreaming. Courtesy of Gordon Stevens.

Legasee: The Veterans' Video Archive. legasee.org.uk.

Ophuls, Marcel, dir. *Le chagrin et la pitié* (*The Sorrow and the Pity*). Télévision Rencontre, 1969.

Index